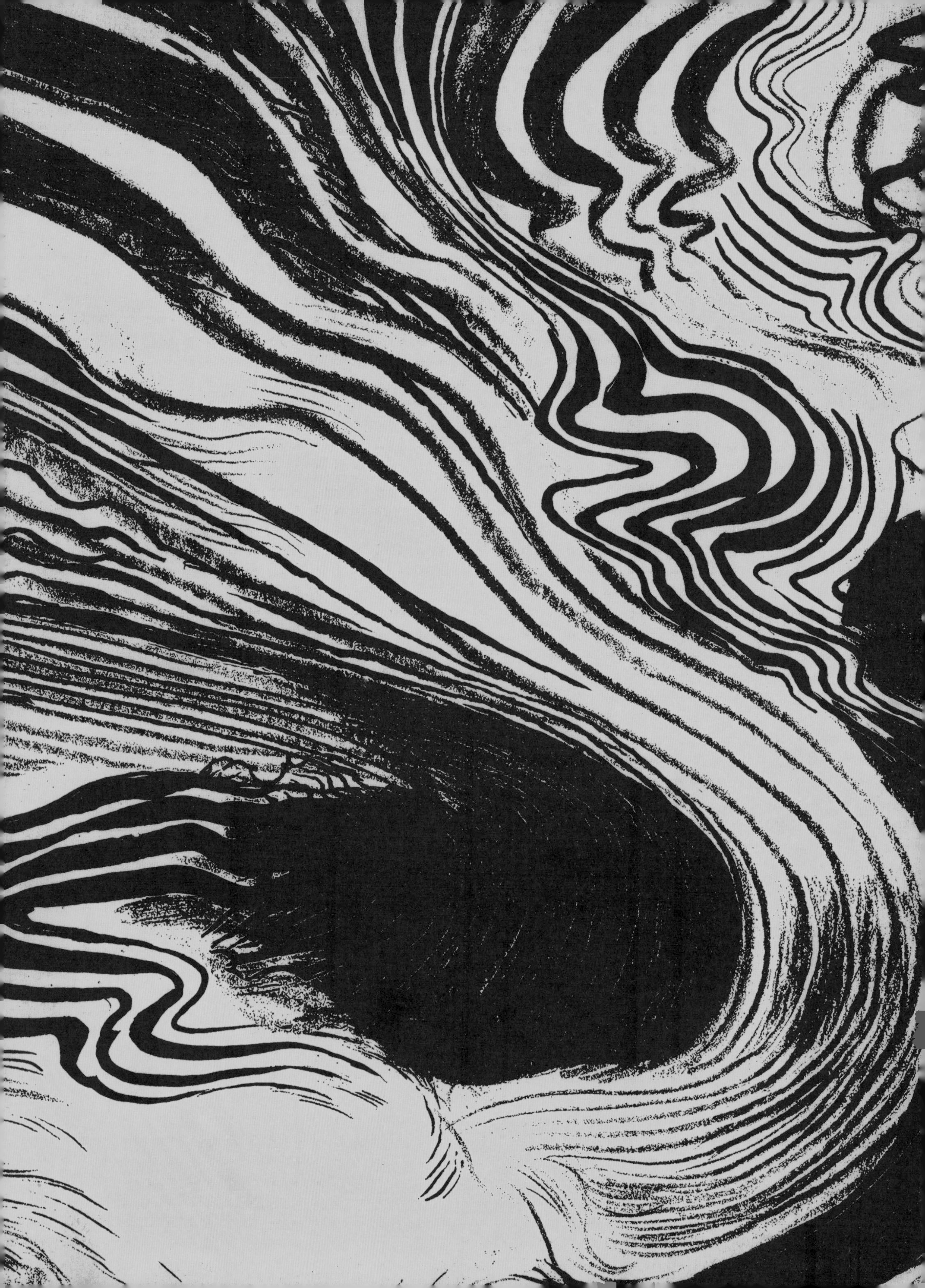

FANTAGRAPHICS BOOKS INC.
7563 Lake City Way NE
Seattle, Washington, 98115
www.fantagraphics.com

Written and illustrated by Mikael Ross
Plot development: Jean-Baptiste Coursaud
Colorist: Claire Paq
Translator: Nika Knight
Designer: Kayla E.
Production: Paul Baresh & C. Hwang
Promotion: Jacquelene Cohen
VP / Associate Publisher / Editor: Eric Reynolds
President / Publisher: Gary Groth

The translation of this work was supported by a grant from the Goethe-Institut.

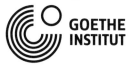

ISBN 978-1-68396-551-0
Library of Congress Control Number 2021950973
First printing: May 2022
Printed in China

GOLDEN BOY

Mikael Ross

translated by
Nika Knight

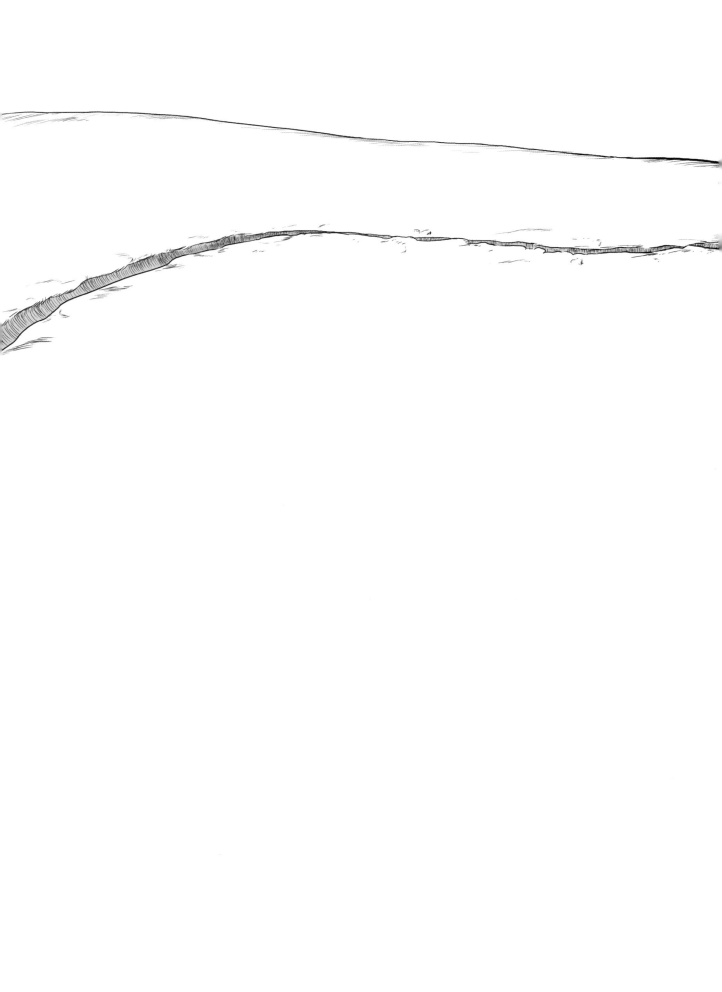

1778

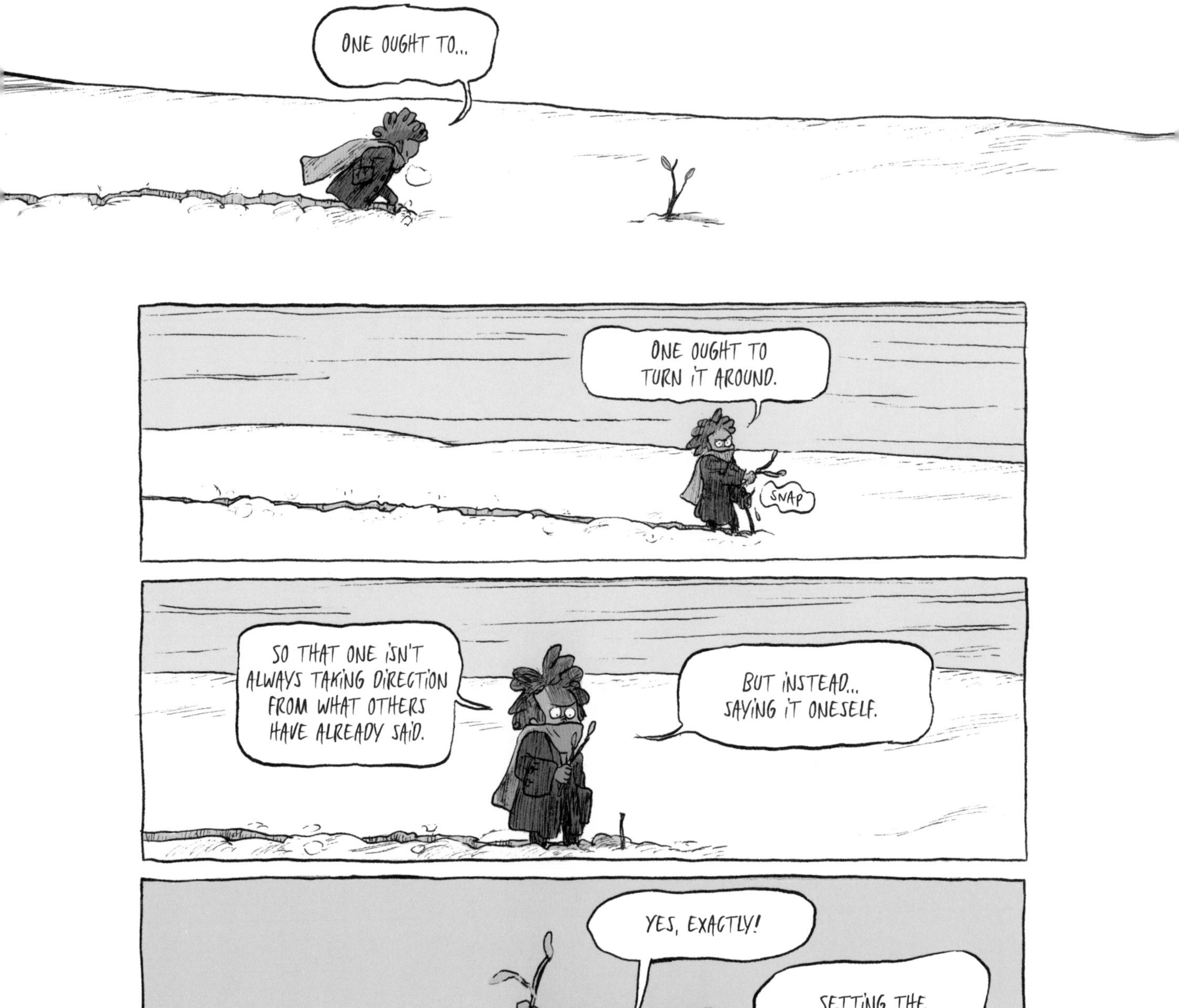
ONE OUGHT TO...
ONE OUGHT TO TURN IT AROUND.
SNAP
SO THAT ONE ISN'T ALWAYS TAKING DIRECTION FROM WHAT OTHERS HAVE ALREADY SAID.
BUT INSTEAD... SAYING IT ONESELF.
YES, EXACTLY!
SETTING THE NOTE ONESELF!

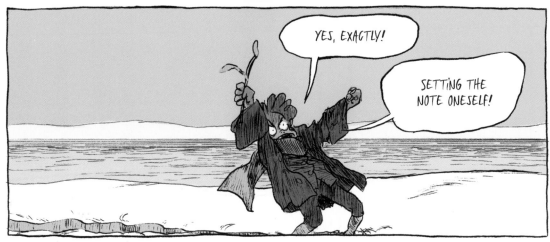

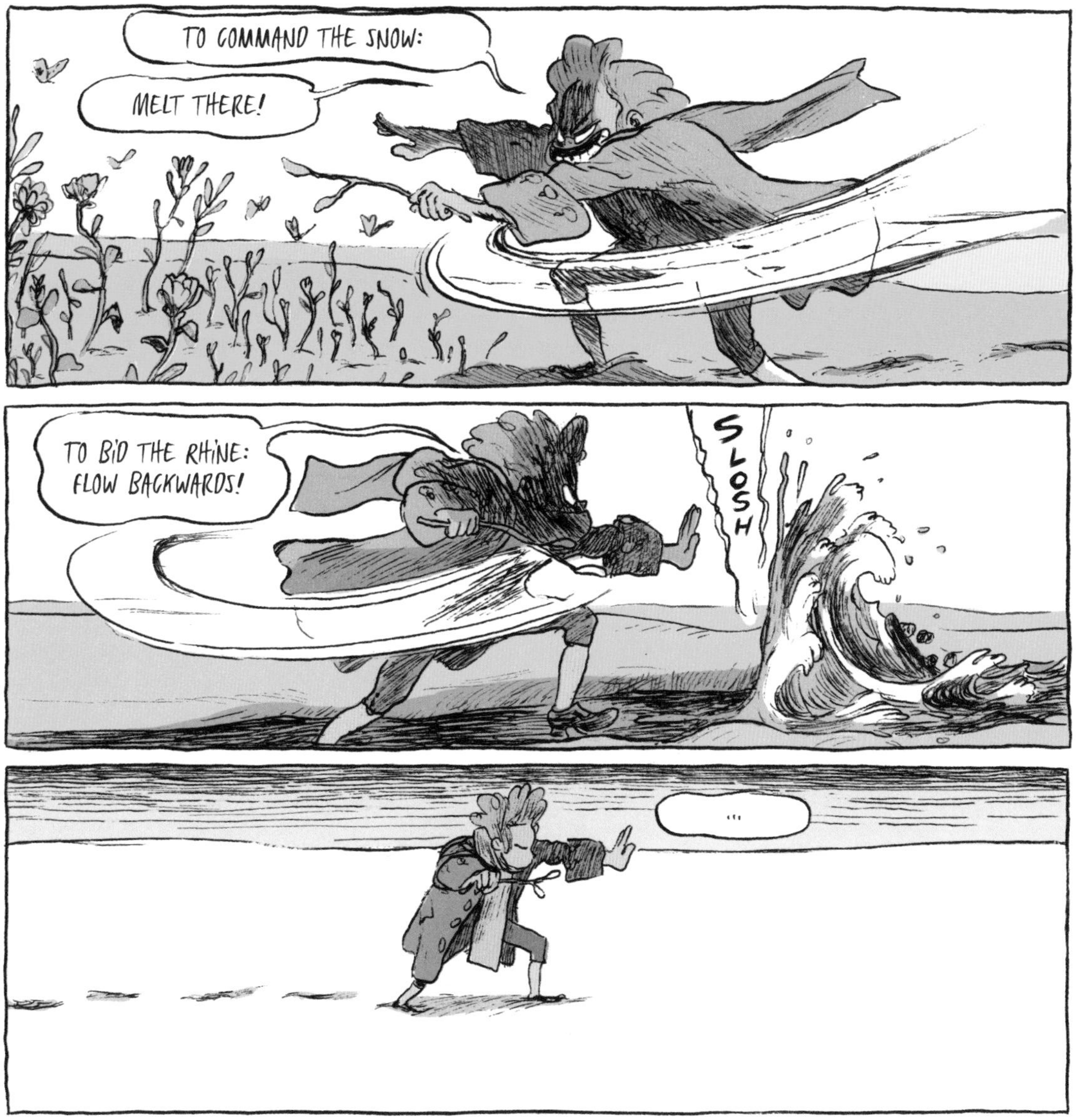
TO COMMAND THE SNOW:
MELT THERE!
TO BID THE RHINE: FLOW BACKWARDS!
SLOSH
...

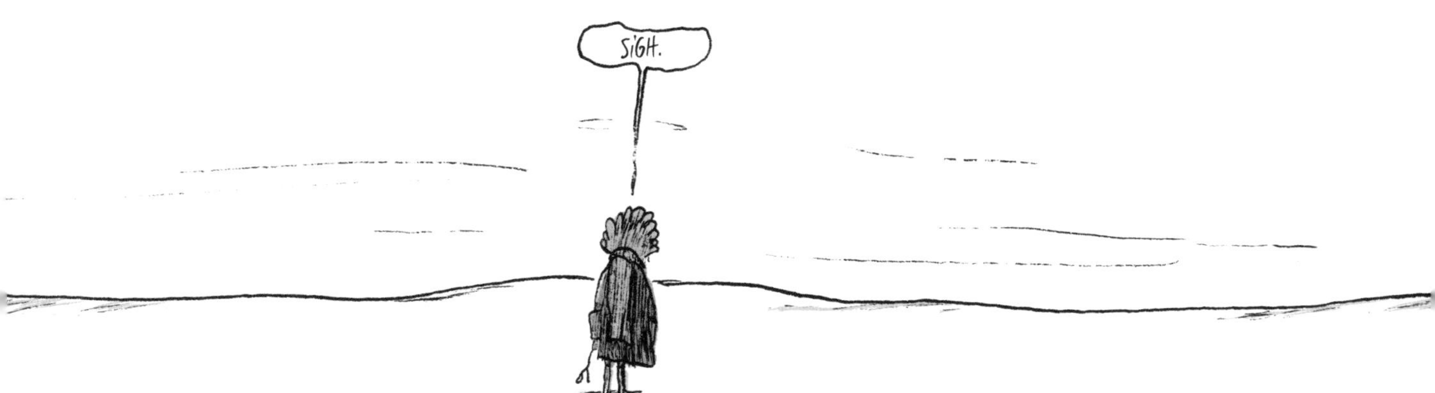
SIGH.

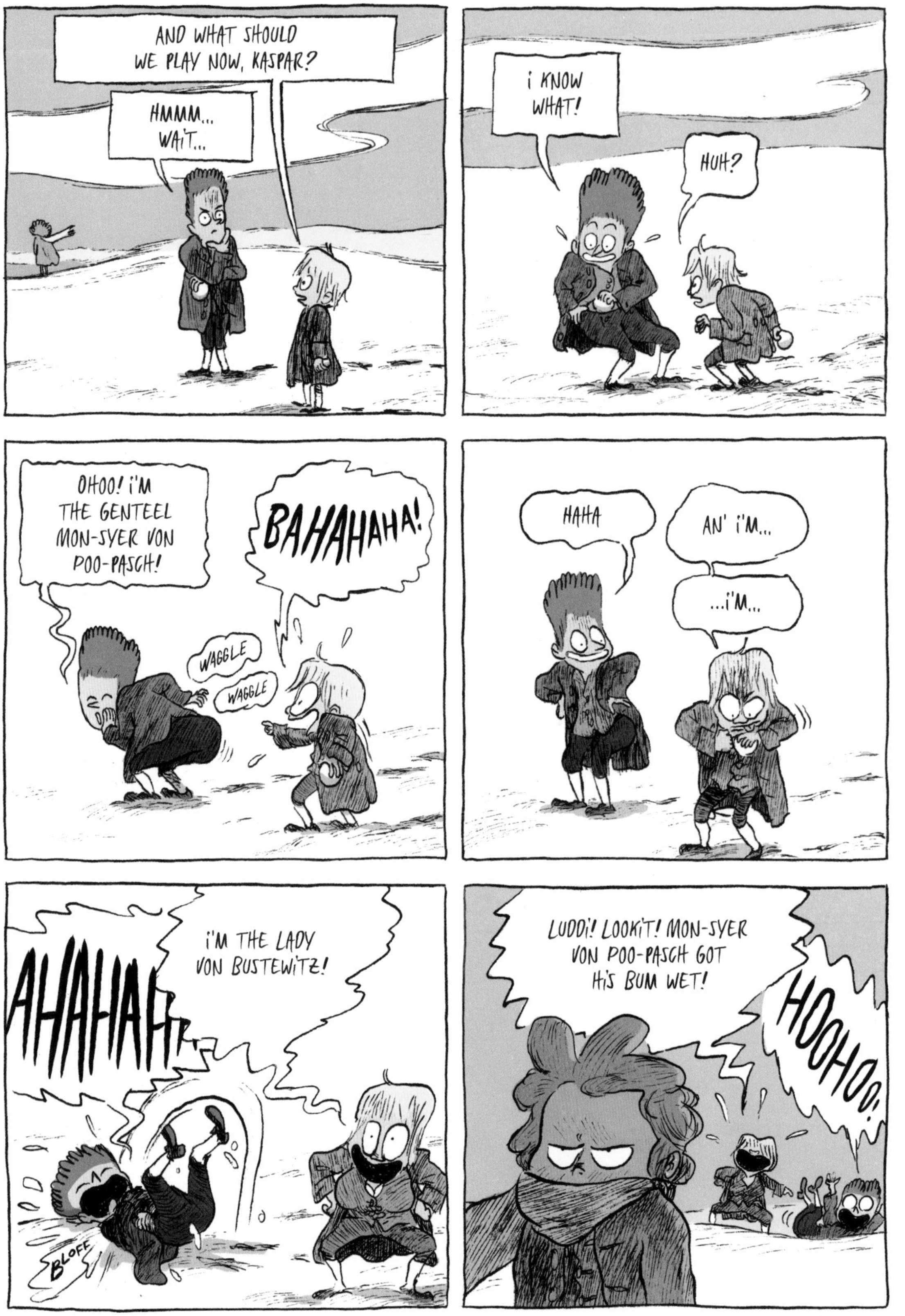
AND WHAT SHOULD WE PLAY NOW, KASPAR?
HMMM... WAIT...
I KNOW WHAT!
HUH?
OHOO! I'M THE GENTEEL MON-SYER VON POO-PASCH!
BAHAHAHA!
WAGGLE
WAGGLE
HAHA
AN' I'M...
...I'M...
AHAHAH
I'M THE LADY VON BUSTEWITZ!
BLOFF
LUDDI! LOOKIT! MON-SYER VON POO-PASCH GOT HIS BUM WET!
HOOHOO!

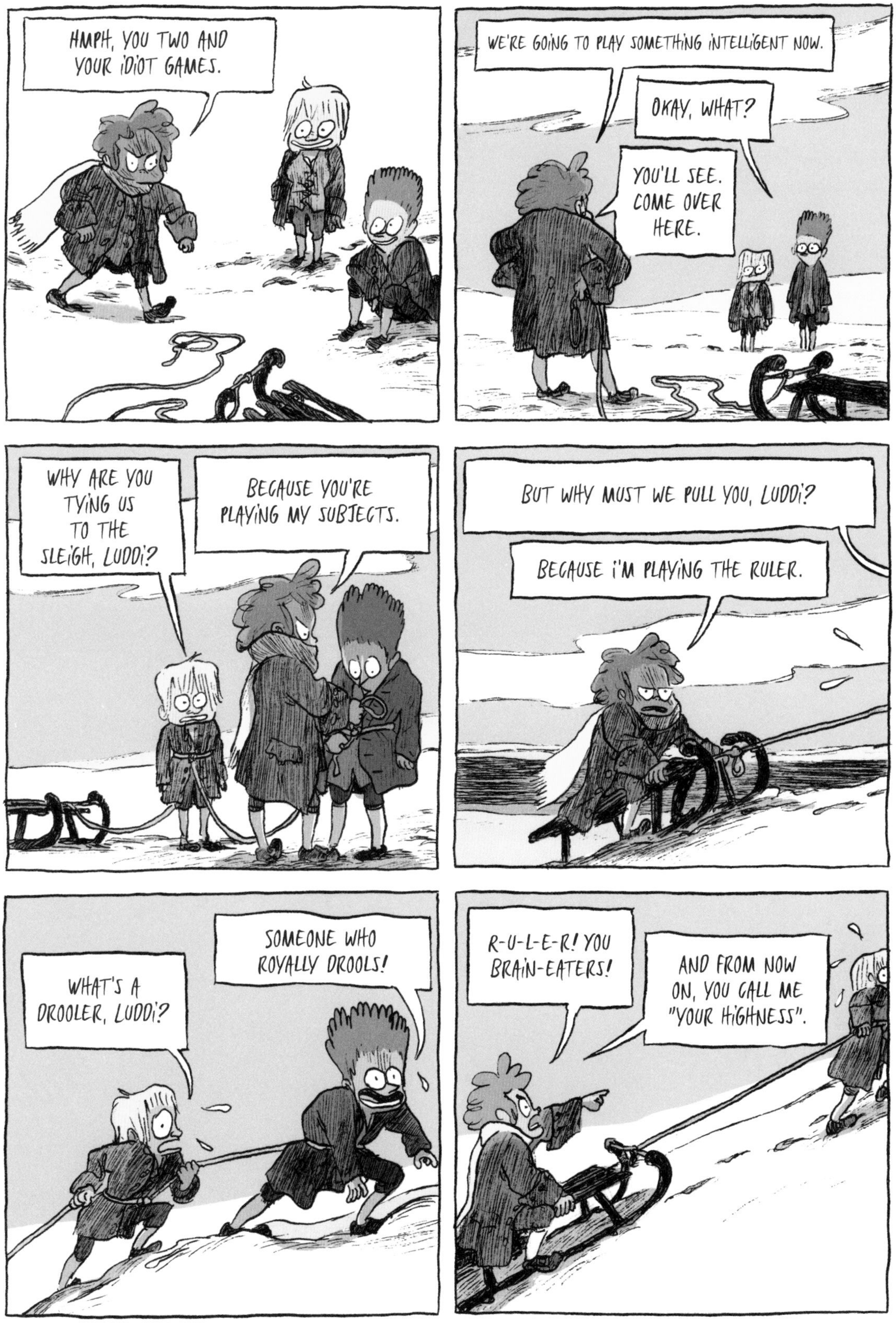
HMPH, YOU TWO AND YOUR iDiOT GAMES.
WE'RE GOiNG TO PLAY SOMETHiNG iNTELLiGENT NOW.
OKAY, WHAT?
YOU'LL SEE. COME OVER HERE.
WHY ARE YOU TYiNG US TO THE SLEiGH, LUDDi?
BECAUSE YOU'RE PLAYiNG MY SUBJECTS.
BUT WHY MUST WE PULL YOU, LUDDi?
BECAUSE i'M PLAYiNG THE RULER.
WHAT'S A DROOLER, LUDDi?
SOMEONE WHO ROYALLY DROOLS!
R-U-L-E-R! YOU BRAiN-EATERS!
AND FROM NOW ON, YOU CALL ME "YOUR HiGHNESS".

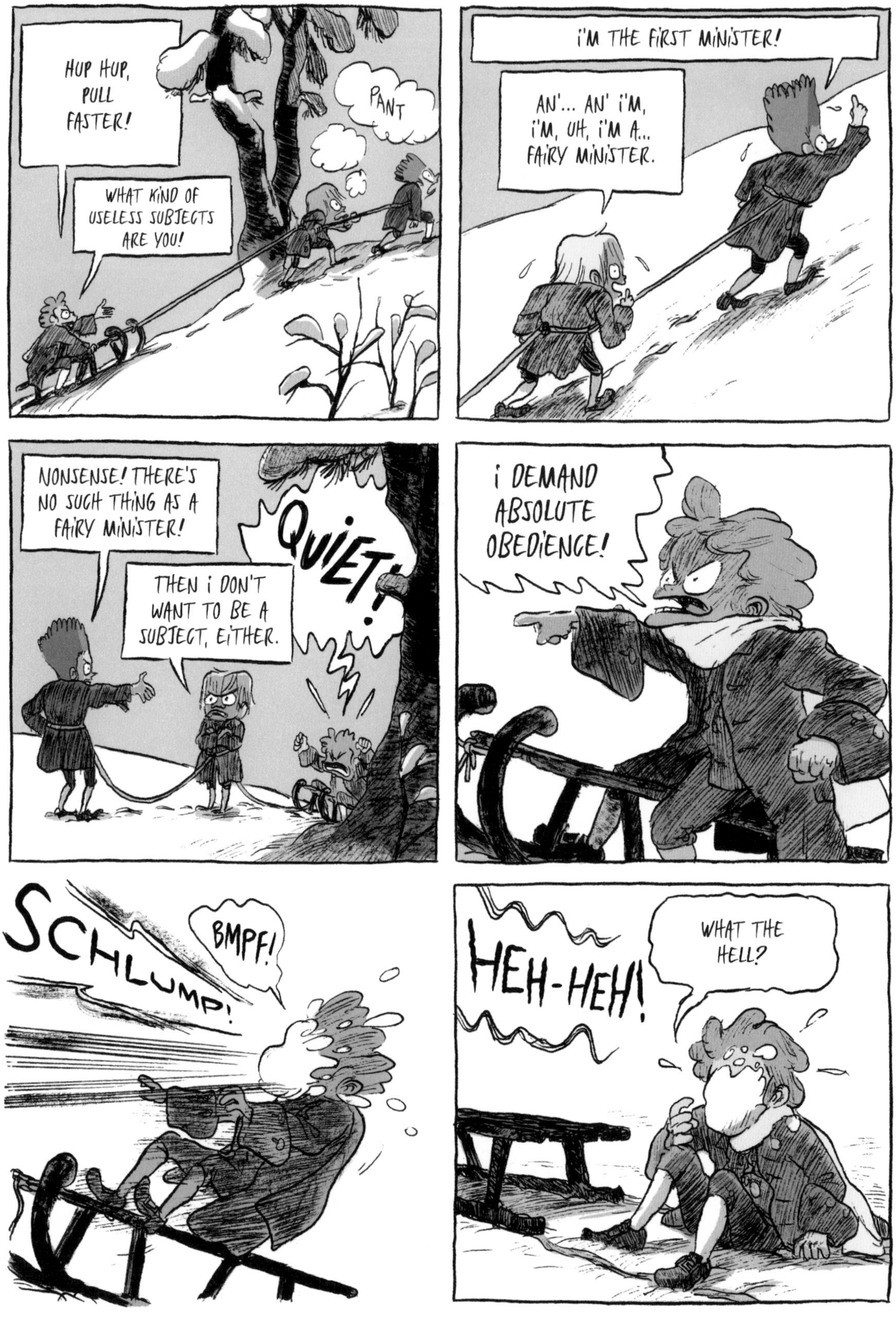
HUP HUP, PULL FASTER!
WHAT KIND OF USELESS SUBJECTS ARE YOU!
PANT
I'M THE FIRST MINISTER!
AN'... AN' I'M, I'M, UH, I'M A... FAIRY MINISTER.
NONSENSE! THERE'S NO SUCH THING AS A FAIRY MINISTER!
THEN I DON'T WANT TO BE A SUBJECT, EITHER.
QUIET!
I DEMAND ABSOLUTE OBEDIENCE!
SCHLUMP!
BMPF!
HEH-HEH!
WHAT THE HELL?

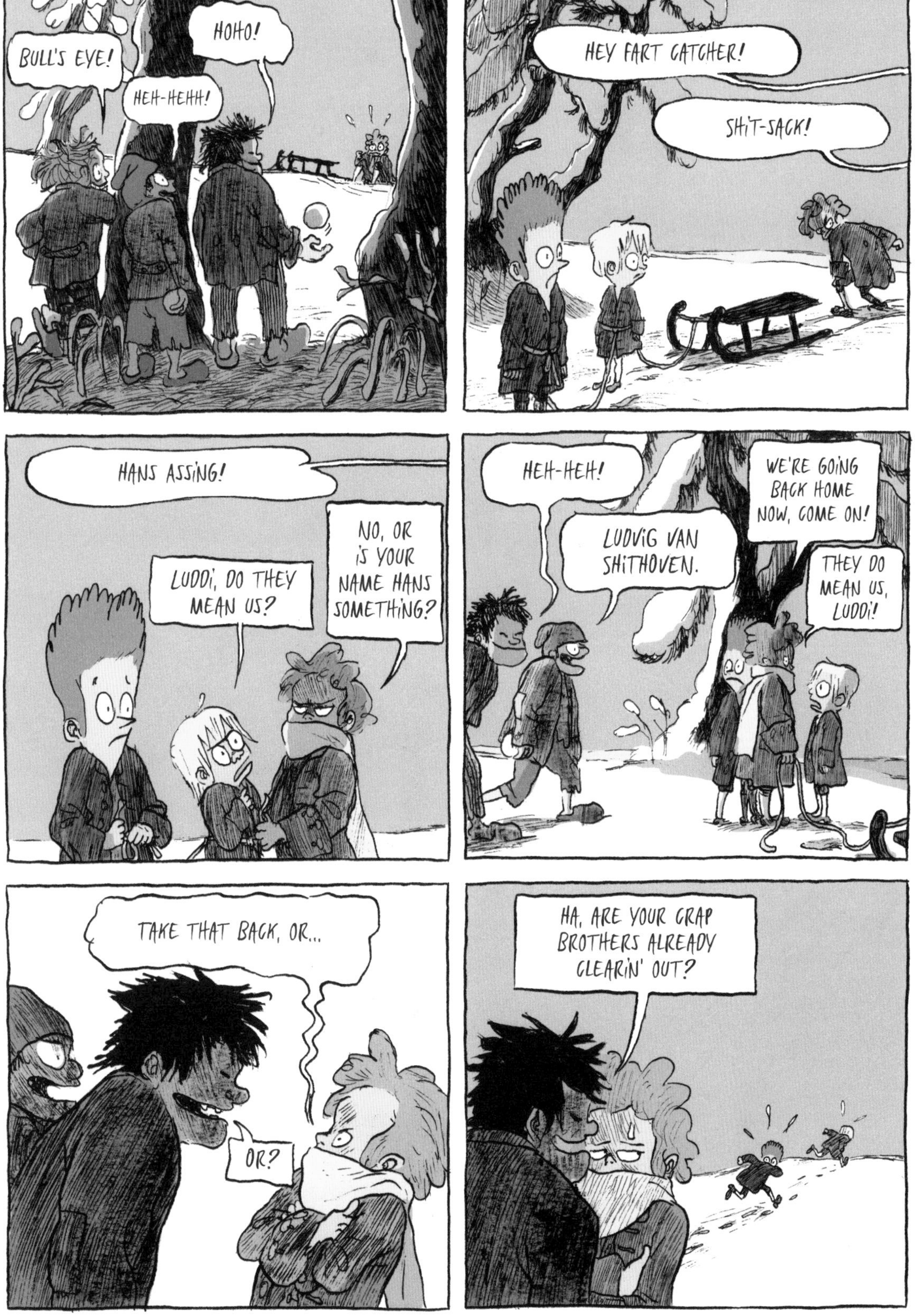
BULL'S EYE!
HOHO!
HEH-HEHH!
HEY FART CATCHER!
SHIT-SACK!
HANS ASSING!
LUDDI, DO THEY MEAN US?
NO, OR IS YOUR NAME HANS SOMETHING?
HEH-HEH!
LUDVIG VAN SHITHOVEN.
WE'RE GOING BACK HOME NOW, COME ON!
THEY DO MEAN US, LUDDI!
TAKE THAT BACK, OR...
OR?
HA, ARE YOUR CRAP BROTHERS ALREADY CLEARIN' OUT?

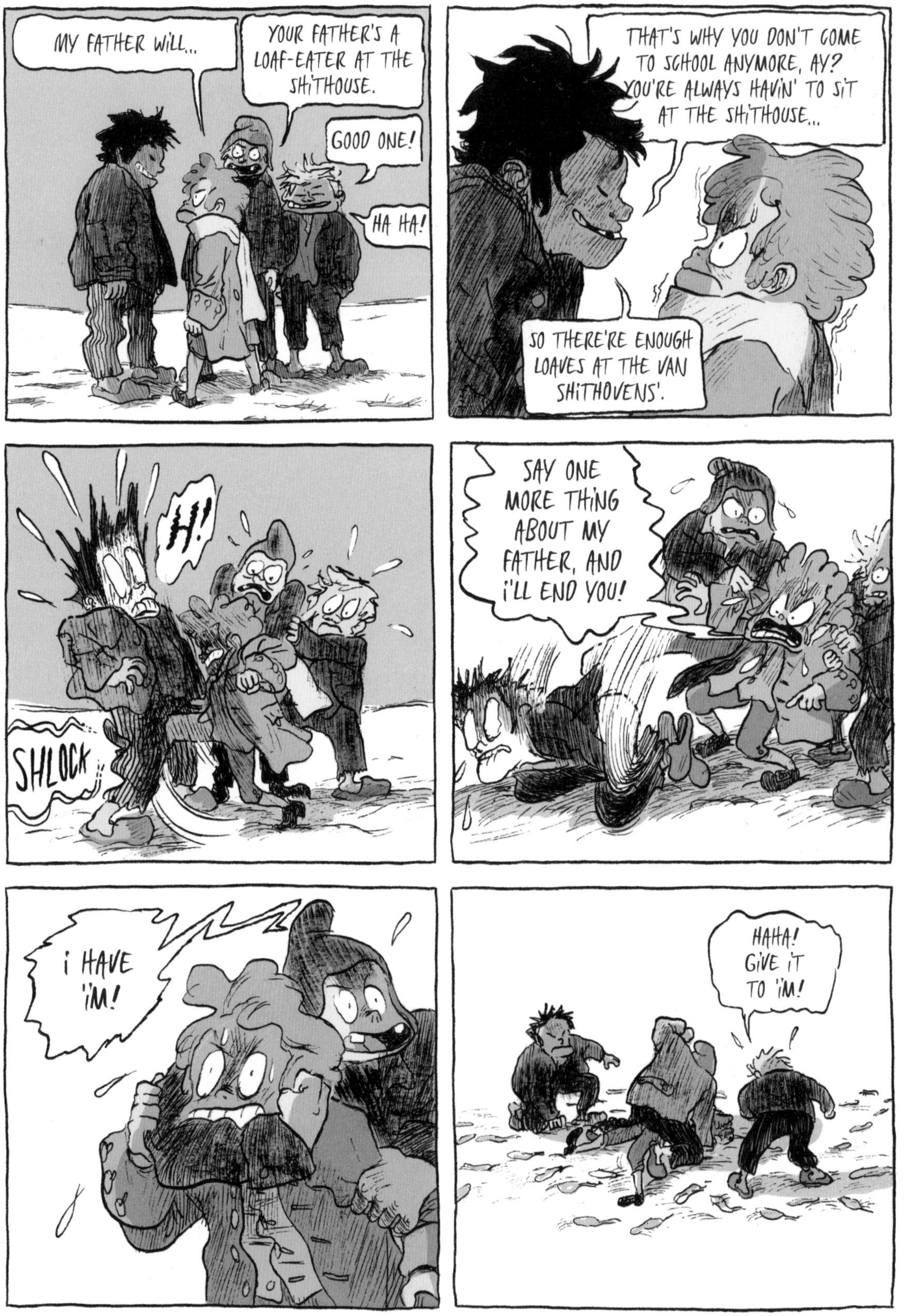
MY FATHER WILL...
YOUR FATHER'S A LOAF-EATER AT THE SHITHOUSE.
GOOD ONE!
HA HA!
THAT'S WHY YOU DON'T COME TO SCHOOL ANYMORE, AY? YOU'RE ALWAYS HAVIN' TO SIT AT THE SHITHOUSE...
SO THERE'RE ENOUGH LOAVES AT THE VAN SHITHOVENS'.
H!
SHLOCK
SAY ONE MORE THING ABOUT MY FATHER, AND I'LL END YOU!
I HAVE 'IM!
HAHA! GIVE IT TO 'IM!

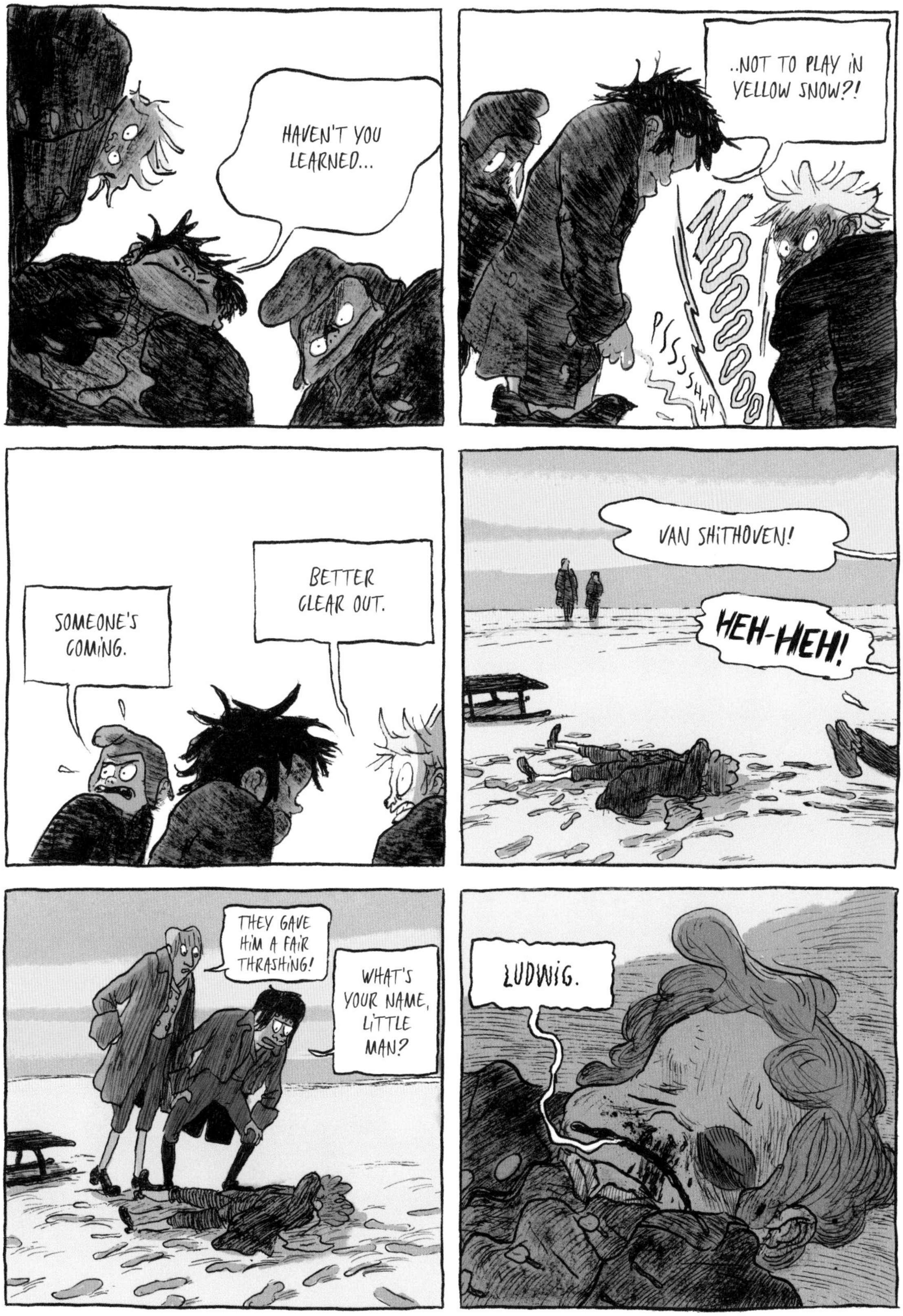
HAVEN'T YOU LEARNED...
..NOT TO PLAY iN YELLOW SNOW?!
NOOOOOOO
PSSSSHHP
SOMEONE'S COMiNG.
BETTER CLEAR OUT.
VAN SHiTHOVEN!
HEH-HEH!
THEY GAVE HiM A FAiR THRASHiNG!
WHAT'S YOUR NAME, LiTTLE MAN?
LUDWiG.

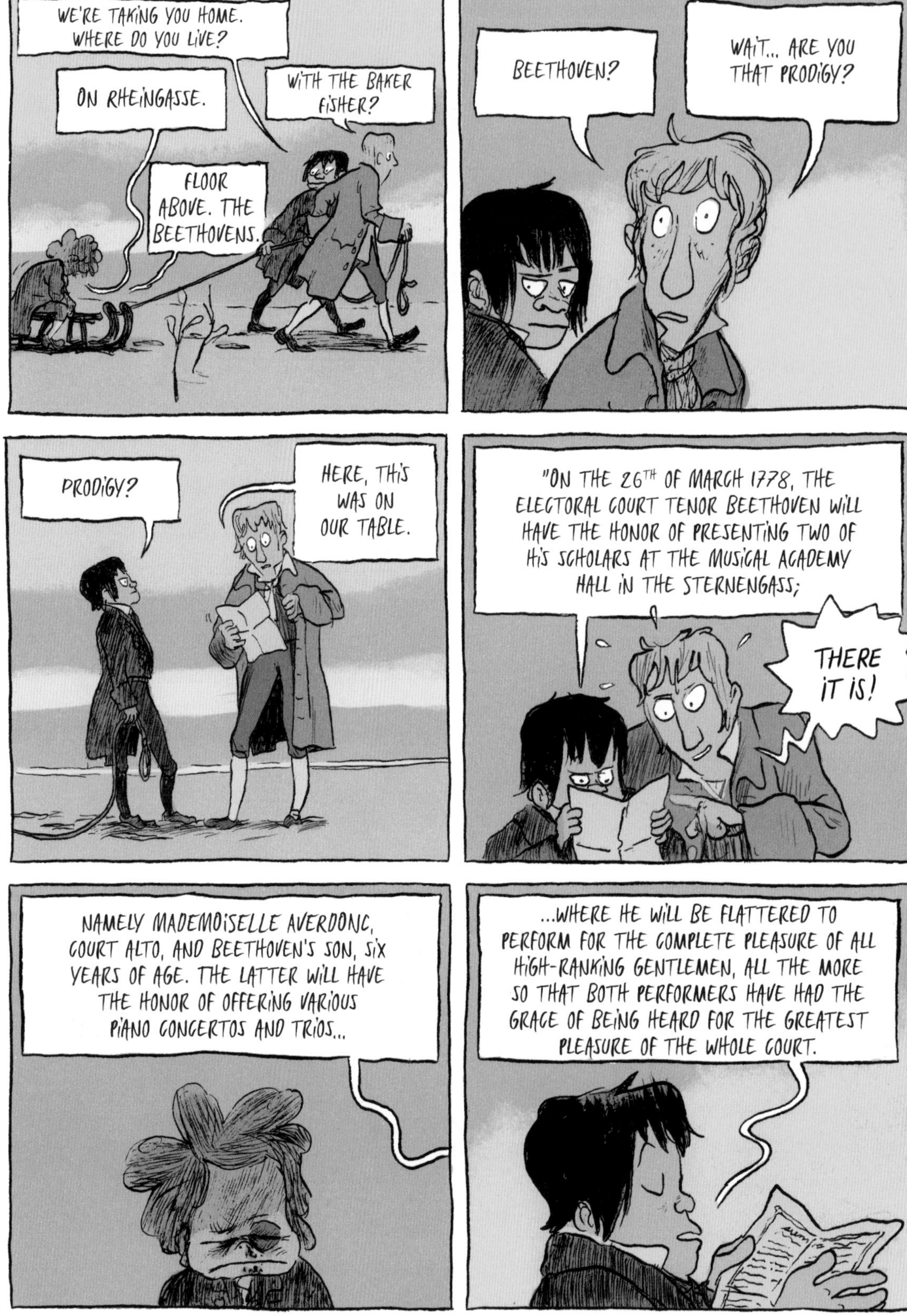
WE'RE TAKING YOU HOME. WHERE DO YOU LIVE?
ON RHEINGASSE.
WITH THE BAKER FISHER?
FLOOR ABOVE. THE BEETHOVENS.
BEETHOVEN?
WAIT... ARE YOU THAT PRODIGY?
PRODIGY?
HERE, THIS WAS ON OUR TABLE.
"ON THE 26TH OF MARCH 1778, THE ELECTORAL COURT TENOR BEETHOVEN WILL HAVE THE HONOR OF PRESENTING TWO OF HIS SCHOLARS AT THE MUSICAL ACADEMY HALL IN THE STERNENGASS;
THERE IT IS!
NAMELY MADEMOISELLE AVERDONC, COURT ALTO, AND BEETHOVEN'S SON, SIX YEARS OF AGE. THE LATTER WILL HAVE THE HONOR OF OFFERING VARIOUS PIANO CONCERTOS AND TRIOS...
...WHERE HE WILL BE FLATTERED TO PERFORM FOR THE COMPLETE PLEASURE OF ALL HIGH-RANKING GENTLEMEN, ALL THE MORE SO THAT BOTH PERFORMERS HAVE HAD THE GRACE OF BEING HEARD FOR THE GREATEST PLEASURE OF THE WHOLE COURT.

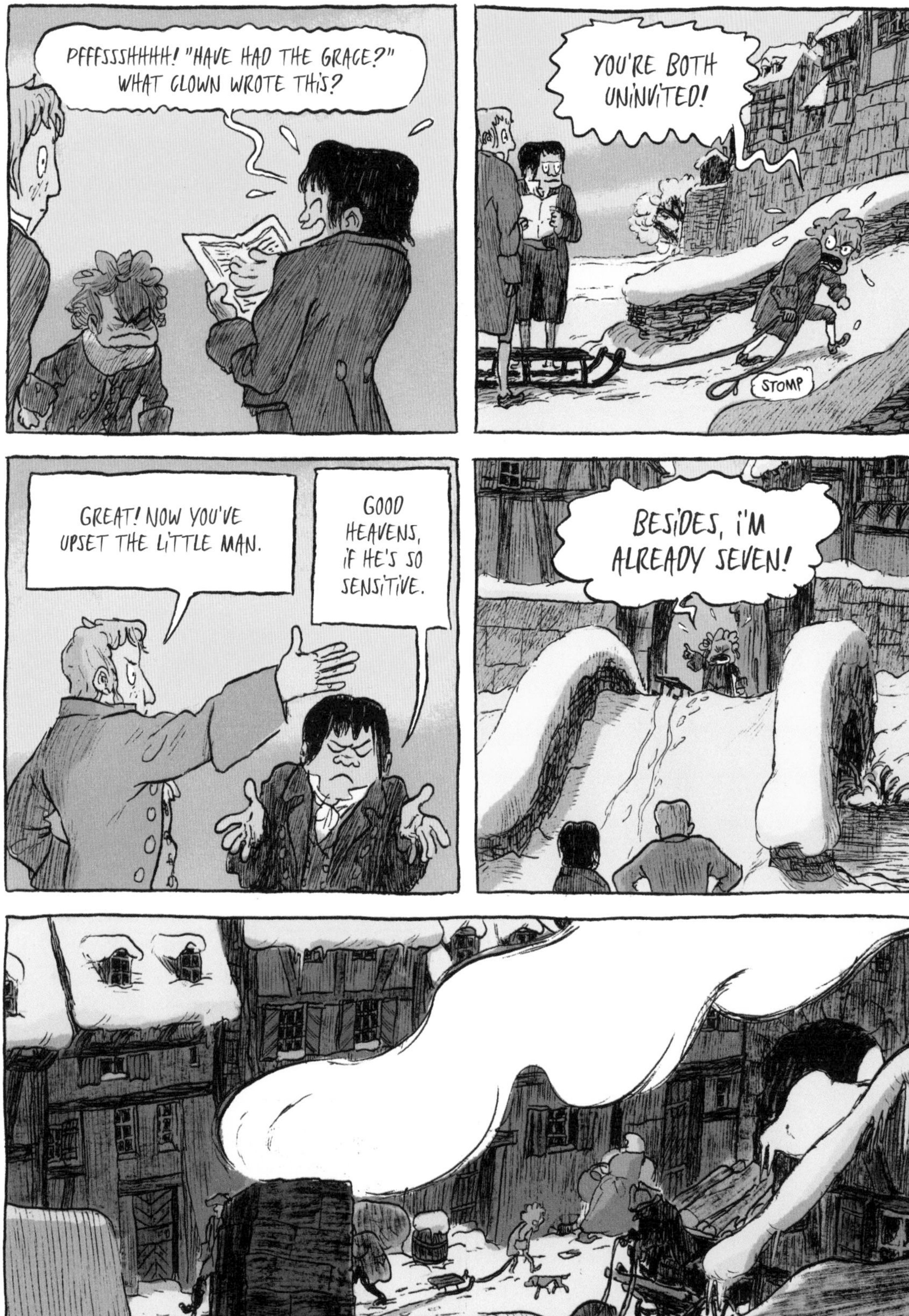
PFFFSSSHHHH! "HAVE HAD THE GRACE?" WHAT CLOWN WROTE THIS?
YOU'RE BOTH UNINVITED!
STOMP
GREAT! NOW YOU'VE UPSET THE LITTLE MAN.
GOOD HEAVENS, IF HE'S SO SENSITIVE.
BESIDES, I'M ALREADY SEVEN!

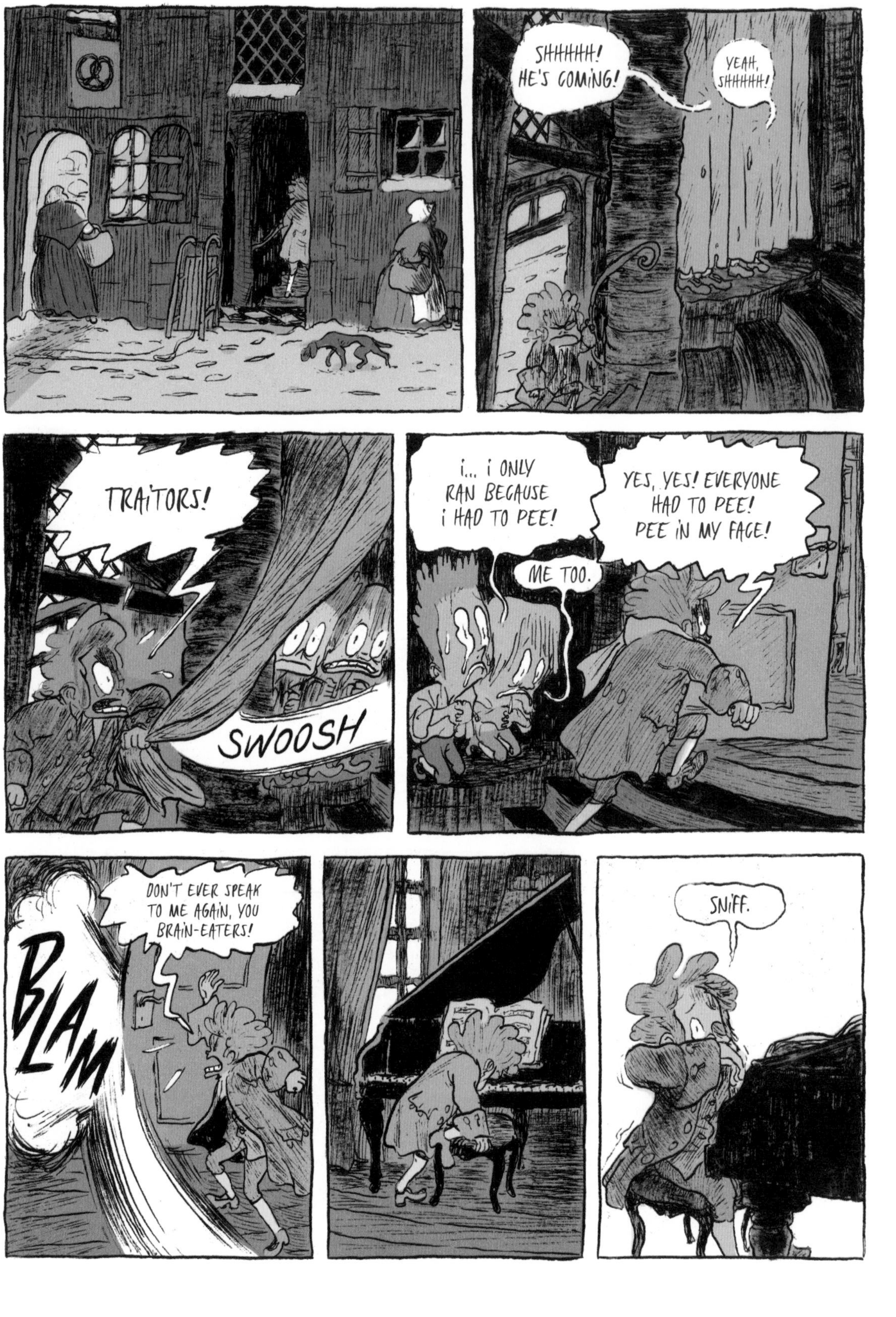
SHHHHH! HE'S COMING!
YEAH, SHHHHH!
TRAITORS!
SWOOSH
I... I ONLY RAN BECAUSE I HAD TO PEE!
ME TOO.
YES, YES! EVERYONE HAD TO PEE! PEE IN MY FACE!
BLAM
DON'T EVER SPEAK TO ME AGAIN, YOU BRAIN-EATERS!
SNIFF.

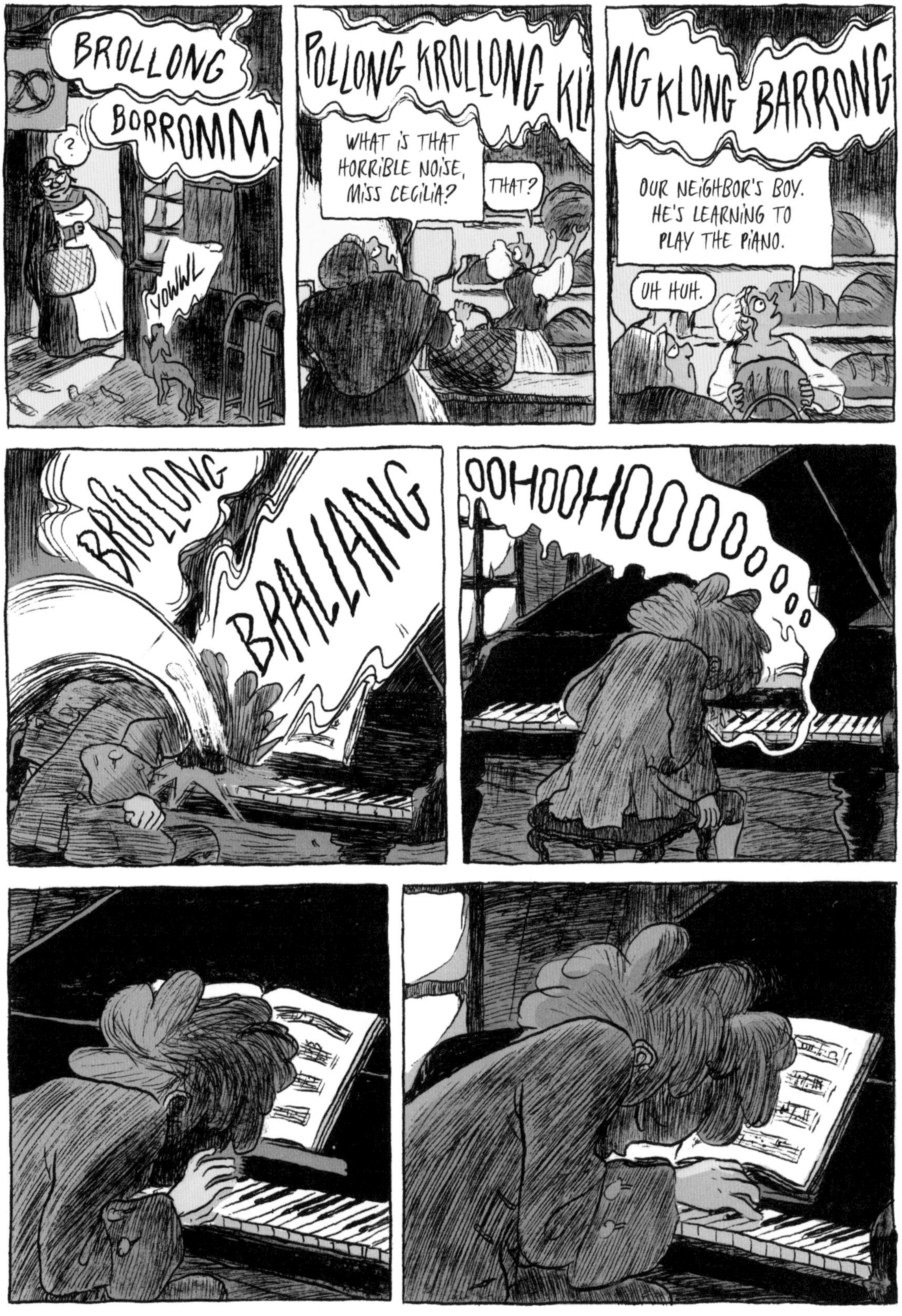
BROLLONG
BORROMM
?
YOWWL
POLLONG KROLLONG KLA
WHAT IS THAT HORRIBLE NOISE, MISS CECILIA?
THAT?
NG KLONG BARRONG
OUR NEIGHBOR'S BOY. HE'S LEARNING TO PLAY THE PIANO.
UH HUH.
BROLLONG
BRALLANG
OOHOOHOOOOOooooo

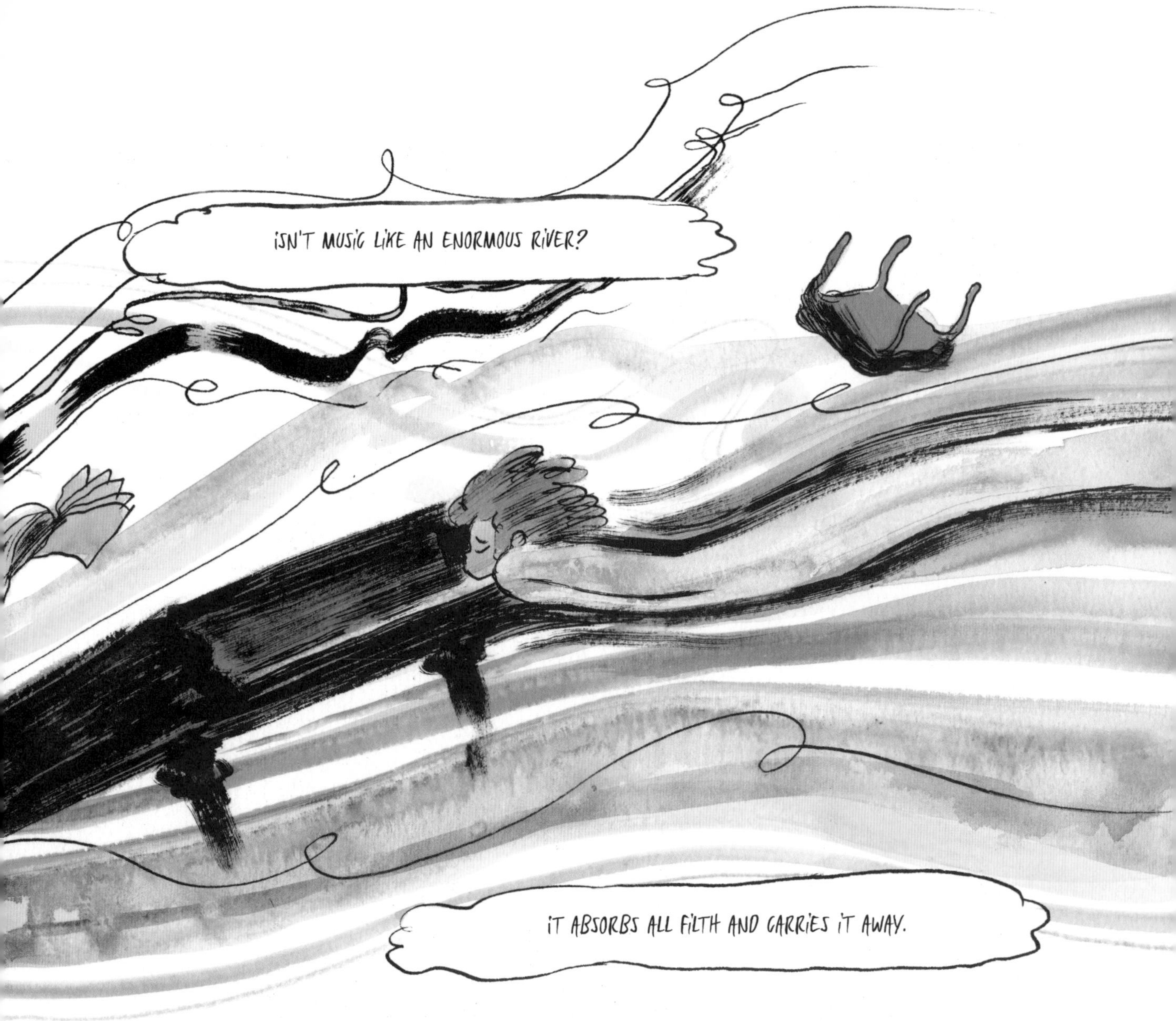
ISN'T MUSIC LIKE AN ENORMOUS RIVER?
IT ABSORBS ALL FILTH AND CARRIES IT AWAY.
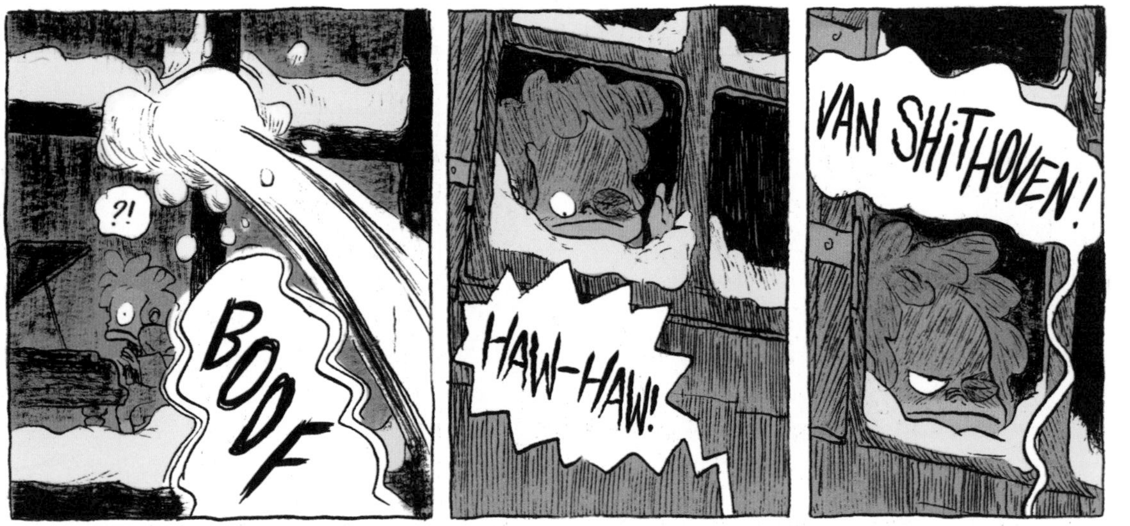
?!
BOOF
HAW-HAW!
VAN SHITHOVEN!

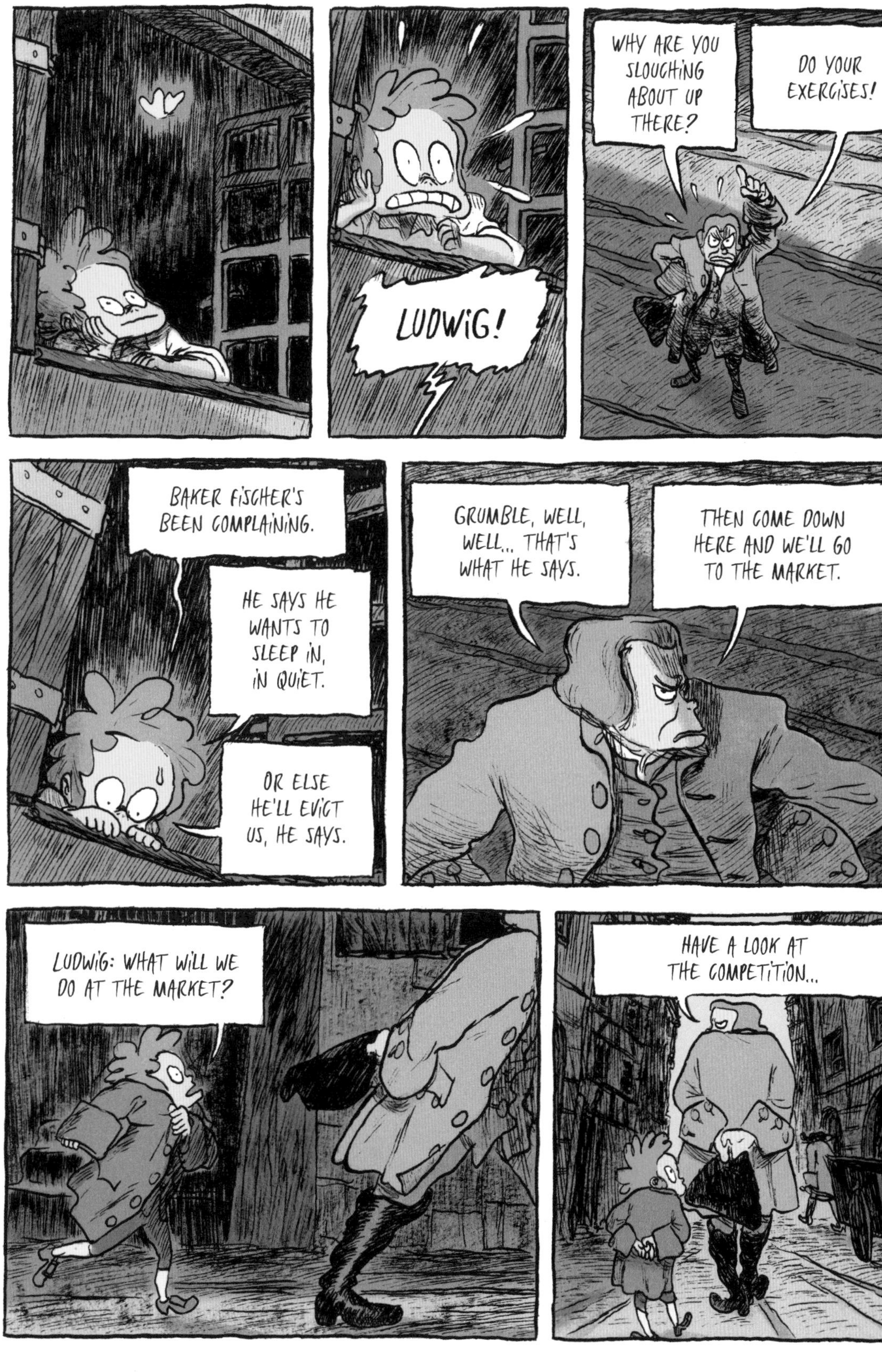
LUDWIG!
WHY ARE YOU SLOUCHING ABOUT UP THERE?
DO YOUR EXERCISES!
BAKER FISCHER'S BEEN COMPLAINING.
HE SAYS HE WANTS TO SLEEP IN, IN QUIET.
OR ELSE HE'LL EVICT US, HE SAYS.
GRUMBLE, WELL, WELL... THAT'S WHAT HE SAYS.
THEN COME DOWN HERE AND WE'LL GO TO THE MARKET.
LUDWIG: WHAT WILL WE DO AT THE MARKET?
HAVE A LOOK AT THE COMPETITION...

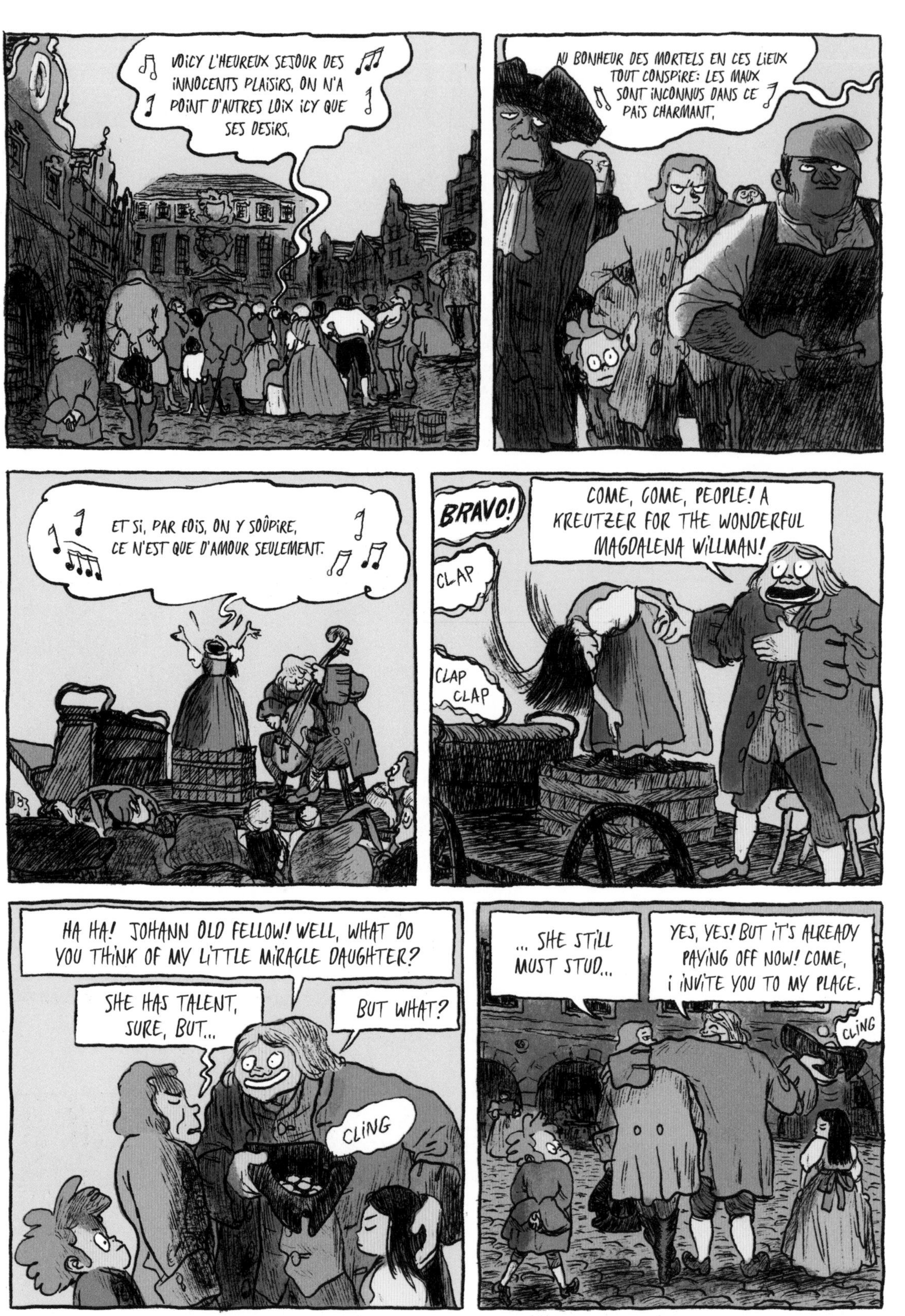
VOICY L'HEUREUX SEJOUR DES INNOCENTS PLAISIRS, ON N'A POINT D'AUTRES LOIX ICY QUE SES DESIRS.
AU BONHEUR DES MORTELS EN CES LIEUX TOUT CONSPIRE: LES MAUX SONT INCONNUS DANS CE PAIS CHARMANT,
ET SI, PAR FOIS, ON Y SOÛPIRE, CE N'EST QUE D'AMOUR SEULEMENT.
BRAVO!
COME, COME, PEOPLE! A KREUTZER FOR THE WONDERFUL MAGDALENA WILLMAN!
CLAP
CLAP CLAP
HA HA! JOHANN OLD FELLOW! WELL, WHAT DO YOU THINK OF MY LITTLE MIRACLE DAUGHTER?
SHE HAS TALENT, SURE, BUT...
BUT WHAT?
CLING
... SHE STILL MUST STUD...
YES, YES! BUT IT'S ALREADY PAYING OFF NOW! COME, I INVITE YOU TO MY PLACE.
CLING

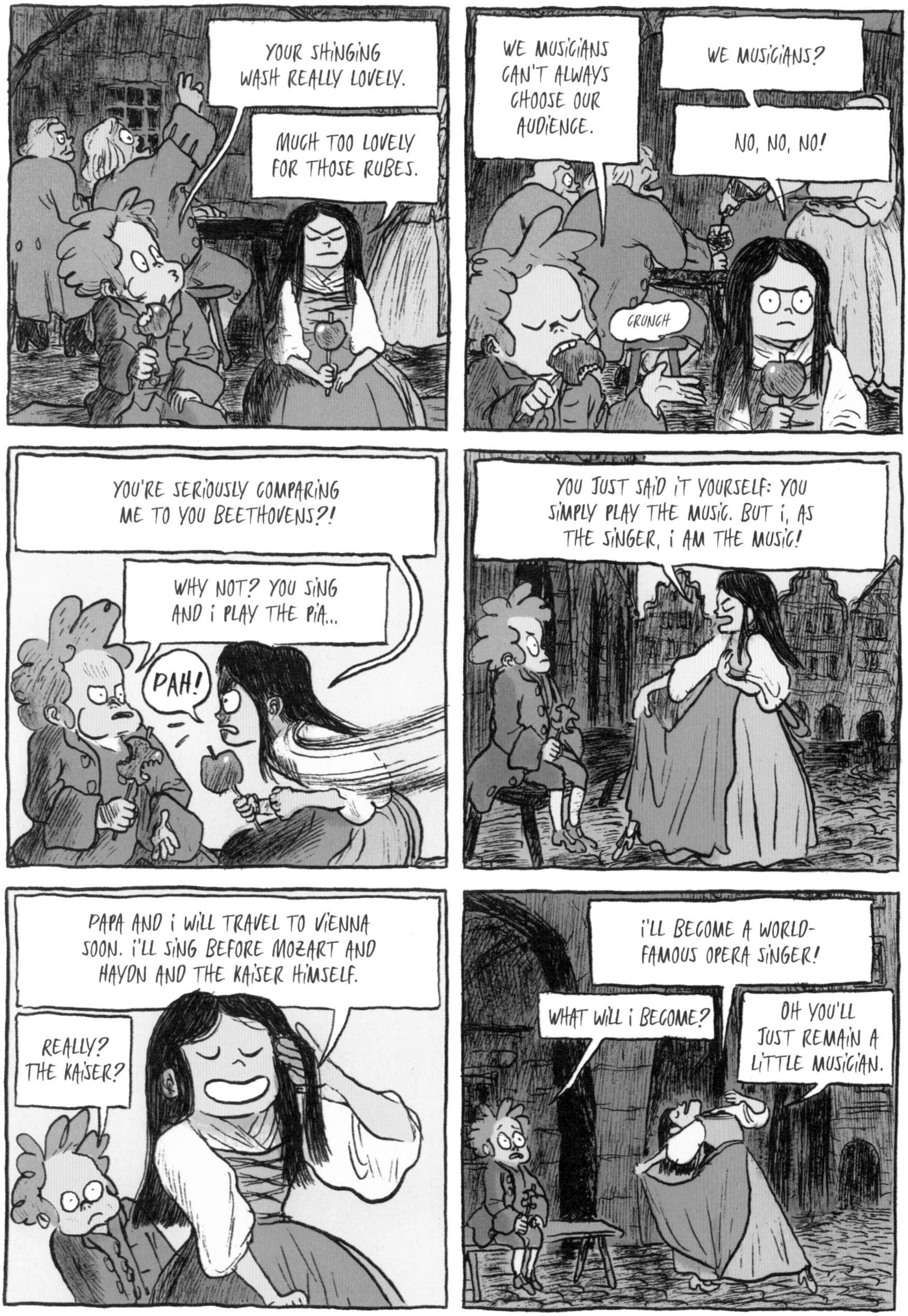
YOUR SHINGING WASH REALLY LOVELY.
MUCH TOO LOVELY FOR THOSE RUBES.
WE MUSICIANS CAN'T ALWAYS CHOOSE OUR AUDIENCE.
WE MUSICIANS?
NO, NO, NO!
CRUNCH
YOU'RE SERIOUSLY COMPARING ME TO YOU BEETHOVENS?!
WHY NOT? YOU SING AND I PLAY THE PIA...
PAH!
YOU JUST SAID IT YOURSELF: YOU SIMPLY PLAY THE MUSIC. BUT I, AS THE SINGER, I AM THE MUSIC!
PAPA AND I WILL TRAVEL TO VIENNA SOON. I'LL SING BEFORE MOZART AND HAYDN AND THE KAISER HIMSELF.
REALLY? THE KAISER?
I'LL BECOME A WORLD-FAMOUS OPERA SINGER!
WHAT WILL I BECOME?
OH YOU'LL JUST REMAIN A LITTLE MUSICIAN.

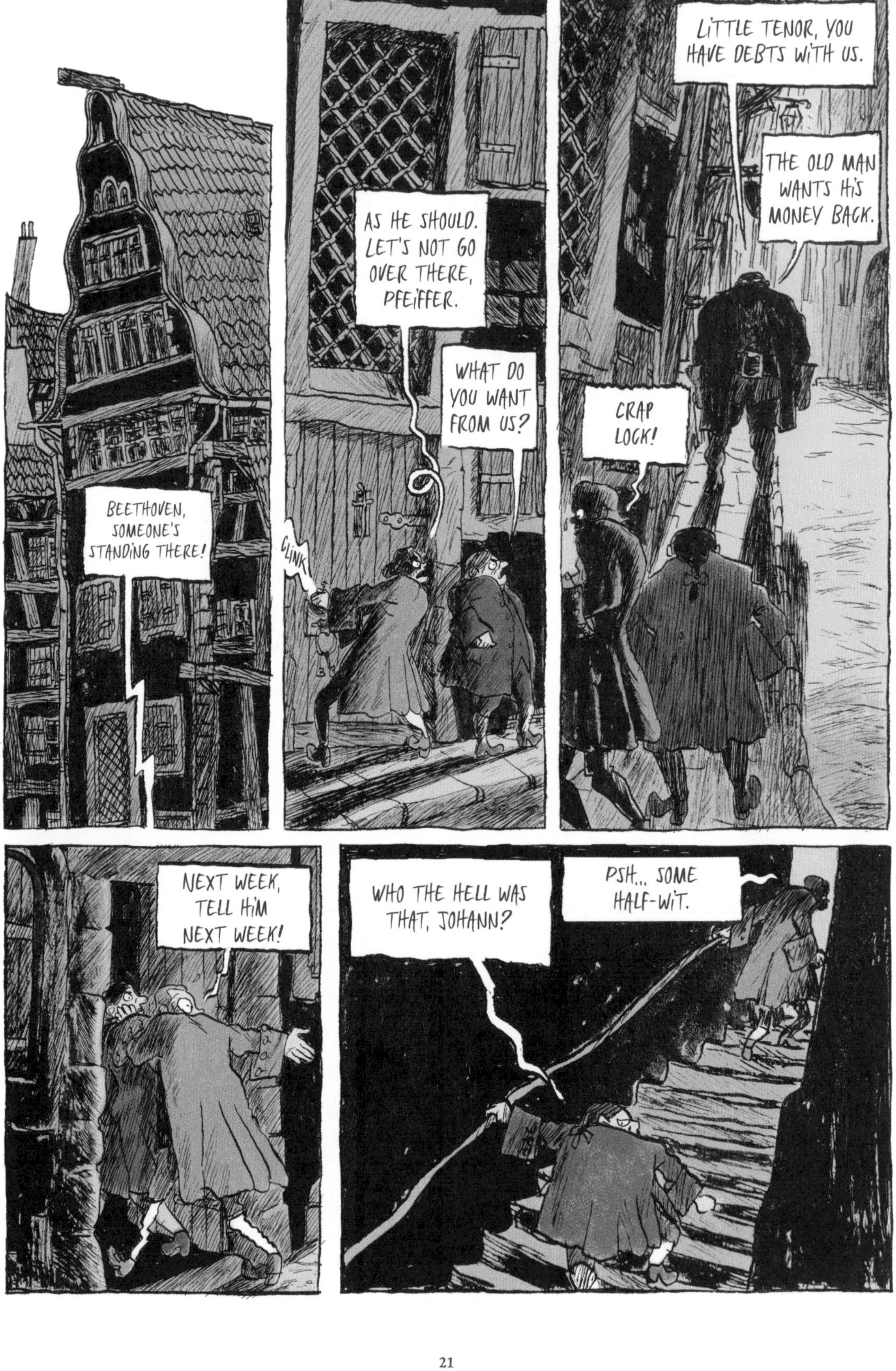
BEETHOVEN, SOMEONE'S STANDING THERE!
AS HE SHOULD. LET'S NOT GO OVER THERE, PFEIFFER.
WHAT DO YOU WANT FROM US?
CLINK
LITTLE TENOR, YOU HAVE DEBTS WITH US.
THE OLD MAN WANTS HIS MONEY BACK.
CRAP LOCK!
NEXT WEEK, TELL HIM NEXT WEEK!
WHO THE HELL WAS THAT, JOHANN?
PSH... SOME HALF-WIT.

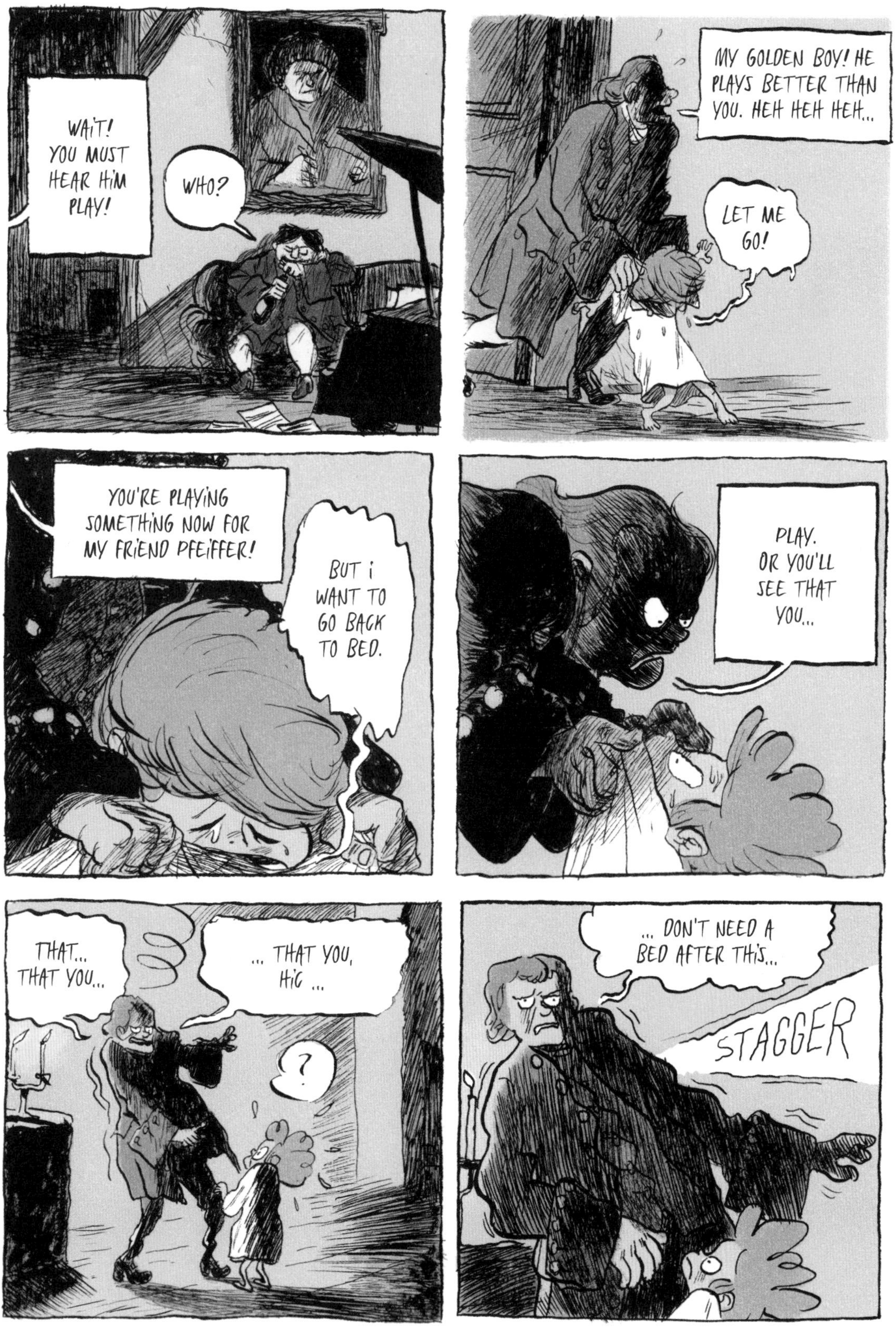
WAIT! YOU MUST HEAR HIM PLAY!
WHO?
MY GOLDEN BOY! HE PLAYS BETTER THAN YOU. HEH HEH HEH...
LET ME GO!
YOU'RE PLAYING SOMETHING NOW FOR MY FRIEND PFEIFFER!
BUT I WANT TO GO BACK TO BED.
PLAY. OR YOU'LL SEE THAT YOU...
THAT... THAT YOU...
... THAT YOU, HIC ...
?
... DON'T NEED A BED AFTER THIS...
STAGGER

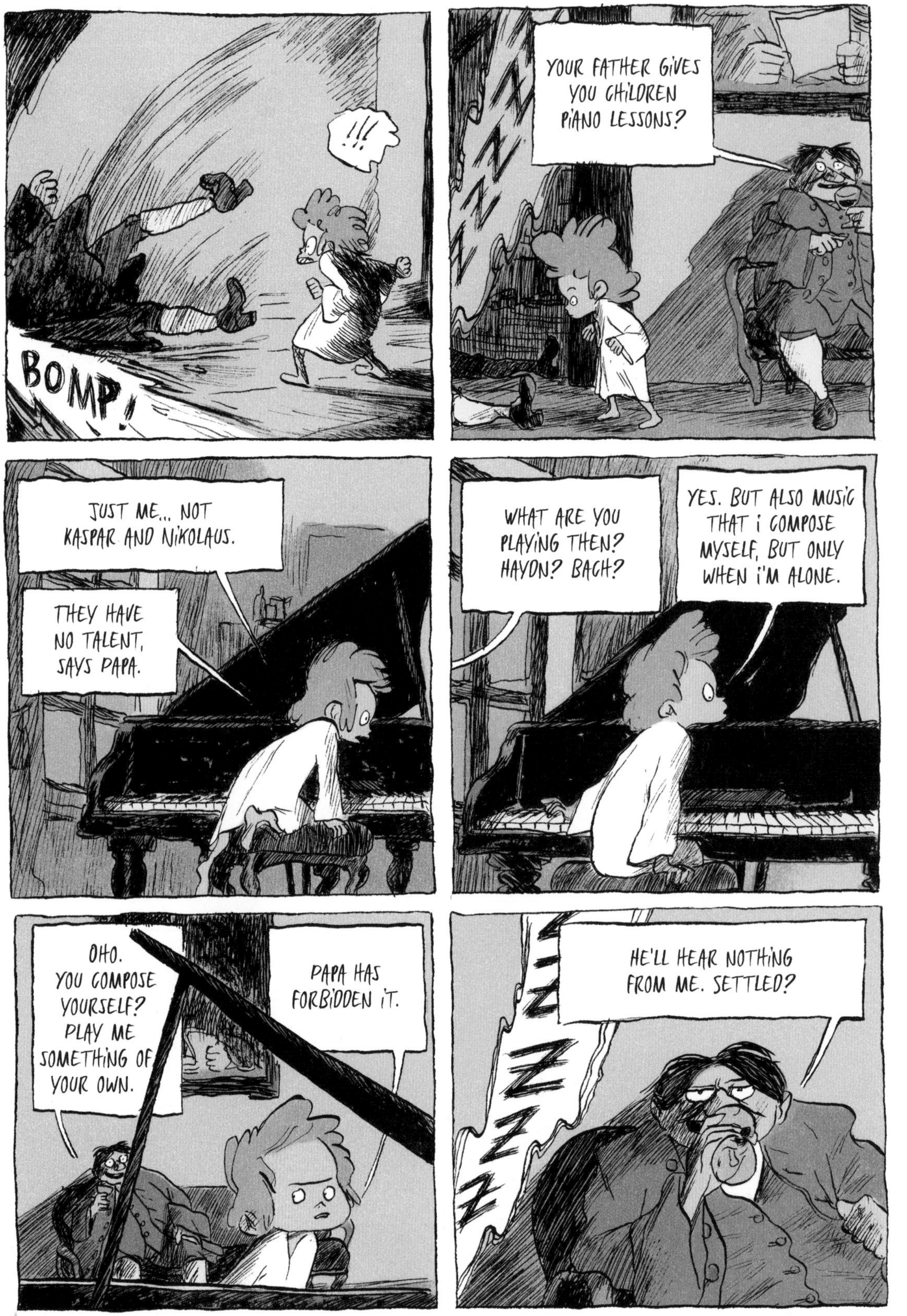

!!!
BOMP!
ZZZZZZ
YOUR FATHER GIVES YOU CHILDREN PIANO LESSONS?
JUST ME... NOT KASPAR AND NIKOLAUS.
THEY HAVE NO TALENT, SAYS PAPA.
WHAT ARE YOU PLAYING THEN? HAYDN? BACH?
YES. BUT ALSO MUSIC THAT I COMPOSE MYSELF, BUT ONLY WHEN I'M ALONE.
OHO. YOU COMPOSE YOURSELF? PLAY ME SOMETHING OF YOUR OWN.
PAPA HAS FORBIDDEN IT.
HE'LL HEAR NOTHING FROM ME. SETTLED?
ZZZZZZ

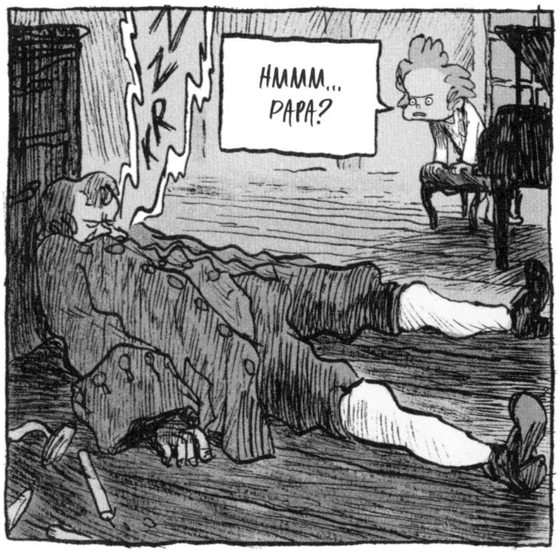
ZZZ
KR
HMMM... PAPA?

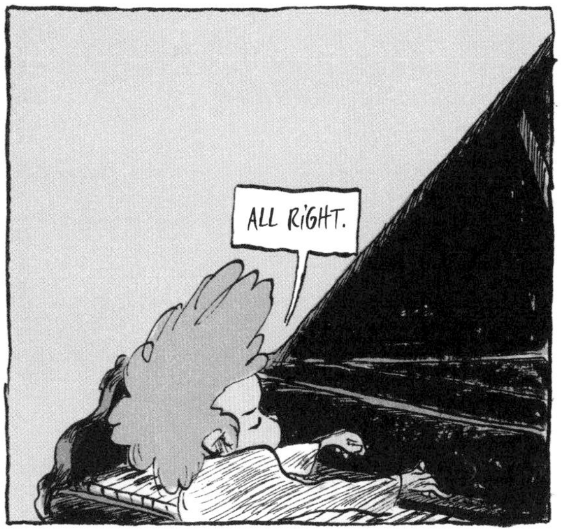
ALL RIGHT.

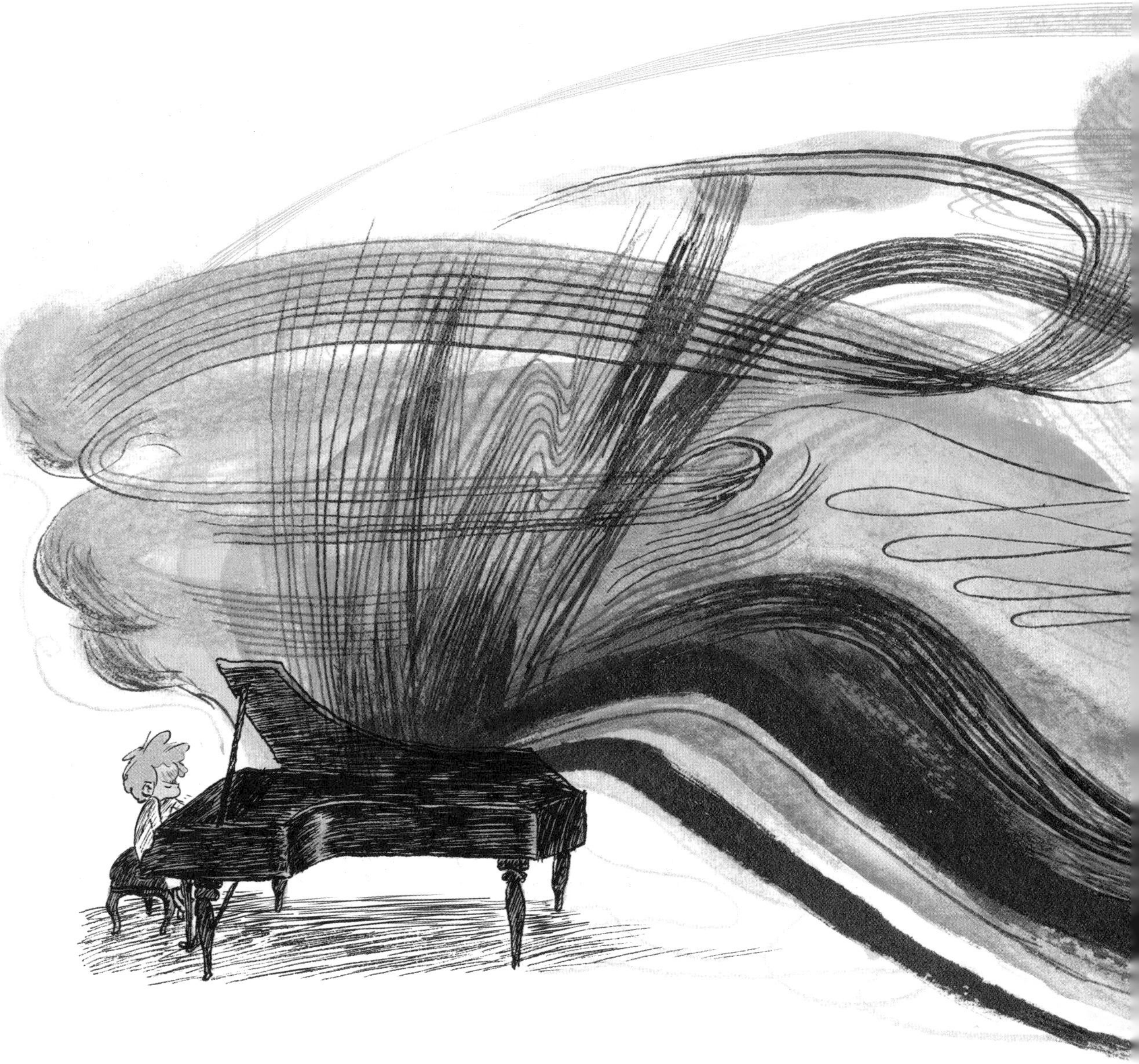

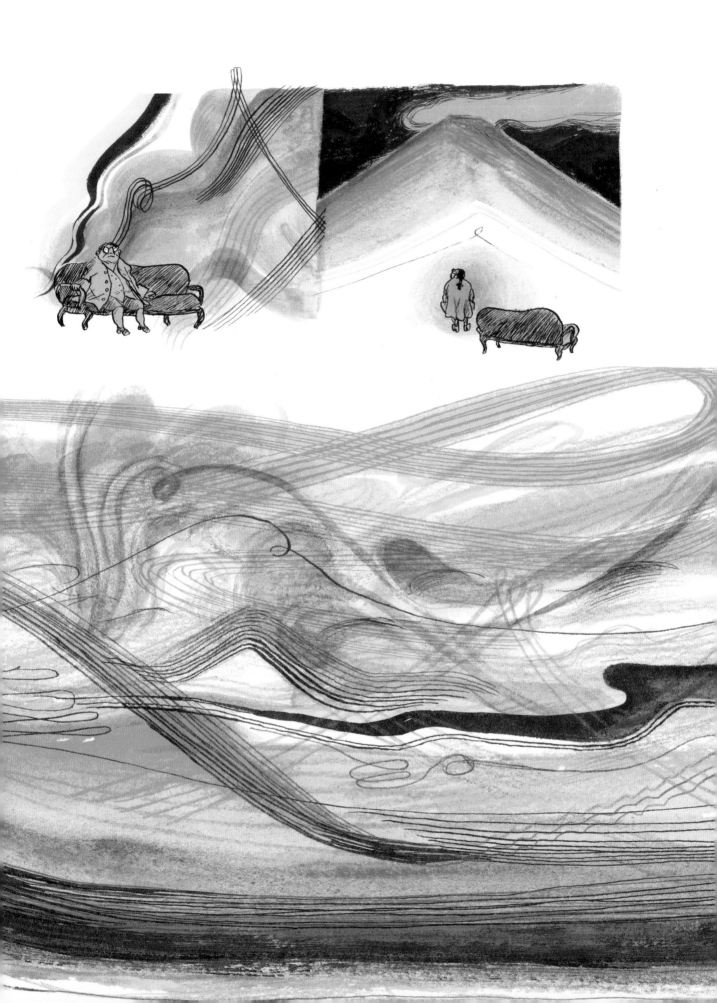

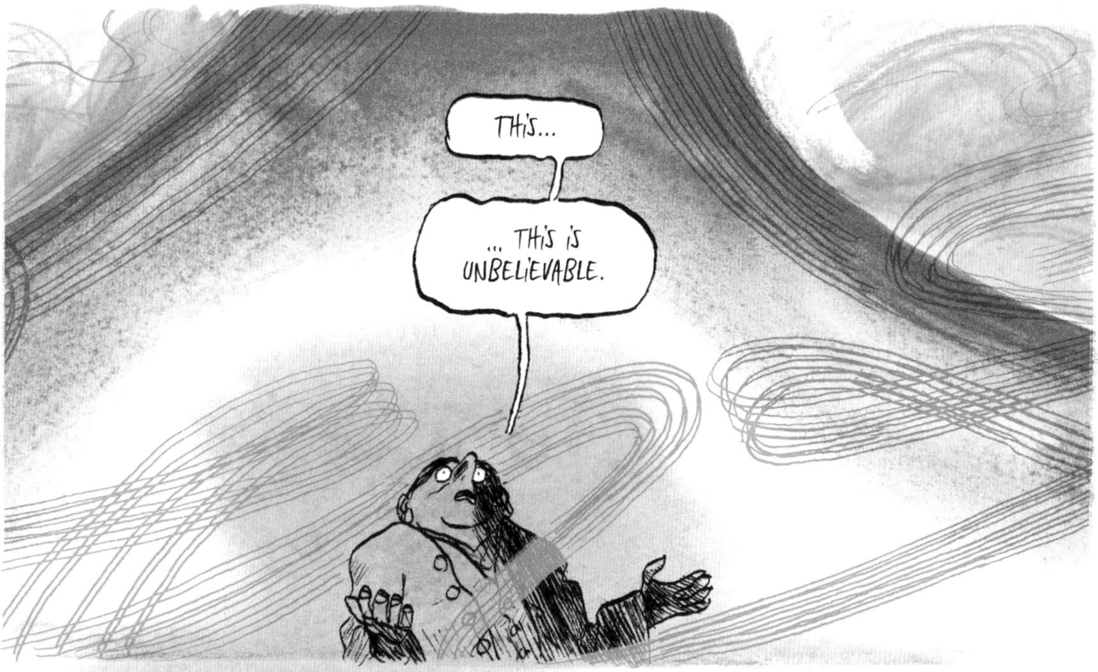
THis...
... THis is UNBELIEVABLE.

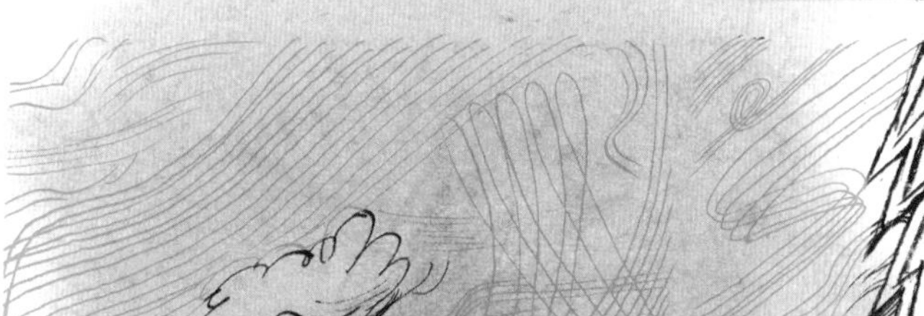

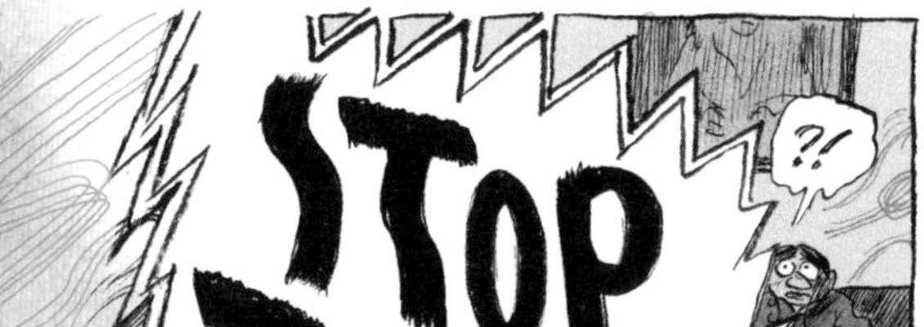
STOP THAT!
?!

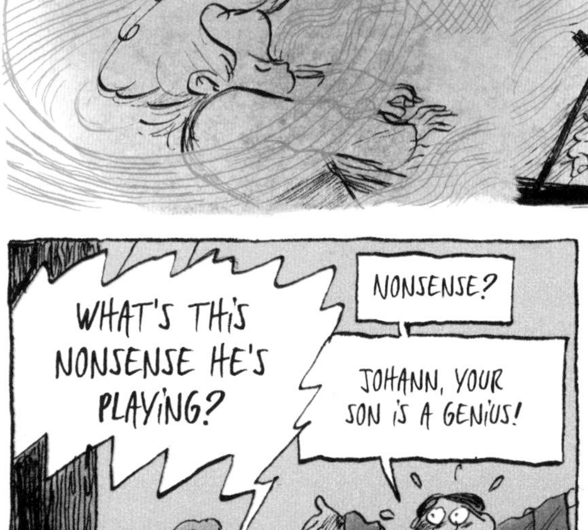
WHAT'S THis NONSENSE HE'S PLAYiNG?
NONSENSE?
JOHANN, YOUR SON iS A GENiUS!

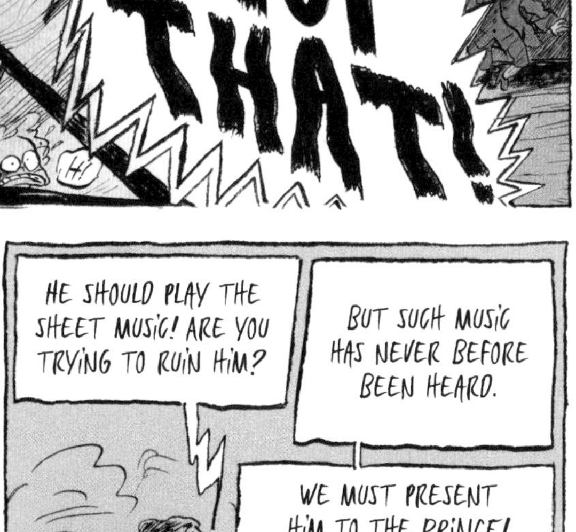
HE SHOULD PLAY THE SHEET MUSiC! ARE YOU TRYiNG TO RUiN HiM?
BUT SUCH MUSiC HAS NEVER BEFORE BEEN HEARD.
WE MUST PRESENT HiM TO THE PRiNCE!

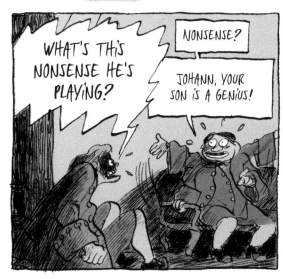

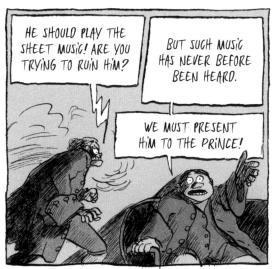

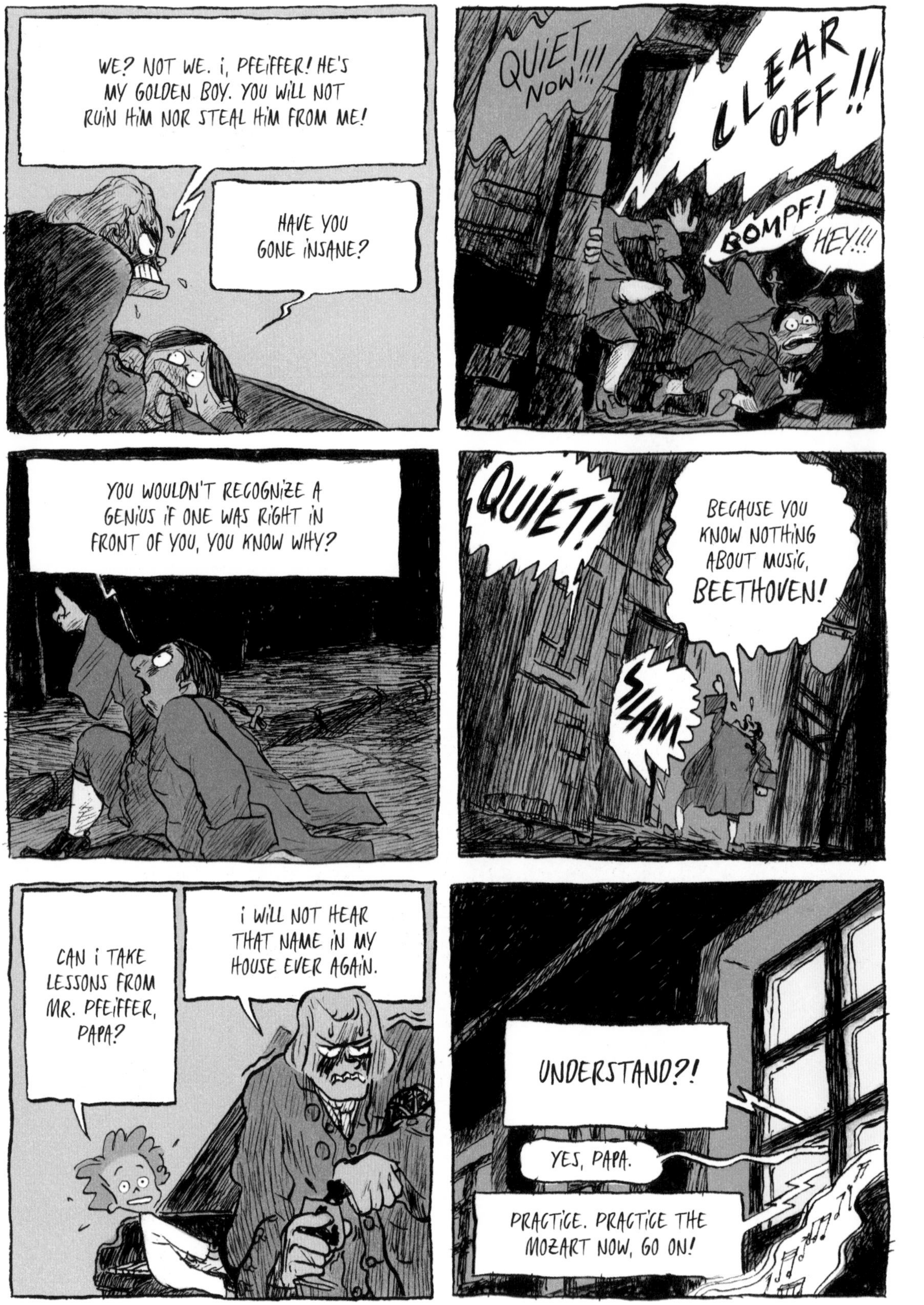

WE? NOT WE. I, PFEIFFER! HE'S MY GOLDEN BOY. YOU WILL NOT RUIN HIM NOR STEAL HIM FROM ME!
HAVE YOU GONE INSANE?
QUIET NOW!!!
CLEAR OFF!!
BOMPF!
HEY!!!
YOU WOULDN'T RECOGNIZE A GENIUS IF ONE WAS RIGHT IN FRONT OF YOU, YOU KNOW WHY?
QUIET!
BECAUSE YOU KNOW NOTHING ABOUT MUSIC, BEETHOVEN!
SLAM
CAN I TAKE LESSONS FROM MR. PFEIFFER, PAPA?
I WILL NOT HEAR THAT NAME IN MY HOUSE EVER AGAIN.
UNDERSTAND?!
YES, PAPA.
PRACTICE. PRACTICE THE MOZART NOW, GO ON!

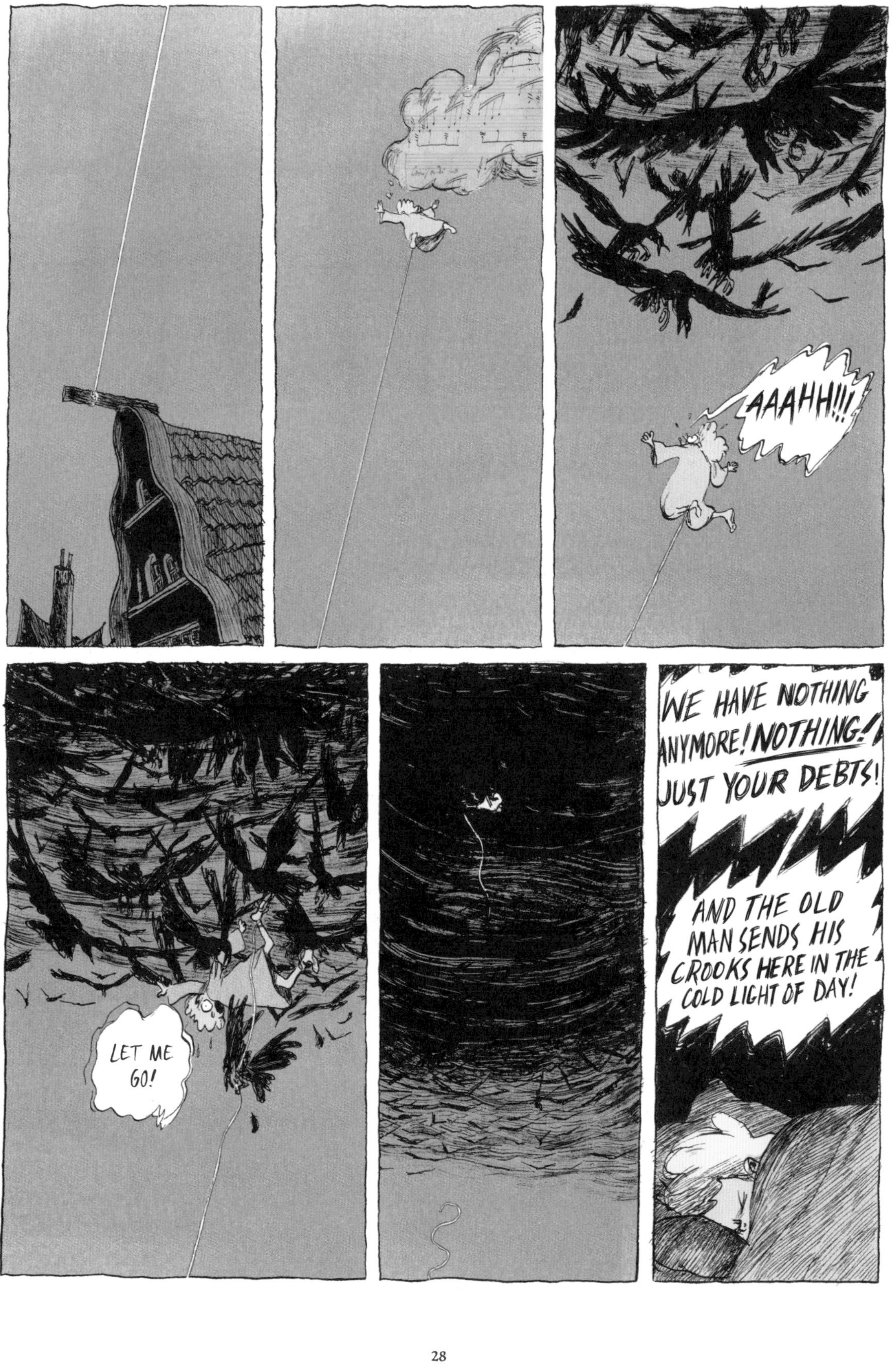
AAAHH!!!
LET ME GO!
WE HAVE NOTHING ANYMORE! NOTHING! JUST YOUR DEBTS!
AND THE OLD MAN SENDS HIS CROOKS HERE IN THE COLD LIGHT OF DAY!

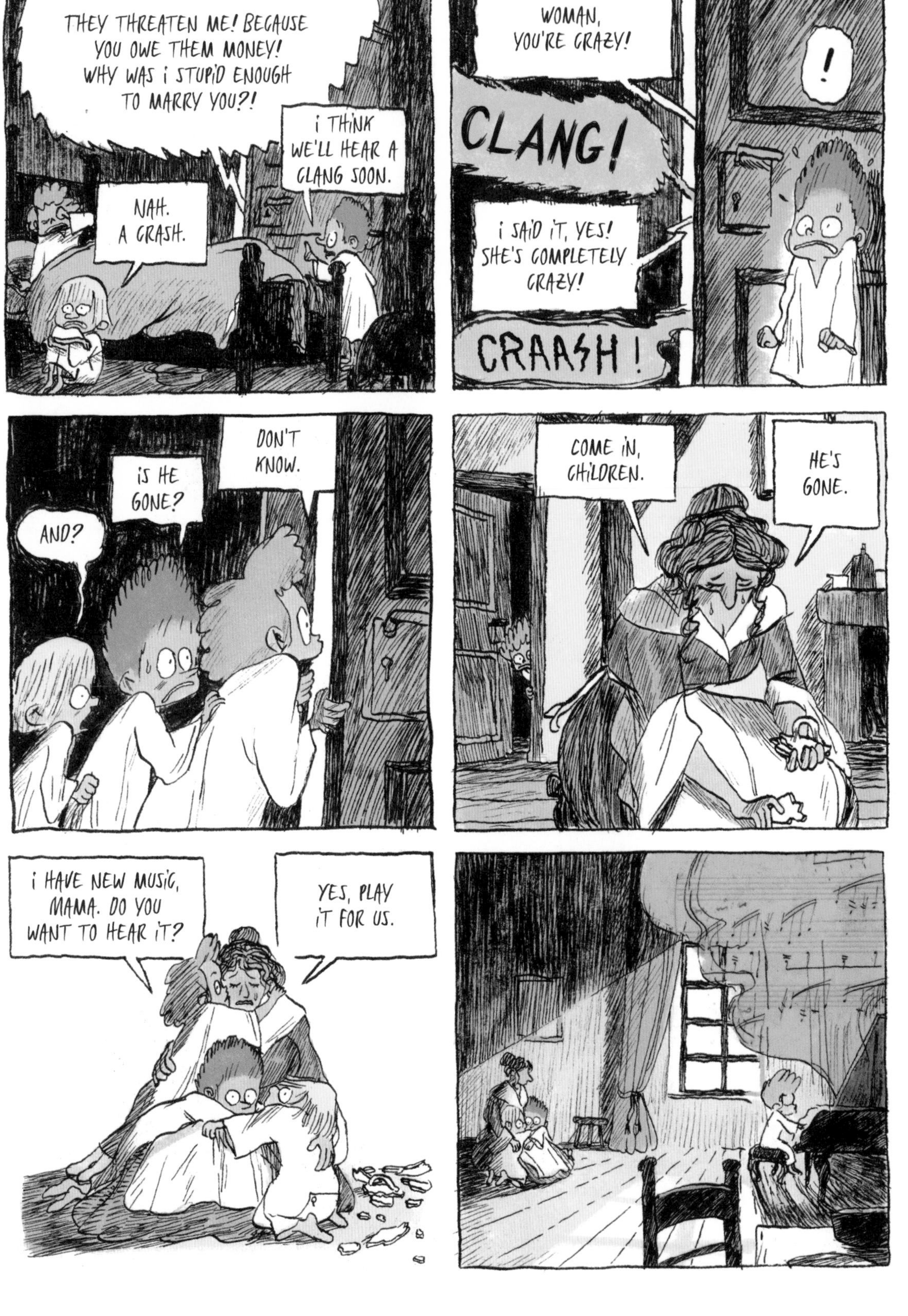
THEY THREATEN ME! BECAUSE YOU OWE THEM MONEY! WHY WAS I STUPID ENOUGH TO MARRY YOU?!
I THINK WE'LL HEAR A CLANG SOON.
NAH. A CRASH.
WOMAN, YOU'RE CRAZY!
CLANG!
I SAID IT, YES! SHE'S COMPLETELY CRAZY!
CRAASH!
!
DON'T KNOW.
IS HE GONE?
AND?
COME IN, CHILDREN.
HE'S GONE.
I HAVE NEW MUSIC, MAMA. DO YOU WANT TO HEAR IT?
YES, PLAY IT FOR US.

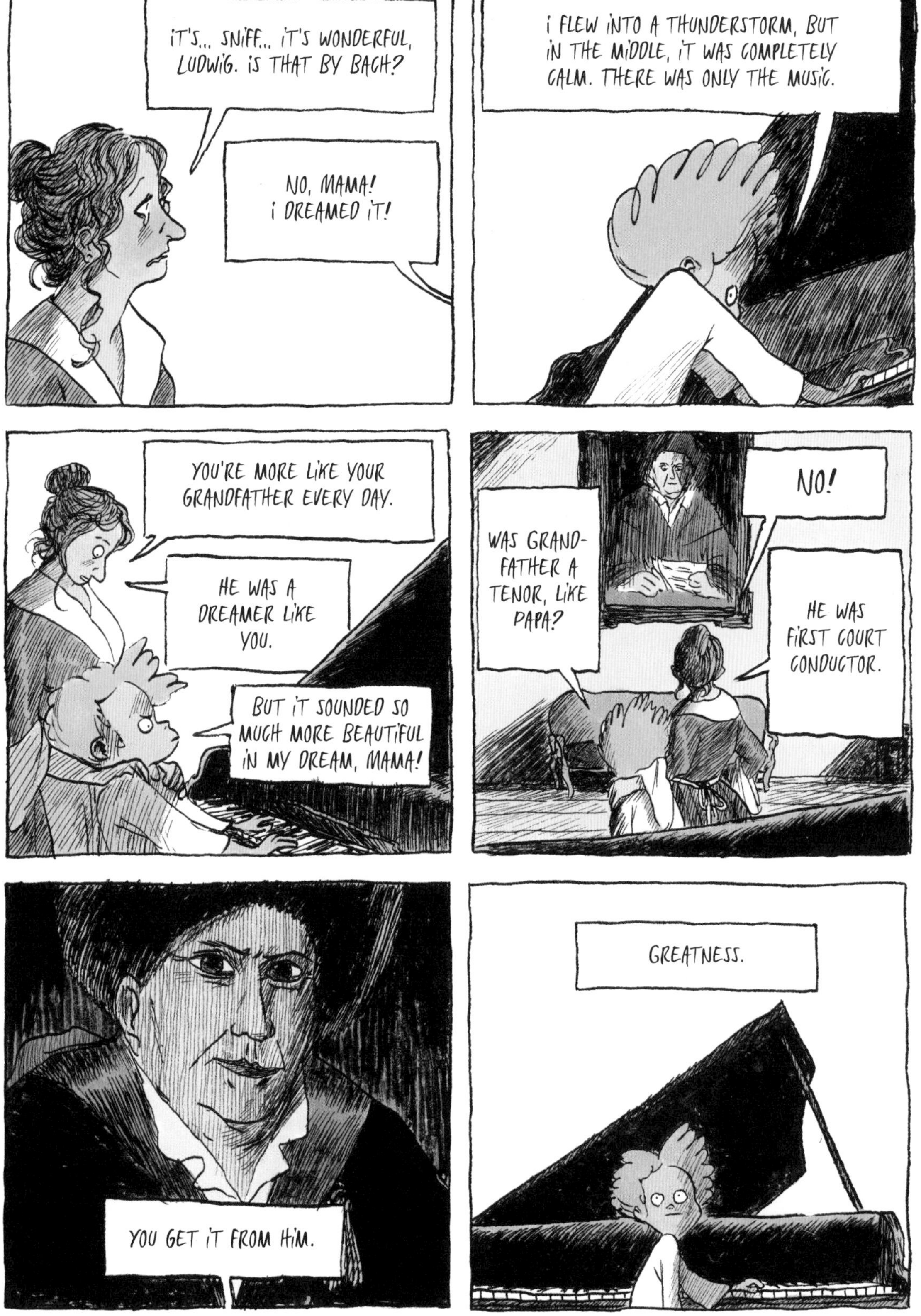
IT'S... SNIFF... IT'S WONDERFUL, LUDWIG. IS THAT BY BACH?
NO, MAMA! I DREAMED IT!
I FLEW INTO A THUNDERSTORM, BUT IN THE MIDDLE, IT WAS COMPLETELY CALM. THERE WAS ONLY THE MUSIC.
YOU'RE MORE LIKE YOUR GRANDFATHER EVERY DAY.
HE WAS A DREAMER LIKE YOU.
BUT IT SOUNDED SO MUCH MORE BEAUTIFUL IN MY DREAM, MAMA!
WAS GRANDFATHER A TENOR, LIKE PAPA?
NO!
HE WAS FIRST COURT CONDUCTOR.
YOU GET IT FROM HIM.
GREATNESS.

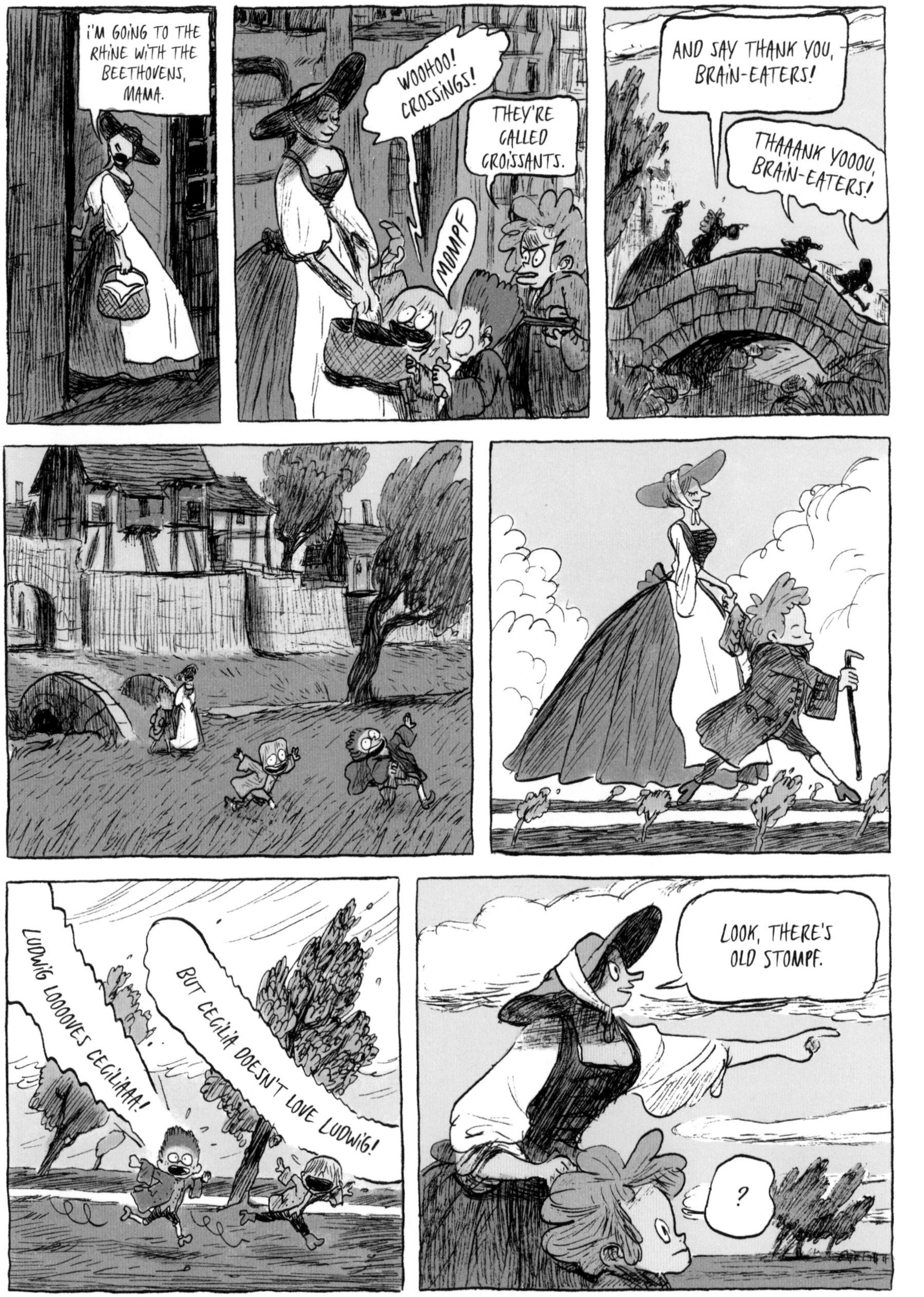
I'M GOING TO THE RHINE WITH THE BEETHOVENS, MAMA.
WOOHOO! CROSSINGS!
THEY'RE CALLED CROISSANTS.
MOMPF
AND SAY THANK YOU, BRAIN-EATERS!
THAAANK YOOOU, BRAIN-EATERS!
LUDWIG LOOOOVES CECILIAAA!
BUT CECILIA DOESN'T LOVE LUDWIG!
LOOK, THERE'S OLD STOMPF.
?

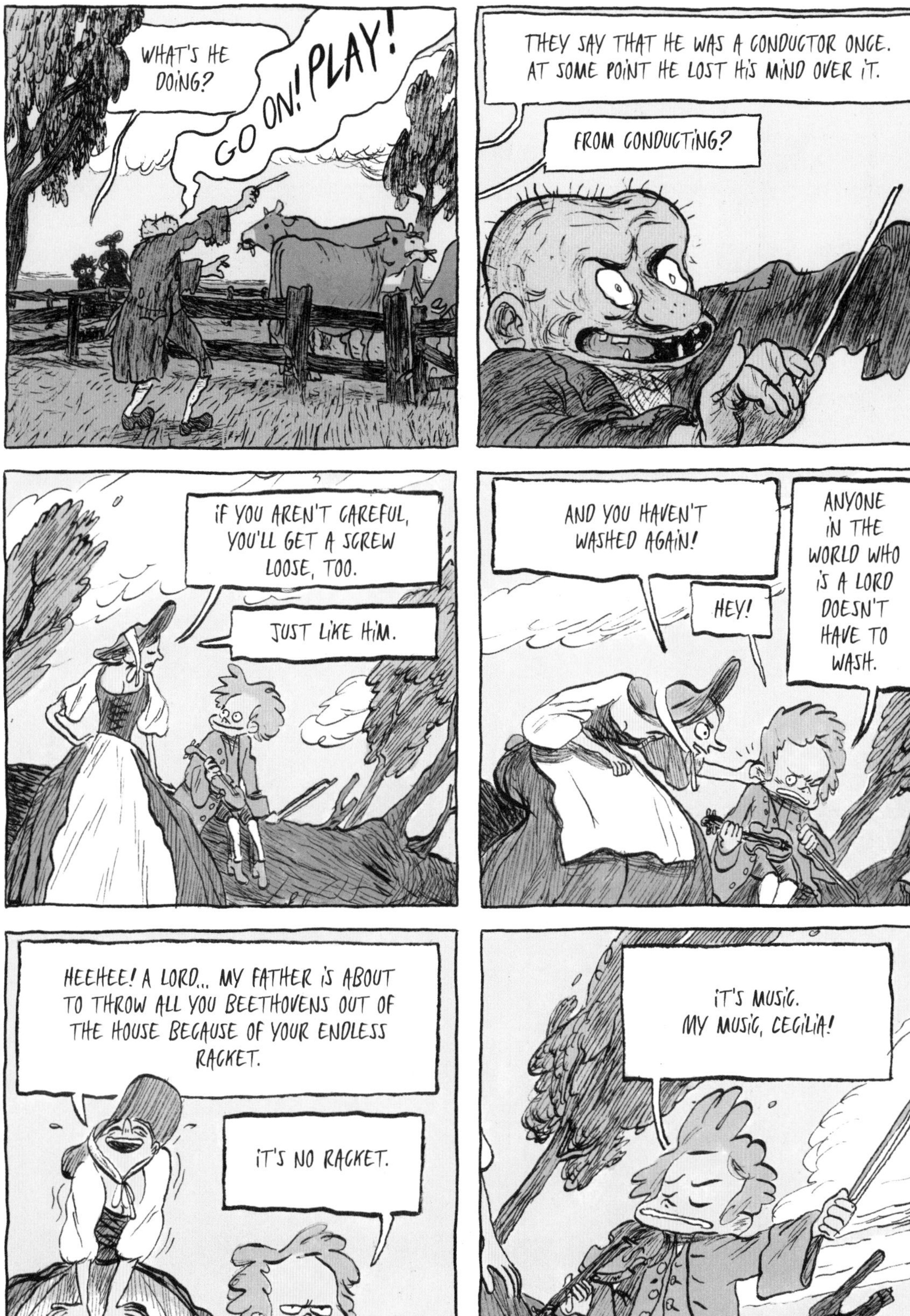
WHAT'S HE DOING?
GO ON! PLAY!
THEY SAY THAT HE WAS A CONDUCTOR ONCE. AT SOME POINT HE LOST HIS MIND OVER IT.
FROM CONDUCTING?
IF YOU AREN'T CAREFUL, YOU'LL GET A SCREW LOOSE, TOO.
JUST LIKE HIM.
AND YOU HAVEN'T WASHED AGAIN!
HEY!
ANYONE IN THE WORLD WHO IS A LORD DOESN'T HAVE TO WASH.
HEEHEE! A LORD... MY FATHER IS ABOUT TO THROW ALL YOU BEETHOVENS OUT OF THE HOUSE BECAUSE OF YOUR ENDLESS RACKET.
IT'S NO RACKET.
IT'S MUSIC. MY MUSIC, CECILIA!

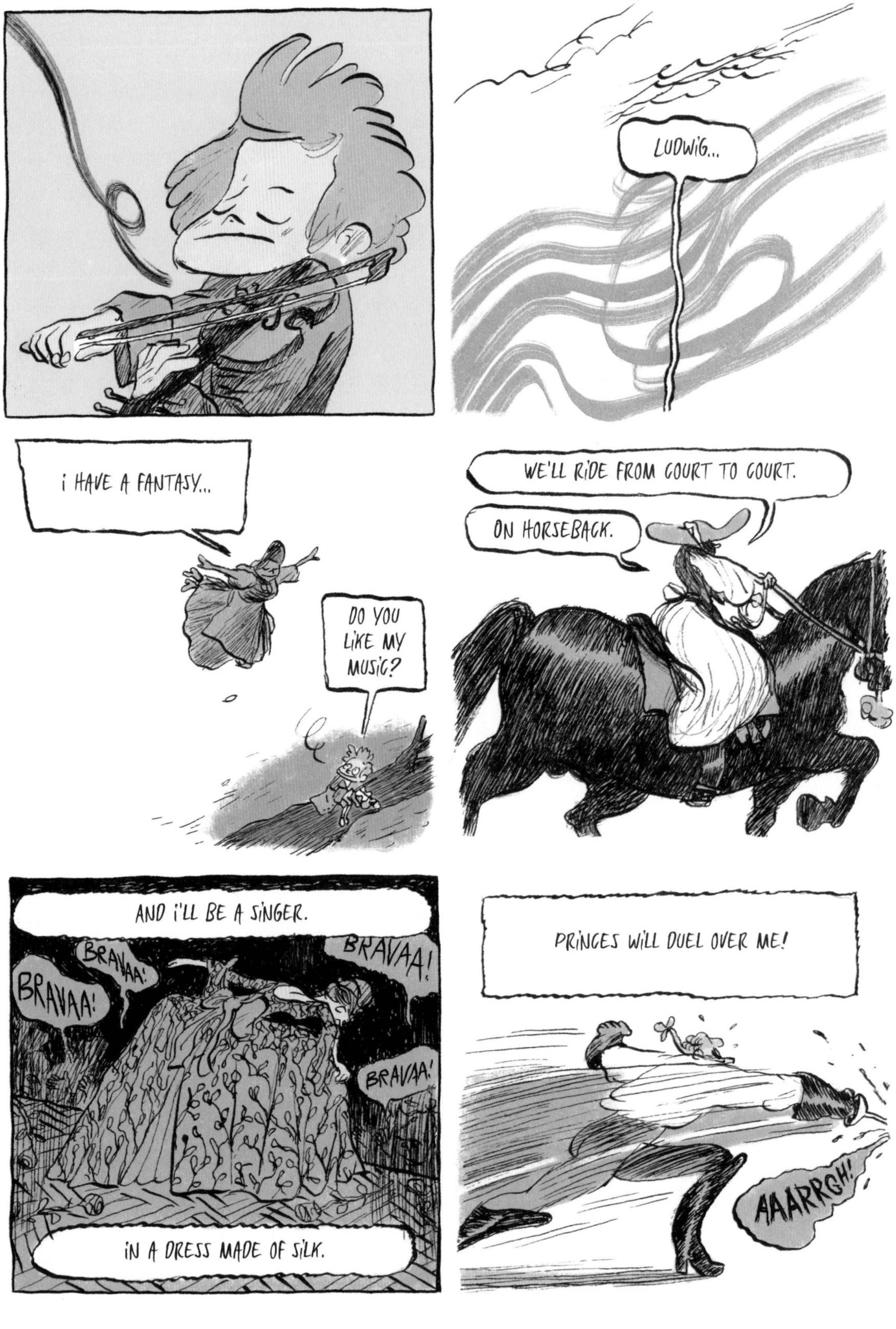
LUDWIG...
I HAVE A FANTASY...
DO YOU LIKE MY MUSIC?
WE'LL RIDE FROM COURT TO COURT.
ON HORSEBACK.
AND I'LL BE A SINGER.
BRAVAA!
BRAVAA!
BRAVAA!
BRAVAA!
IN A DRESS MADE OF SILK.
PRINCES WILL DUEL OVER ME!
AAARRGH!

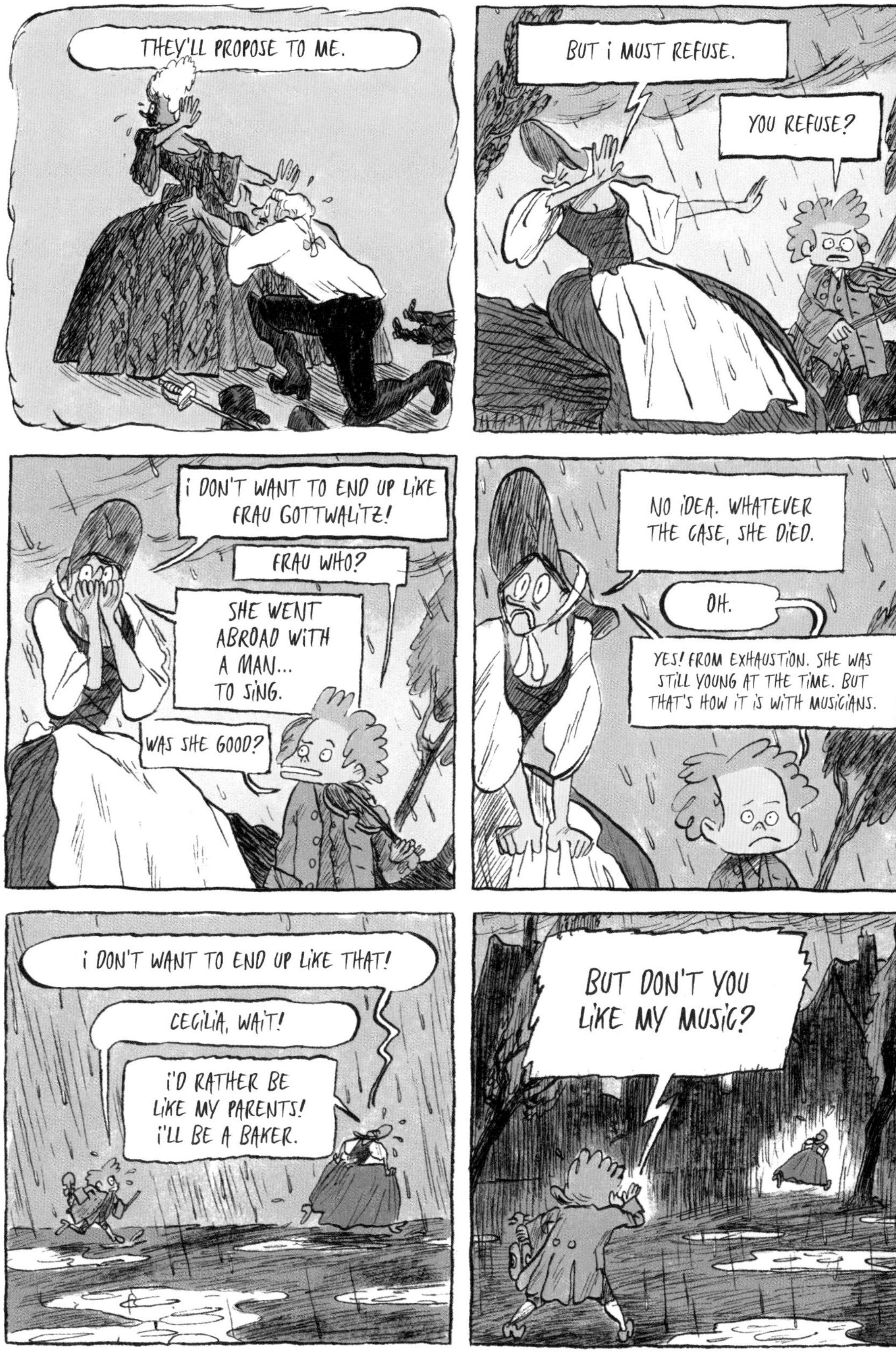
THEY'LL PROPOSE TO ME.
BUT I MUST REFUSE.
YOU REFUSE?
I DON'T WANT TO END UP LIKE FRAU GOTTWALITZ!
FRAU WHO?
SHE WENT ABROAD WITH A MAN... TO SING.
WAS SHE GOOD?
NO IDEA. WHATEVER THE CASE, SHE DIED.
OH.
YES! FROM EXHAUSTION. SHE WAS STILL YOUNG AT THE TIME. BUT THAT'S HOW IT IS WITH MUSICIANS.
I DON'T WANT TO END UP LIKE THAT!
CECILIA, WAIT!
I'D RATHER BE LIKE MY PARENTS! I'LL BE A BAKER.
BUT DON'T YOU LIKE MY MUSIC?

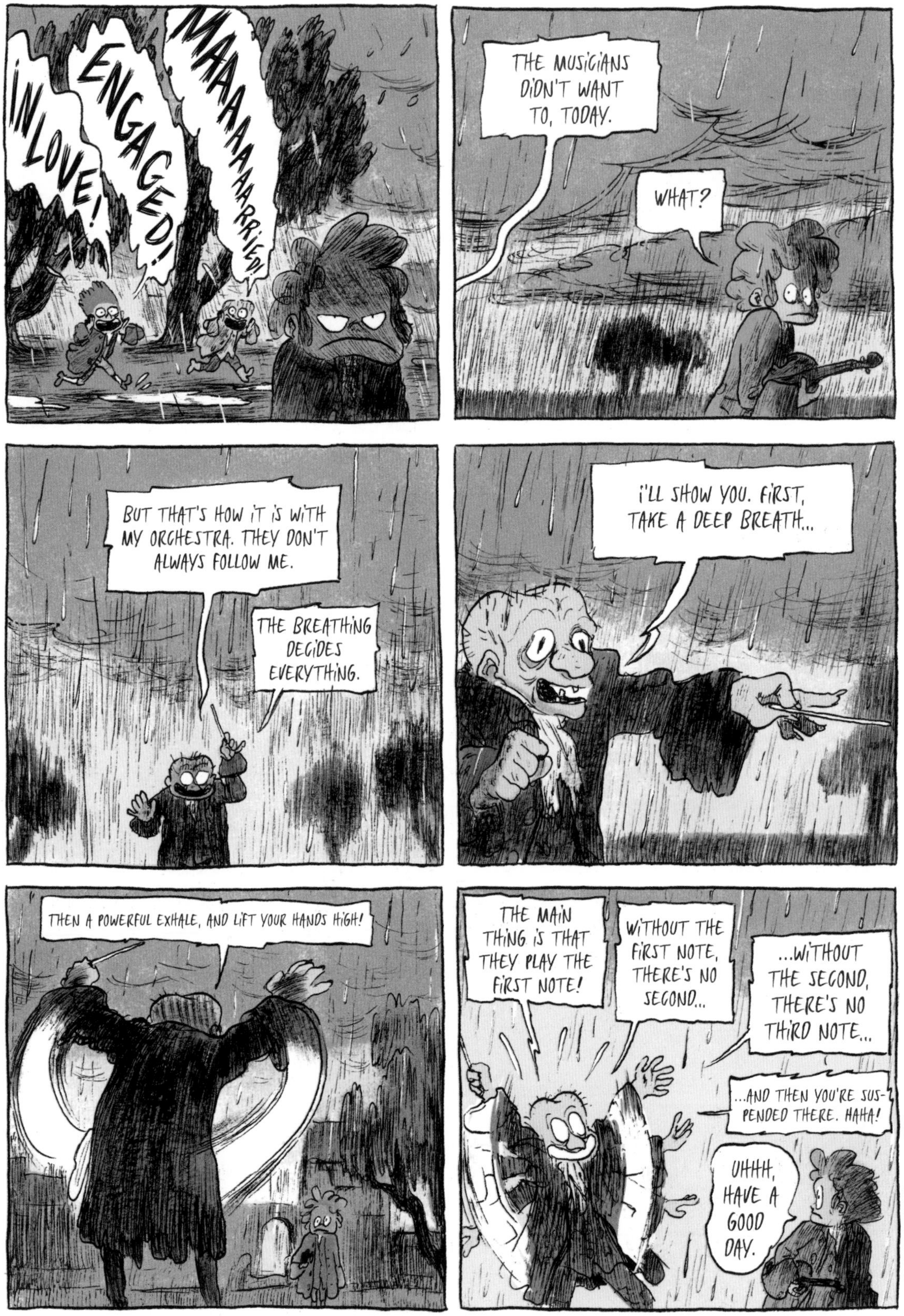
IN LOVE!
ENGAGED!
MAAAAAAAARRIED!
THE MUSICIANS DIDN'T WANT TO, TODAY.
WHAT?
BUT THAT'S HOW IT IS WITH MY ORCHESTRA. THEY DON'T ALWAYS FOLLOW ME.
THE BREATHING DECIDES EVERYTHING.
I'LL SHOW YOU. FIRST, TAKE A DEEP BREATH...
THEN A POWERFUL EXHALE, AND LIFT YOUR HANDS HIGH!
THE MAIN THING IS THAT THEY PLAY THE FIRST NOTE!
WITHOUT THE FIRST NOTE, THERE'S NO SECOND...
...WITHOUT THE SECOND, THERE'S NO THIRD NOTE...
...AND THEN YOU'RE SUS-PENDED THERE. HAHA!
UHHH, HAVE A GOOD DAY.

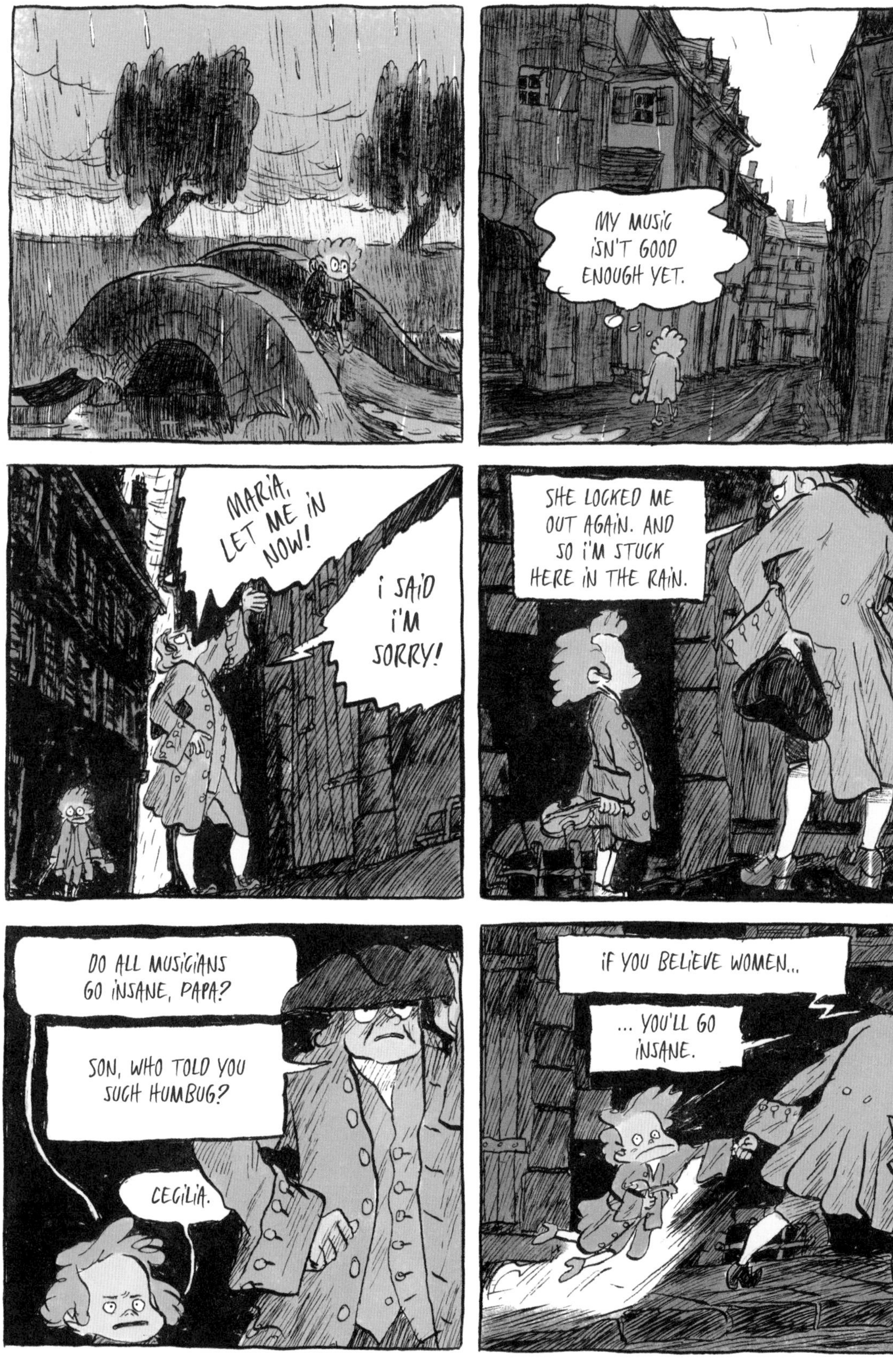
MY MUSIC ISN'T GOOD ENOUGH YET.
MARIA, LET ME IN NOW!
I SAID I'M SORRY!
SHE LOCKED ME OUT AGAIN. AND SO I'M STUCK HERE IN THE RAIN.
DO ALL MUSICIANS GO INSANE, PAPA?
SON, WHO TOLD YOU SUCH HUMBUG?
CECILIA.
IF YOU BELIEVE WOMEN...
... YOU'LL GO INSANE.

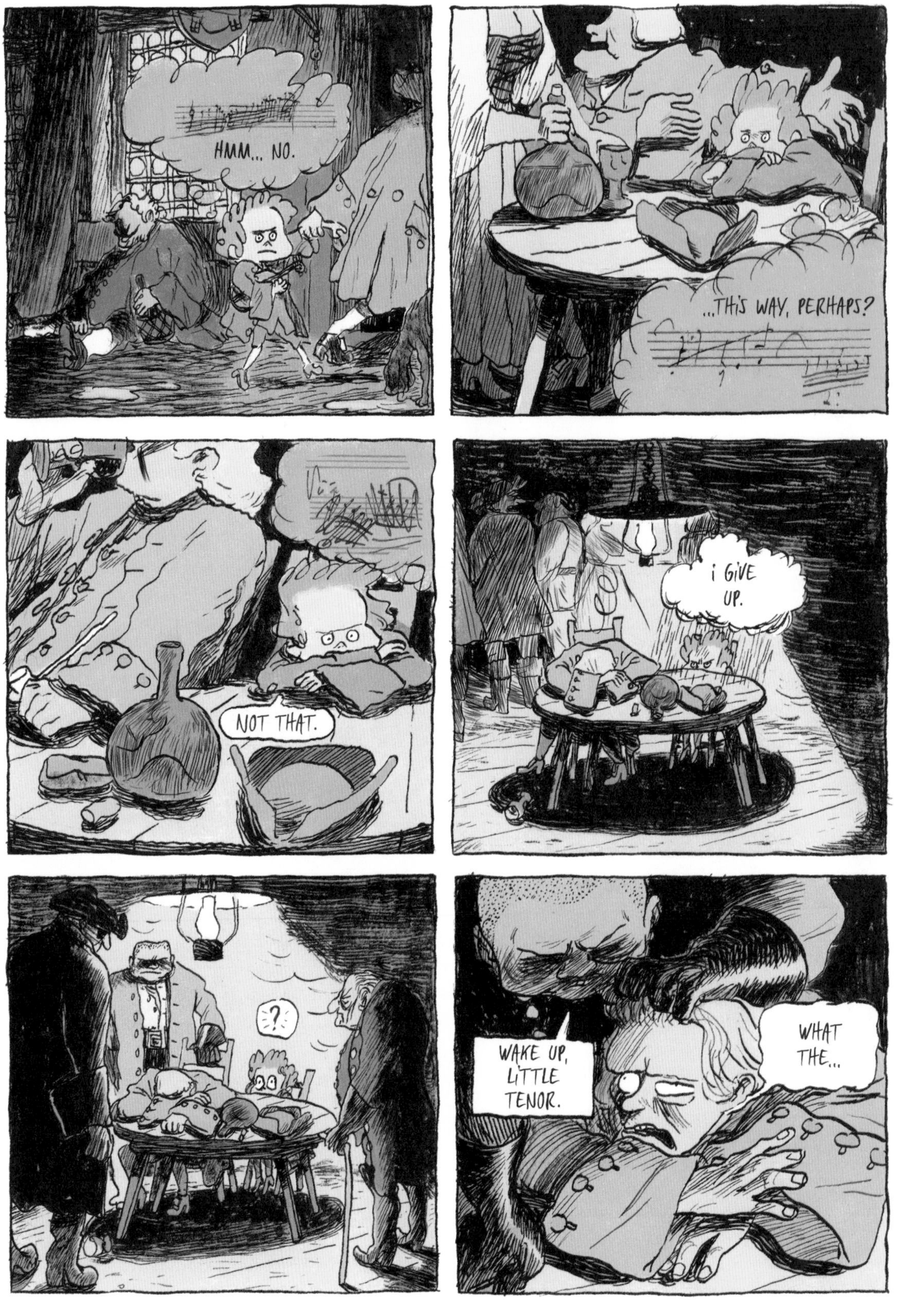
HMM... NO.
...THIS WAY, PERHAPS?
NOT THAT.
I GIVE UP.
?
WAKE UP, LITTLE TENOR.
WHAT THE...

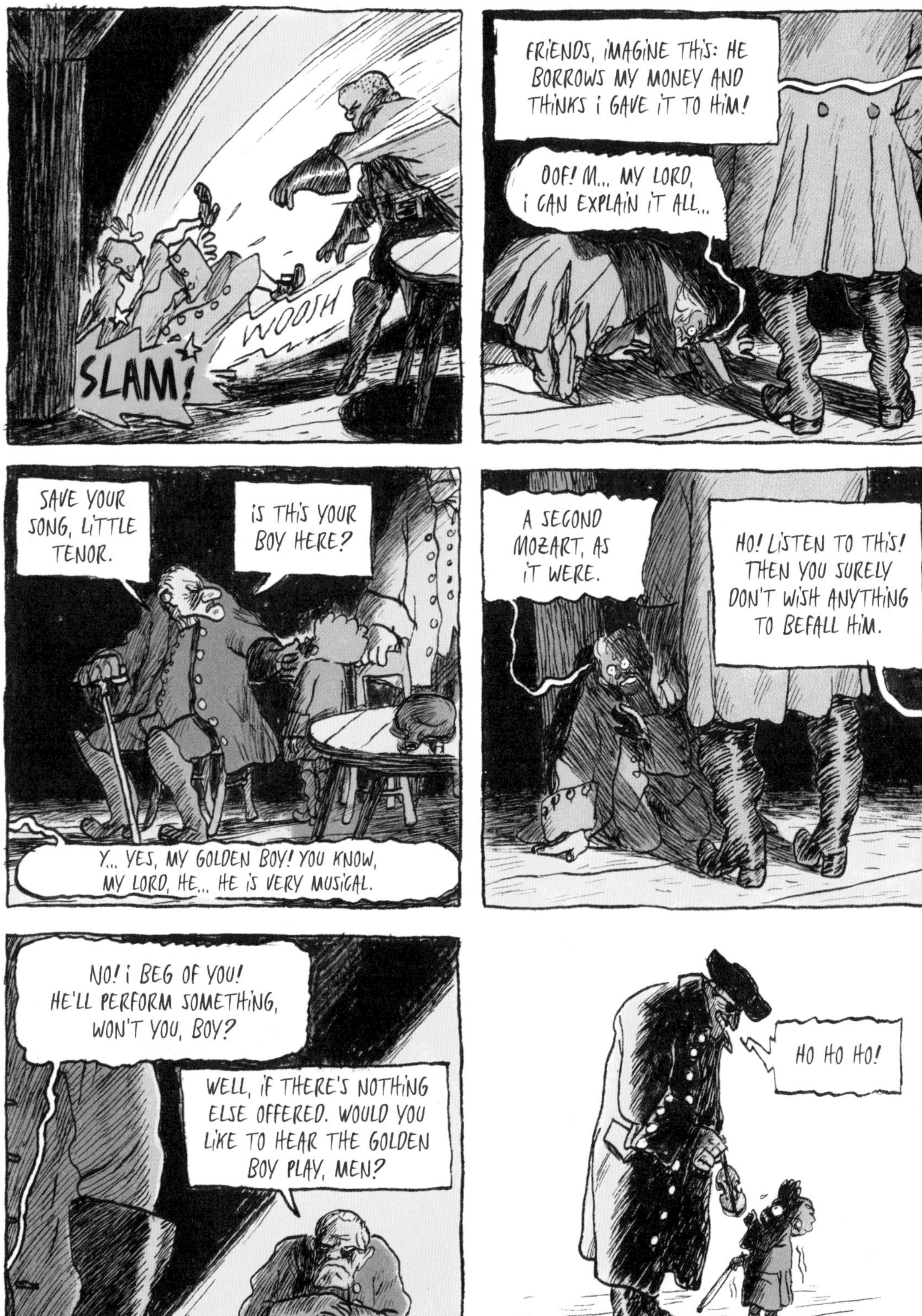
SLAM!
WOOSH
FRIENDS, IMAGINE THIS: HE BORROWS MY MONEY AND THINKS I GAVE IT TO HIM!
OOF! M... MY LORD, I CAN EXPLAIN IT ALL...
SAVE YOUR SONG, LITTLE TENOR.
IS THIS YOUR BOY HERE?
Y... YES, MY GOLDEN BOY! YOU KNOW, MY LORD, HE... HE IS VERY MUSICAL.
A SECOND MOZART, AS IT WERE.
HO! LISTEN TO THIS! THEN YOU SURELY DON'T WISH ANYTHING TO BEFALL HIM.
NO! I BEG OF YOU! HE'LL PERFORM SOMETHING, WON'T YOU, BOY?
WELL, IF THERE'S NOTHING ELSE OFFERED. WOULD YOU LIKE TO HEAR THE GOLDEN BOY PLAY, MEN?
HO HO HO!

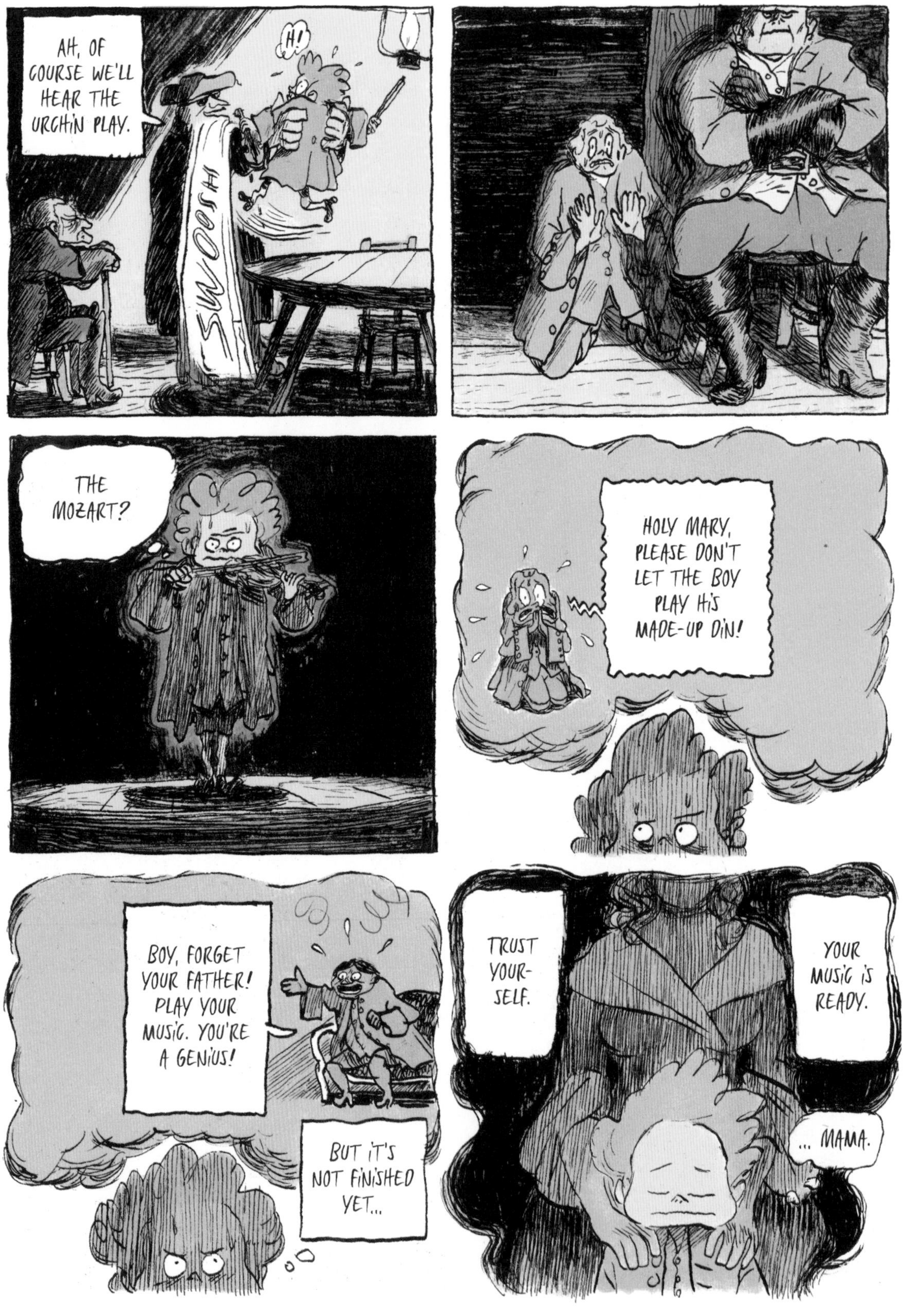
AH, OF COURSE WE'LL HEAR THE URCHIN PLAY.
H!
SWOOSH
THE MOZART?
HOLY MARY, PLEASE DON'T LET THE BOY PLAY HIS MADE-UP DIN!
BOY, FORGET YOUR FATHER! PLAY YOUR MUSIC. YOU'RE A GENIUS!
BUT IT'S NOT FINISHED YET...
TRUST YOURSELF.
YOUR MUSIC IS READY.
... MAMA.

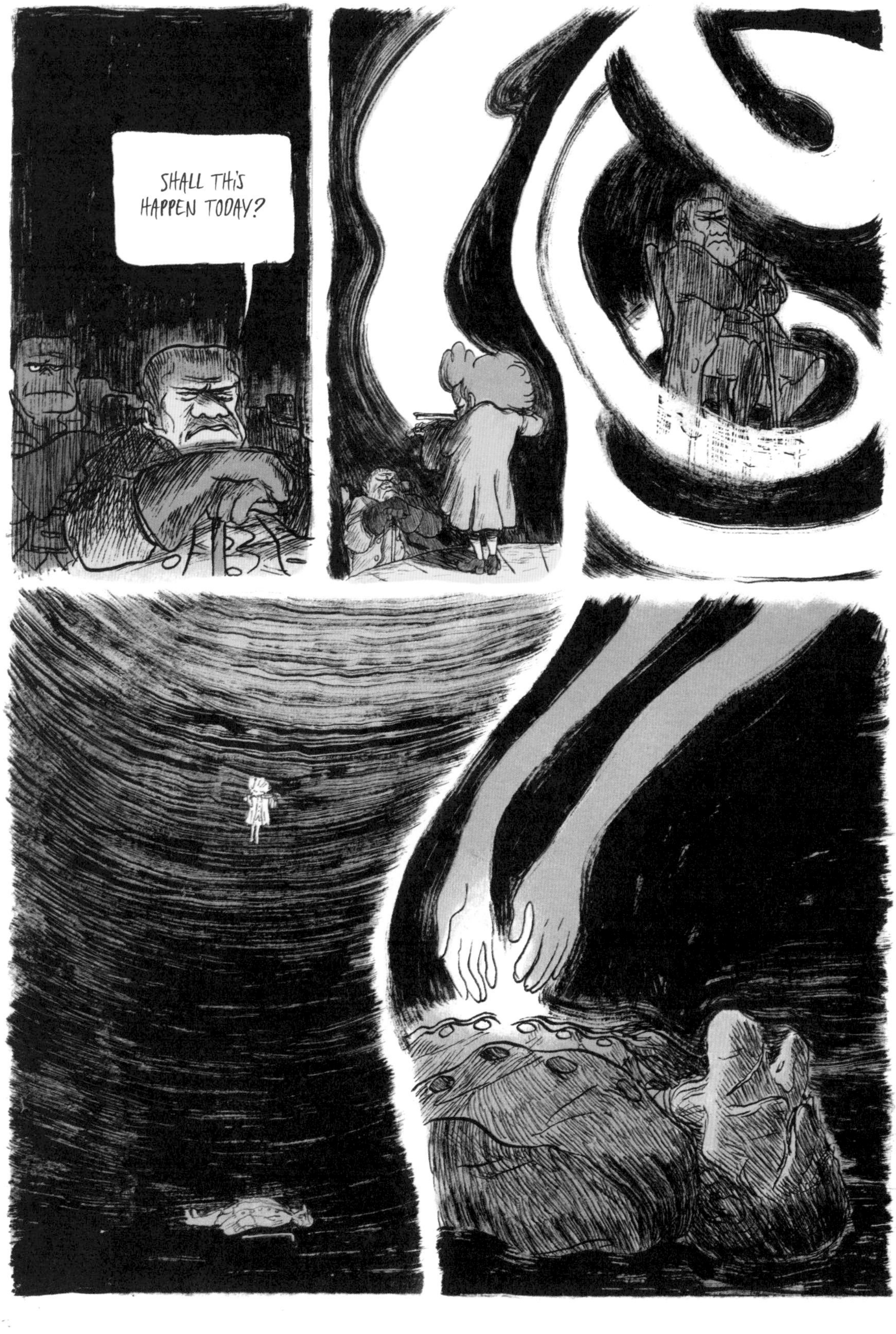
SHALL THIS HAPPEN TODAY?

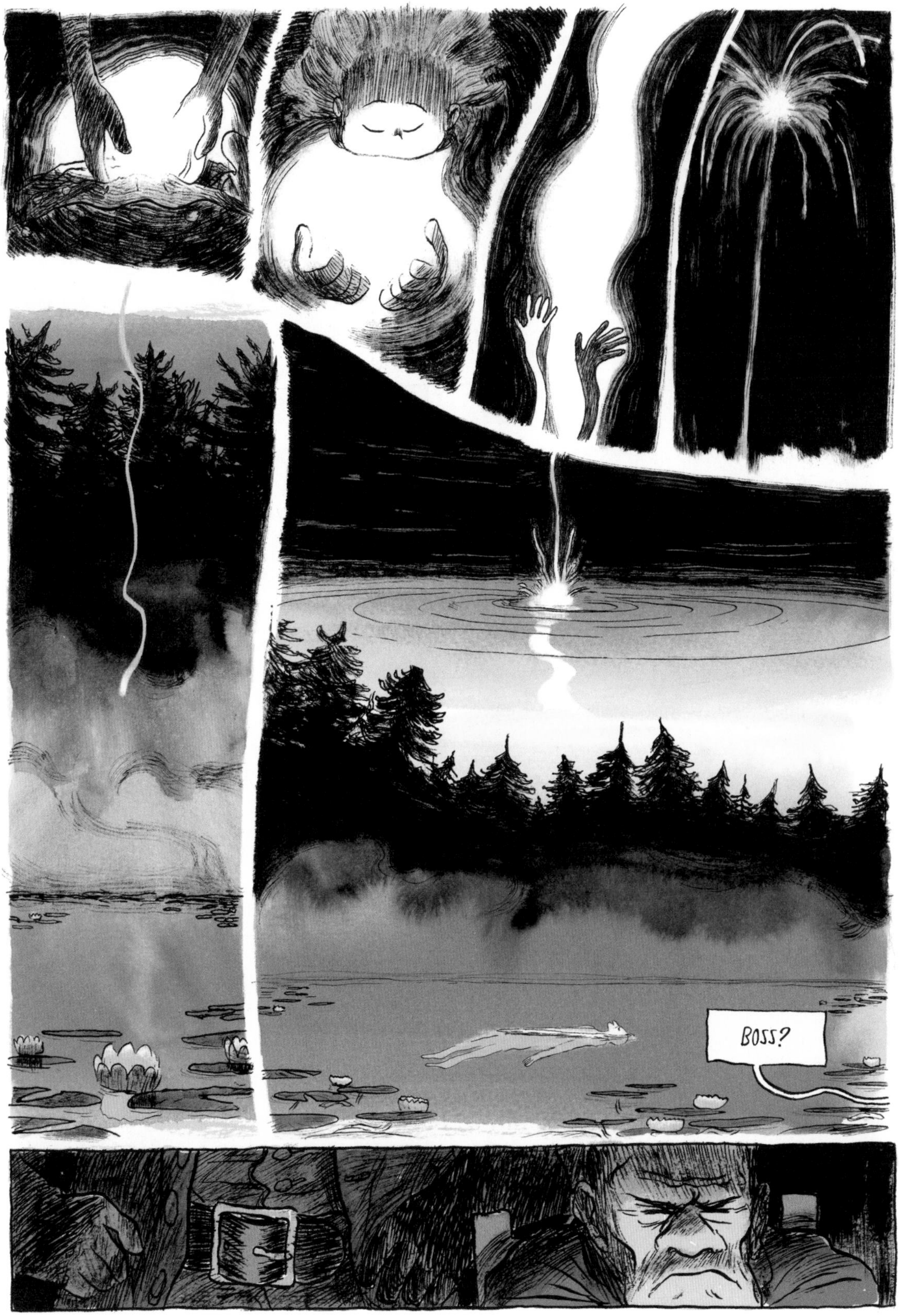
BOSS?

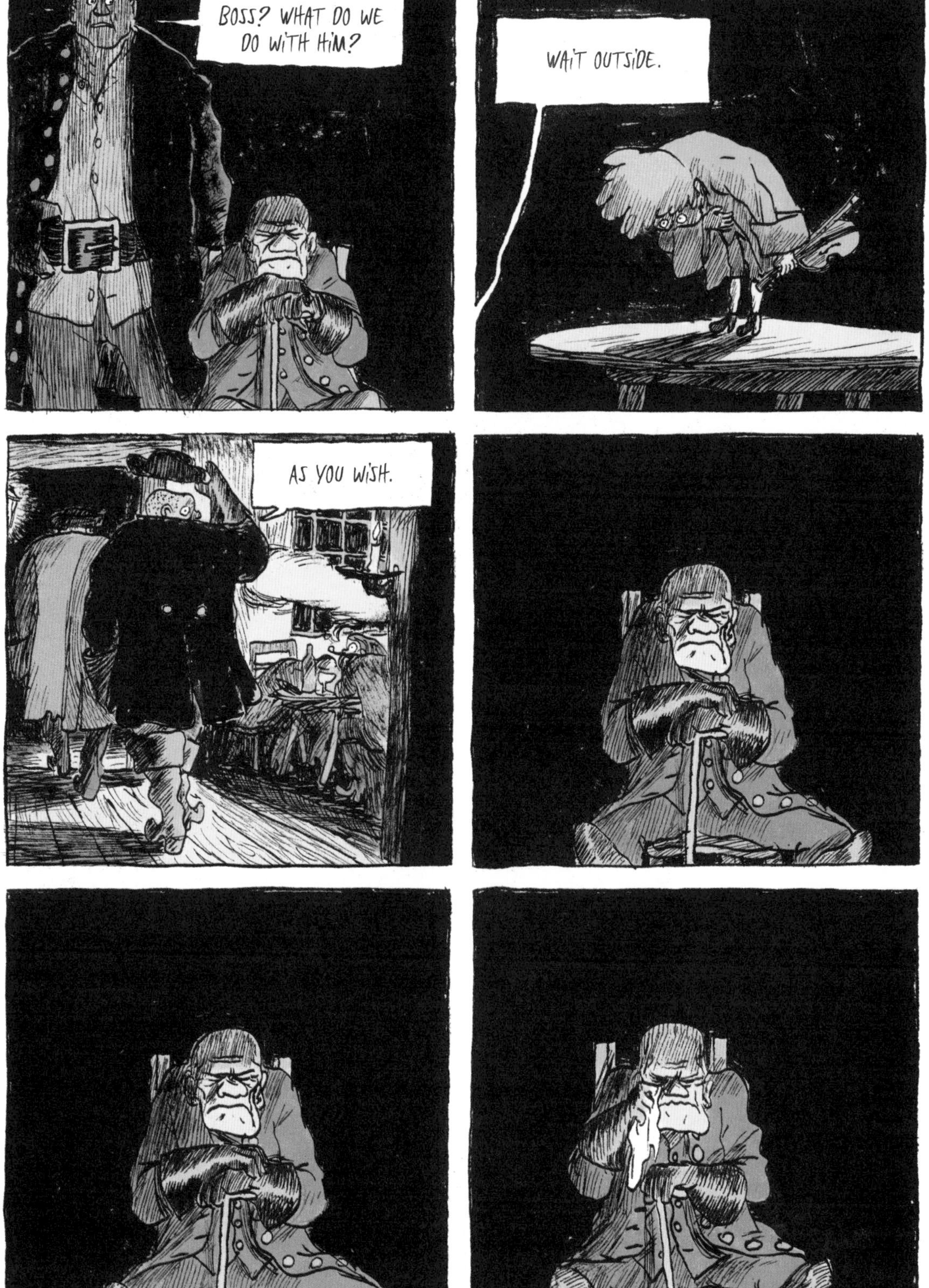
BOSS? WHAT DO WE DO WITH HIM?
WAIT OUTSIDE.
AS YOU WISH.

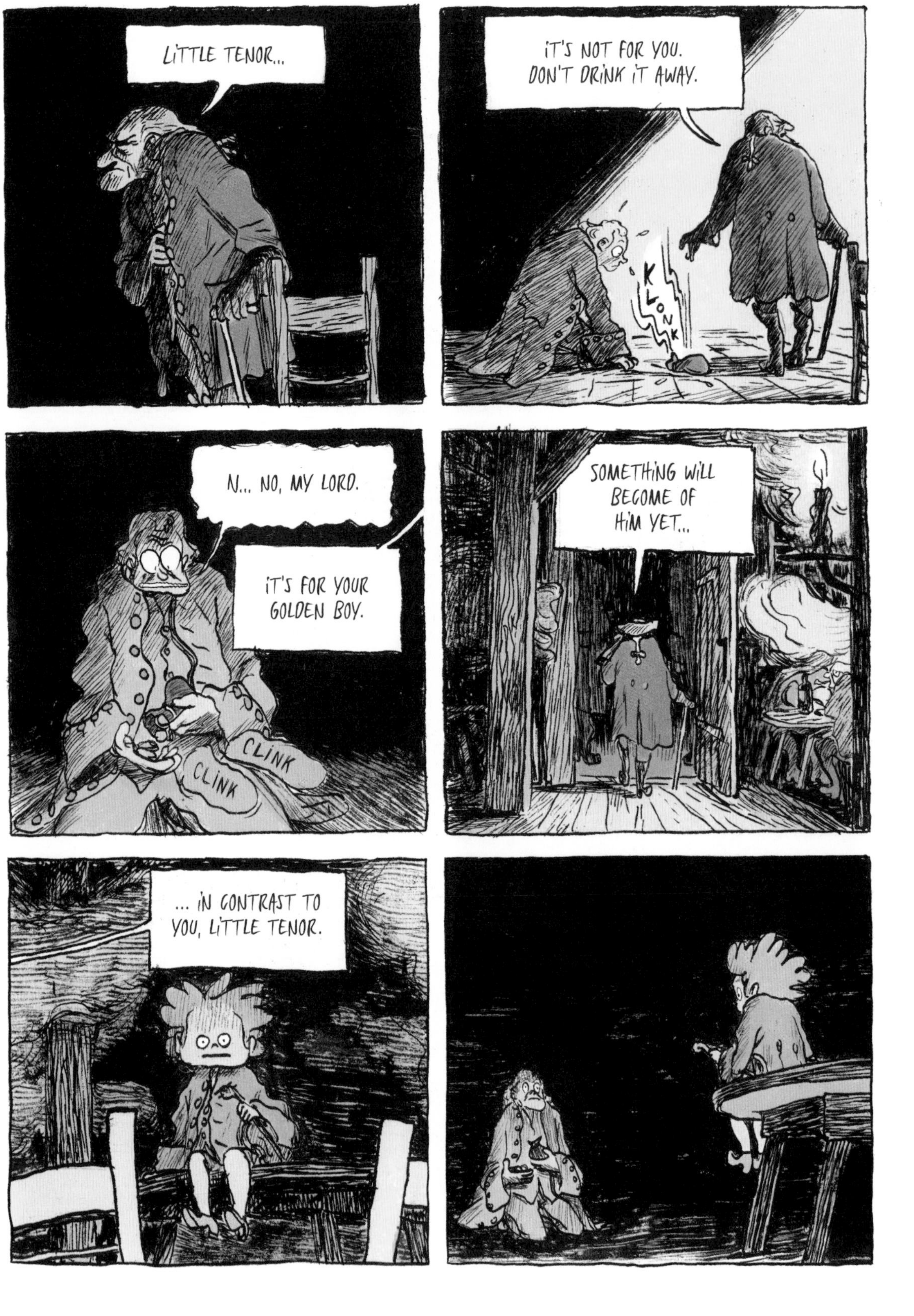
LITTLE TENOR...
IT'S NOT FOR YOU. DON'T DRINK IT AWAY.
KLONK
N... NO, MY LORD.
IT'S FOR YOUR GOLDEN BOY.
CLINK
CLINK
SOMETHING WILL BECOME OF HIM YET...
... IN CONTRAST TO YOU, LITTLE TENOR.

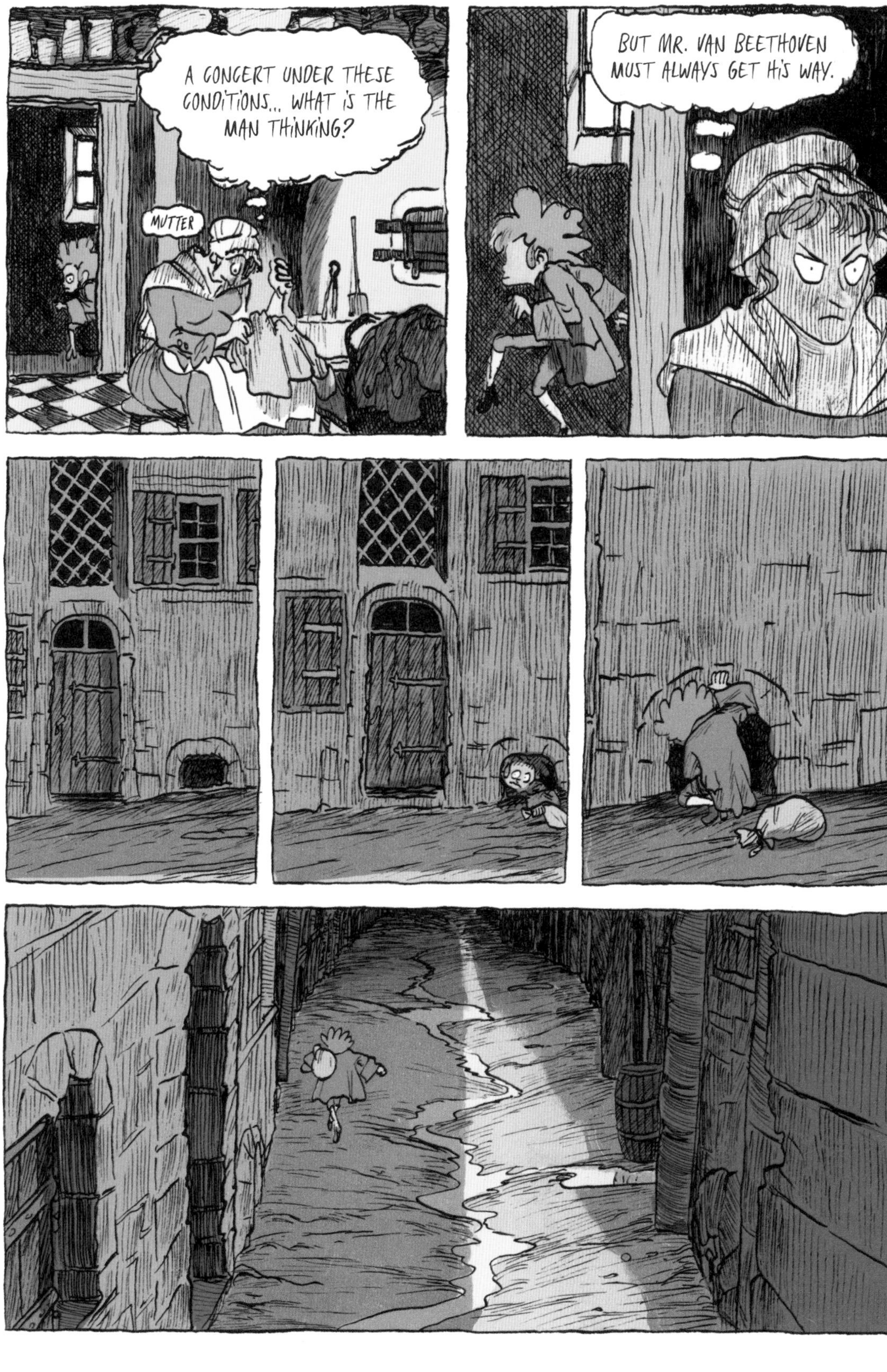
A CONCERT UNDER THESE CONDITIONS... WHAT IS THE MAN THINKING?
MUTTER
BUT MR. VAN BEETHOVEN MUST ALWAYS GET HIS WAY.

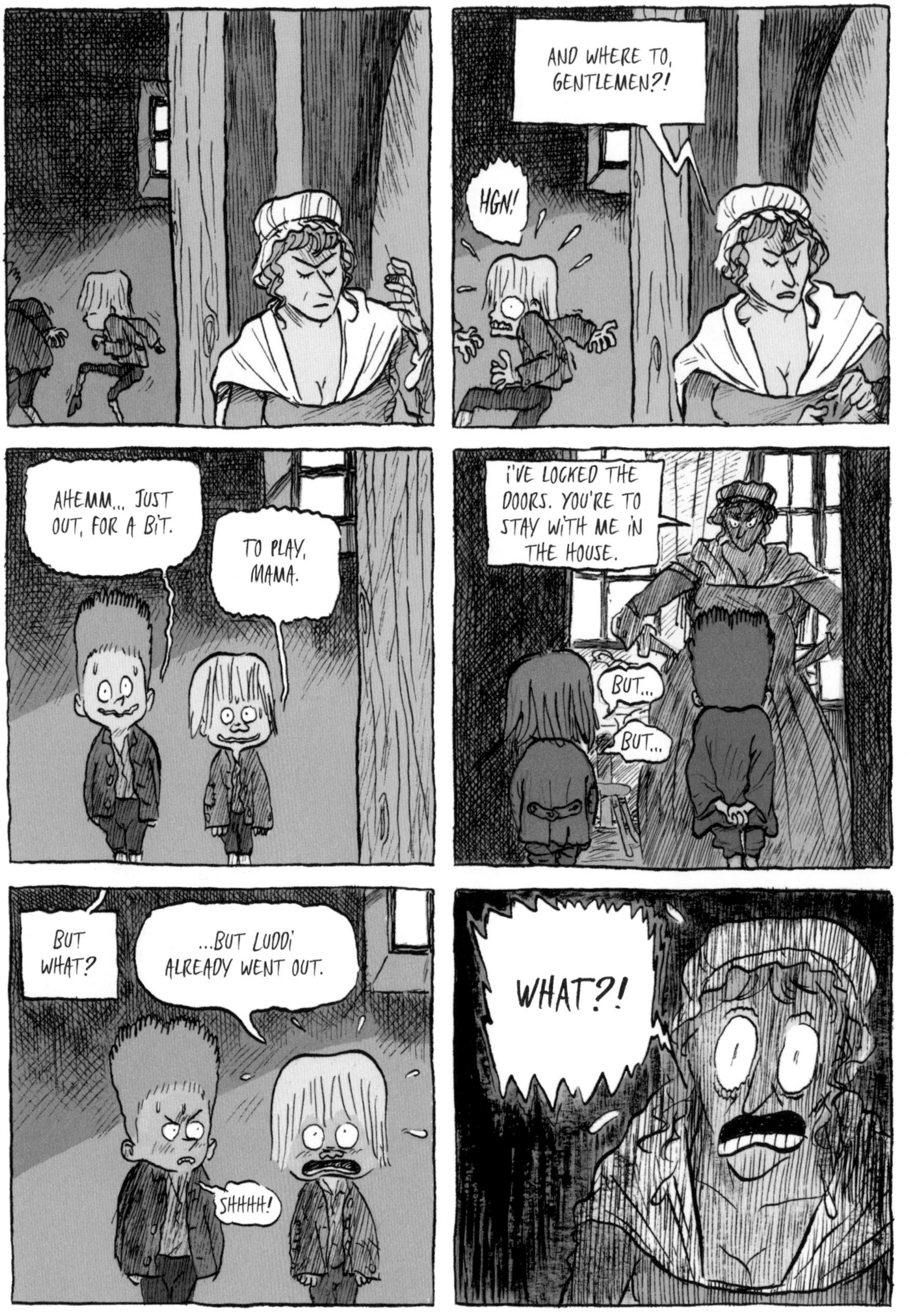
AND WHERE TO, GENTLEMEN?!
HGN!
AHEMM... JUST OUT, FOR A BIT.
TO PLAY, MAMA.
I'VE LOCKED THE DOORS. YOU'RE TO STAY WITH ME IN THE HOUSE.
BUT...
BUT...
BUT WHAT?
...BUT LUDDI ALREADY WENT OUT.
SHHHH!
WHAT?!

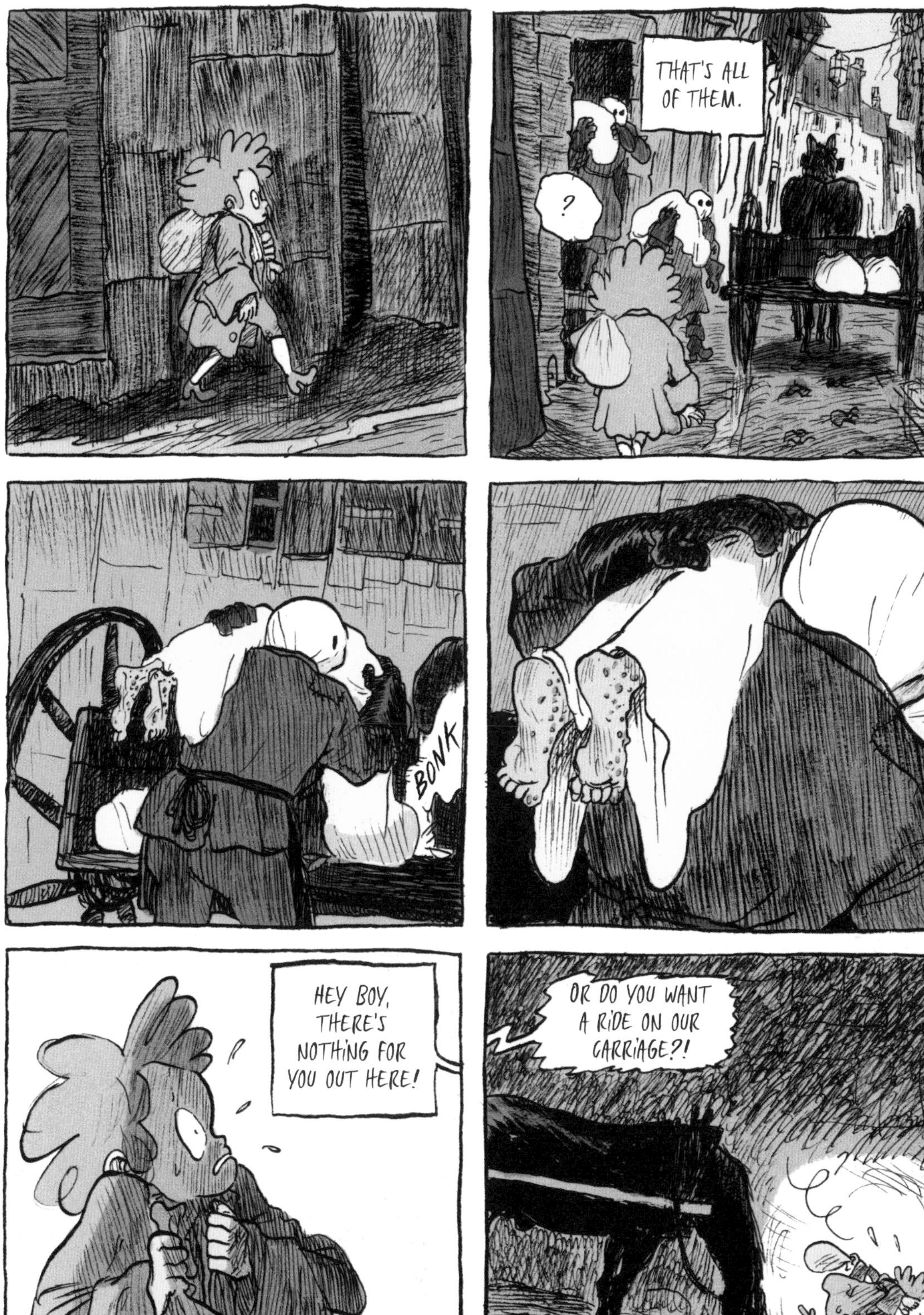
THAT'S ALL OF THEM.
?
BONK
HEY BOY, THERE'S NOTHING FOR YOU OUT HERE!
OR DO YOU WANT A RIDE ON OUR CARRIAGE?!

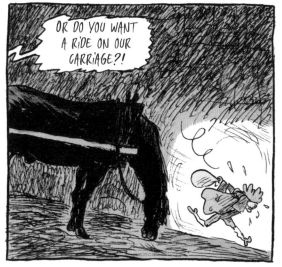

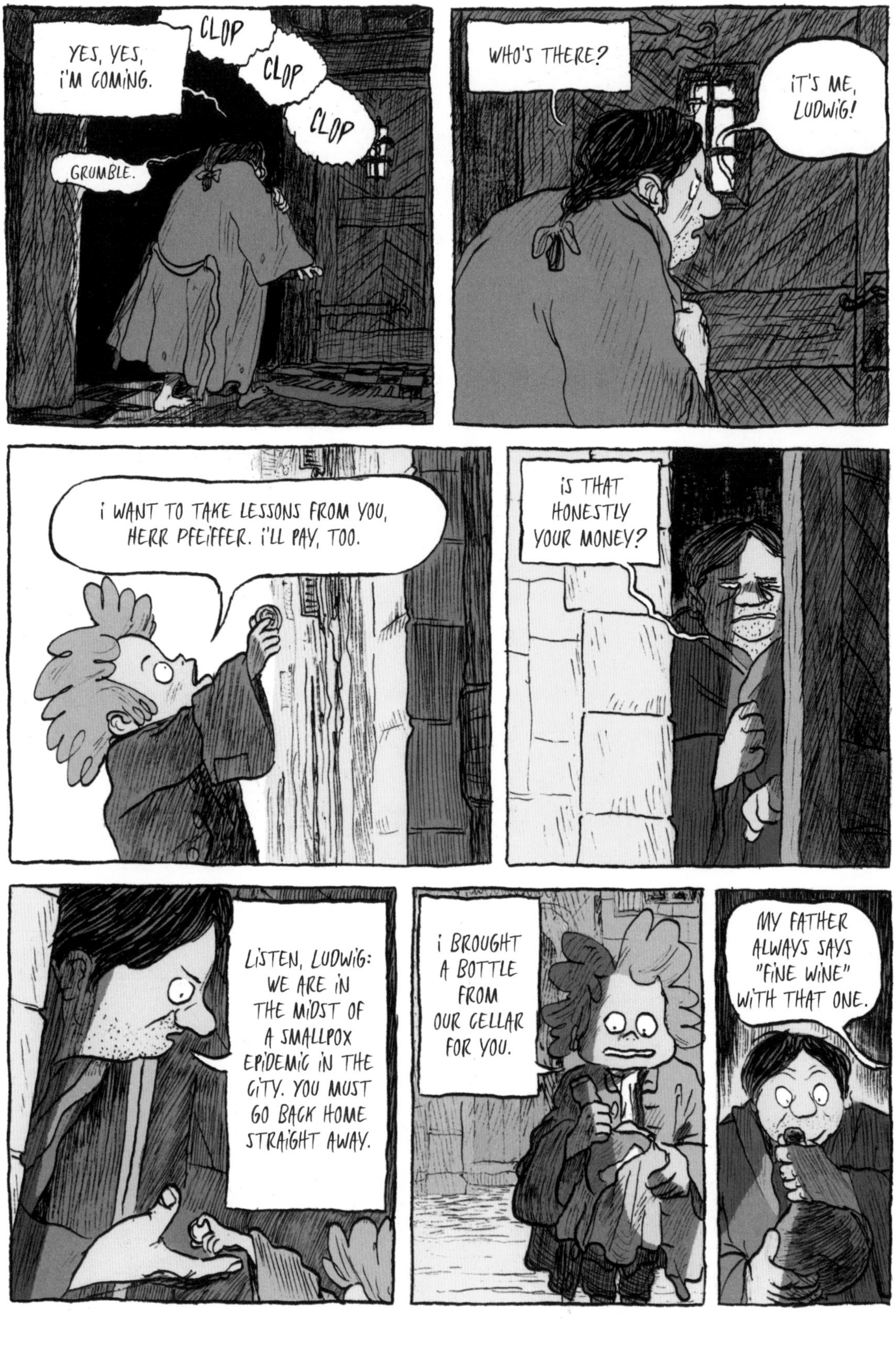
YES, YES, I'M COMING.
CLOP
CLOP
CLOP
GRUMBLE.
WHO'S THERE?
IT'S ME, LUDWIG!
I WANT TO TAKE LESSONS FROM YOU, HERR PFEIFFER. I'LL PAY, TOO.
IS THAT HONESTLY YOUR MONEY?
LISTEN, LUDWIG: WE ARE IN THE MIDST OF A SMALLPOX EPIDEMIC IN THE CITY. YOU MUST GO BACK HOME STRAIGHT AWAY.
I BROUGHT A BOTTLE FROM OUR CELLAR FOR YOU.
MY FATHER ALWAYS SAYS "FINE WINE" WITH THAT ONE.

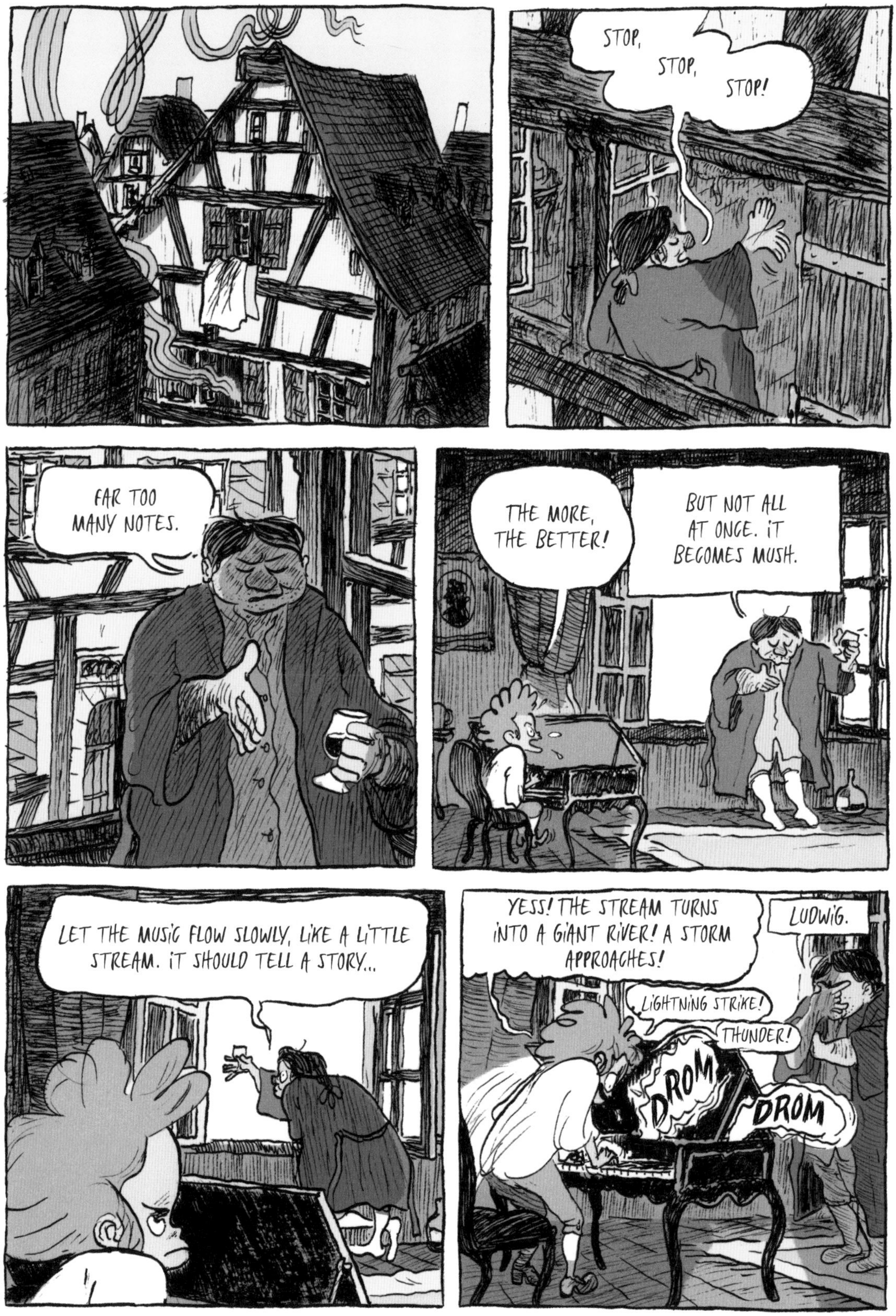
STOP, STOP, STOP!
FAR TOO MANY NOTES.
THE MORE, THE BETTER!
BUT NOT ALL AT ONCE. IT BECOMES MUSH.
LET THE MUSIC FLOW SLOWLY, LIKE A LITTLE STREAM. IT SHOULD TELL A STORY...
YESS! THE STREAM TURNS INTO A GIANT RIVER! A STORM APPROACHES!
LIGHTNING STRIKE!
THUNDER!
DROM
DROM
LUDWIG.

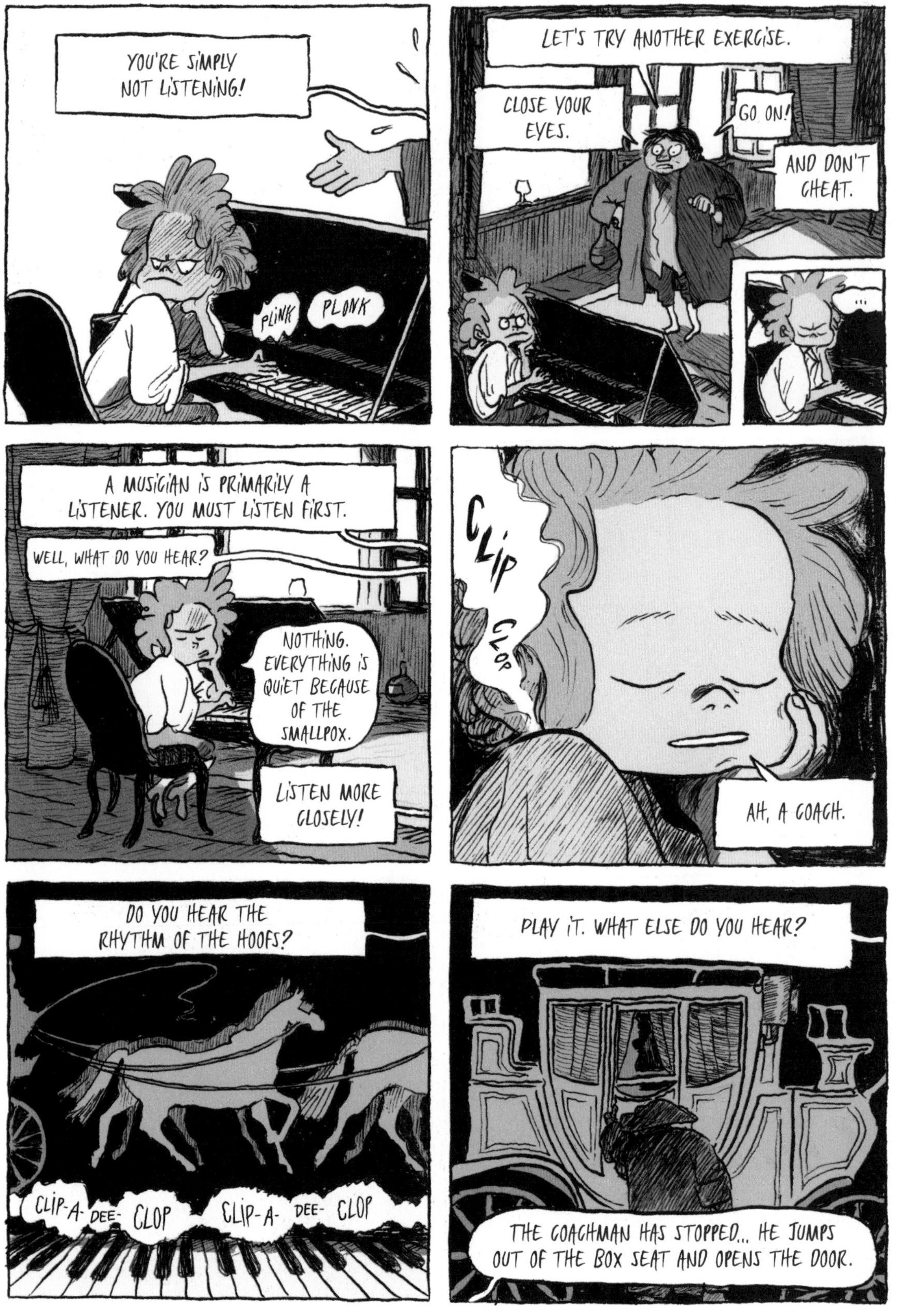
YOU'RE SIMPLY NOT LISTENING!
PLINK
PLONK
LET'S TRY ANOTHER EXERCISE.
CLOSE YOUR EYES.
GO ON!
AND DON'T CHEAT.
...
A MUSICIAN IS PRIMARILY A LISTENER. YOU MUST LISTEN FIRST.
WELL, WHAT DO YOU HEAR?
NOTHING. EVERYTHING IS QUIET BECAUSE OF THE SMALLPOX.
LISTEN MORE CLOSELY!
CLIP
CLOP
AH, A COACH.
DO YOU HEAR THE RHYTHM OF THE HOOFS?
CLIP-A- DEE- CLOP
CLIP-A- DEE- CLOP
PLAY IT. WHAT ELSE DO YOU HEAR?
THE COACHMAN HAS STOPPED... HE JUMPS OUT OF THE BOX SEAT AND OPENS THE DOOR.

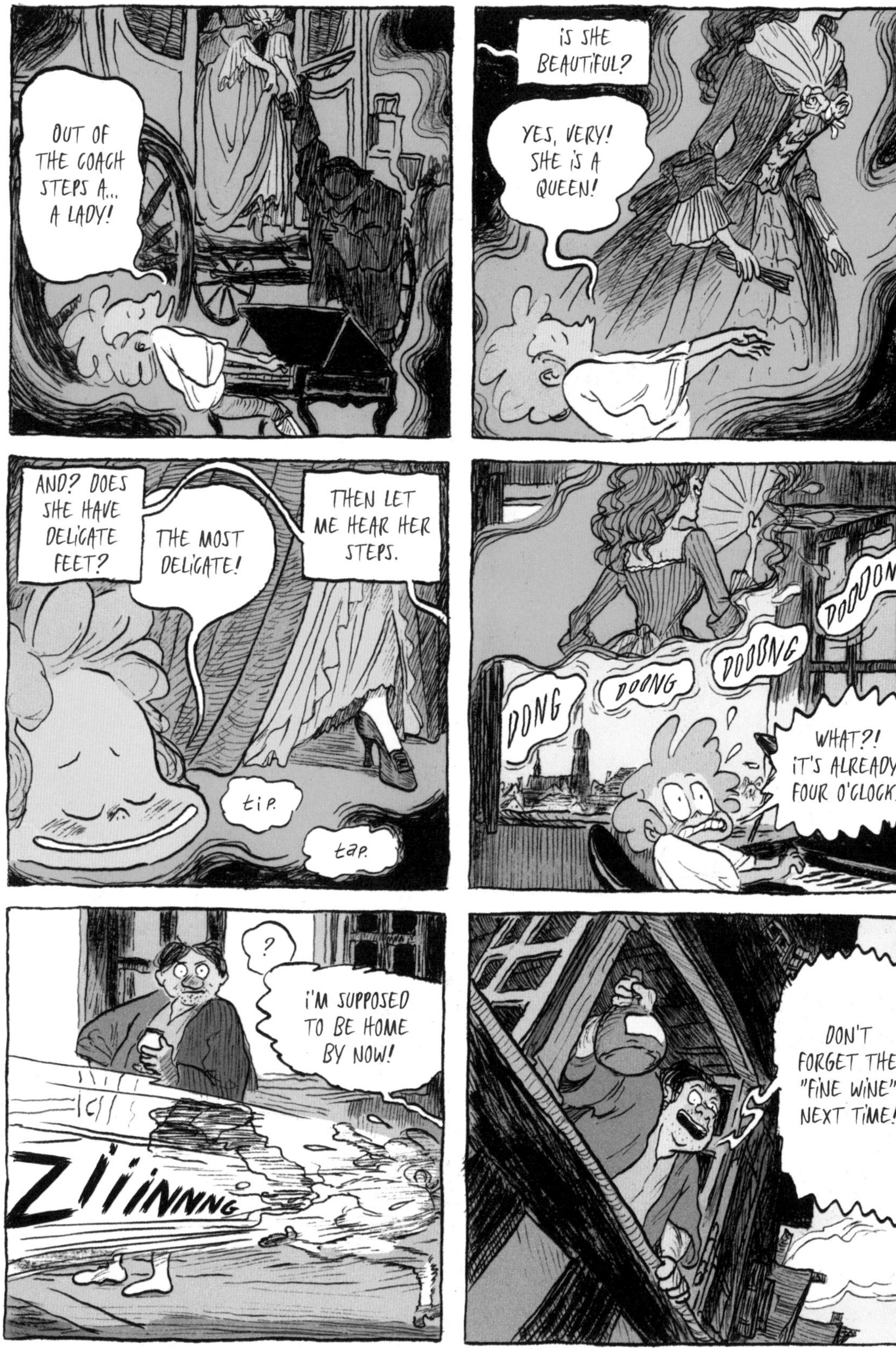
OUT OF THE COACH STEPS A... A LADY!
IS SHE BEAUTIFUL?
YES, VERY! SHE IS A QUEEN!
AND? DOES SHE HAVE DELICATE FEET?
THE MOST DELICATE!
THEN LET ME HEAR HER STEPS.
TIP.
TAP.
DONG
DOONG
DOOONG
DOOOONG
WHAT?! IT'S ALREADY FOUR O'CLOCK!
?
I'M SUPPOSED TO BE HOME BY NOW!
ZIIINNNG
DON'T FORGET THE "FINE WINE" NEXT TIME!

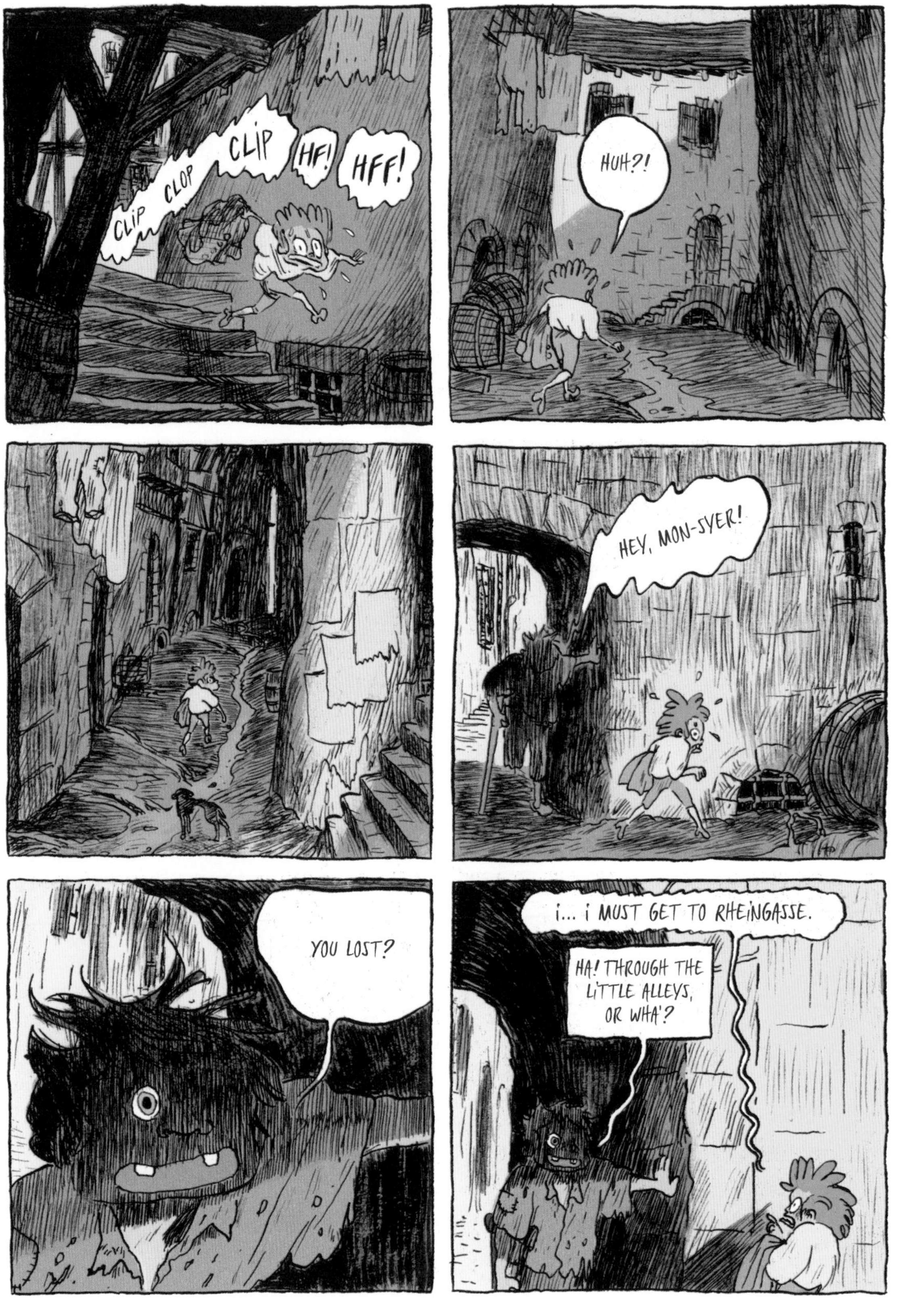
CLIP CLOP CLIP
HF!
HFF!
HUH?!
HEY, MON-SYER!
YOU LOST?
i... i MUST GET TO RHEiNGASSE.
HA! THROUGH THE LiTTLE ALLEYS, OR WHA'?

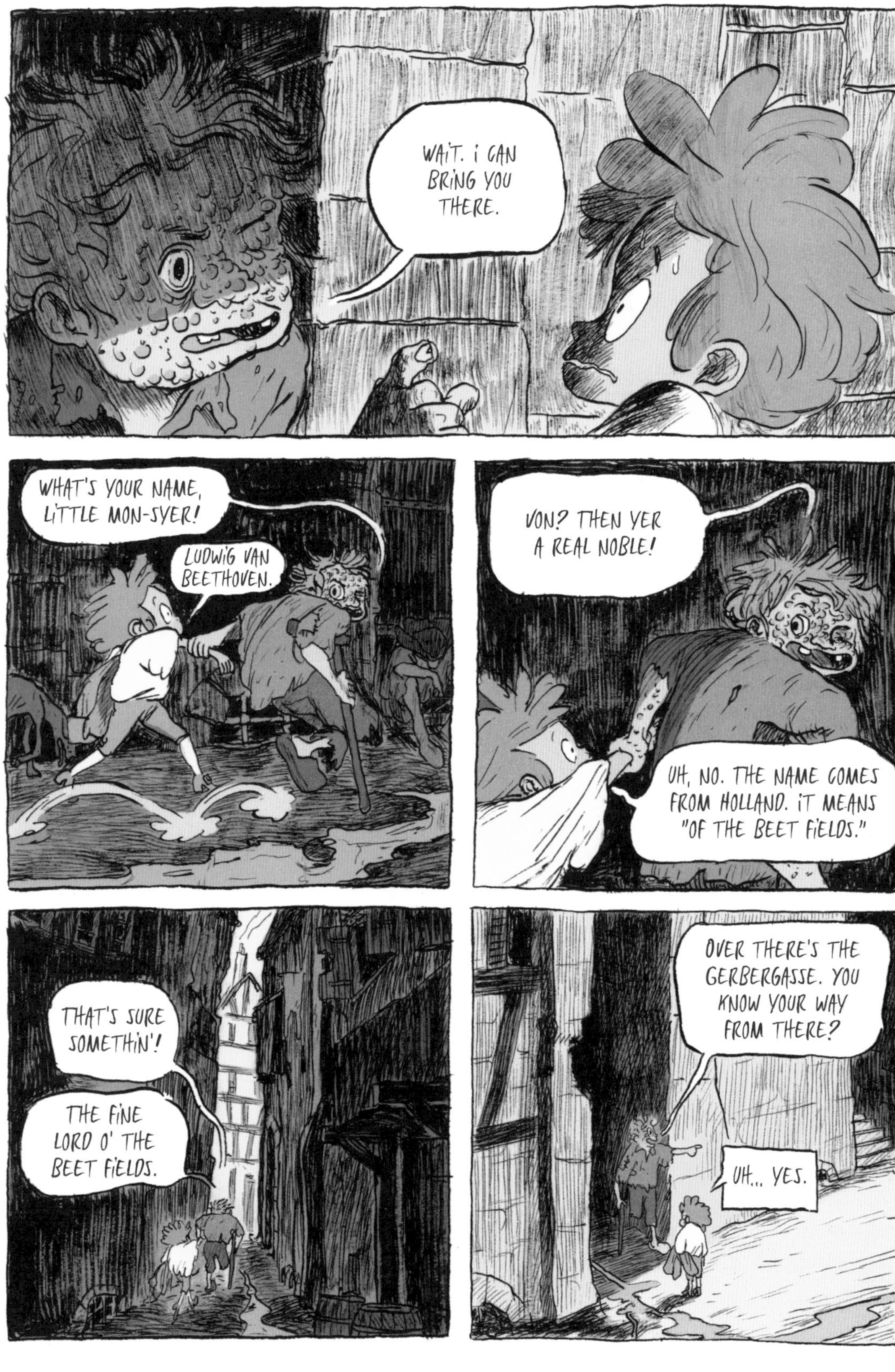
WAIT. I CAN BRING YOU THERE.
WHAT'S YOUR NAME, LITTLE MON-SYER!
LUDWIG VAN BEETHOVEN.
VON? THEN YER A REAL NOBLE!
UH, NO. THE NAME COMES FROM HOLLAND. IT MEANS "OF THE BEET FIELDS."
THAT'S SURE SOMETHIN'!
THE FINE LORD O' THE BEET FIELDS.
OVER THERE'S THE GERBERGASSE. YOU KNOW YOUR WAY FROM THERE?
UH... YES.

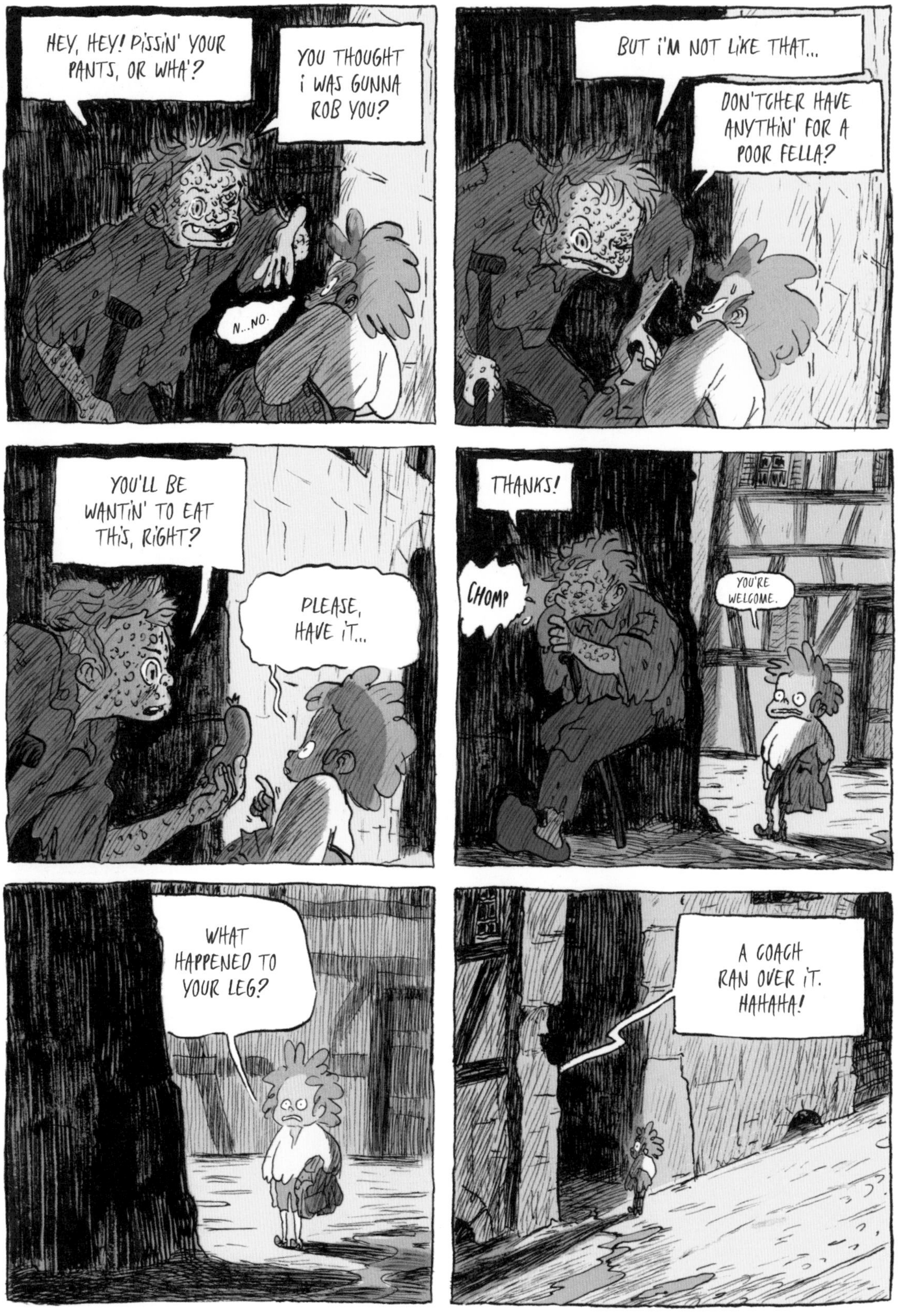
HEY, HEY! PISSIN' YOUR PANTS, OR WHA'?
YOU THOUGHT I WAS GUNNA ROB YOU?
N...NO.
BUT I'M NOT LIKE THAT...
DON'TCHER HAVE ANYTHIN' FOR A POOR FELLA?
YOU'LL BE WANTIN' TO EAT THIS, RIGHT?
PLEASE, HAVE IT...
THANKS!
CHOMP
YOU'RE WELCOME.
WHAT HAPPENED TO YOUR LEG?
A COACH RAN OVER IT. HAHAHA!

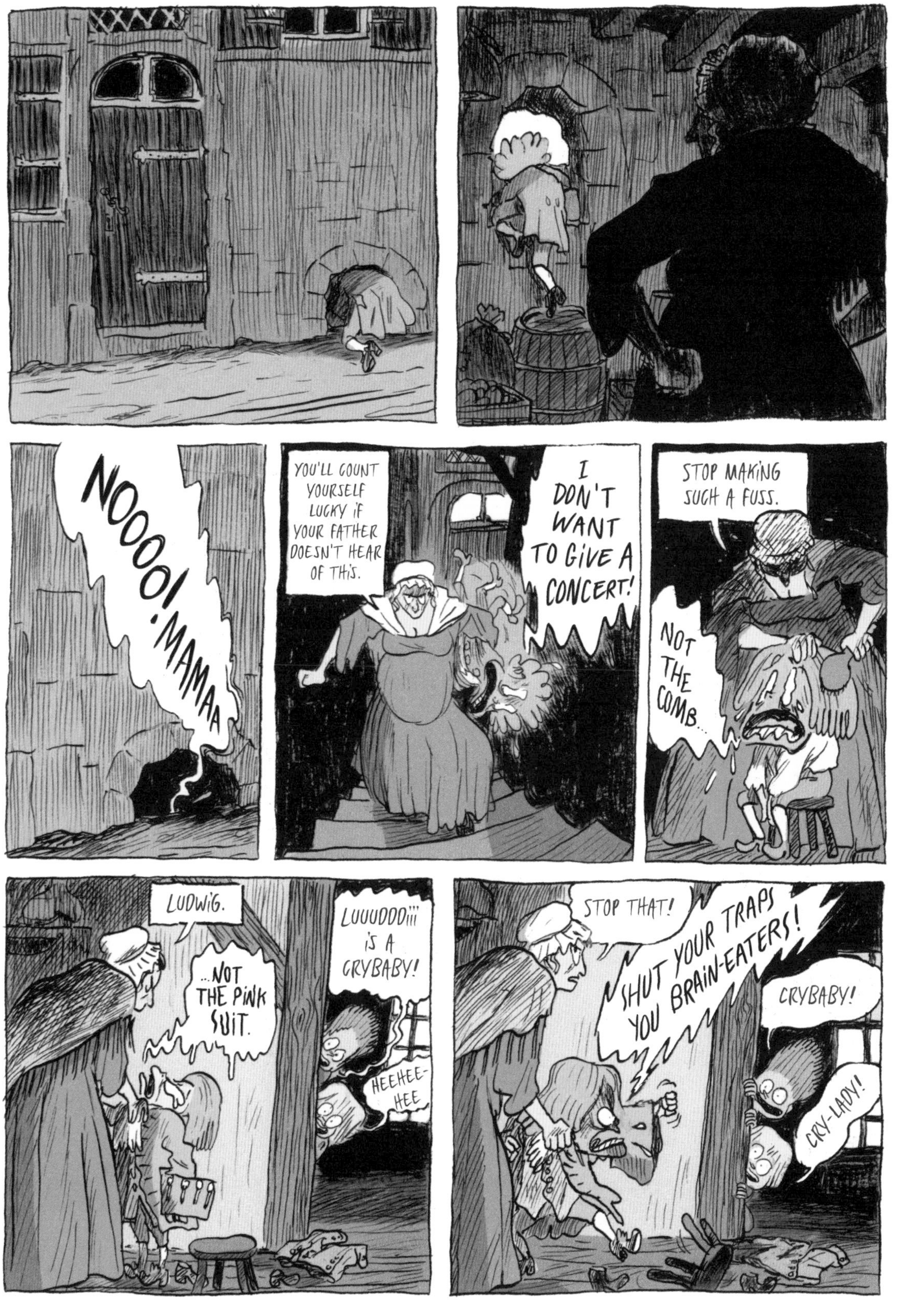
NOOOO! MAMAAA
YOU'LL COUNT YOURSELF LUCKY IF YOUR FATHER DOESN'T HEAR OF THIS.
I DON'T WANT TO GIVE A CONCERT!
STOP MAKING SUCH A FUSS.
NOT THE COMB...
LUDWIG.
...NOT THE PINK SUIT.
LUUUDDDiii is A CRYBABY!
HEEHEE-HEE
STOP THAT!
SHUT YOUR TRAPS YOU BRAIN-EATERS!
CRYBABY!
CRY-LADY!

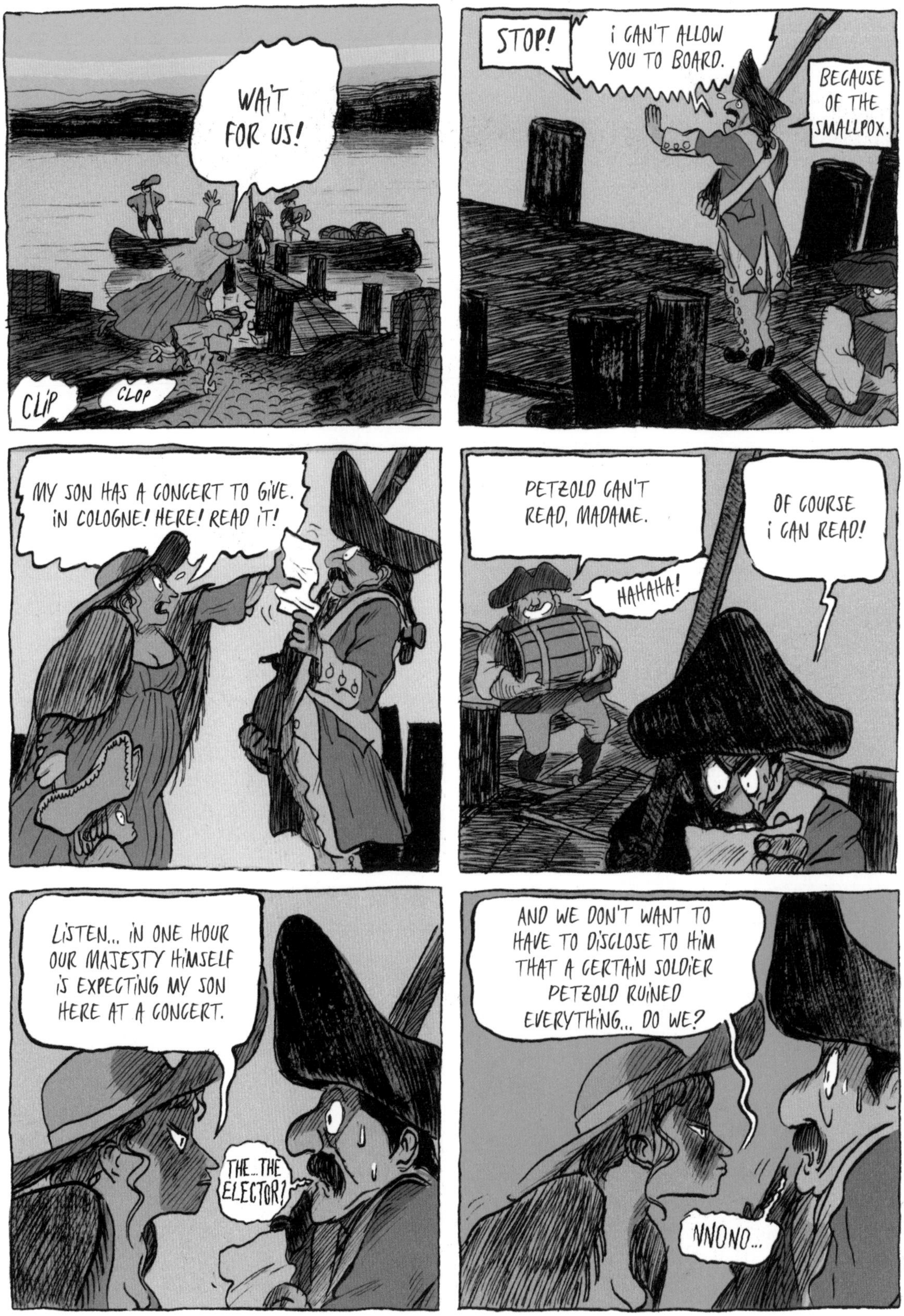
WAIT FOR US!
CLIP
CLOP
STOP!
I CAN'T ALLOW YOU TO BOARD.
BECAUSE OF THE SMALLPOX.
MY SON HAS A CONCERT TO GIVE. IN COLOGNE! HERE! READ IT!
PETZOLD CAN'T READ, MADAME.
HAHAHA!
OF COURSE I CAN READ!
LISTEN... IN ONE HOUR OUR MAJESTY HIMSELF IS EXPECTING MY SON HERE AT A CONCERT.
THE... THE ELECTOR?
AND WE DON'T WANT TO HAVE TO DISCLOSE TO HIM THAT A CERTAIN SOLDIER PETZOLD RUINED EVERYTHING... DO WE?
NNONO...

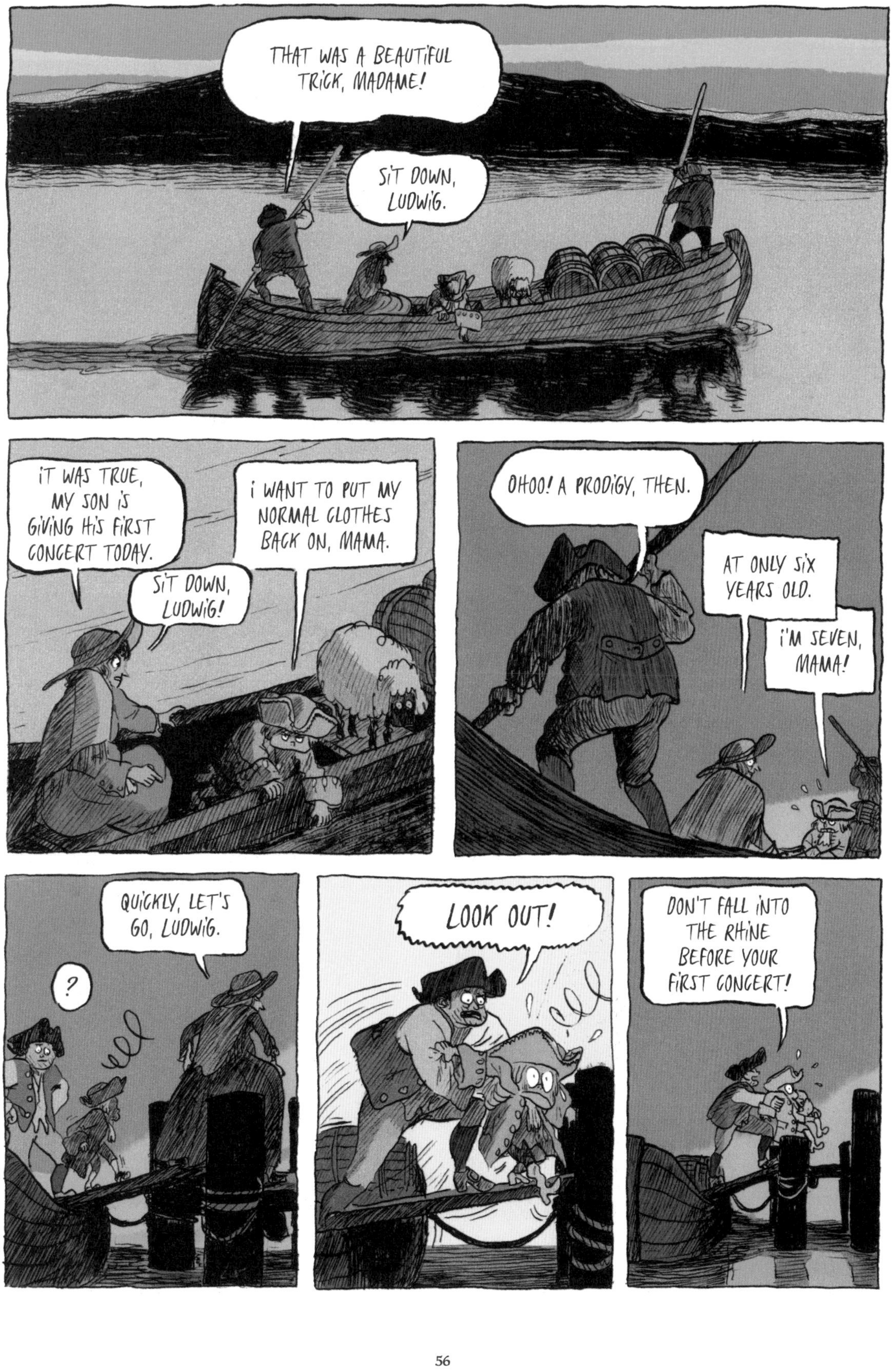
THAT WAS A BEAUTIFUL TRICK, MADAME!
SIT DOWN, LUDWIG.
IT WAS TRUE, MY SON IS GIVING HIS FIRST CONCERT TODAY.
SIT DOWN, LUDWIG!
I WANT TO PUT MY NORMAL CLOTHES BACK ON, MAMA.
OHOO! A PRODIGY, THEN.
AT ONLY SIX YEARS OLD.
I'M SEVEN, MAMA!
QUICKLY, LET'S GO, LUDWIG.
?
LOOK OUT!
DON'T FALL INTO THE RHINE BEFORE YOUR FIRST CONCERT!

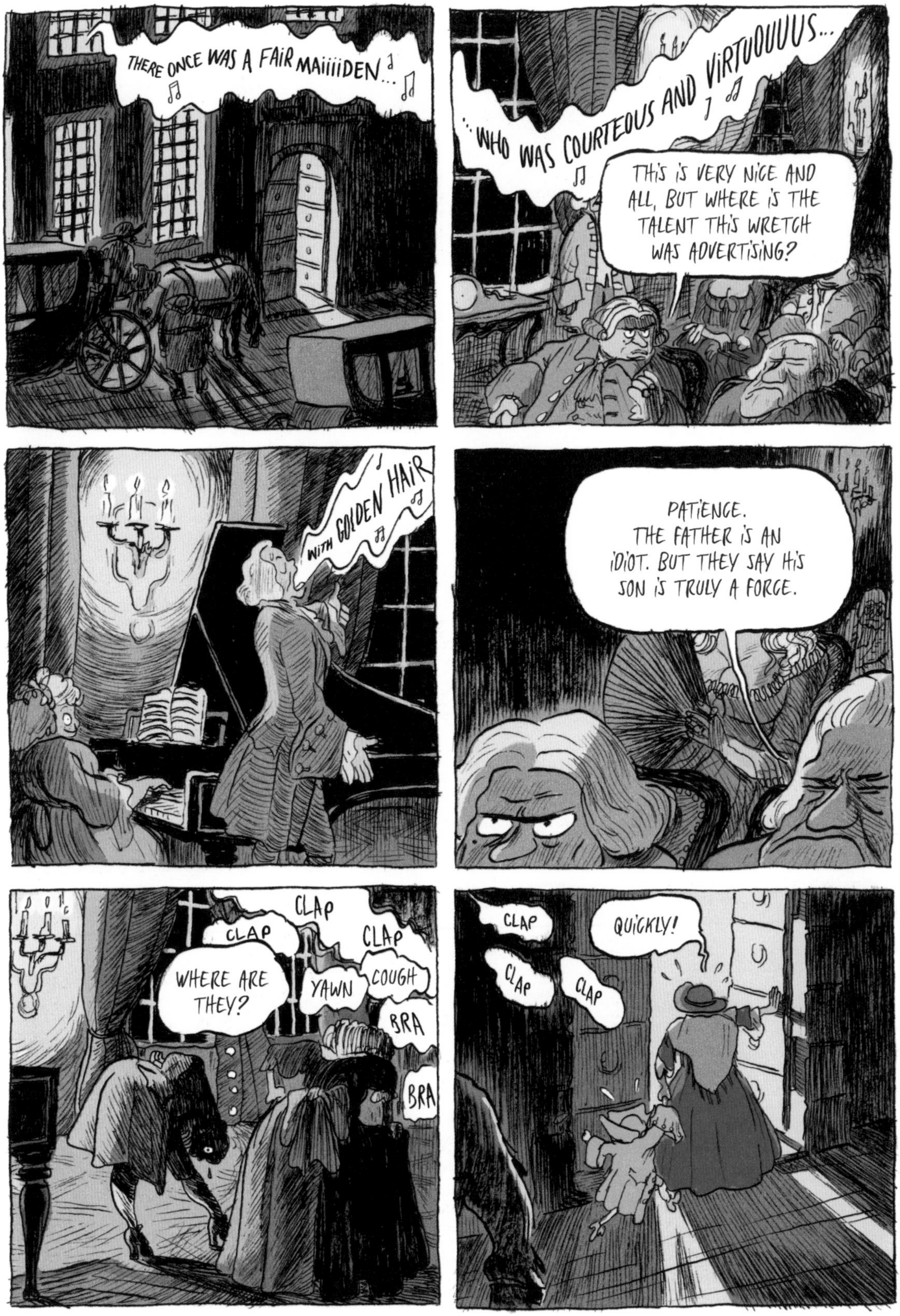
THERE ONCE WAS A FAIR MAiiiiDEN...
...WHO WAS COURTEOUS AND ViRTUOUUUS...
THis is VERY NiCE AND ALL, BUT WHERE is THE TALENT THis WRETCH WAS ADVERTiSiNG?
WiTH GOLDEN HAiR
PATiENCE. THE FATHER is AN iDiOT. BUT THEY SAY His SON is TRULY A FORCE.
CLAP
CLAP
CLAP
WHERE ARE THEY?
YAWN
COUGH
BRA
BRA
CLAP
CLAP
CLAP
QUiCKLY!

LUDWIG, YOU'RE SUPPOSED TO PLAY NOW.
MAMA, I FEEL DIFFERENT...
WHERE THE HELL WERE YOU HIDING?
REALLY, MAMA...
ARE YOU TRYING TO RUIN ME?
IS THAT IT?
HUFF! JOHANN, THE FERRY WAS LATE.
VERY DIFFERENT...
BLAAARGH
SPLASH

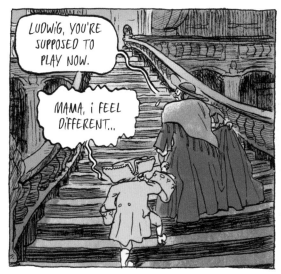

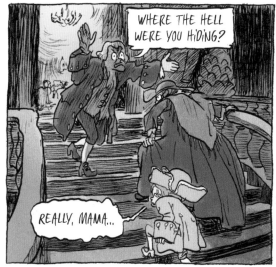

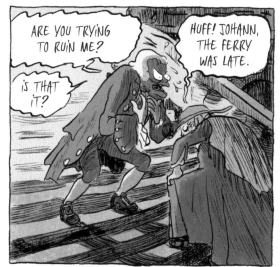

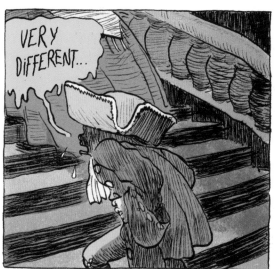

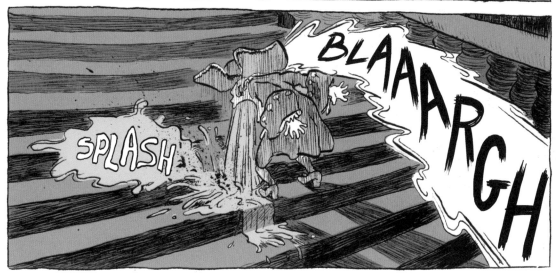

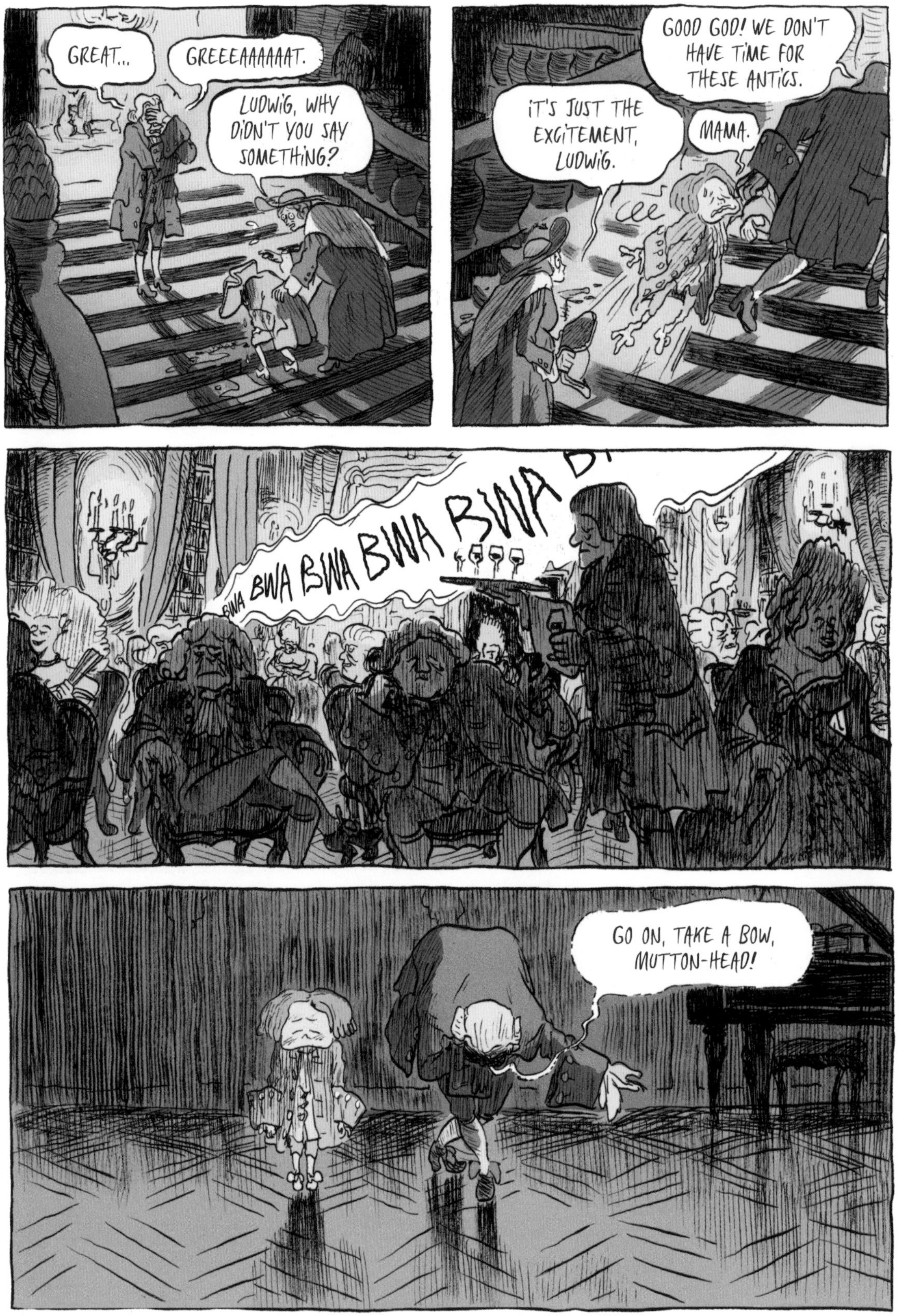
GREAT...
GREEEAAAAAAT.
LUDWIG, WHY DIDN'T YOU SAY SOMETHING?
GOOD GOD! WE DON'T HAVE TIME FOR THESE ANTICS.
IT'S JUST THE EXCITEMENT, LUDWIG.
MAMA.
BWA BWA BWA BWA BWA B
GO ON, TAKE A BOW, MUTTON-HEAD!

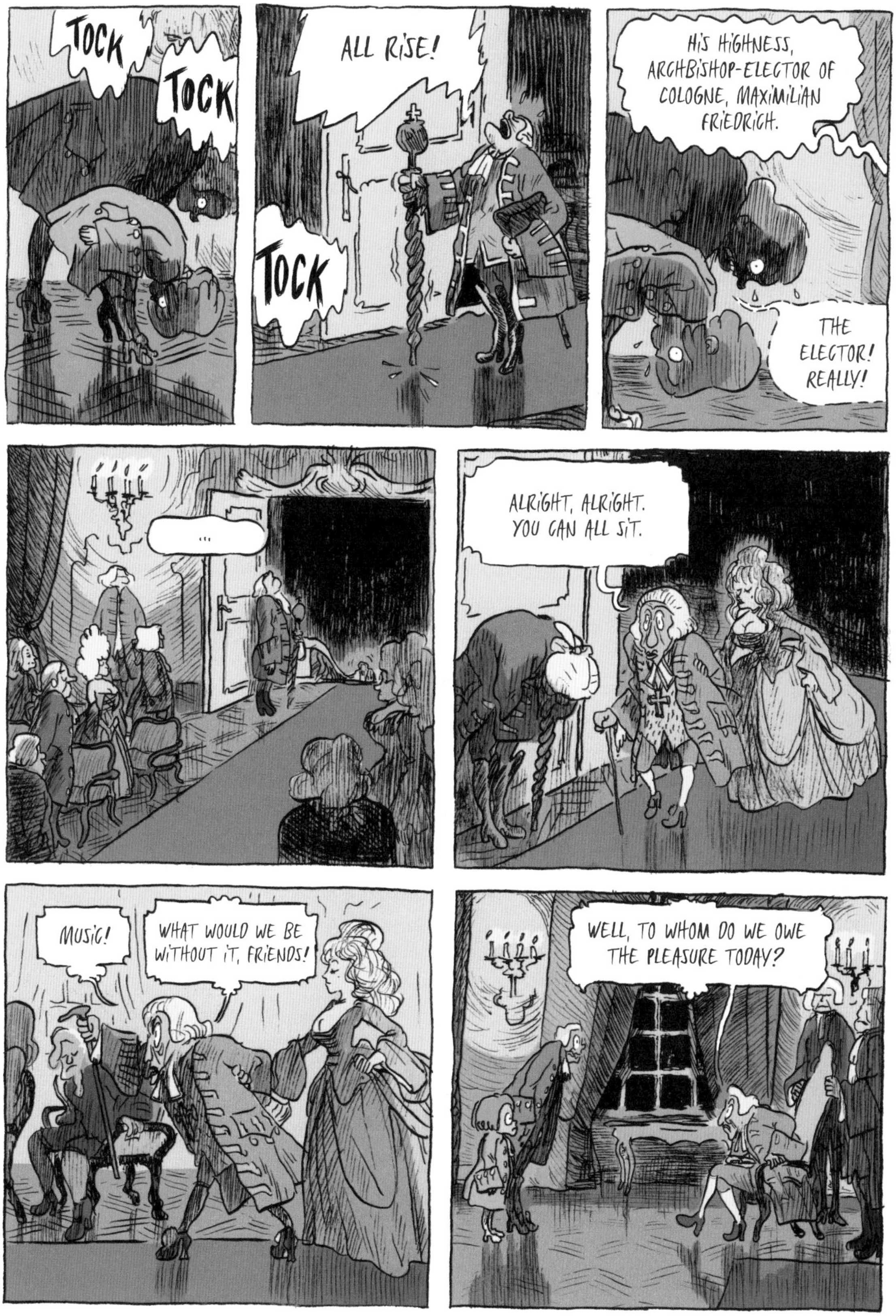
TOCK
TOCK
ALL RISE!
TOCK
HIS HIGHNESS, ARCHBISHOP-ELECTOR OF COLOGNE, MAXIMILIAN FRIEDRICH.
THE ELECTOR! REALLY!
...
ALRIGHT, ALRIGHT. YOU CAN ALL SIT.
MUSIC!
WHAT WOULD WE BE WITHOUT IT, FRIENDS!
WELL, TO WHOM DO WE OWE THE PLEASURE TODAY?

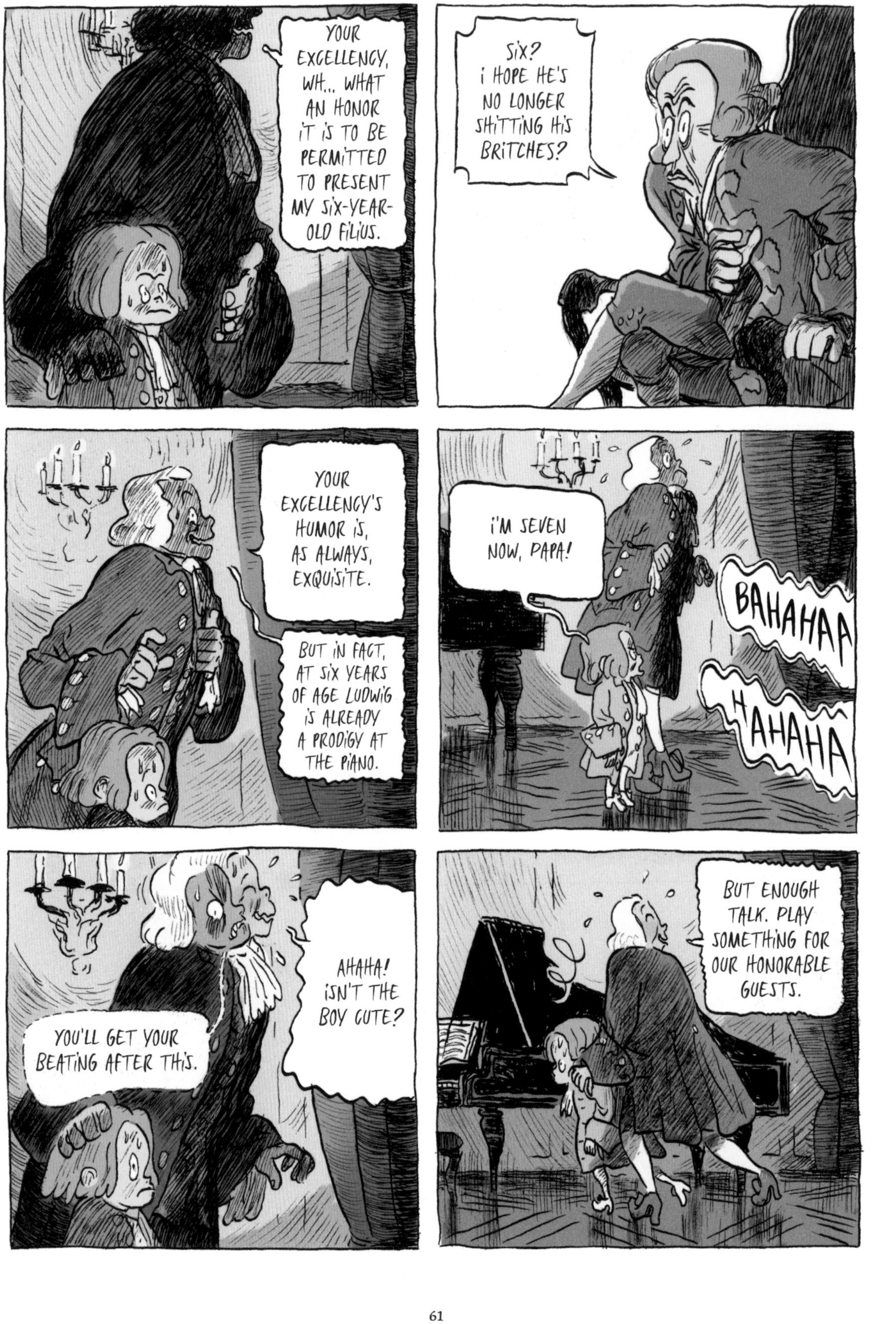
YOUR EXCELLENCY, WH... WHAT AN HONOR IT IS TO BE PERMITTED TO PRESENT MY SIX-YEAR-OLD FILIUS.
SIX? I HOPE HE'S NO LONGER SHITTING HIS BRITCHES?
YOUR EXCELLENCY'S HUMOR IS, AS ALWAYS, EXQUISITE.
BUT IN FACT, AT SIX YEARS OF AGE LUDWIG IS ALREADY A PRODIGY AT THE PIANO.
I'M SEVEN NOW, PAPA!
BAHAHAA
HAHAHA
YOU'LL GET YOUR BEATING AFTER THIS.
AHAHA! ISN'T THE BOY CUTE?
BUT ENOUGH TALK. PLAY SOMETHING FOR OUR HONORABLE GUESTS.

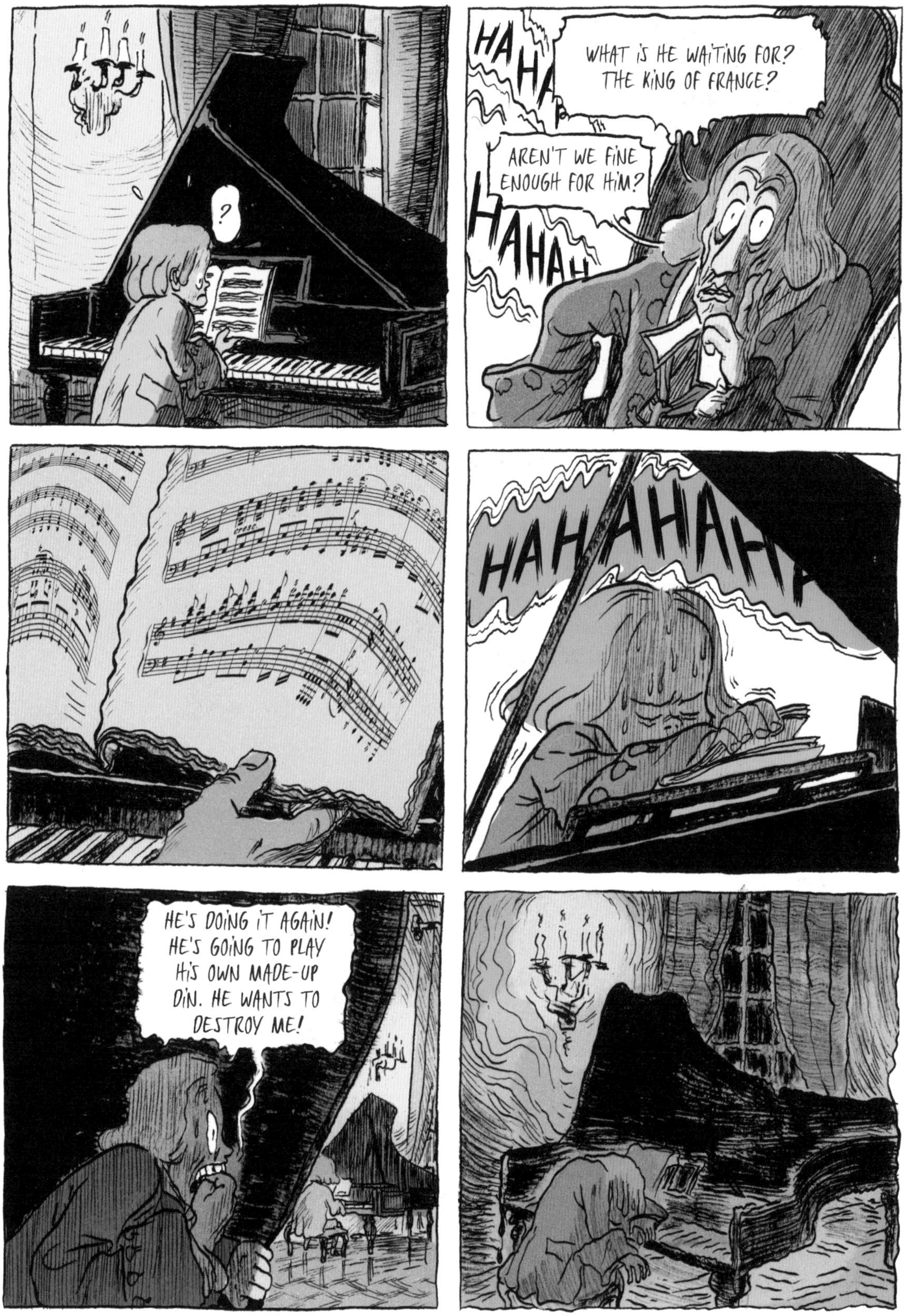
?
HAHAHAHAHAH
WHAT iS HE WAiTiNG FOR? THE KiNG OF FRANCE?
AREN'T WE FiNE ENOUGH FOR HiM?
HAHAHAHAH
HE'S DOiNG iT AGAiN! HE'S GOiNG TO PLAY HiS OWN MADE-UP DiN. HE WANTS TO DESTROY ME!

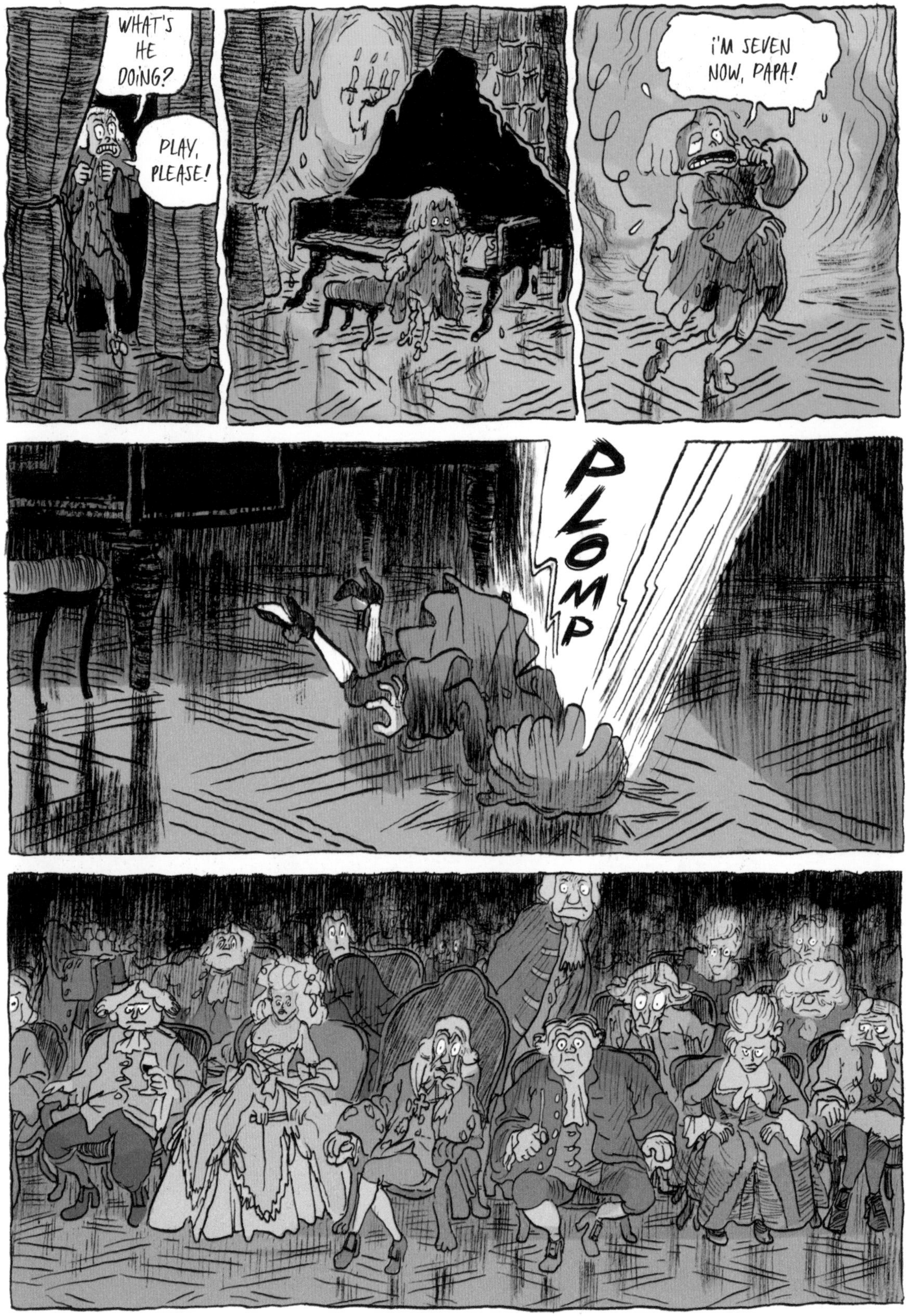
WHAT'S HE DOING?
PLAY, PLEASE!
I'M SEVEN NOW, PAPA!
PLOMP

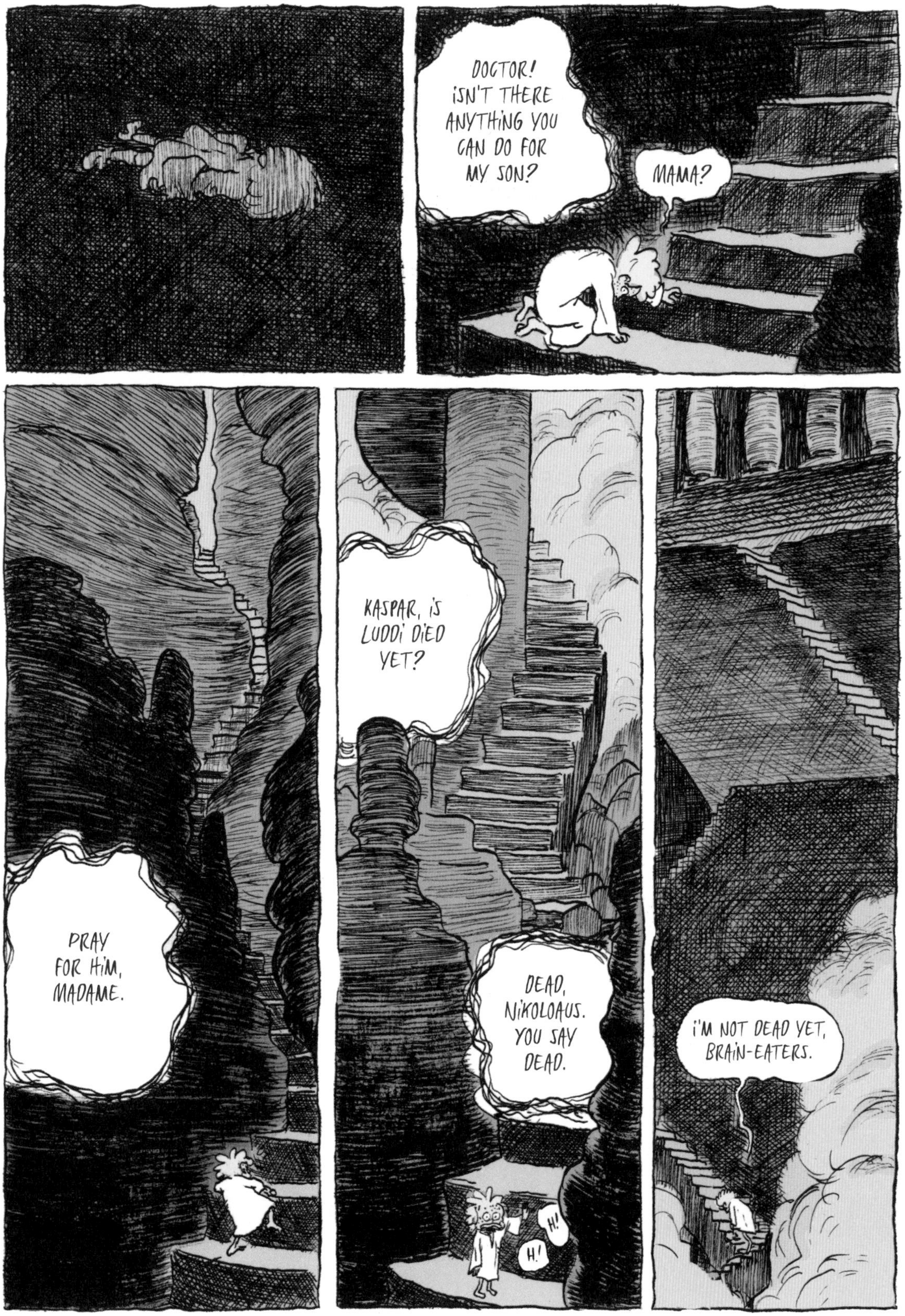
DOCTOR! ISN'T THERE ANYTHING YOU CAN DO FOR MY SON?
MAMA?
PRAY FOR HIM, MADAME.
KASPAR, IS LUDDI DIED YET?
DEAD, NIKOLOAUS. YOU SAY DEAD.
H!
H!
I'M NOT DEAD YET, BRAIN-EATERS.

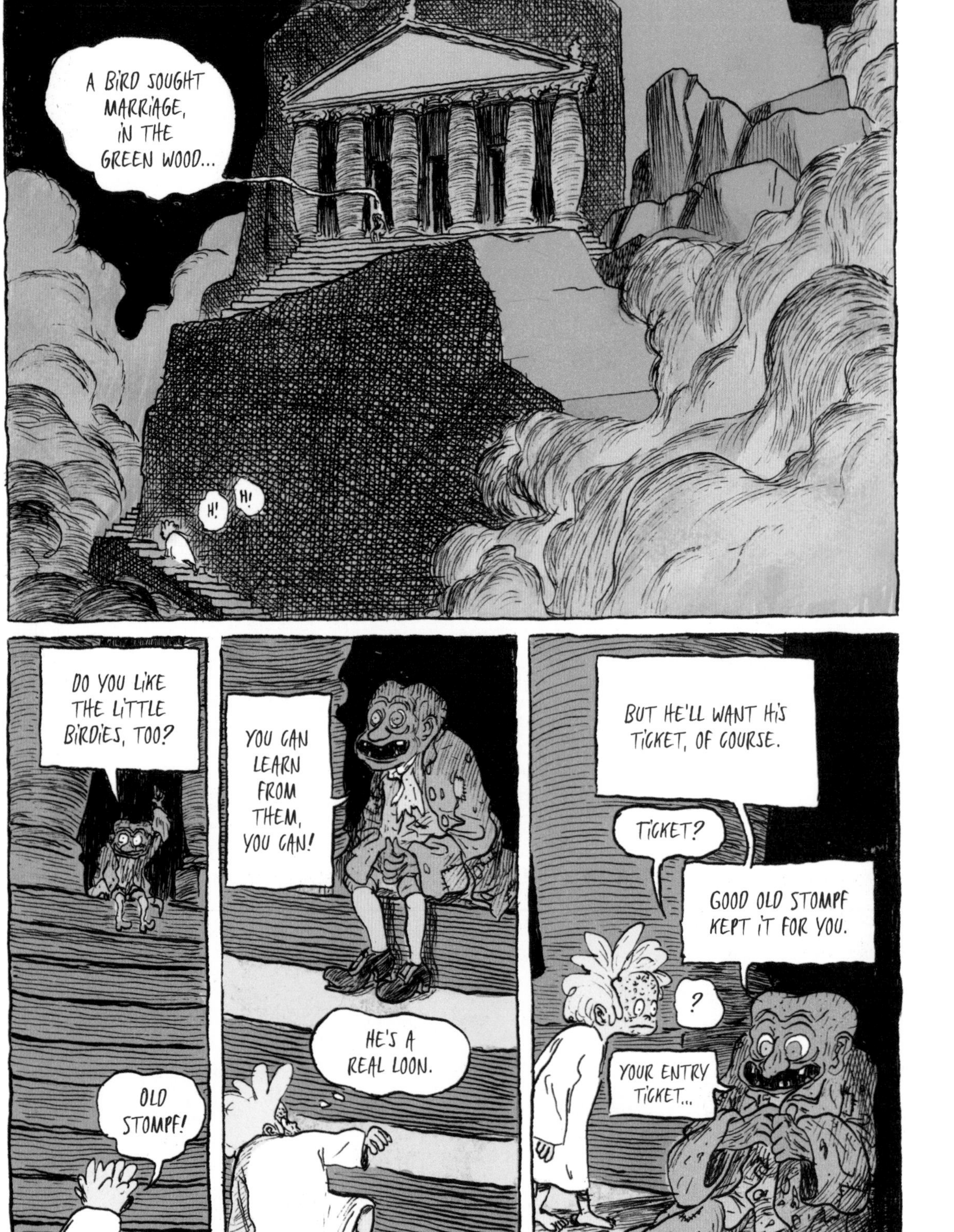
A BIRD SOUGHT MARRIAGE, IN THE GREEN WOOD...
H!
H!
DO YOU LIKE THE LITTLE BIRDIES, TOO?
OLD STOMPF!
YOU CAN LEARN FROM THEM, YOU CAN!
HE'S A REAL LOON.
BUT HE'LL WANT HIS TICKET, OF COURSE.
TICKET?
GOOD OLD STOMPF KEPT IT FOR YOU.
?
YOUR ENTRY TICKET...

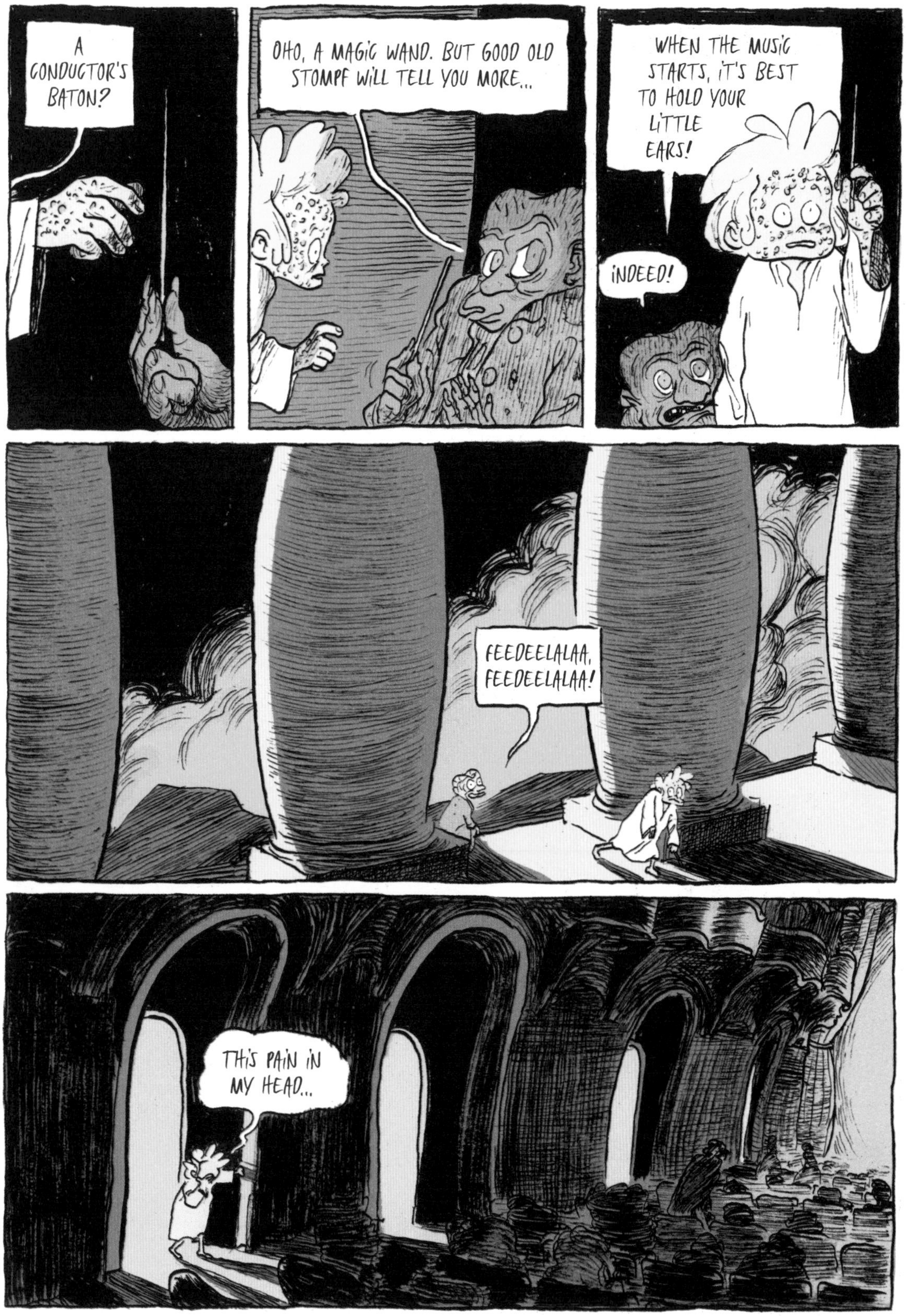
A CONDUCTOR'S BATON?
OHO, A MAGIC WAND. BUT GOOD OLD STOMPF WILL TELL YOU MORE...
WHEN THE MUSIC STARTS, IT'S BEST TO HOLD YOUR LITTLE EARS!
INDEED!
FEEDEELALAA, FEEDEELALAA!
THIS PAIN IN MY HEAD...

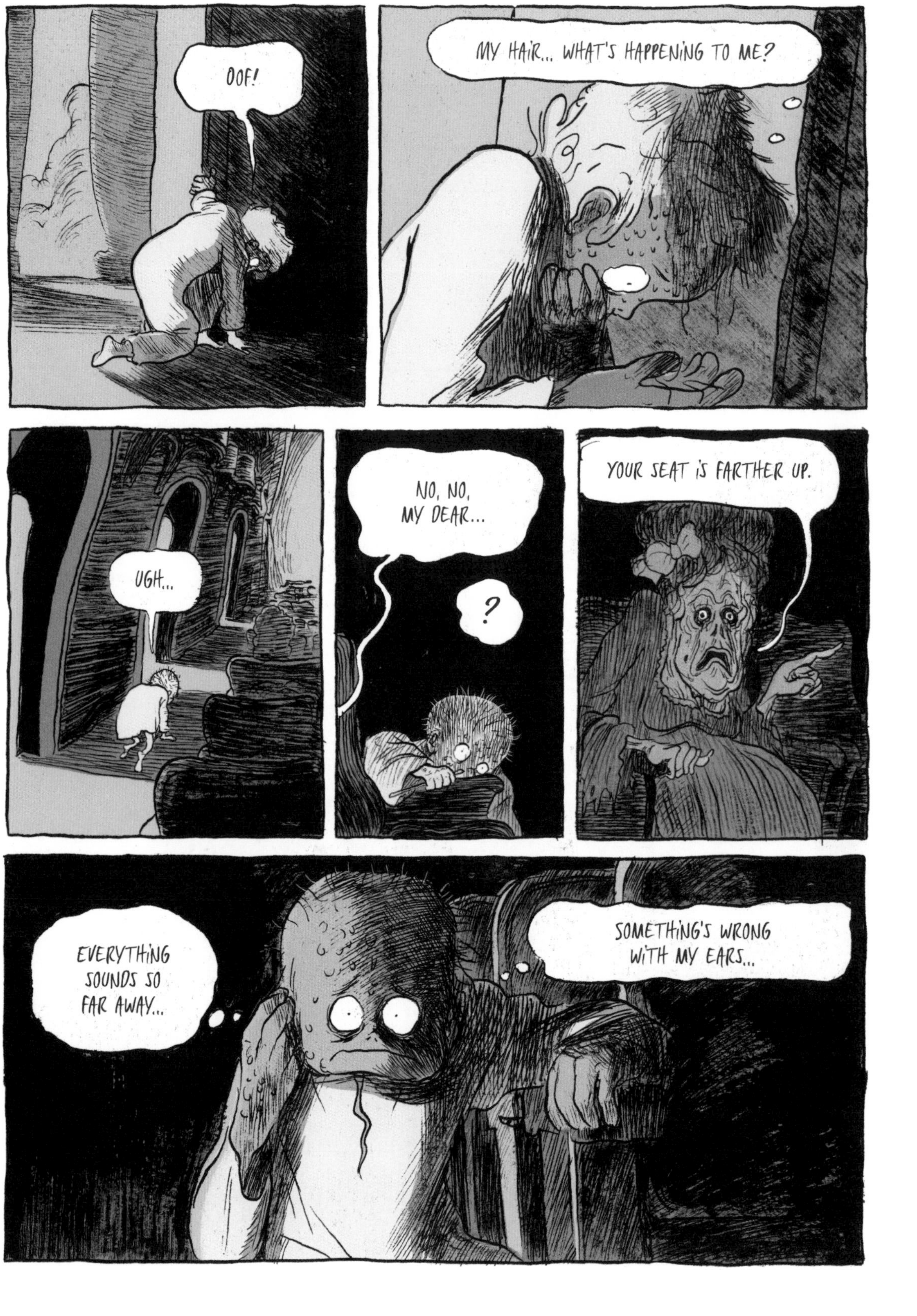
OOF!
MY HAIR... WHAT'S HAPPENING TO ME?
UGH...
NO, NO, MY DEAR...
?
YOUR SEAT IS FARTHER UP.
EVERYTHING SOUNDS SO FAR AWAY...
SOMETHING'S WRONG WITH MY EARS...

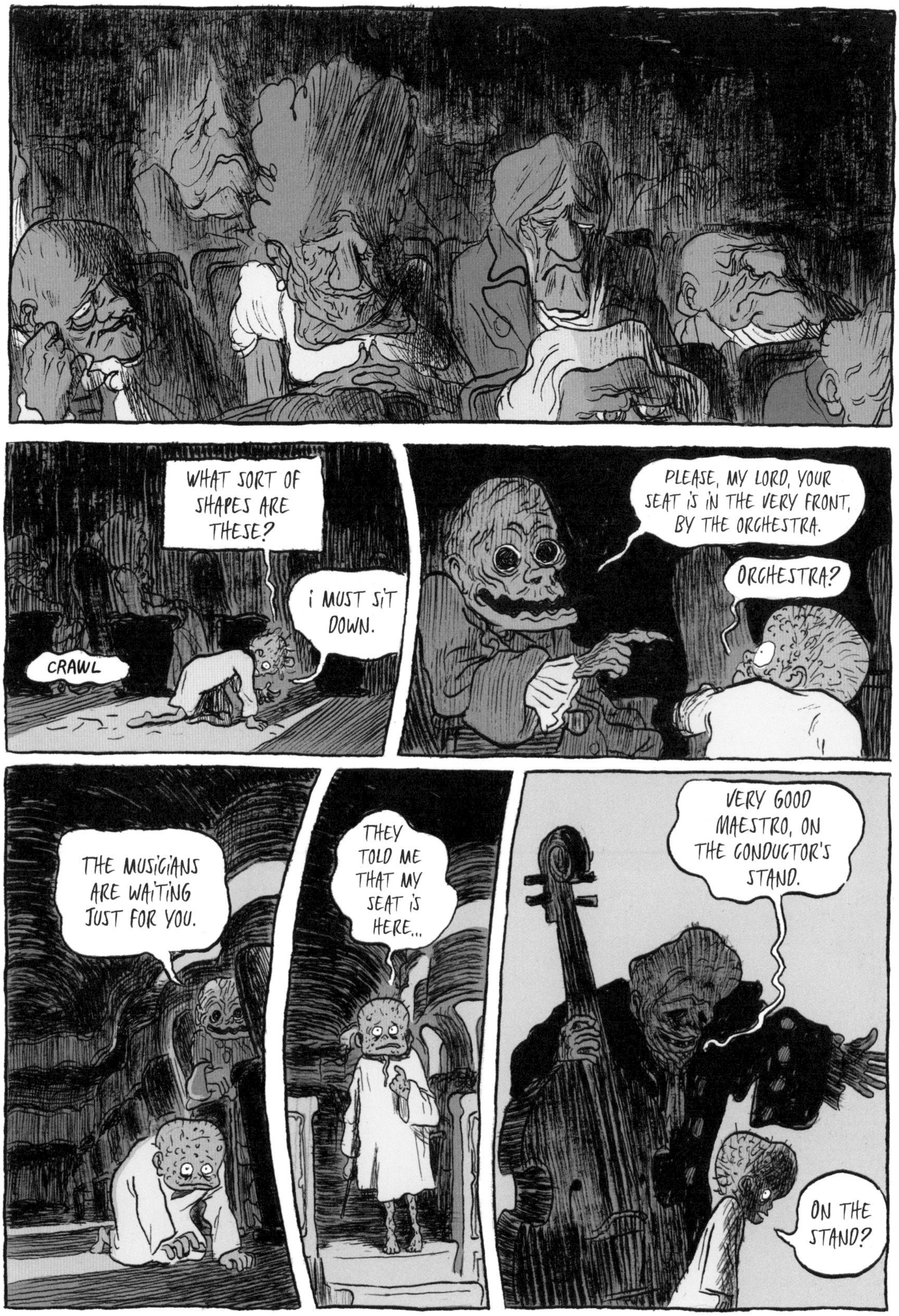
WHAT SORT OF SHAPES ARE THESE?
I MUST SIT DOWN.
CRAWL
PLEASE, MY LORD, YOUR SEAT IS IN THE VERY FRONT, BY THE ORCHESTRA.
ORCHESTRA?
THE MUSICIANS ARE WAITING JUST FOR YOU.
THEY TOLD ME THAT MY SEAT IS HERE...
VERY GOOD MAESTRO, ON THE CONDUCTOR'S STAND.
ON THE STAND?

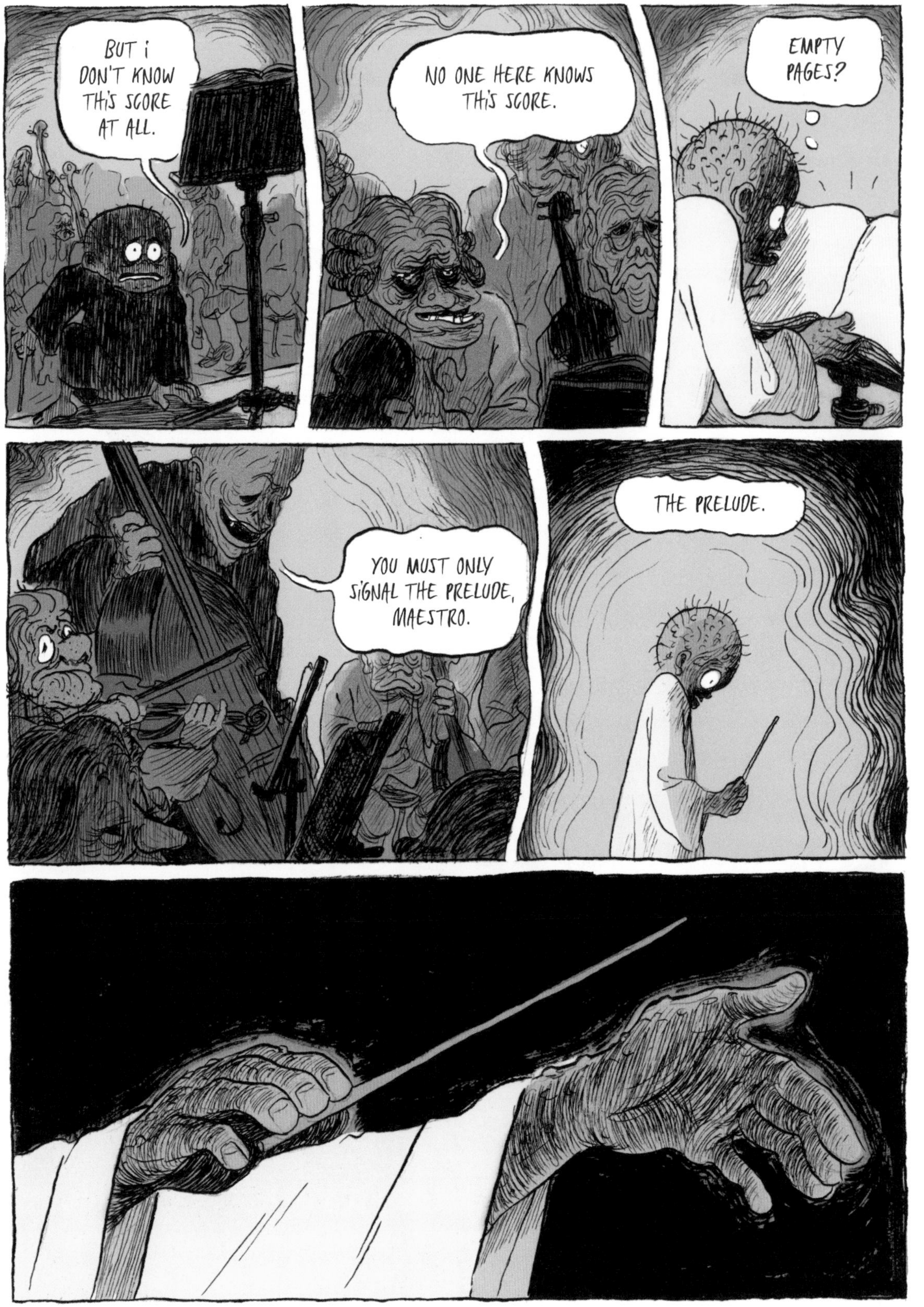
BUT I DON'T KNOW THIS SCORE AT ALL.
NO ONE HERE KNOWS THIS SCORE.
EMPTY PAGES?
YOU MUST ONLY SIGNAL THE PRELUDE, MAESTRO.
THE PRELUDE.

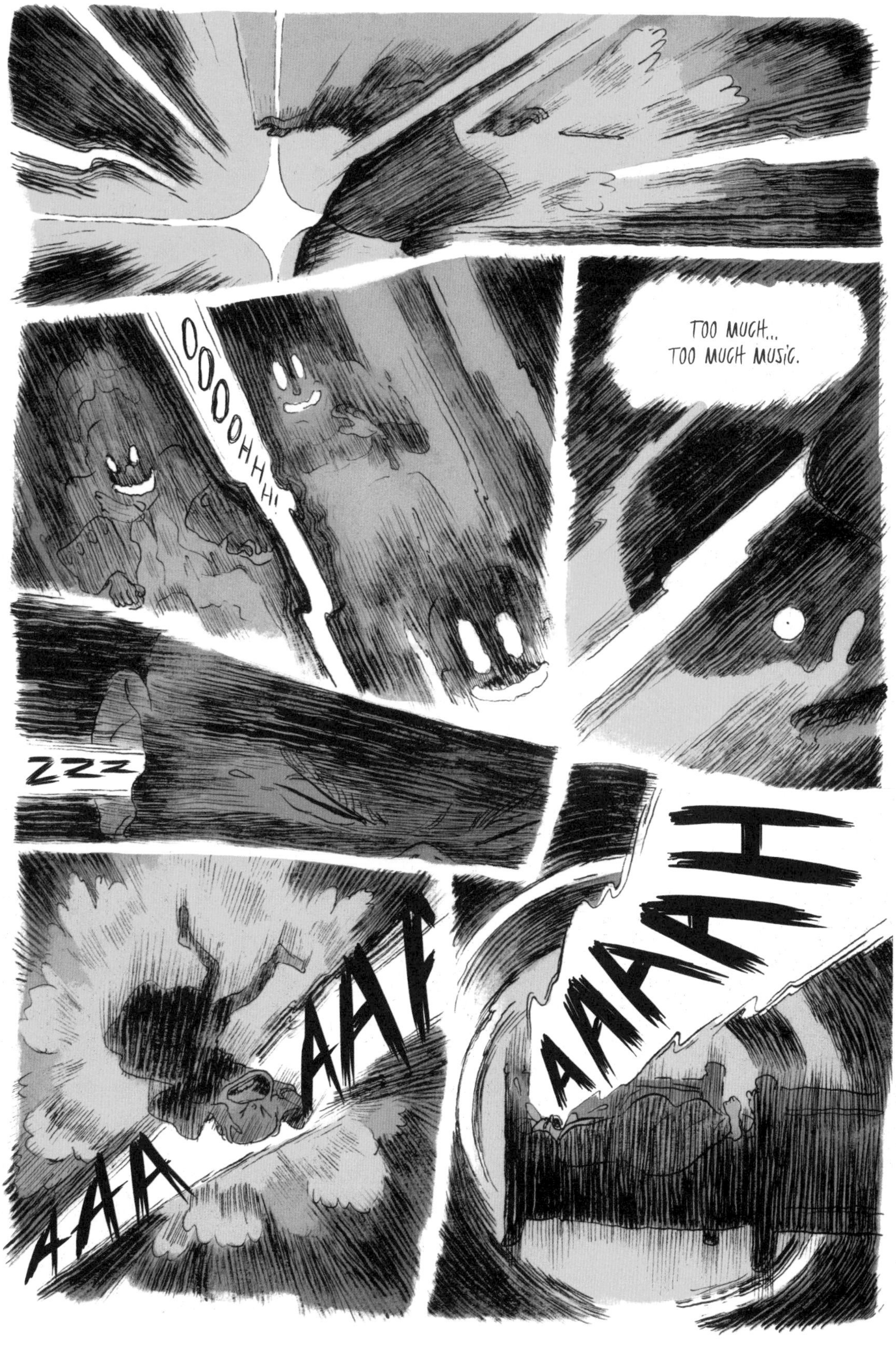
OOOOOOHHHH!
TOO MUCH...
TOO MUCH MUSIC.
ZZZ
AAAAAAAAAAAAH

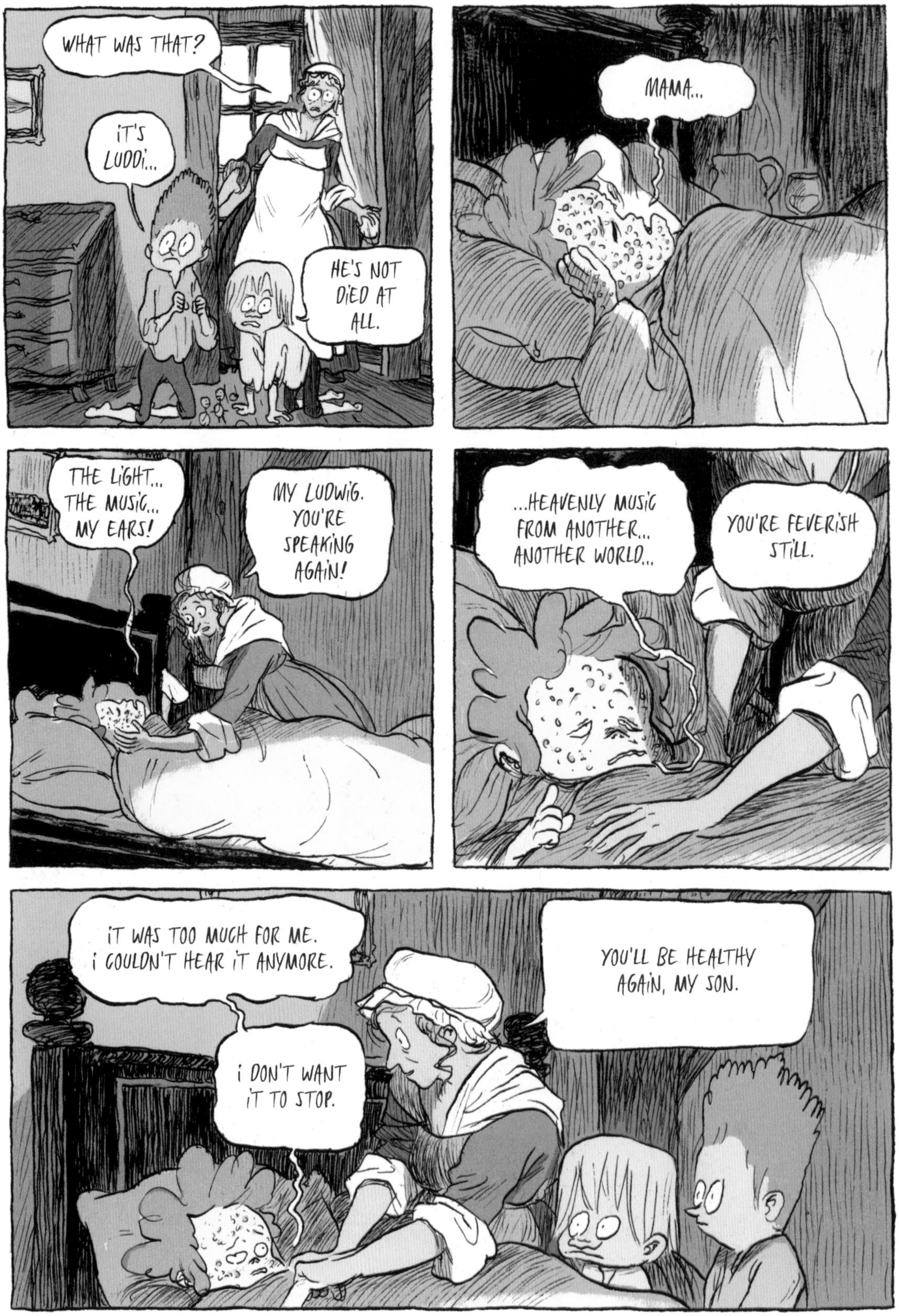
WHAT WAS THAT?
IT'S LUDDI...
HE'S NOT DIED AT ALL.
MAMA...
THE LIGHT... THE MUSIC... MY EARS!
MY LUDWIG. YOU'RE SPEAKING AGAIN!
...HEAVENLY MUSIC FROM ANOTHER... ANOTHER WORLD...
YOU'RE FEVERISH STILL.
IT WAS TOO MUCH FOR ME. I COULDN'T HEAR IT ANYMORE.
I DON'T WANT IT TO STOP.
YOU'LL BE HEALTHY AGAIN, MY SON.

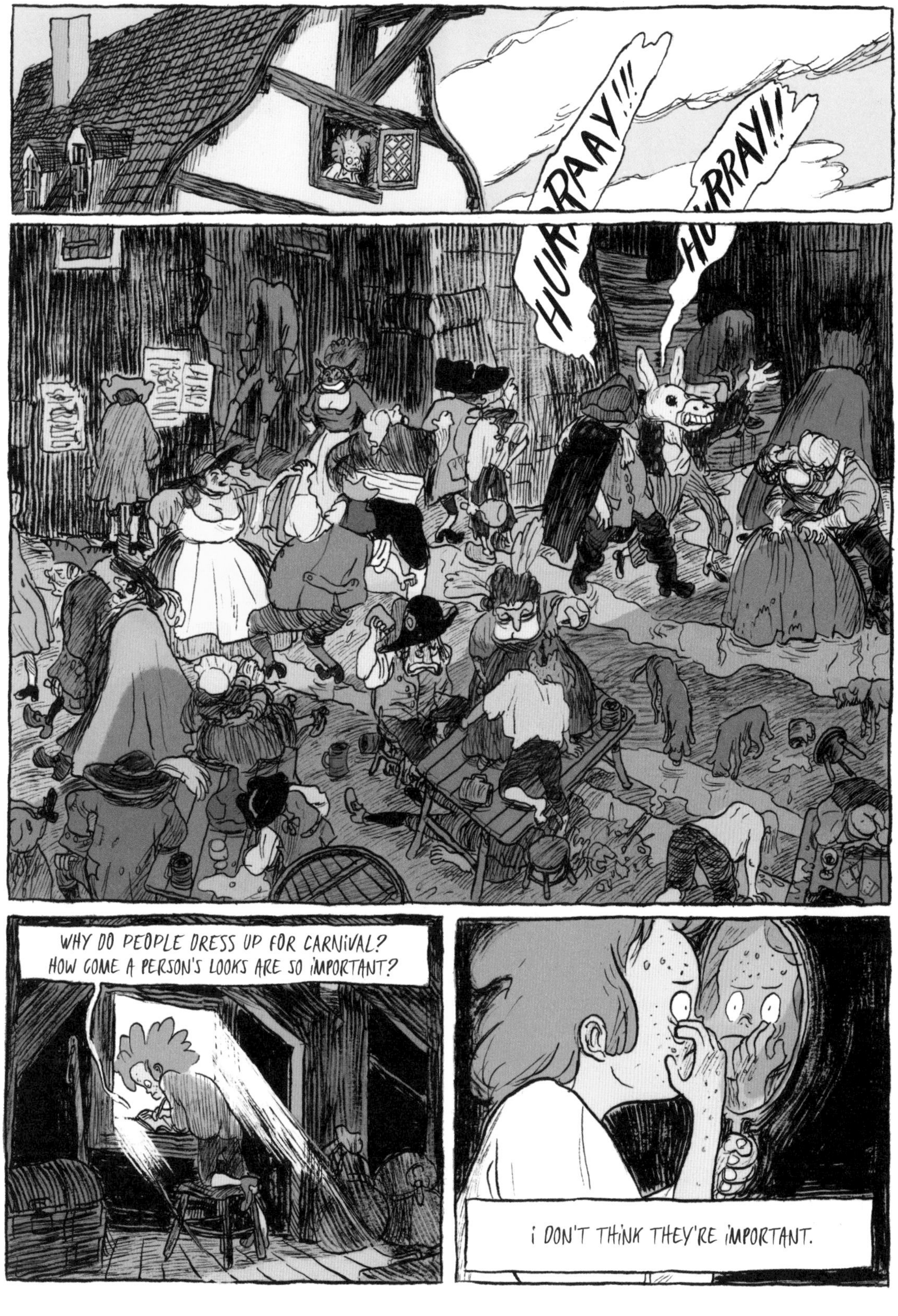
HURRAAY!!!
HURRAY!!!
WHY DO PEOPLE DRESS UP FOR CARNIVAL? HOW COME A PERSON'S LOOKS ARE SO IMPORTANT?
I DON'T THINK THEY'RE IMPORTANT.

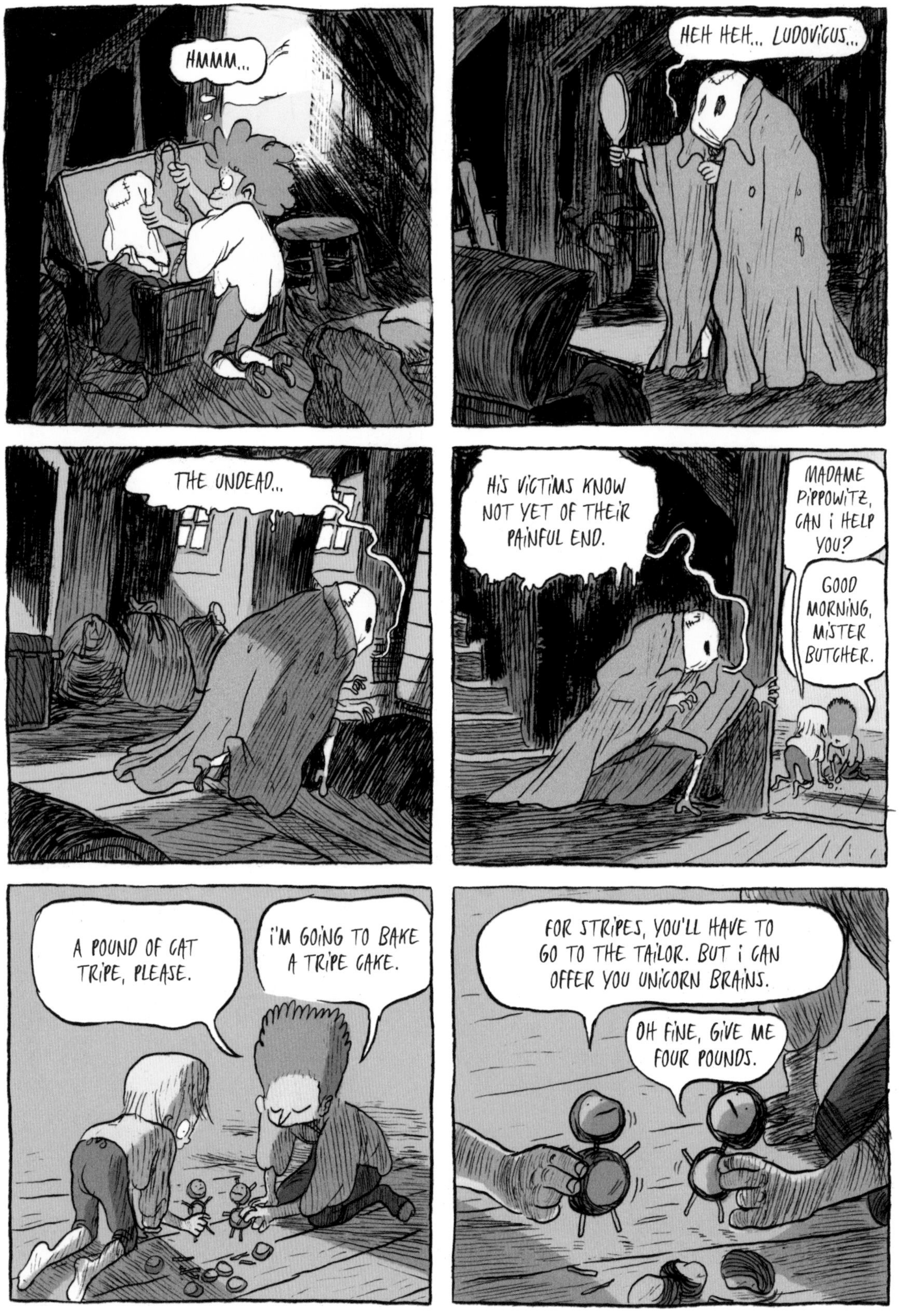
HMMM...
HEH HEH... LUDOVICUS...
THE UNDEAD...
HIS VICTIMS KNOW NOT YET OF THEIR PAINFUL END.
MADAME PIPPOWITZ, CAN I HELP YOU?
GOOD MORNING, MISTER BUTCHER.
A POUND OF CAT TRIPE, PLEASE.
I'M GOING TO BAKE A TRIPE CAKE.
FOR STRIPES, YOU'LL HAVE TO GO TO THE TAILOR. BUT I CAN OFFER YOU UNICORN BRAINS.
OH FINE, GIVE ME FOUR POUNDS.

I WANT TO EAT YOUR BRAINS!
WHO... WHO'S THERE?
D-DID YOU HEAR THAT TOO?
I WANT TO SUCK YOUR SWEET YOUNG BLOOOOD!
TH-THERE! IT'S COMING FROM THE DOOR!
WHERE'S YOUR USELESS FATHER HIDING NOW?
EVERY BONE IN MY BODY HURTS, AND NOW THERE'S THIS CARNIVAL RACKET..
MA-MAMA... TH-THAT ROOM IS HAUNTED!
LUDOVICUUUS...
EEEEK
... THE UNDEAD IS UPON YOU!

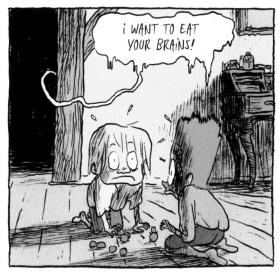

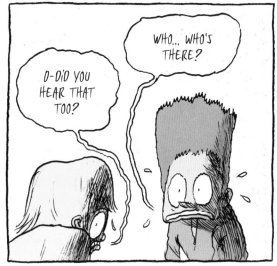

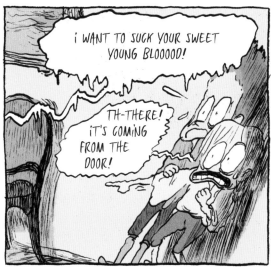

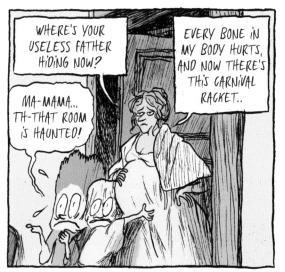

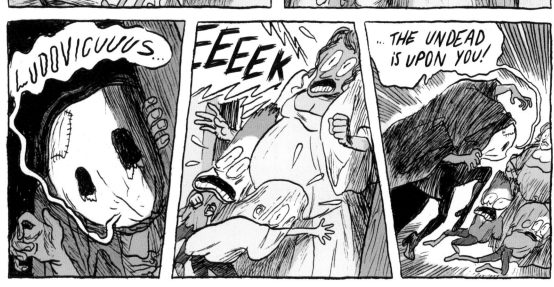

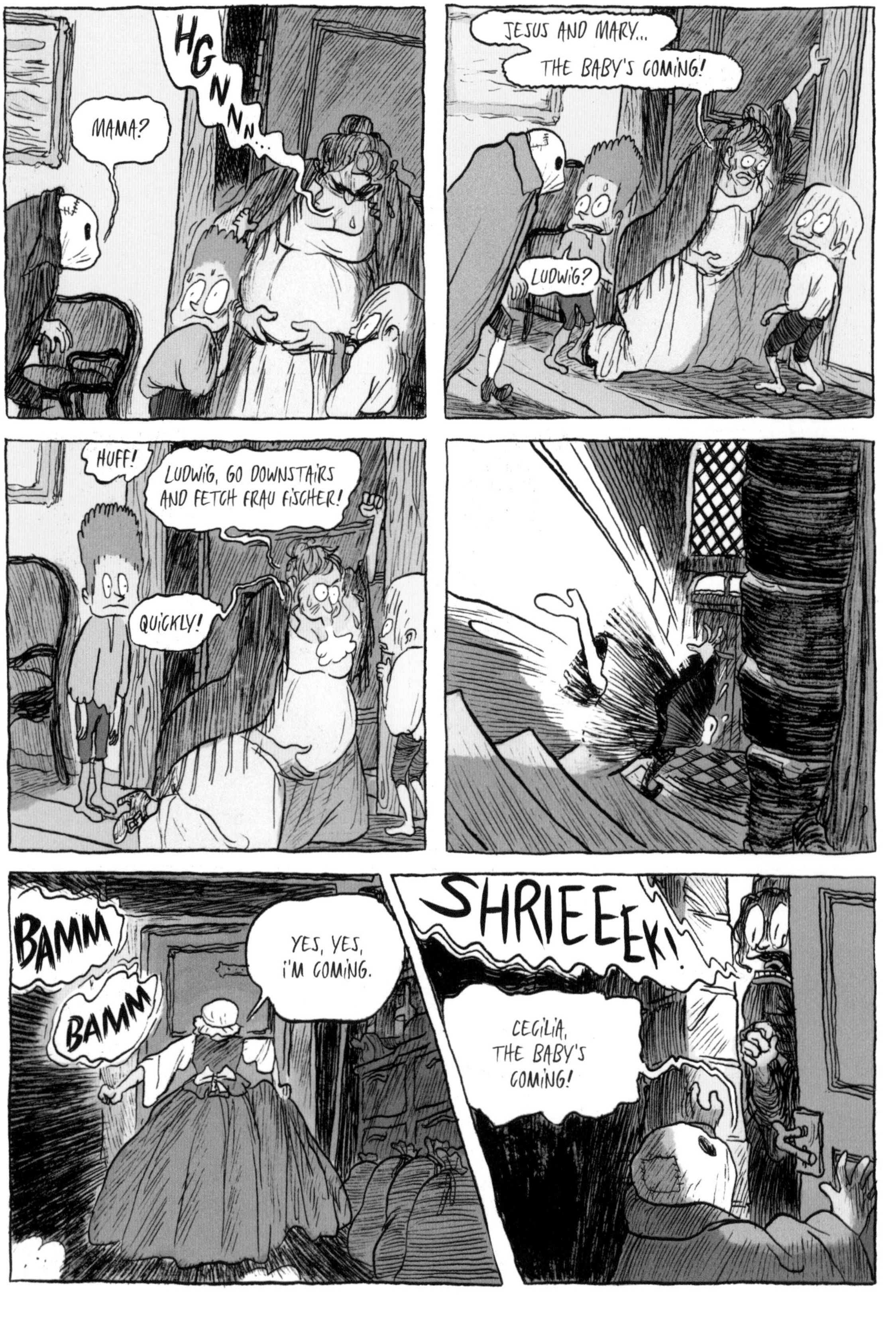
HGNNN...
MAMA?
JESUS AND MARY...
THE BABY'S COMING!
LUDWIG?
HUFF!
LUDWIG, GO DOWNSTAIRS AND FETCH FRAU FISCHER!
QUICKLY!
BAMM
BAMM
YES, YES, I'M COMING.
SHRIEEEEK!
CECILIA, THE BABY'S COMING!

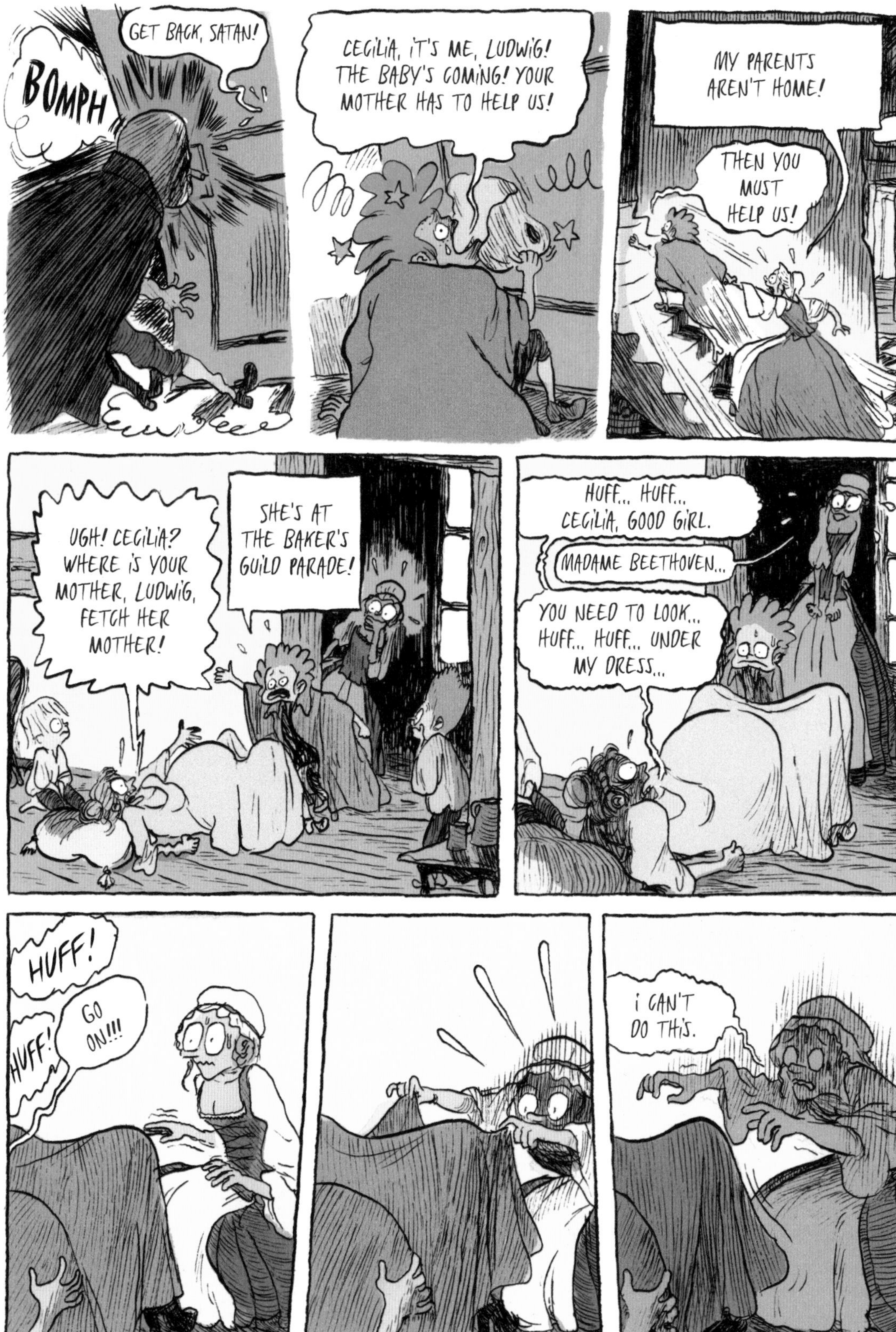
BOMPH
GET BACK, SATAN!
CECILIA, IT'S ME, LUDWIG! THE BABY'S COMING! YOUR MOTHER HAS TO HELP US!
MY PARENTS AREN'T HOME!
THEN YOU MUST HELP US!
UGH! CECILIA? WHERE IS YOUR MOTHER, LUDWIG, FETCH HER MOTHER!
SHE'S AT THE BAKER'S GUILD PARADE!
HUFF... HUFF... CECILIA, GOOD GIRL.
MADAME BEETHOVEN...
YOU NEED TO LOOK... HUFF... HUFF... UNDER MY DRESS...
HUFF!
HUFF!
GO ON!!!
I CAN'T DO THIS.

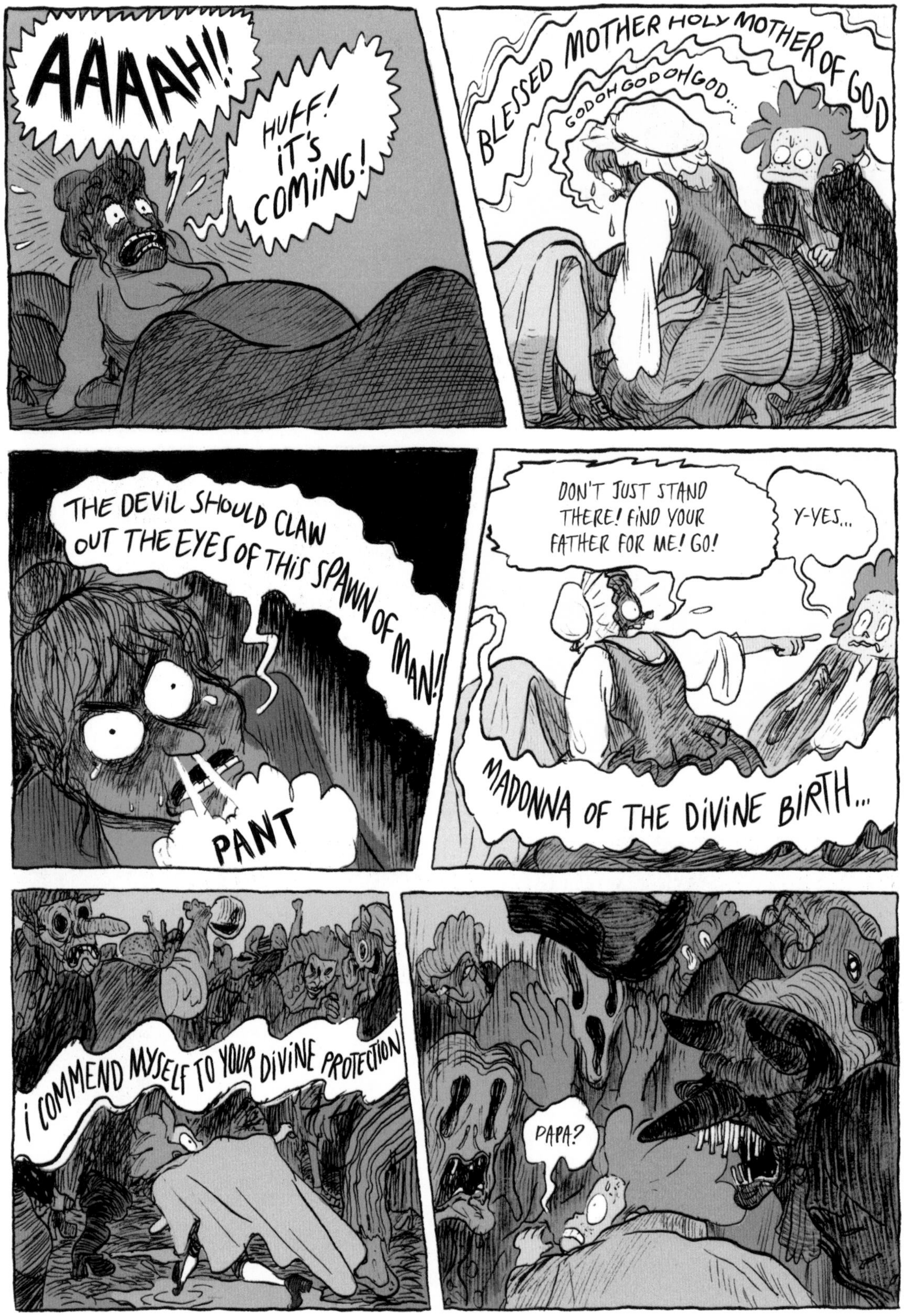
AAAAH!!
HUFF! IT'S COMING!
BLESSED MOTHER HOLY MOTHER OF GOD
GODOHGODOHGOD...
THE DEVIL SHOULD CLAW OUT THE EYES OF THIS SPAWN OF MAN!!
PANT
DON'T JUST STAND THERE! FIND YOUR FATHER FOR ME! GO!
Y-YES...
MADONNA OF THE DIVINE BIRTH...
I COMMEND MYSELF TO YOUR DIVINE PROTECTION
PAPA?

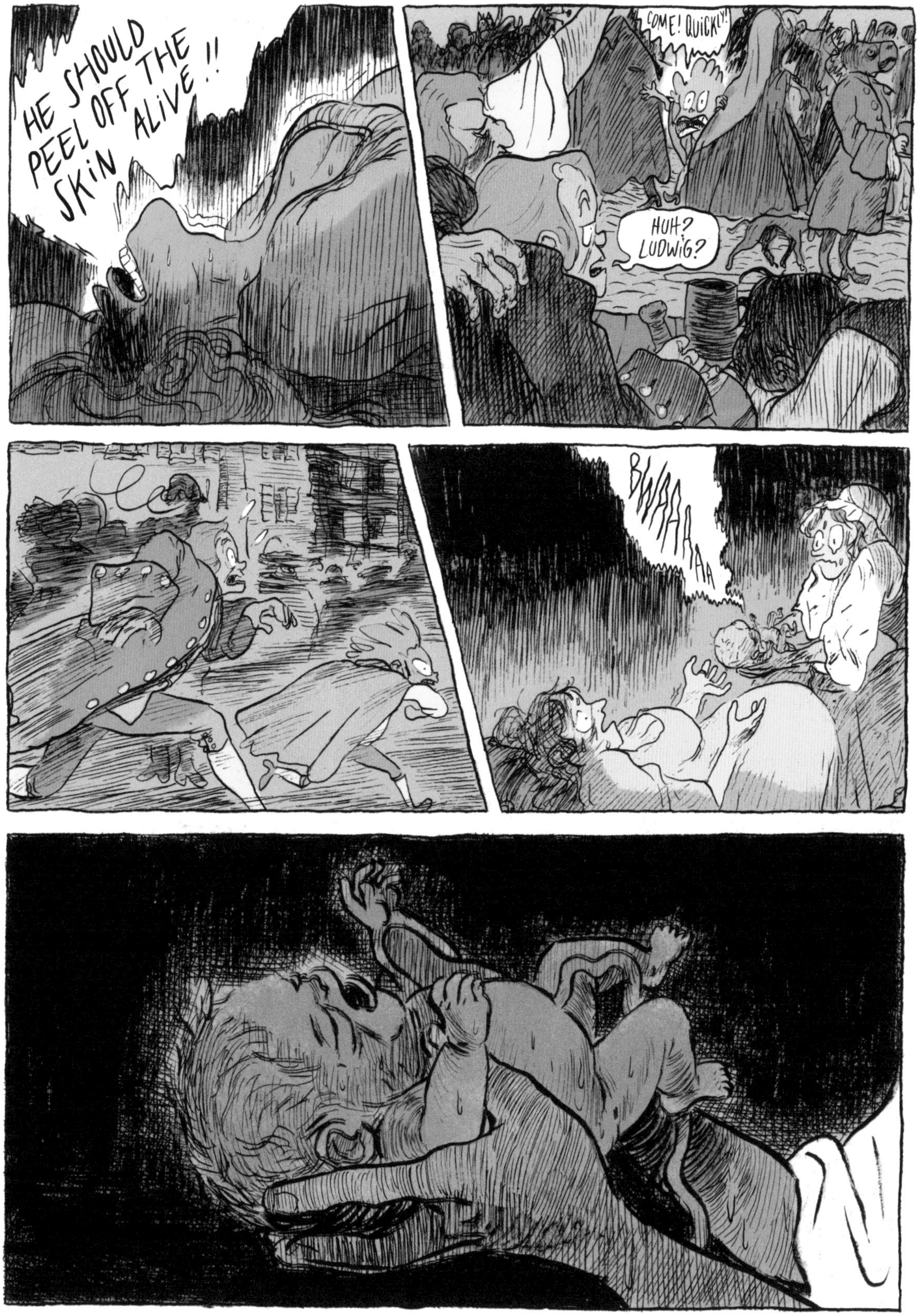
HE SHOULD PEEL OFF THE SKIN ALIVE!!
COME! QUICKLY!
HUH? LUDWIG?
BWAAAAAAA

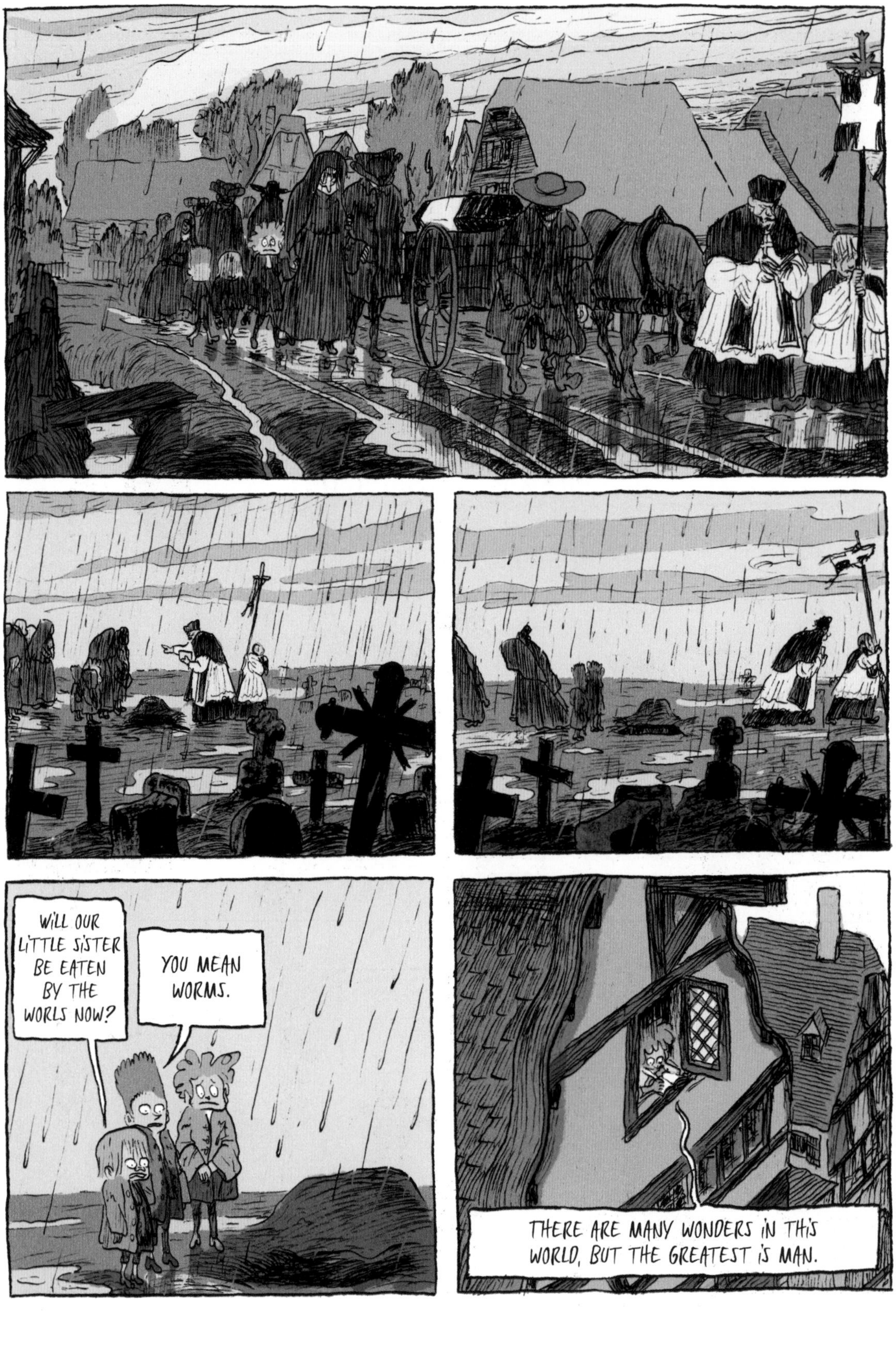
WiLL OUR LiTTLE SiSTER BE EATEN BY THE WORLS NOW?
YOU MEAN WORMS.
THERE ARE MANY WONDERS iN THiS WORLD, BUT THE GREATEST iS MAN.

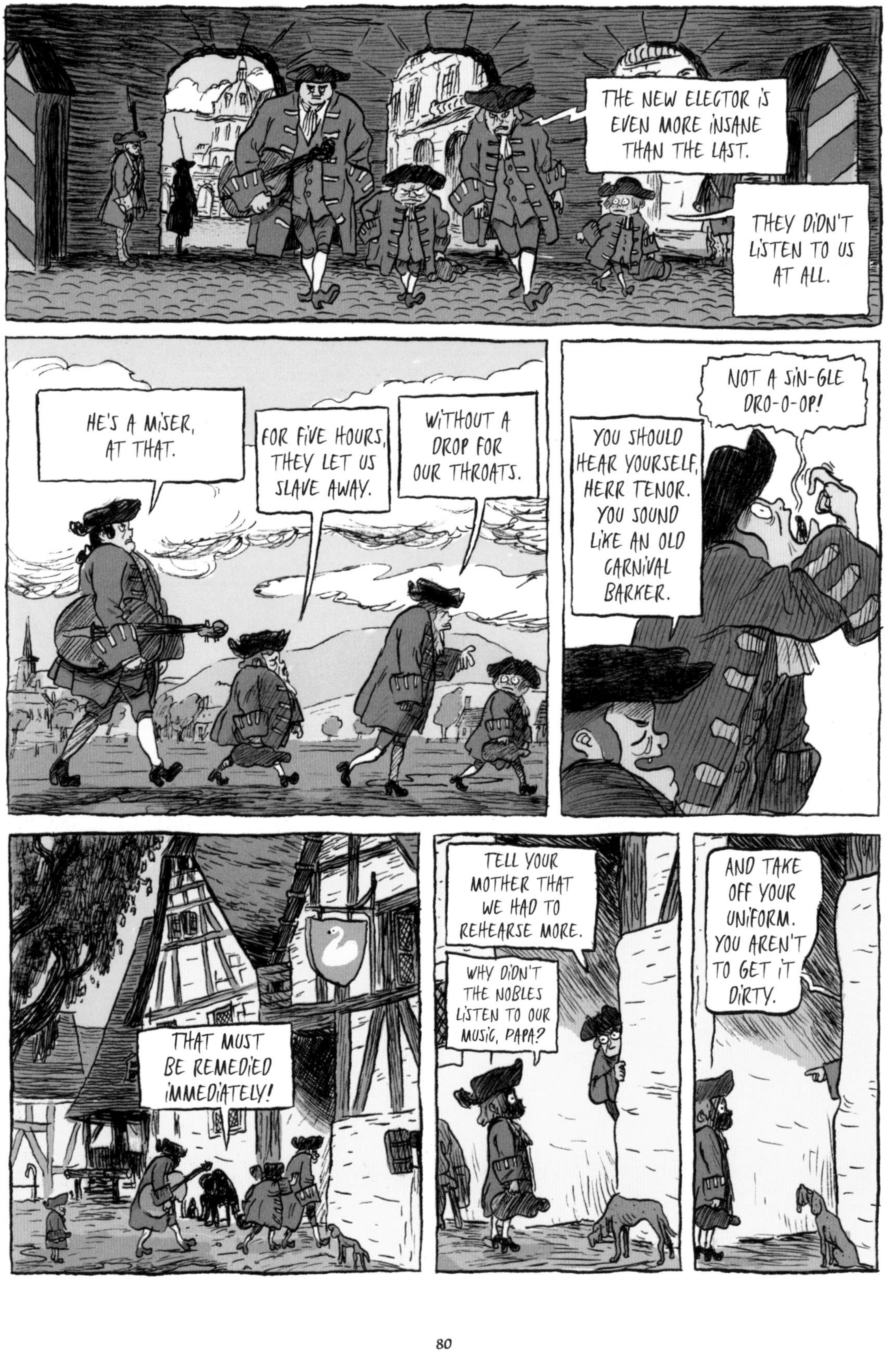
THE NEW ELECTOR is EVEN MORE iNSANE THAN THE LAST.
THEY DiDN'T LiSTEN TO US AT ALL.
HE'S A MiSER, AT THAT.
FOR FiVE HOURS, THEY LET US SLAVE AWAY.
WiTHOUT A DROP FOR OUR THROATS.
NOT A SiN-GLE DRO-O-OP!
YOU SHOULD HEAR YOURSELF, HERR TENOR. YOU SOUND LiKE AN OLD CARNiVAL BARKER.
THAT MUST BE REMEDiED iMMEDiATELY!
TELL YOUR MOTHER THAT WE HAD TO REHEARSE MORE.
WHY DiDN'T THE NOBLES LiSTEN TO OUR MUSiC, PAPA?
AND TAKE OFF YOUR UNiFORM. YOU AREN'T TO GET iT DiRTY.

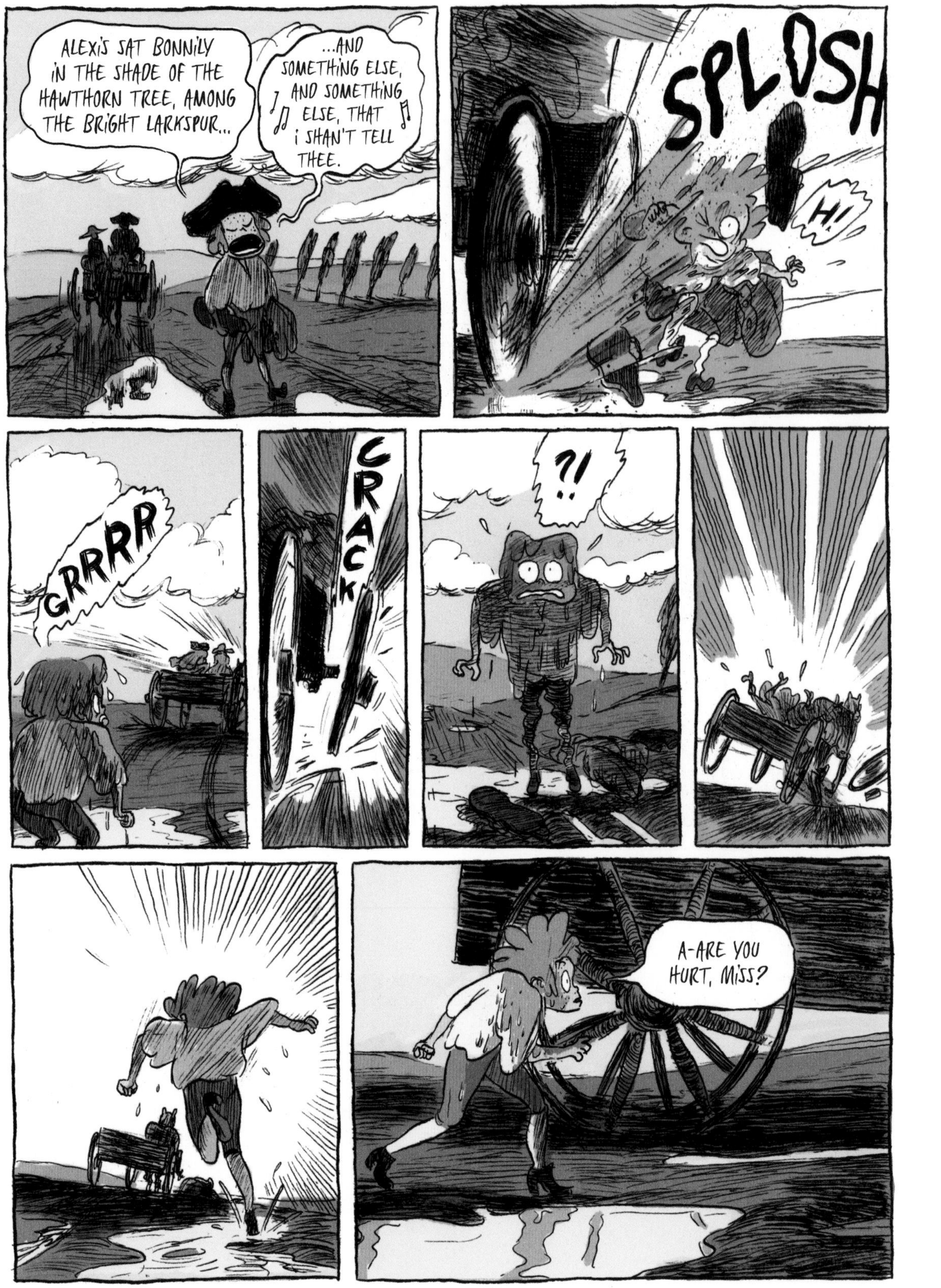
ALEXIS SAT BONNILY IN THE SHADE OF THE HAWTHORN TREE, AMONG THE BRIGHT LARKSPUR...
...AND SOMETHING ELSE, AND SOMETHING ELSE, THAT I SHAN'T TELL THEE.
SPLOSH
H!
GRRRR
CRACK
?!
A-ARE YOU HURT, MISS?

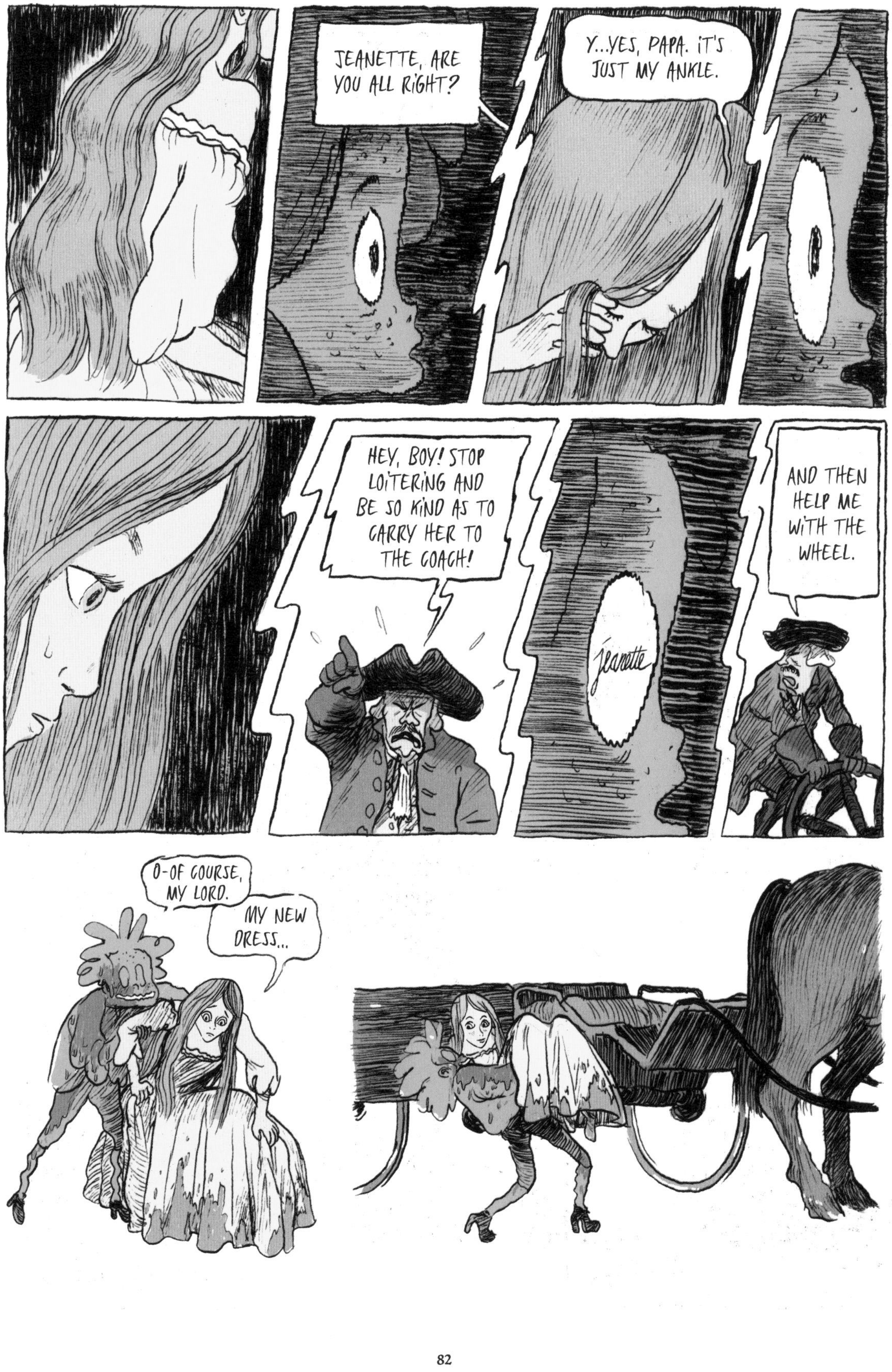
JEANETTE, ARE YOU ALL RIGHT?
Y...YES, PAPA. IT'S JUST MY ANKLE.
HEY, BOY! STOP LOITERING AND BE SO KIND AS TO CARRY HER TO THE COACH!
Jeanette
AND THEN HELP ME WITH THE WHEEL.
O-OF COURSE, MY LORD.
MY NEW DRESS...

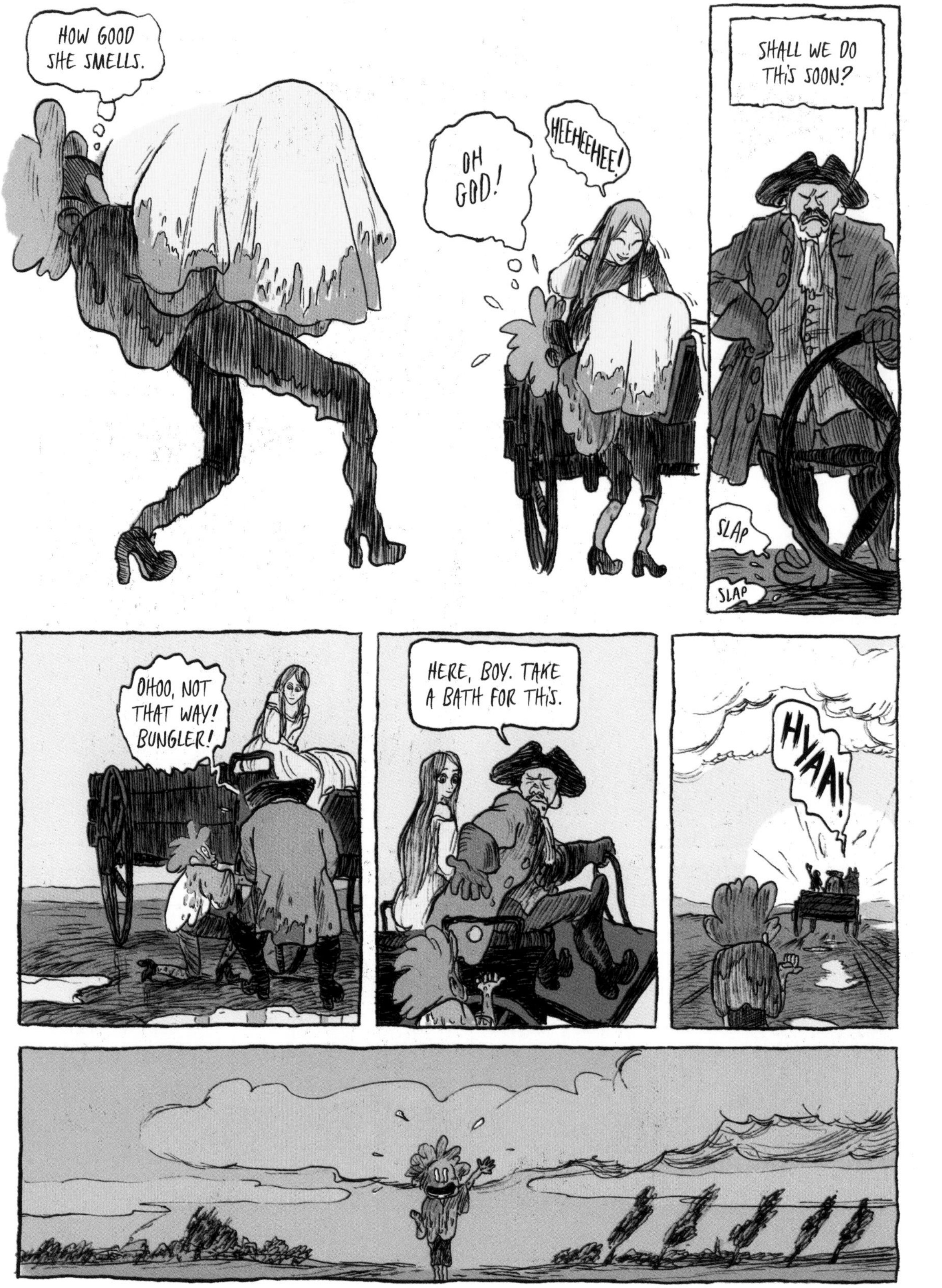
HOW GOOD SHE SMELLS.
OH GOD!
HEEHEEHEE!
SHALL WE DO THIS SOON?
SLAP
SLAP
OHOO, NOT THAT WAY! BUNGLER!
HERE, BOY. TAKE A BATH FOR THIS.
HYAA!

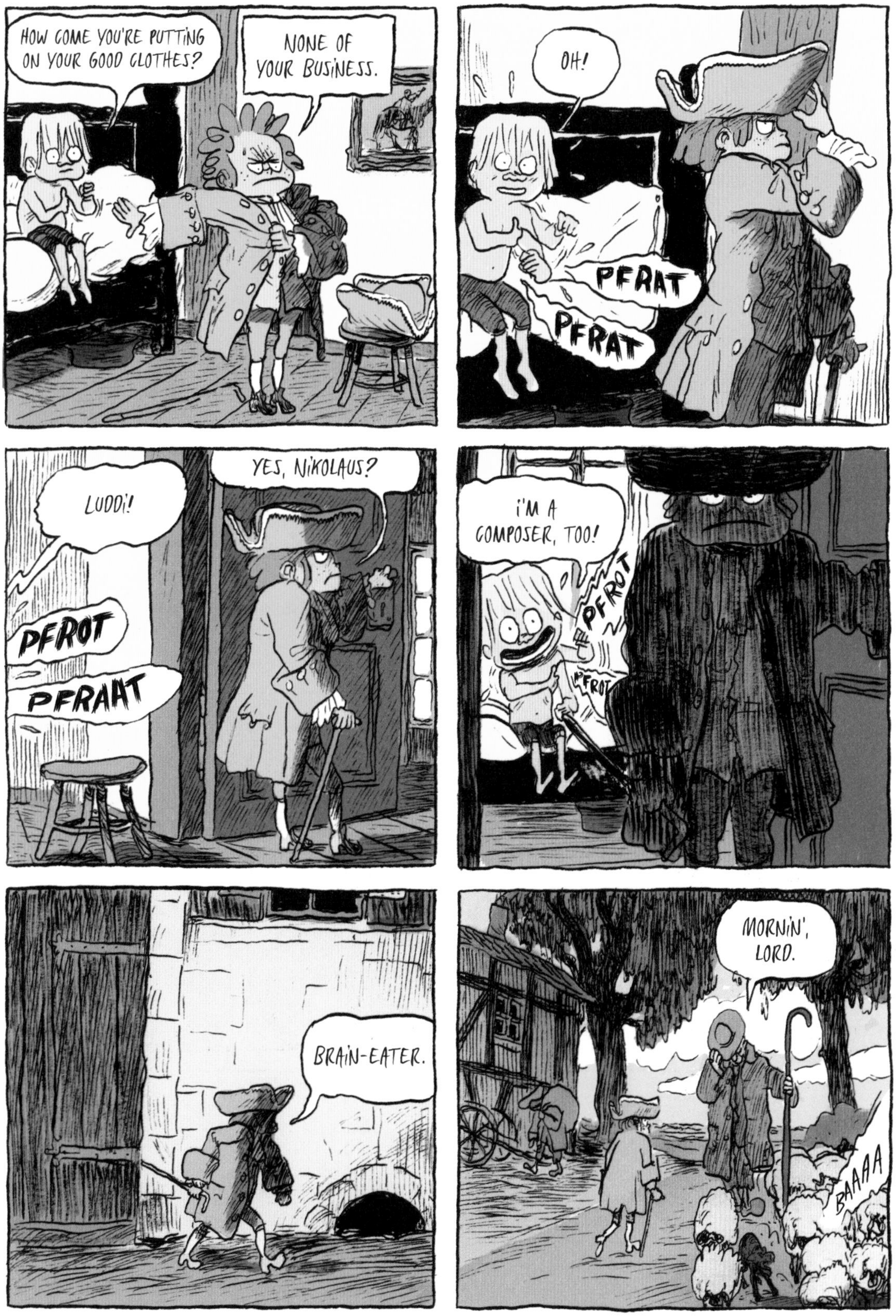

HOW COME YOU'RE PUTTING ON YOUR GOOD CLOTHES?
NONE OF YOUR BUSINESS.
OH!
PFRAT
PFRAT
LUDDI!
YES, NIKOLAUS?
PFROT
PFRAAT
I'M A COMPOSER, TOO!
PFROT
PFROT
BRAIN-EATER.
MORNIN', LORD.
BAAAA

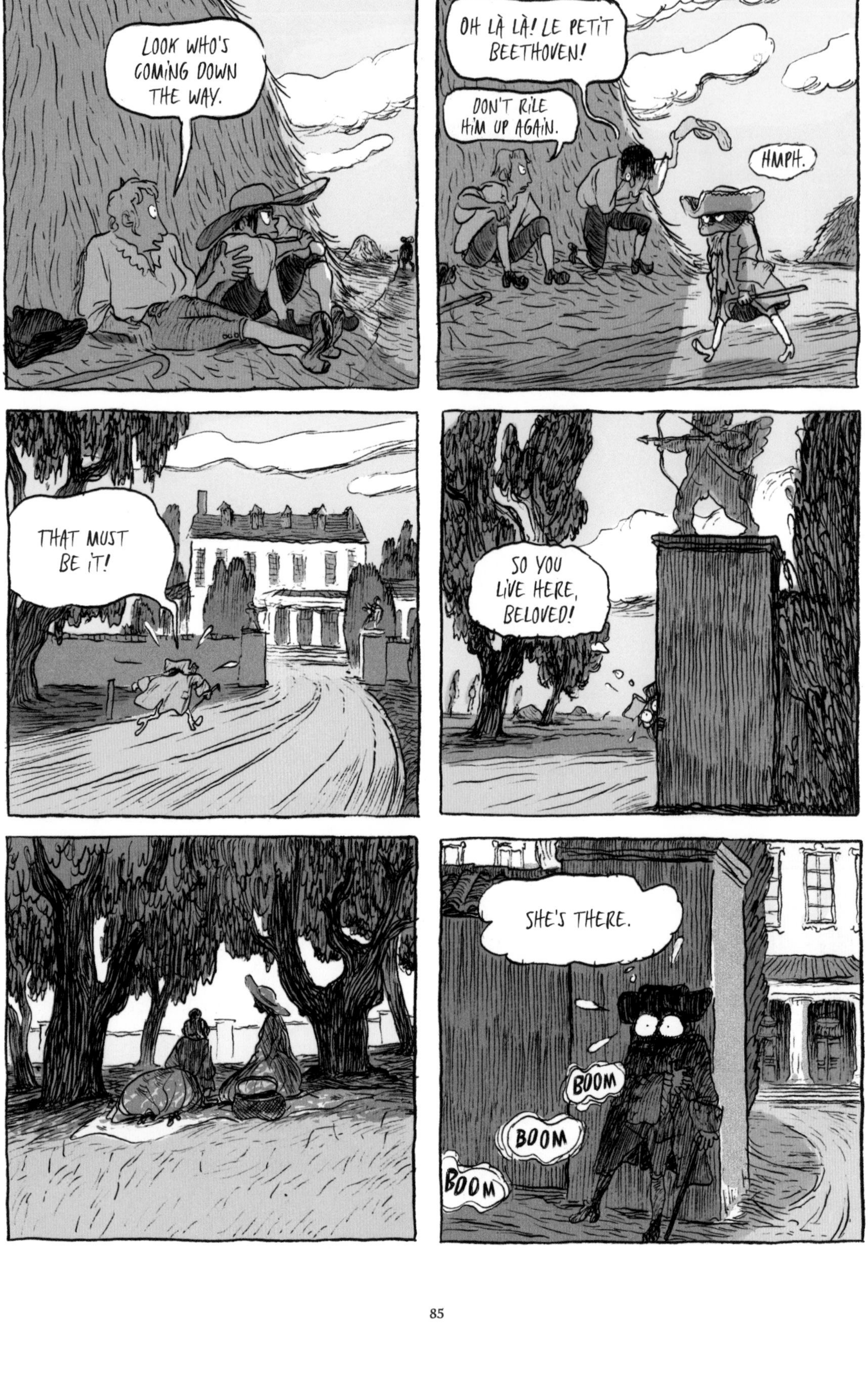
LOOK WHO'S COMING DOWN THE WAY.
OH LÀ LÀ! LE PETIT BEETHOVEN!
DON'T RILE HIM UP AGAIN.
HMPH.
THAT MUST BE IT!
SO YOU LIVE HERE, BELOVED!
SHE'S THERE.
BOOM
BOOM
BOOM

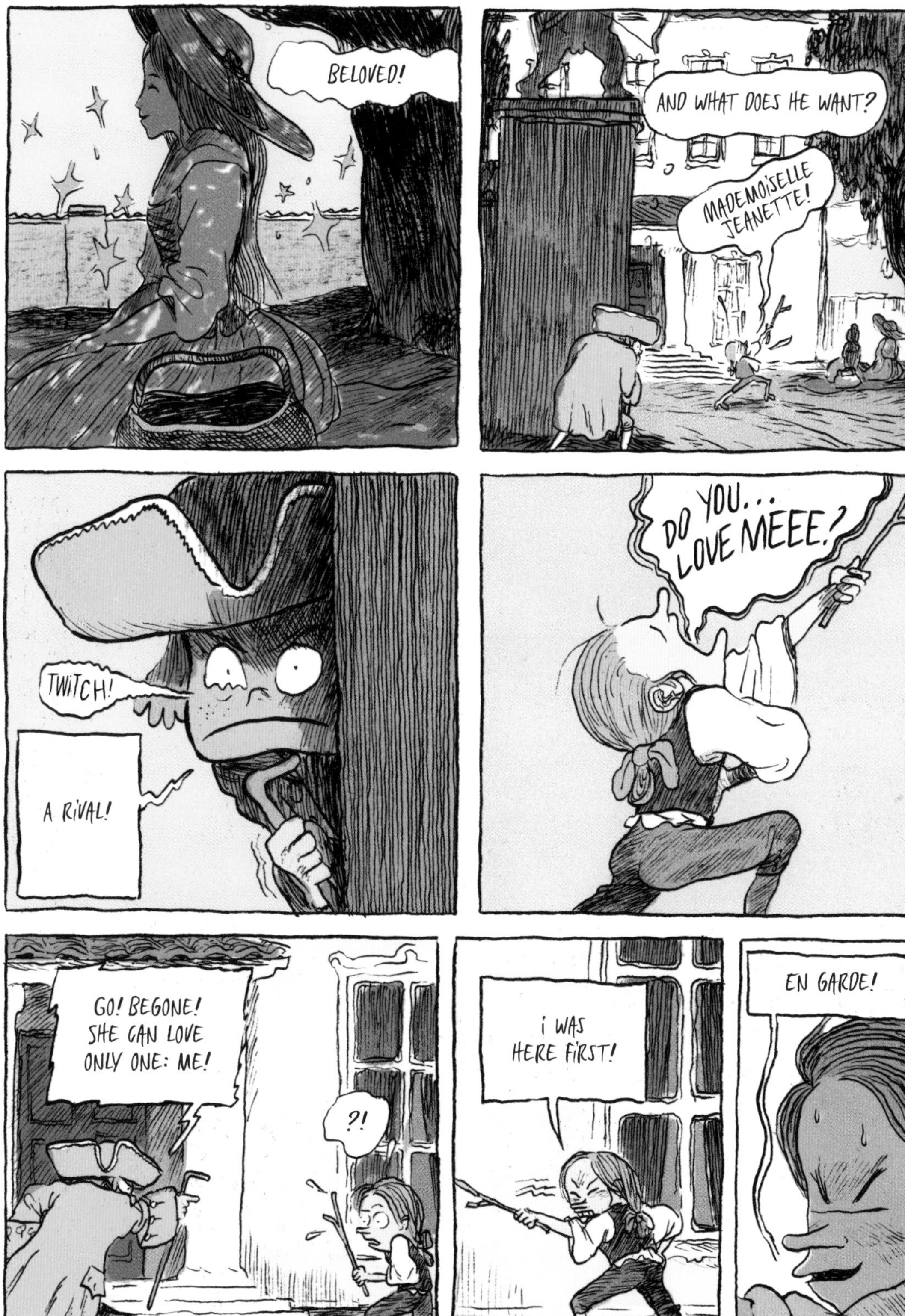
BELOVED!
AND WHAT DOES HE WANT?
MADEMOISELLE JEANETTE!
TWITCH!
A RIVAL!
DO YOU... LOVE MEEE?
GO! BEGONE! SHE CAN LOVE ONLY ONE: ME!
?!
I WAS HERE FIRST!
EN GARDE!

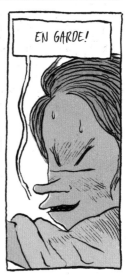

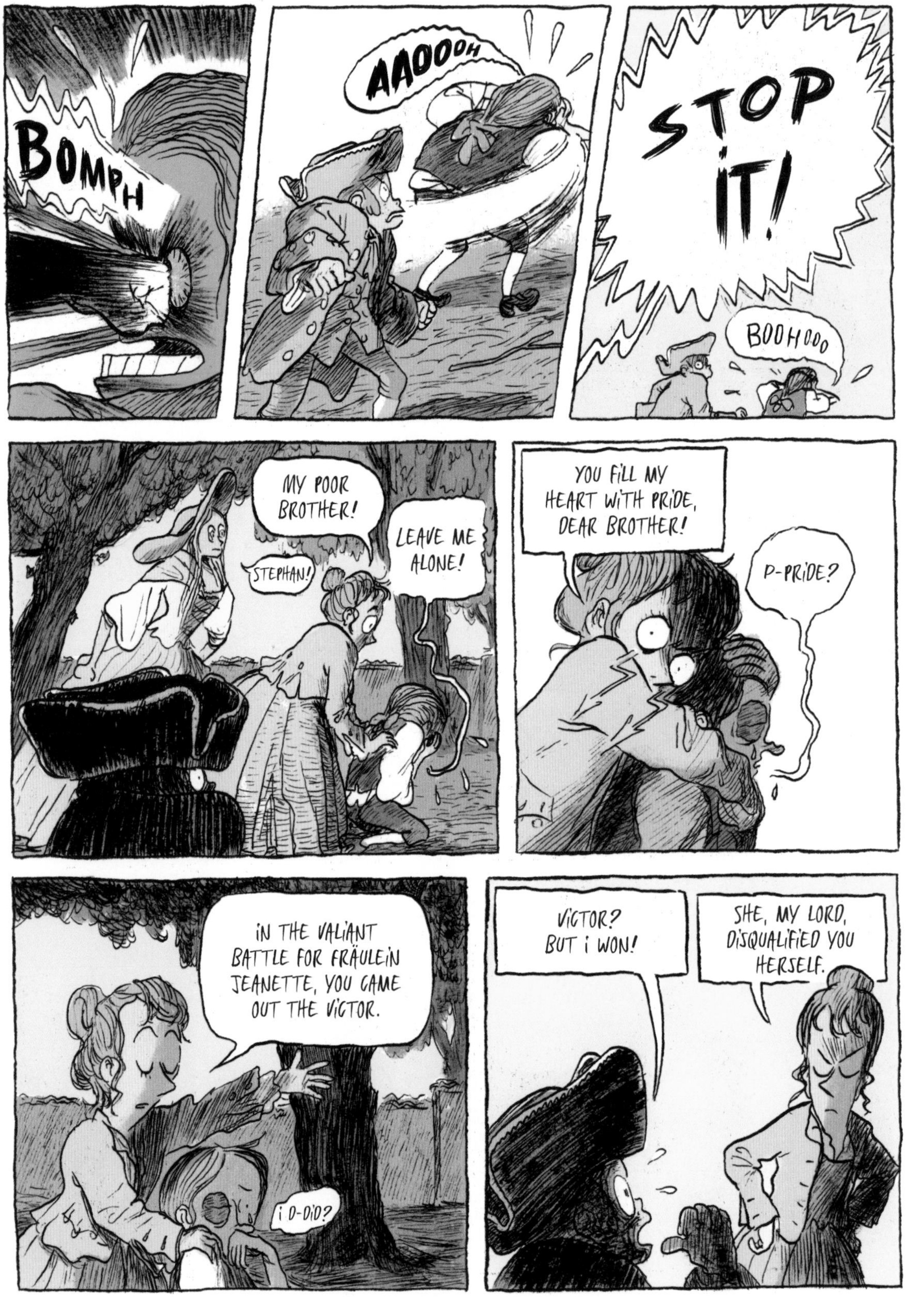
BOMPH
AAOOOH
STOP IT!
BOOHOOO
MY POOR BROTHER!
STEPHAN!
LEAVE ME ALONE!
YOU FILL MY HEART WITH PRIDE, DEAR BROTHER!
P-PRIDE?
IN THE VALIANT BATTLE FOR FRÄULEIN JEANETTE, YOU CAME OUT THE VICTOR.
I D-DID?
VICTOR? BUT I WON!
SHE, MY LORD, DISQUALIFIED YOU HERSELF.

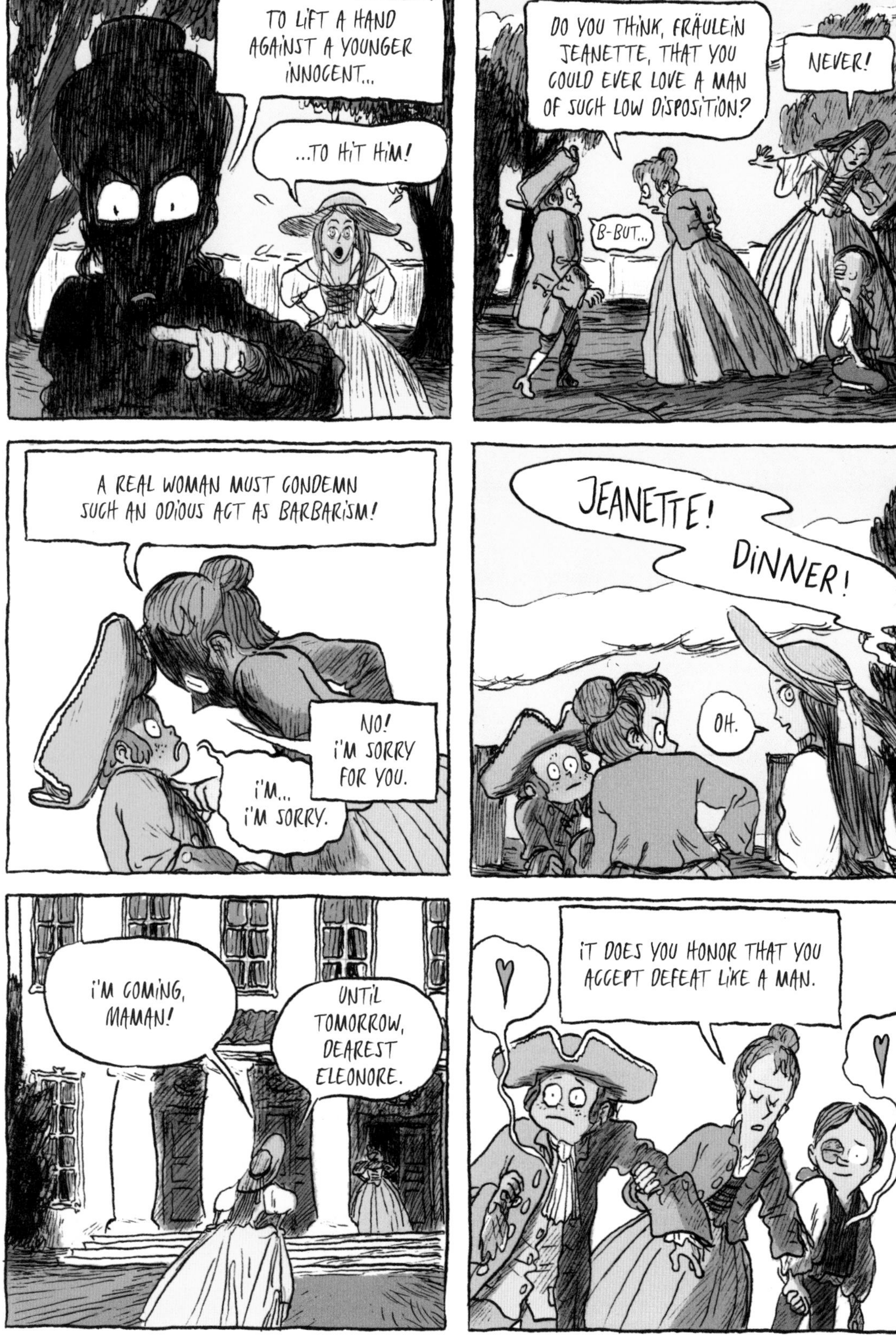
TO LIFT A HAND AGAINST A YOUNGER INNOCENT...
...TO HIT HIM!
DO YOU THINK, FRÄULEIN JEANETTE, THAT YOU COULD EVER LOVE A MAN OF SUCH LOW DISPOSITION?
NEVER!
B-BUT...
A REAL WOMAN MUST CONDEMN SUCH AN ODIOUS ACT AS BARBARISM!
I'M... I'M SORRY.
NO! I'M SORRY FOR YOU.
JEANETTE! DINNER!
OH.
I'M COMING, MAMAN!
UNTIL TOMORROW, DEAREST ELEONORE.
IT DOES YOU HONOR THAT YOU ACCEPT DEFEAT LIKE A MAN.

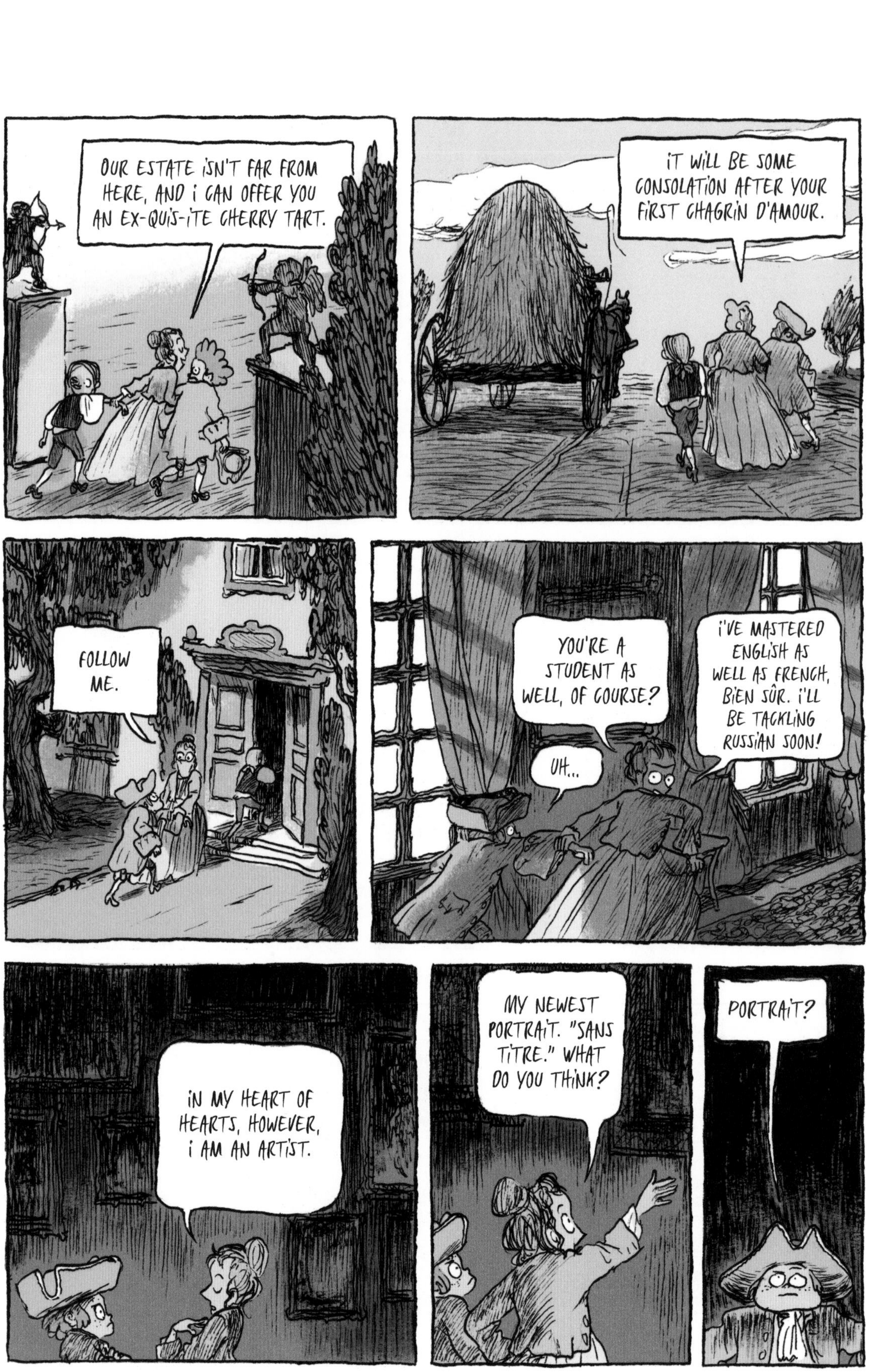
OUR ESTATE iSN'T FAR FROM HERE, AND i CAN OFFER YOU AN EX-QUiS-iTE CHERRY TART.
iT WiLL BE SOME CONSOLATiON AFTER YOUR FiRST CHAGRiN D'AMOUR.
FOLLOW ME.
YOU'RE A STUDENT AS WELL, OF COURSE?
UH...
i'VE MASTERED ENGLiSH AS WELL AS FRENCH, BiEN SÛR. i'LL BE TACKLiNG RUSSiAN SOON!
iN MY HEART OF HEARTS, HOWEVER, i AM AN ARTiST.
MY NEWEST PORTRAiT. "SANS TiTRE." WHAT DO YOU THiNK?
PORTRAiT?

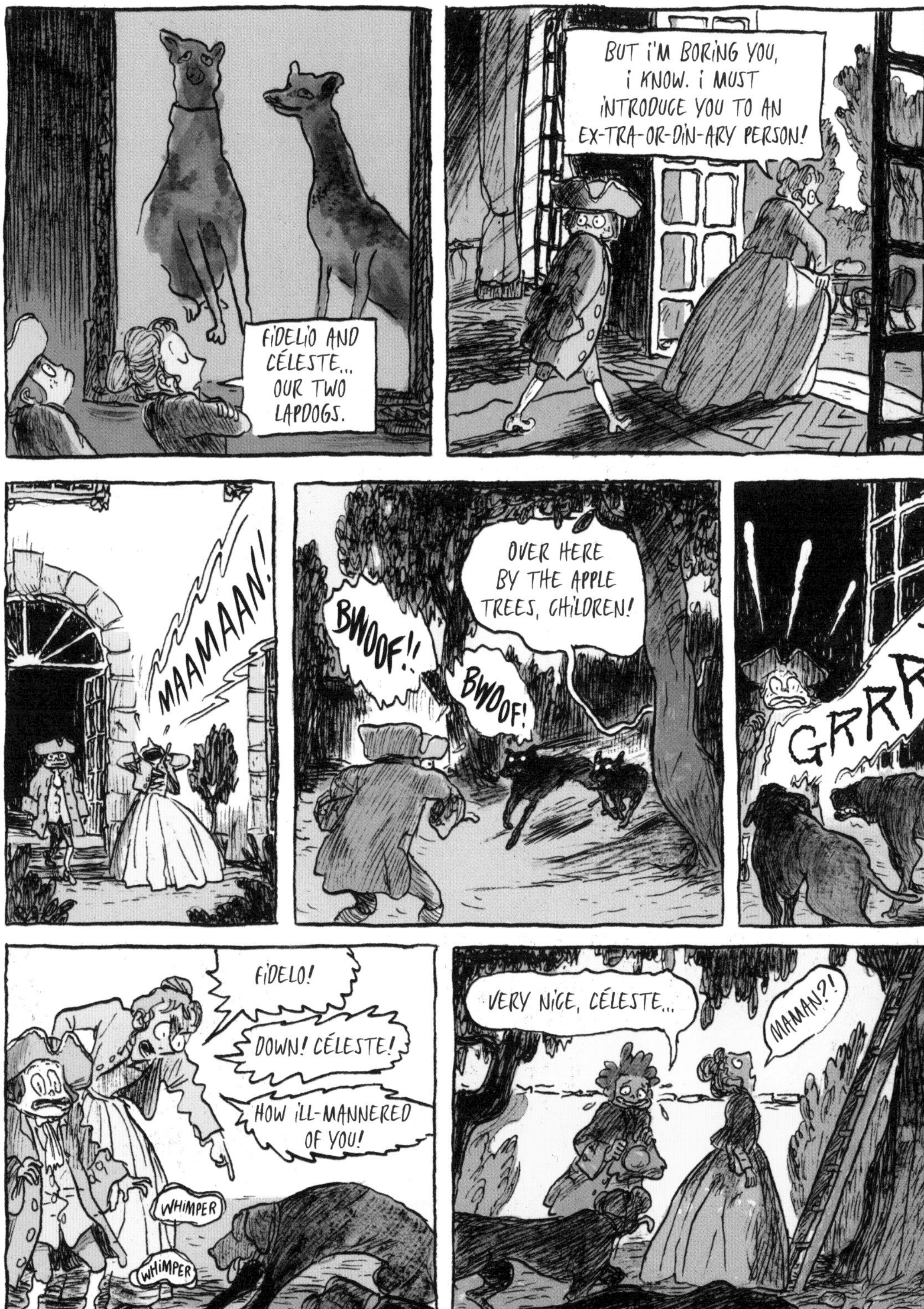
FIDELIO AND CÉLESTE... OUR TWO LAPDOGS.
BUT I'M BORING YOU, I KNOW. I MUST INTRODUCE YOU TO AN EX-TRA-OR-DIN-ARY PERSON!
MAAMAAN!
OVER HERE BY THE APPLE TREES, CHILDREN!
BWOOF!!
BWOOF!
GRRRR
FIDELO!
DOWN! CÉLESTE!
HOW ILL-MANNERED OF YOU!
WHIMPER
WHIMPER
VERY NICE, CÉLESTE...
MAMAN?!

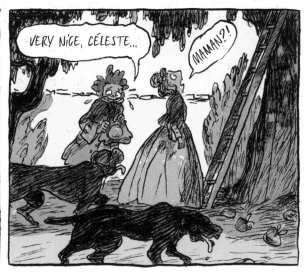

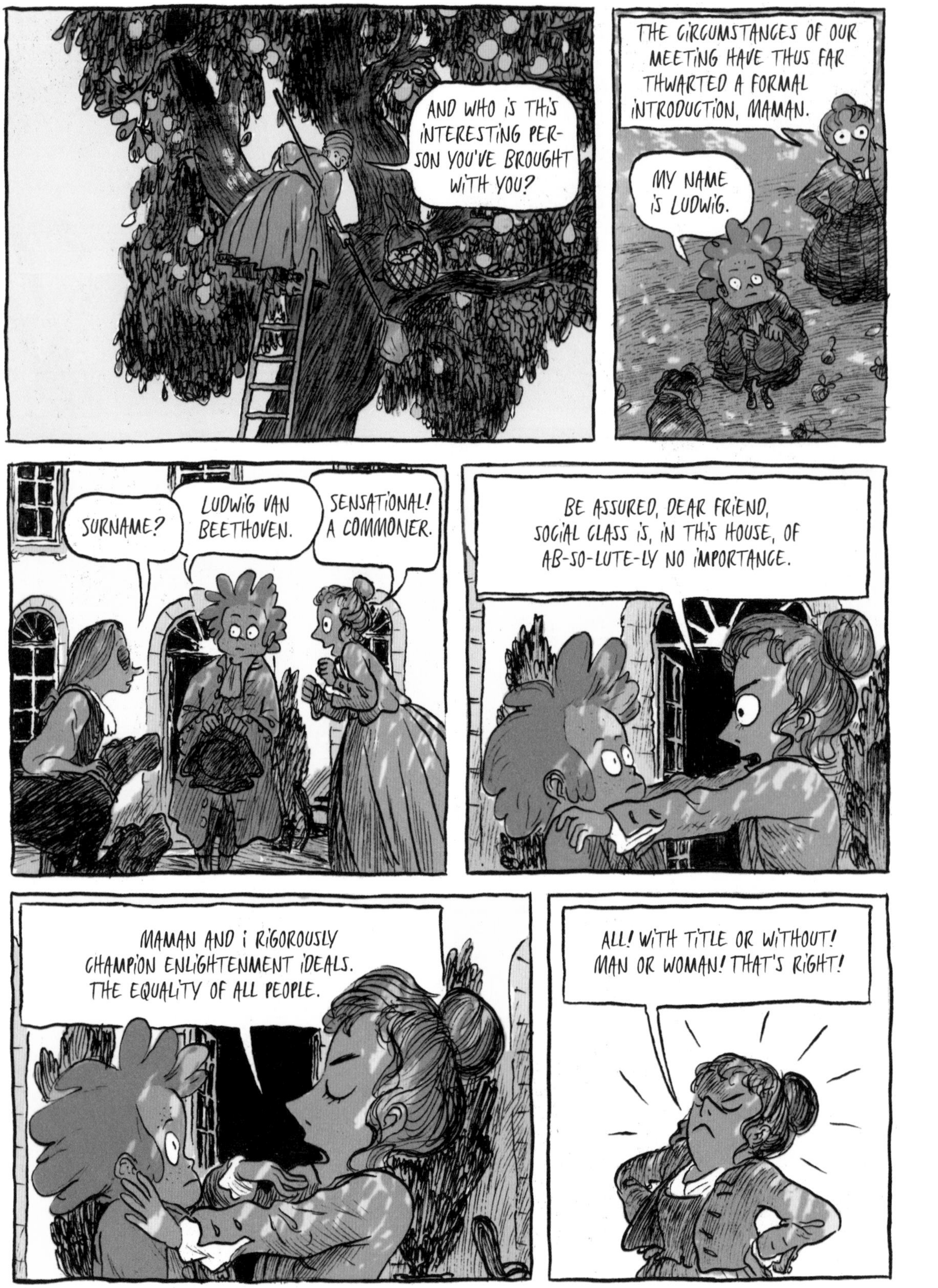
AND WHO IS THIS INTERESTING PERSON YOU'VE BROUGHT WITH YOU?
THE CIRCUMSTANCES OF OUR MEETING HAVE THUS FAR THWARTED A FORMAL INTRODUCTION, MAMAN.
MY NAME IS LUDWIG.
SURNAME?
LUDWIG VAN BEETHOVEN.
SENSATIONAL! A COMMONER.
BE ASSURED, DEAR FRIEND, SOCIAL CLASS IS, IN THIS HOUSE, OF AB-SO-LUTE-LY NO IMPORTANCE.
MAMAN AND I RIGOROUSLY CHAMPION ENLIGHTENMENT IDEALS. THE EQUALITY OF ALL PEOPLE.
ALL! WITH TITLE OR WITHOUT! MAN OR WOMAN! THAT'S RIGHT!

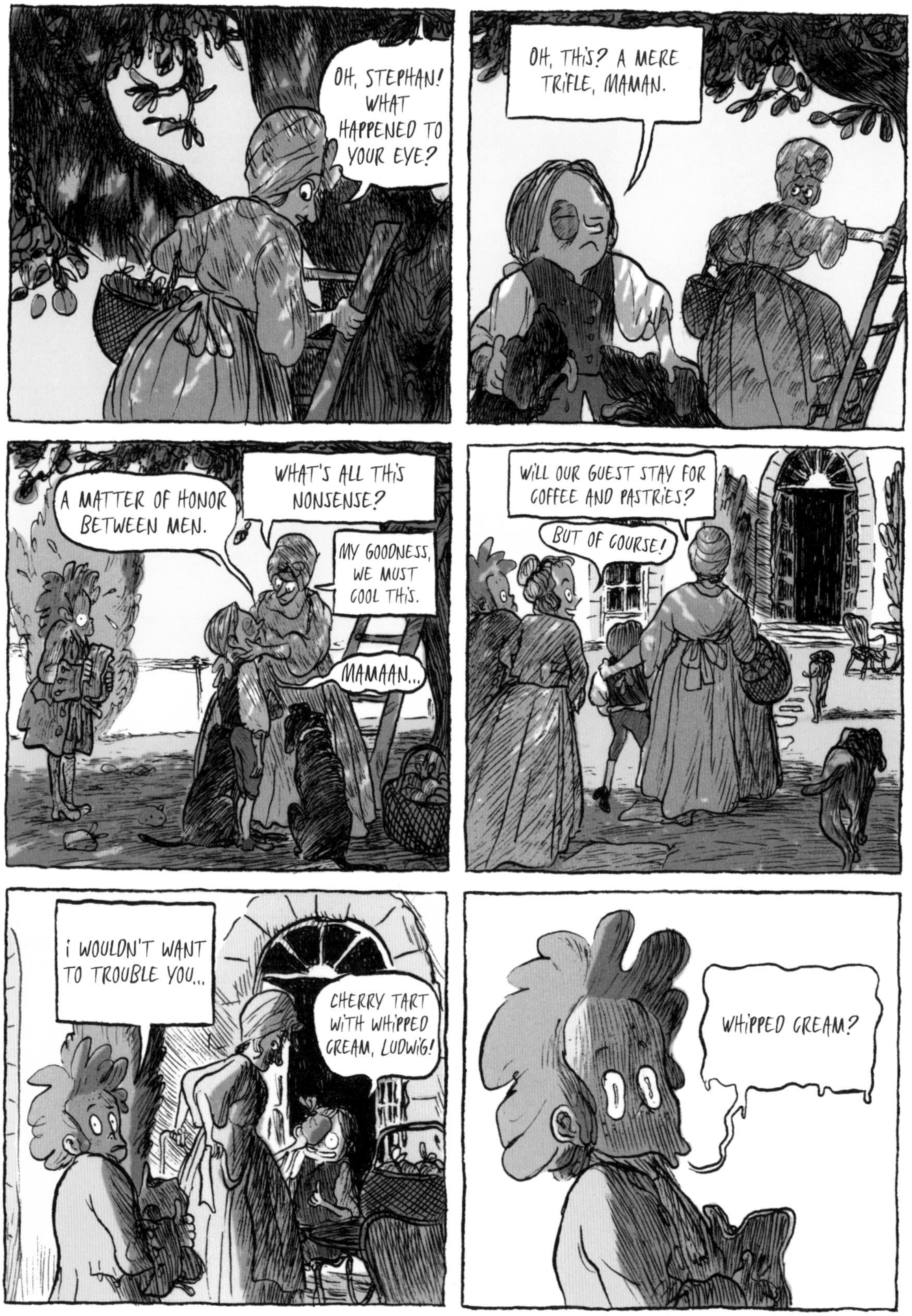
OH, STEPHAN! WHAT HAPPENED TO YOUR EYE?
OH, THIS? A MERE TRIFLE, MAMAN.
A MATTER OF HONOR BETWEEN MEN.
WHAT'S ALL THIS NONSENSE?
MY GOODNESS, WE MUST COOL THIS.
MAMAAN...
WILL OUR GUEST STAY FOR COFFEE AND PASTRIES?
BUT OF COURSE!
I WOULDN'T WANT TO TROUBLE YOU...
CHERRY TART WITH WHIPPED CREAM, LUDWIG!
WHIPPED CREAM?

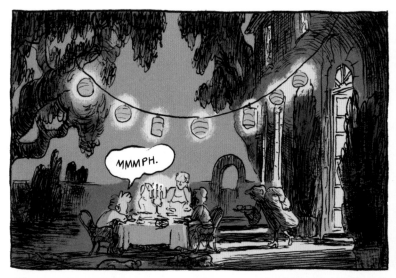

MMMPH.

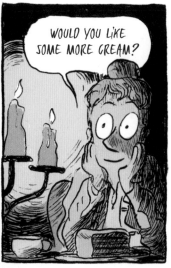

WOULD YOU LIKE SOME MORE CREAM?

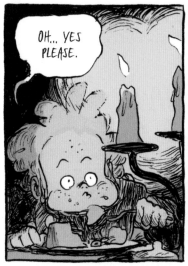

OH... YES PLEASE.

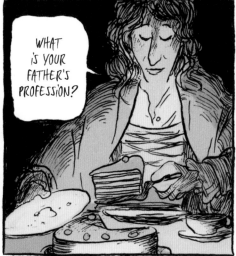

WHAT IS YOUR FATHER'S PROFESSION?

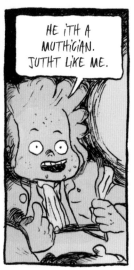

HE ITH A MUTHICIAN. JUTHT LIKE ME.

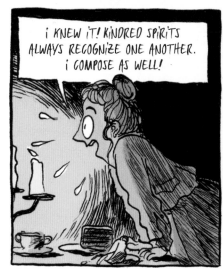

I KNEW IT! KINDRED SPIRITS ALWAYS RECOGNIZE ONE ANOTHER. I COMPOSE AS WELL!

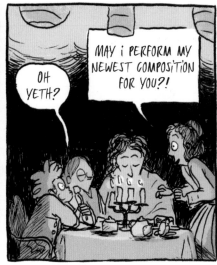

OH YETH?

MAY I PERFORM MY NEWEST COMPOSITION FOR YOU?!

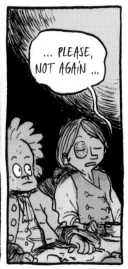

... PLEASE, NOT AGAIN ...

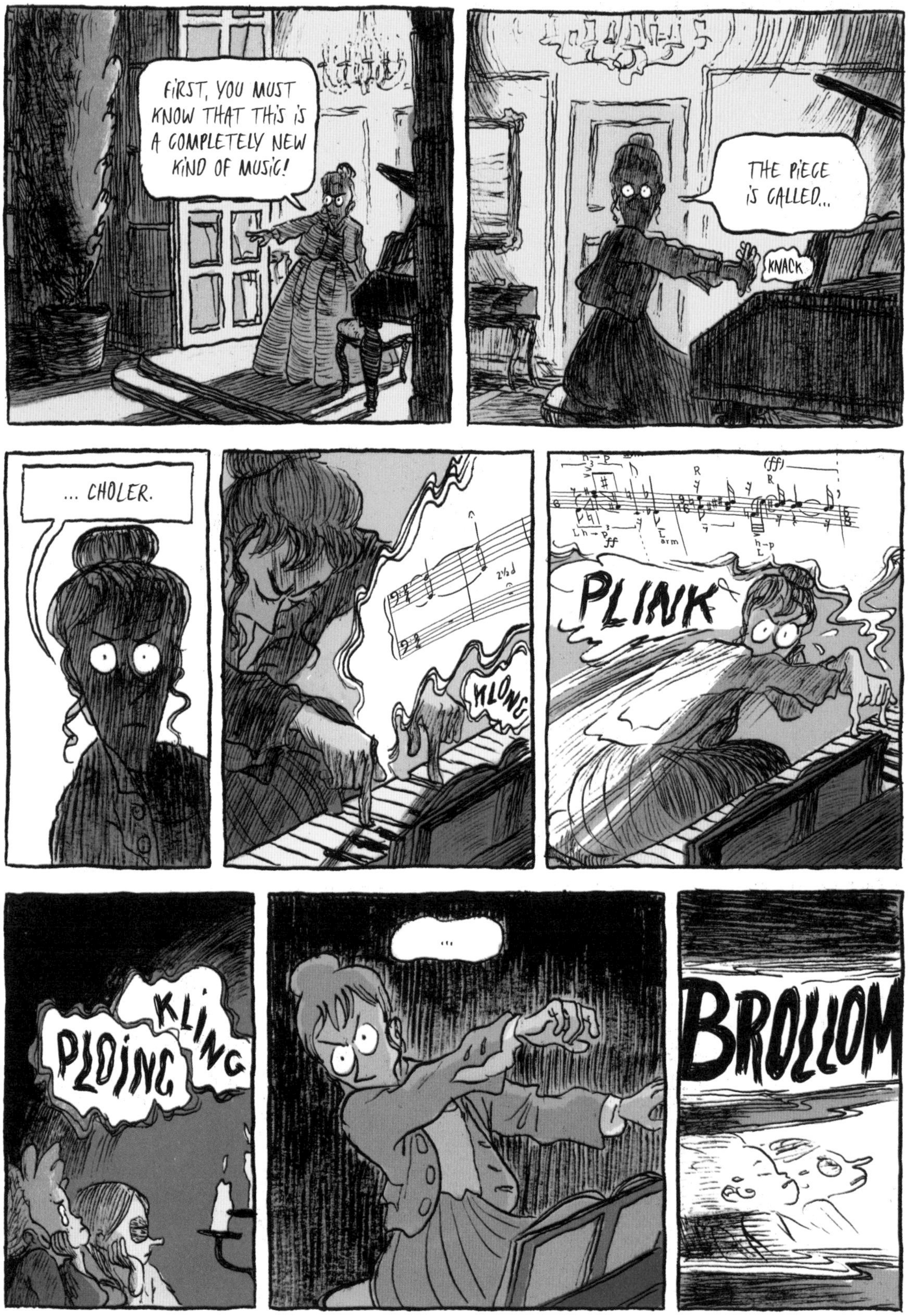
FIRST, YOU MUST KNOW THAT THIS IS A COMPLETELY NEW KIND OF MUSIC!
THE PIECE IS CALLED...
KNACK
... CHOLER.
KLONG
PLINK
PLOING
KLING
...
BROLLOM

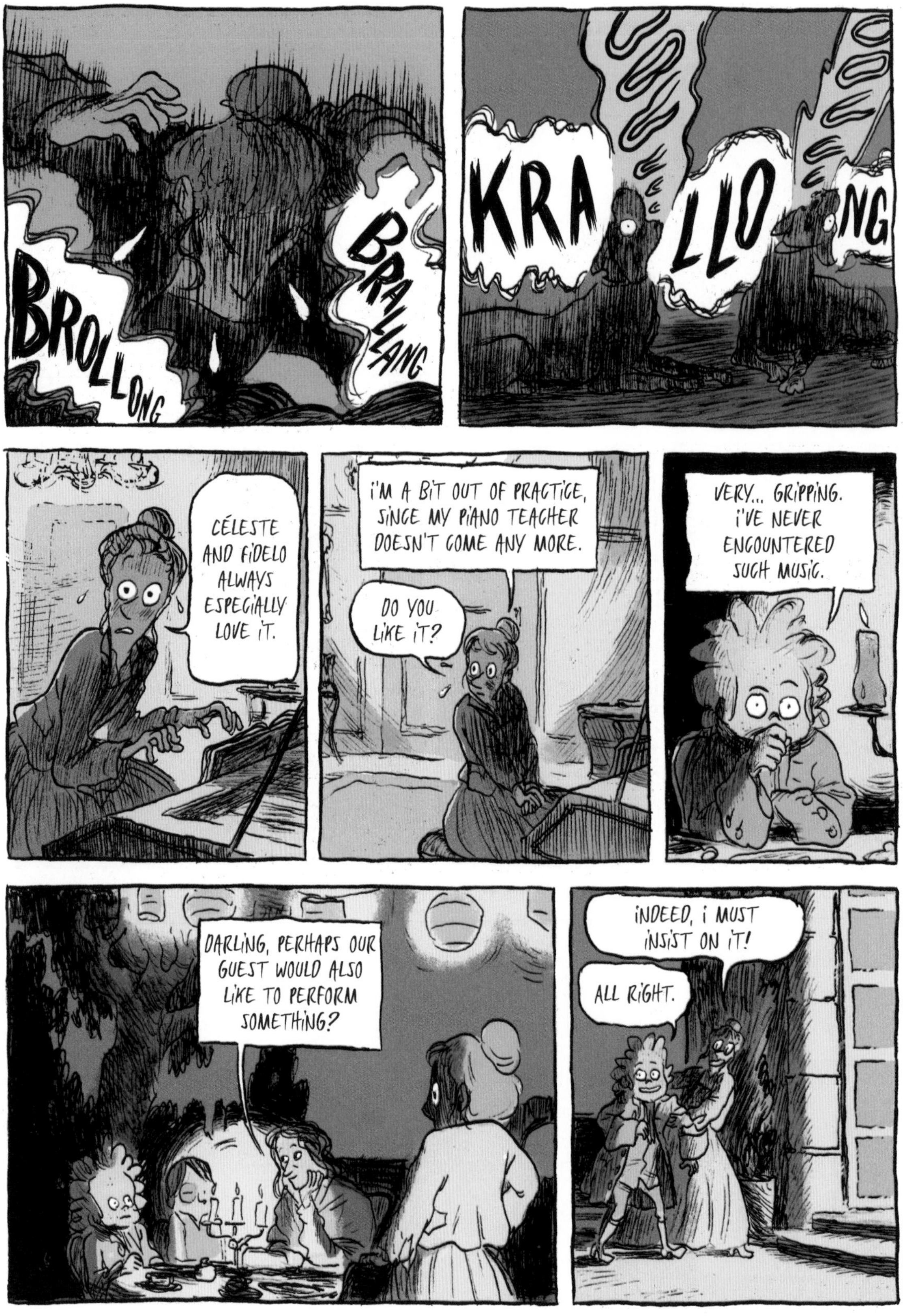
BROLLONG
BRALLANG
KRALLONG
CÉLESTE AND FIDELO ALWAYS ESPECIALLY LOVE IT.
I'M A BIT OUT OF PRACTICE, SINCE MY PIANO TEACHER DOESN'T COME ANY MORE.
DO YOU LIKE IT?
VERY... GRIPPING. I'VE NEVER ENCOUNTERED SUCH MUSIC.
DARLING, PERHAPS OUR GUEST WOULD ALSO LIKE TO PERFORM SOMETHING?
INDEED, I MUST INSIST ON IT!
ALL RIGHT.

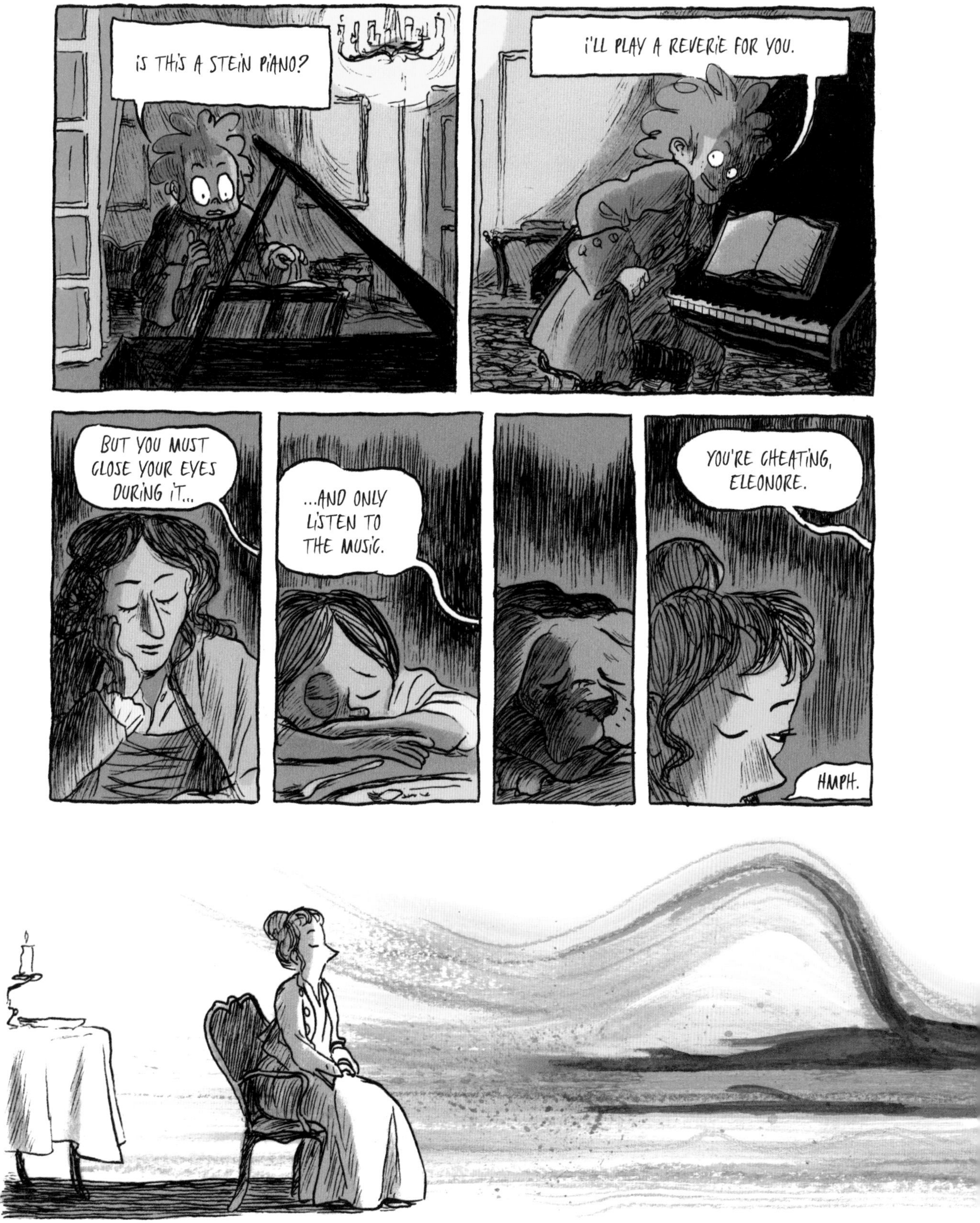
IS THIS A STEIN PIANO?
I'LL PLAY A REVERIE FOR YOU.
BUT YOU MUST CLOSE YOUR EYES DURING IT...
...AND ONLY LISTEN TO THE MUSIC.
YOU'RE CHEATING, ELEONORE.
HMPH.

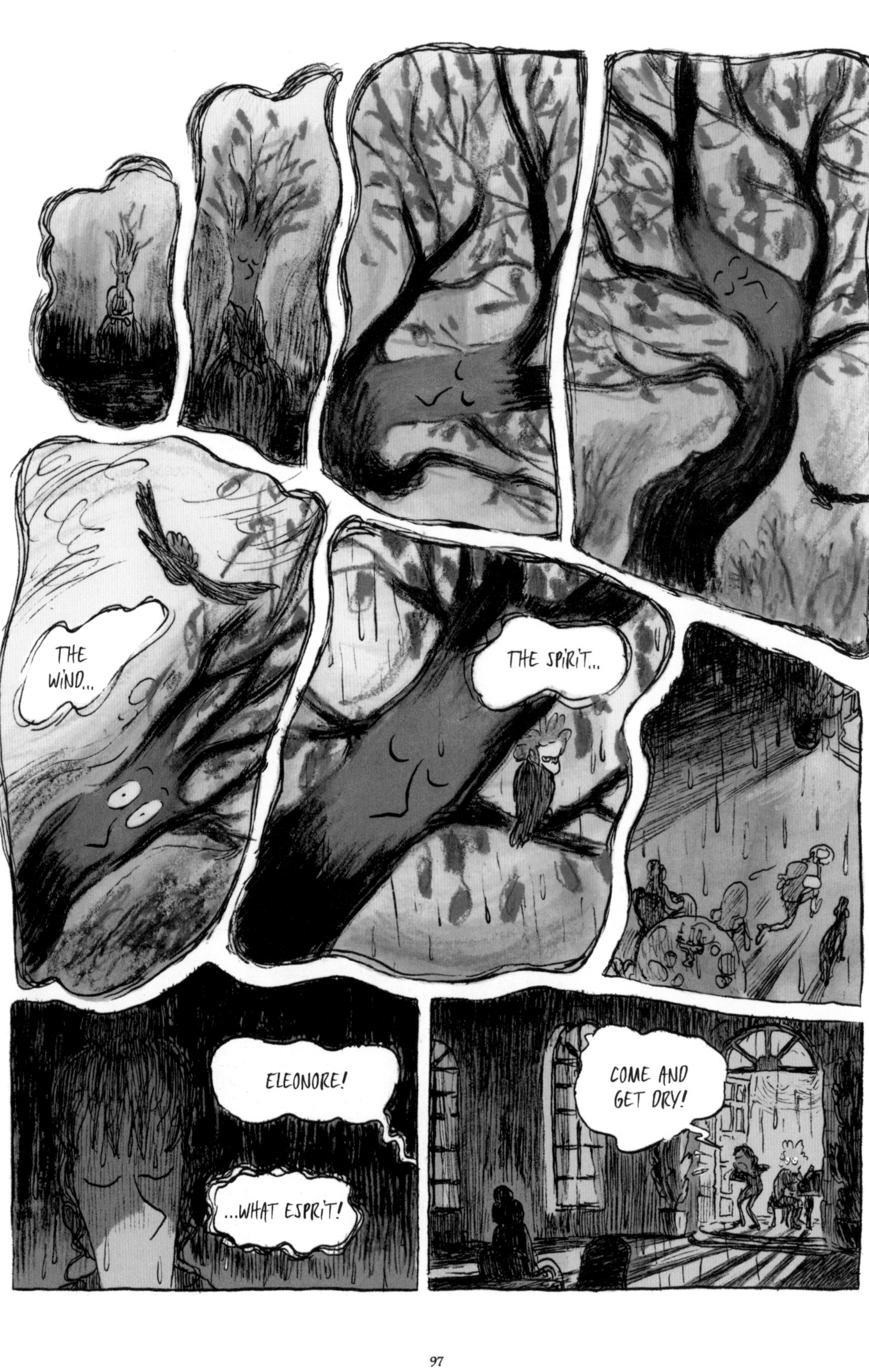
THE WIND...
THE SPIRIT...
ELEONORE!
...WHAT ESPRIT!
COME AND GET DRY!

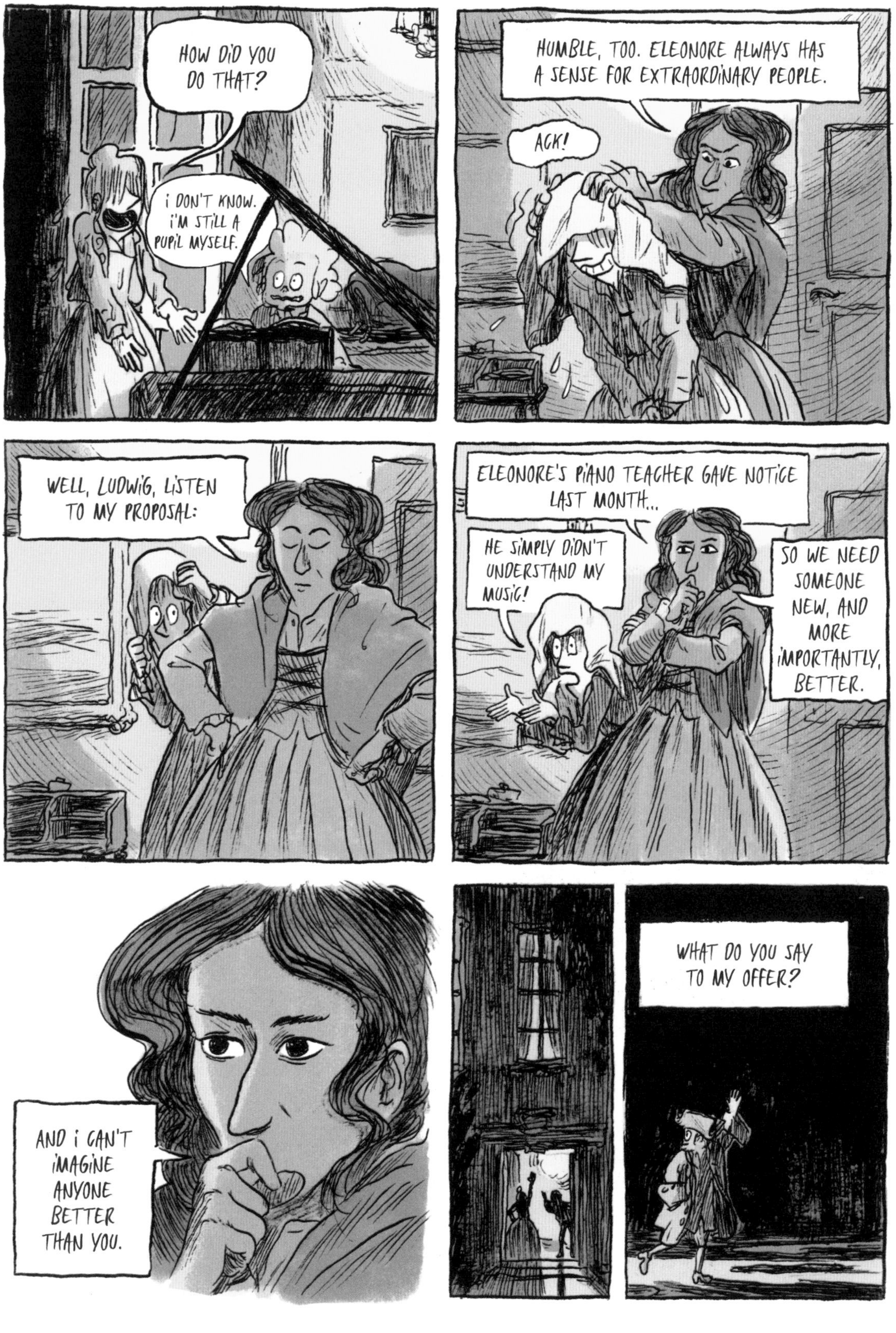
HOW DID YOU DO THAT?
I DON'T KNOW. I'M STILL A PUPIL MYSELF.
HUMBLE, TOO. ELEONORE ALWAYS HAS A SENSE FOR EXTRAORDINARY PEOPLE.
ACK!
WELL, LUDWIG, LISTEN TO MY PROPOSAL:
ELEONORE'S PIANO TEACHER GAVE NOTICE LAST MONTH...
HE SIMPLY DIDN'T UNDERSTAND MY MUSIC!
SO WE NEED SOMEONE NEW, AND MORE IMPORTANTLY, BETTER.
AND I CAN'T IMAGINE ANYONE BETTER THAN YOU.
WHAT DO YOU SAY TO MY OFFER?

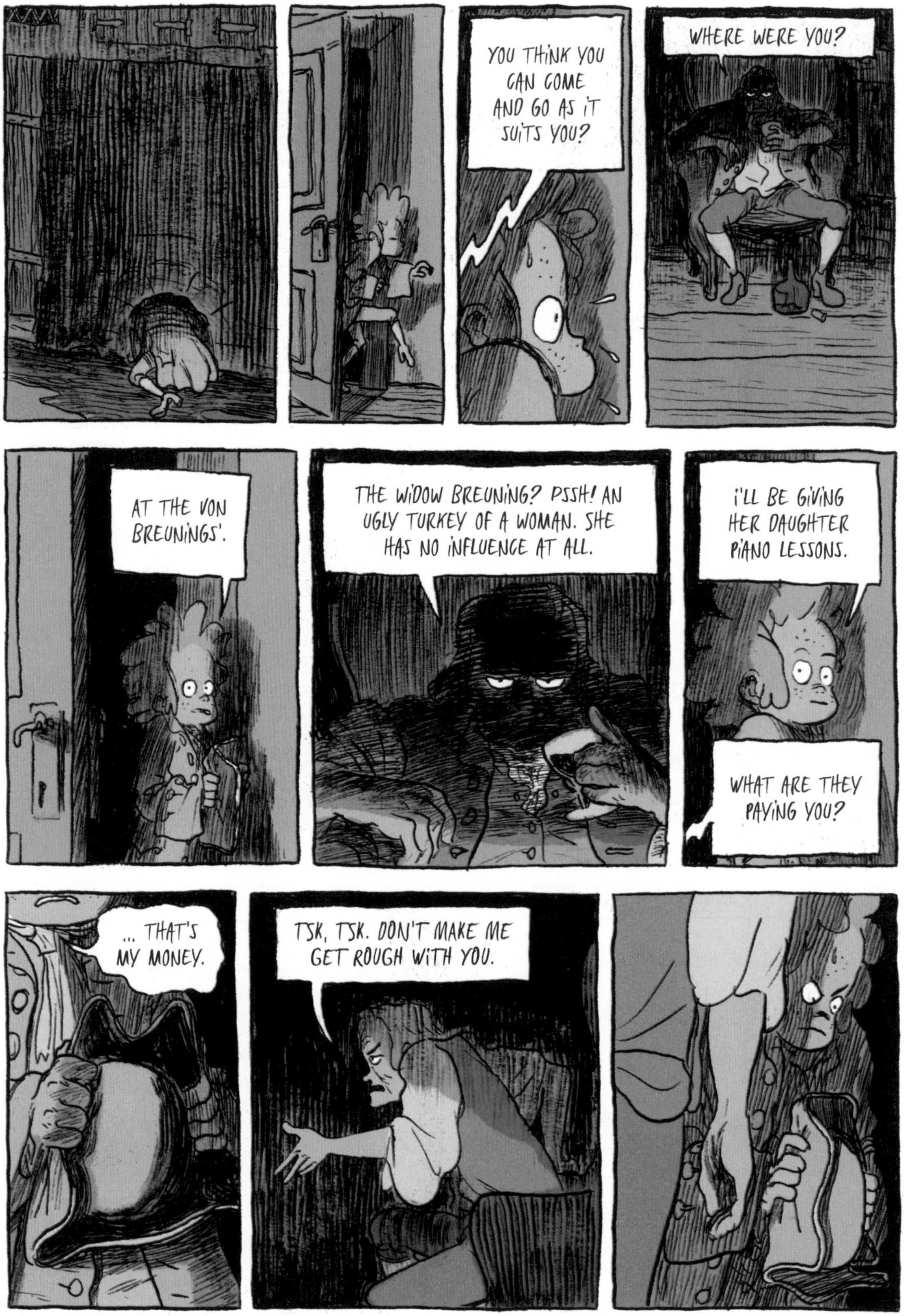
YOU THINK YOU CAN COME AND GO AS IT SUITS YOU?
WHERE WERE YOU?
AT THE VON BREUNINGS'.
THE WIDOW BREUNING? PSSH! AN UGLY TURKEY OF A WOMAN. SHE HAS NO INFLUENCE AT ALL.
I'LL BE GIVING HER DAUGHTER PIANO LESSONS.
WHAT ARE THEY PAYING YOU?
... THAT'S MY MONEY.
TSK, TSK. DON'T MAKE ME GET ROUGH WITH YOU.

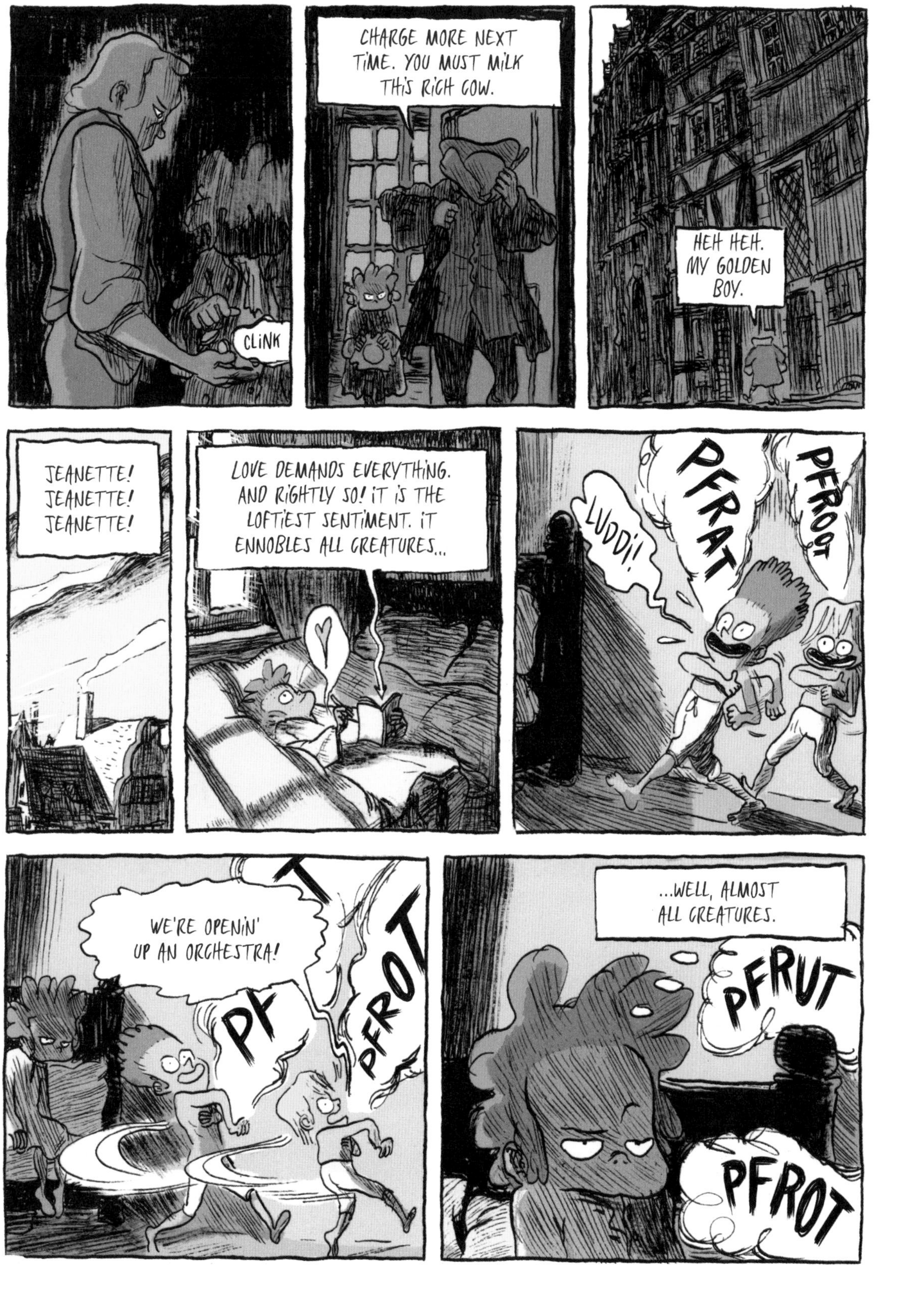
CLINK
CHARGE MORE NEXT TIME. YOU MUST MILK THIS RICH COW.
HEH HEH. MY GOLDEN BOY.
JEANETTE! JEANETTE! JEANETTE!
LOVE DEMANDS EVERYTHING. AND RIGHTLY SO! IT IS THE LOFTIEST SENTIMENT. IT ENNOBLES ALL CREATURES...
LUDDI!
PFRAT
PFROOT
WE'RE OPENIN' UP AN ORCHESTRA!
PFT
PFROT
...WELL, ALMOST ALL CREATURES.
PFRUT
PFROT

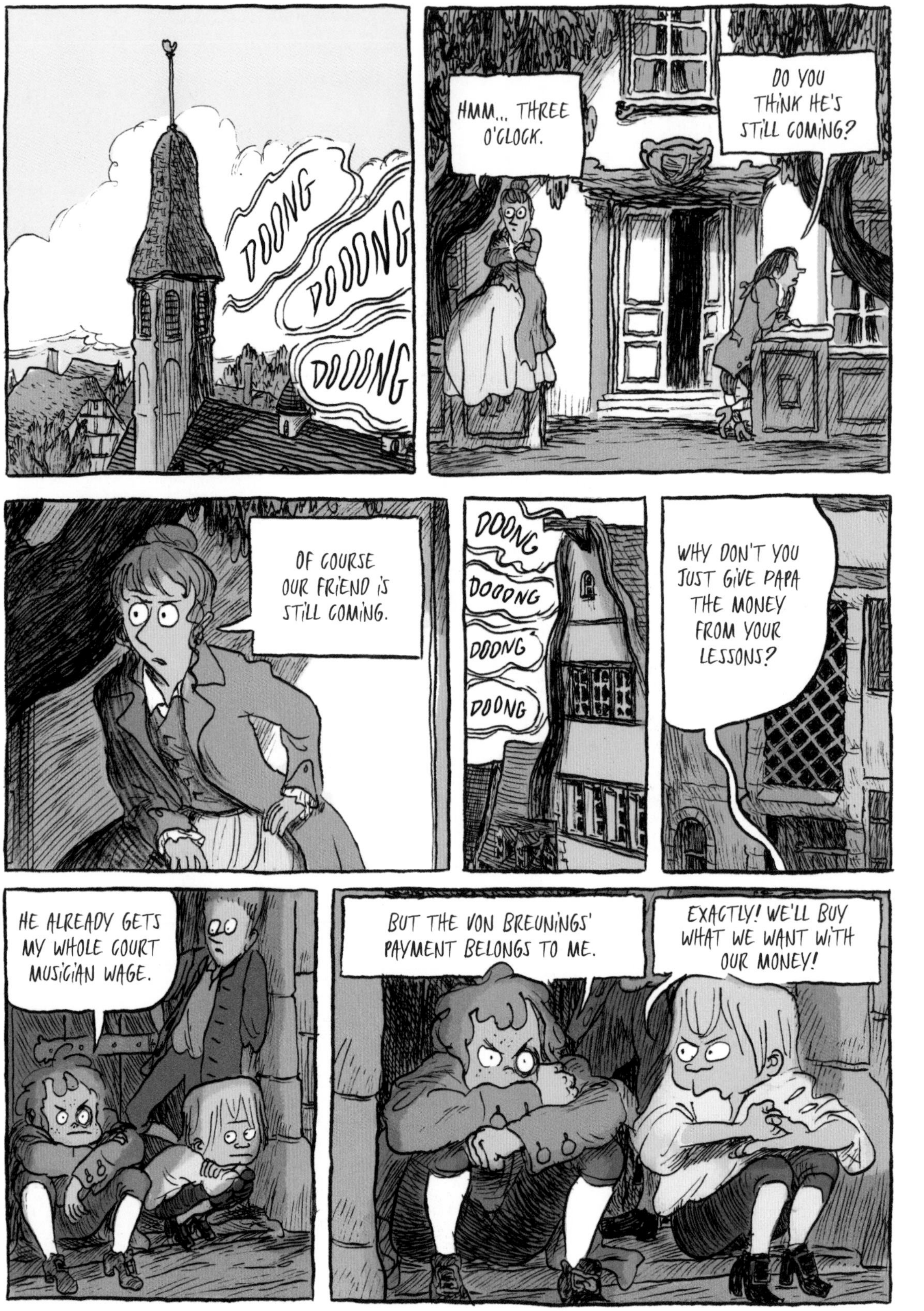
DOOONG
DOOONG
DOOONG
HMM... THREE O'CLOCK.
DO YOU THINK HE'S STILL COMING?
OF COURSE OUR FRIEND IS STILL COMING.
DOONG
DOOONG
DOONG
DOONG
WHY DON'T YOU JUST GIVE PAPA THE MONEY FROM YOUR LESSONS?
HE ALREADY GETS MY WHOLE COURT MUSICIAN WAGE.
BUT THE VON BREUNINGS' PAYMENT BELONGS TO ME.
EXACTLY! WE'LL BUY WHAT WE WANT WITH OUR MONEY!

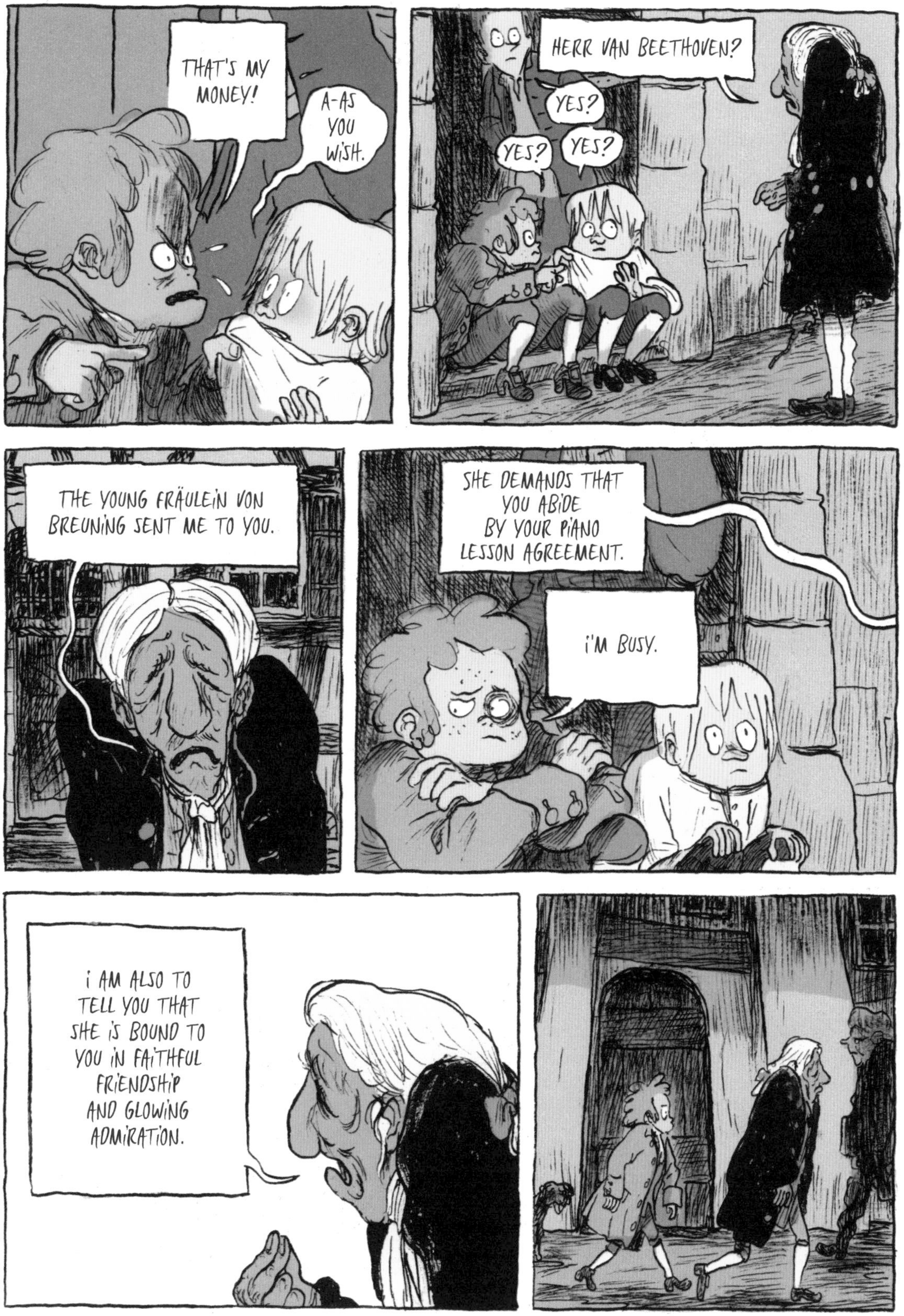
THAT'S MY MONEY!
A-AS YOU WISH.
HERR VAN BEETHOVEN?
YES?
YES?
YES?
THE YOUNG FRÄULEIN VON BREUNING SENT ME TO YOU.
SHE DEMANDS THAT YOU ABIDE BY YOUR PIANO LESSON AGREEMENT.
I'M BUSY.
I AM ALSO TO TELL YOU THAT SHE IS BOUND TO YOU IN FAITHFUL FRIENDSHIP AND GLOWING ADMIRATION.

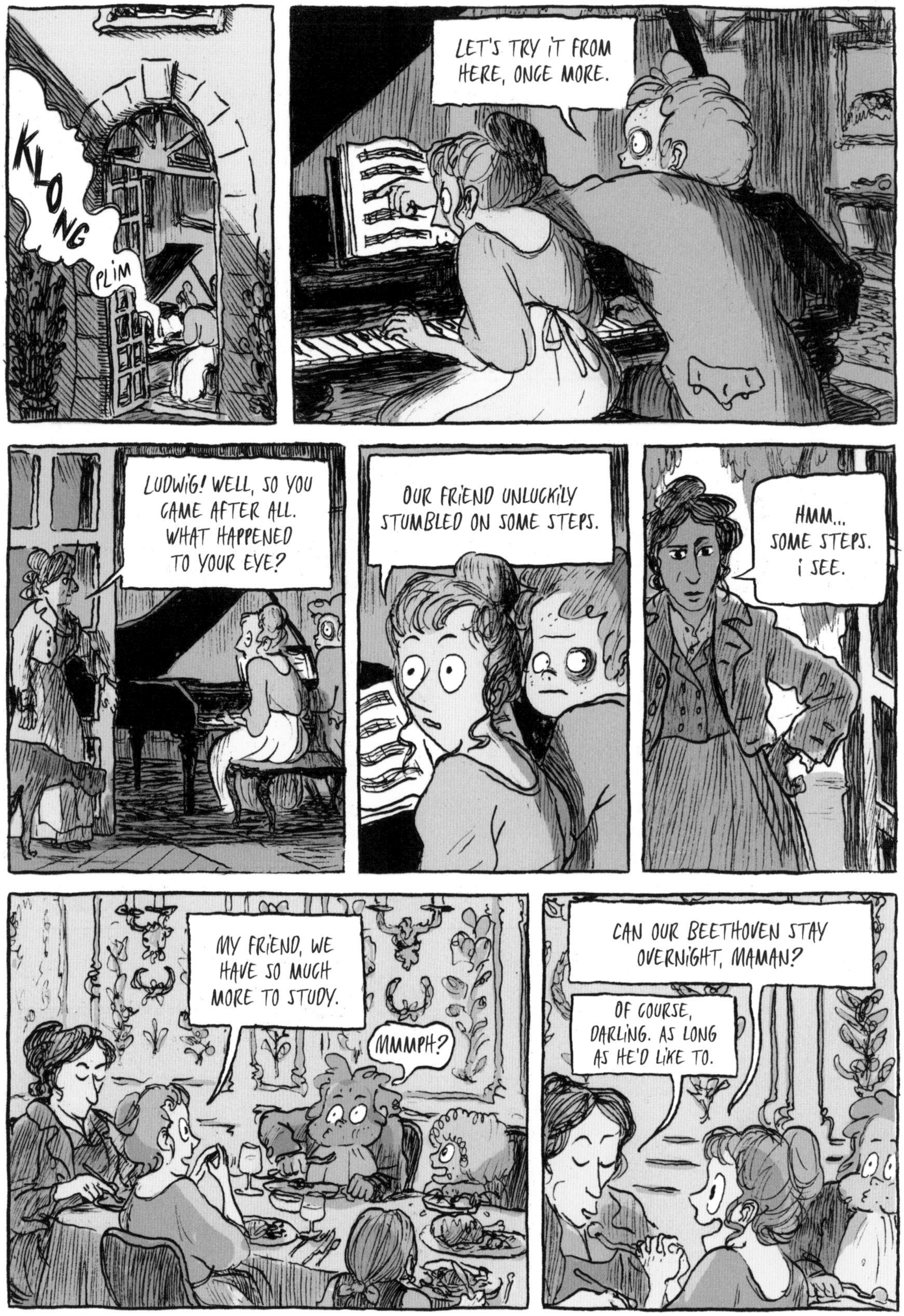
KLONG
PLIM
LET'S TRY IT FROM HERE, ONCE MORE.
LUDWIG! WELL, SO YOU CAME AFTER ALL. WHAT HAPPENED TO YOUR EYE?
OUR FRIEND UNLUCKILY STUMBLED ON SOME STEPS.
HMM... SOME STEPS. I SEE.
MY FRIEND, WE HAVE SO MUCH MORE TO STUDY.
MMMPH?
CAN OUR BEETHOVEN STAY OVERNIGHT, MAMAN?
OF COURSE, DARLING. AS LONG AS HE'D LIKE TO.

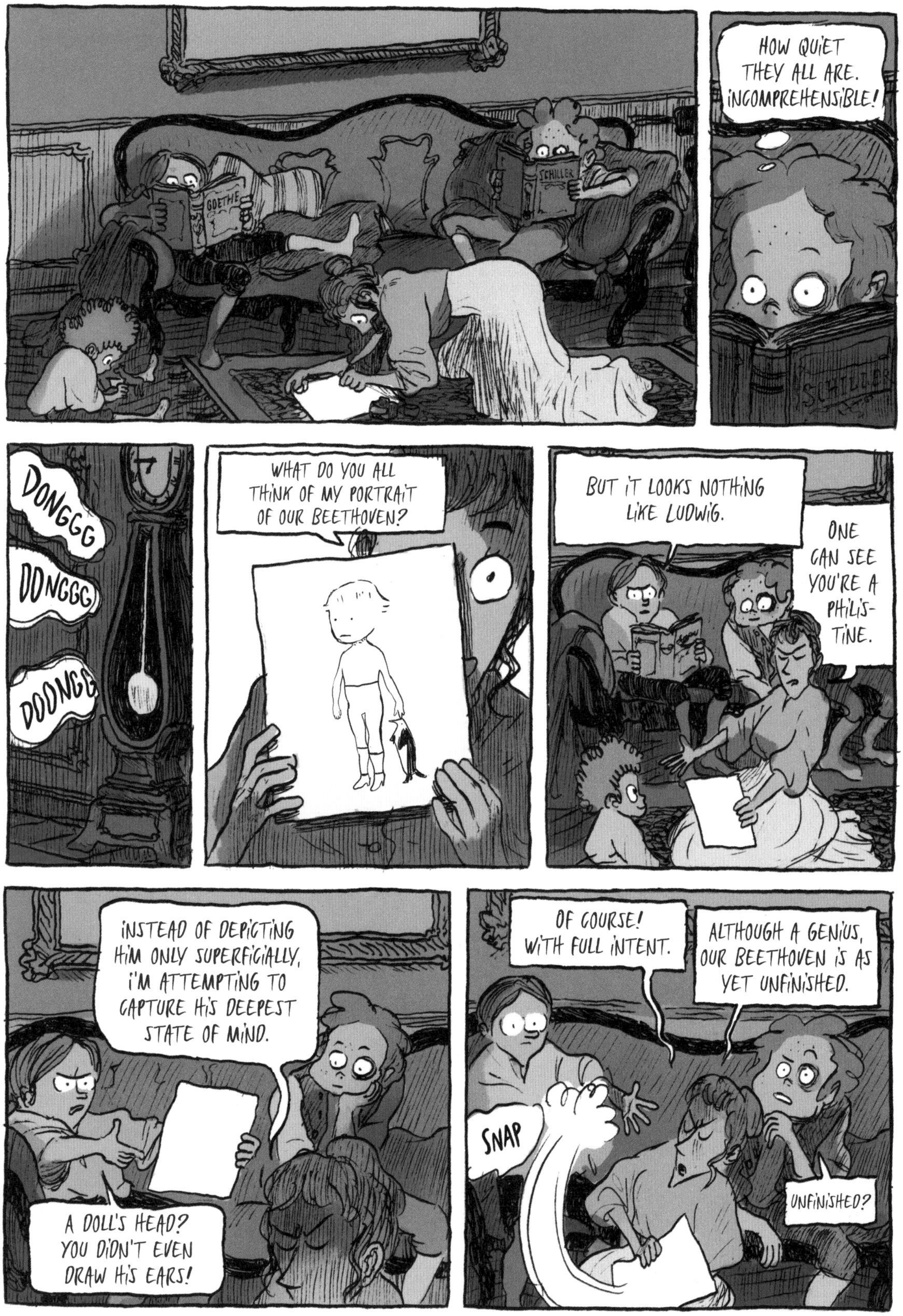
HOW QUIET THEY ALL ARE. INCOMPREHENSIBLE!
DONGGG
DONGGG
DOONGG
WHAT DO YOU ALL THINK OF MY PORTRAIT OF OUR BEETHOVEN?
BUT IT LOOKS NOTHING LIKE LUDWIG.
ONE CAN SEE YOU'RE A PHILIS-TINE.
INSTEAD OF DEPICTING HIM ONLY SUPERFICIALLY, I'M ATTEMPTING TO CAPTURE HIS DEEPEST STATE OF MIND.
A DOLL'S HEAD? YOU DIDN'T EVEN DRAW HIS EARS!
OF COURSE! WITH FULL INTENT.
ALTHOUGH A GENIUS, OUR BEETHOVEN IS AS YET UNFINISHED.
SNAP
UNFINISHED?

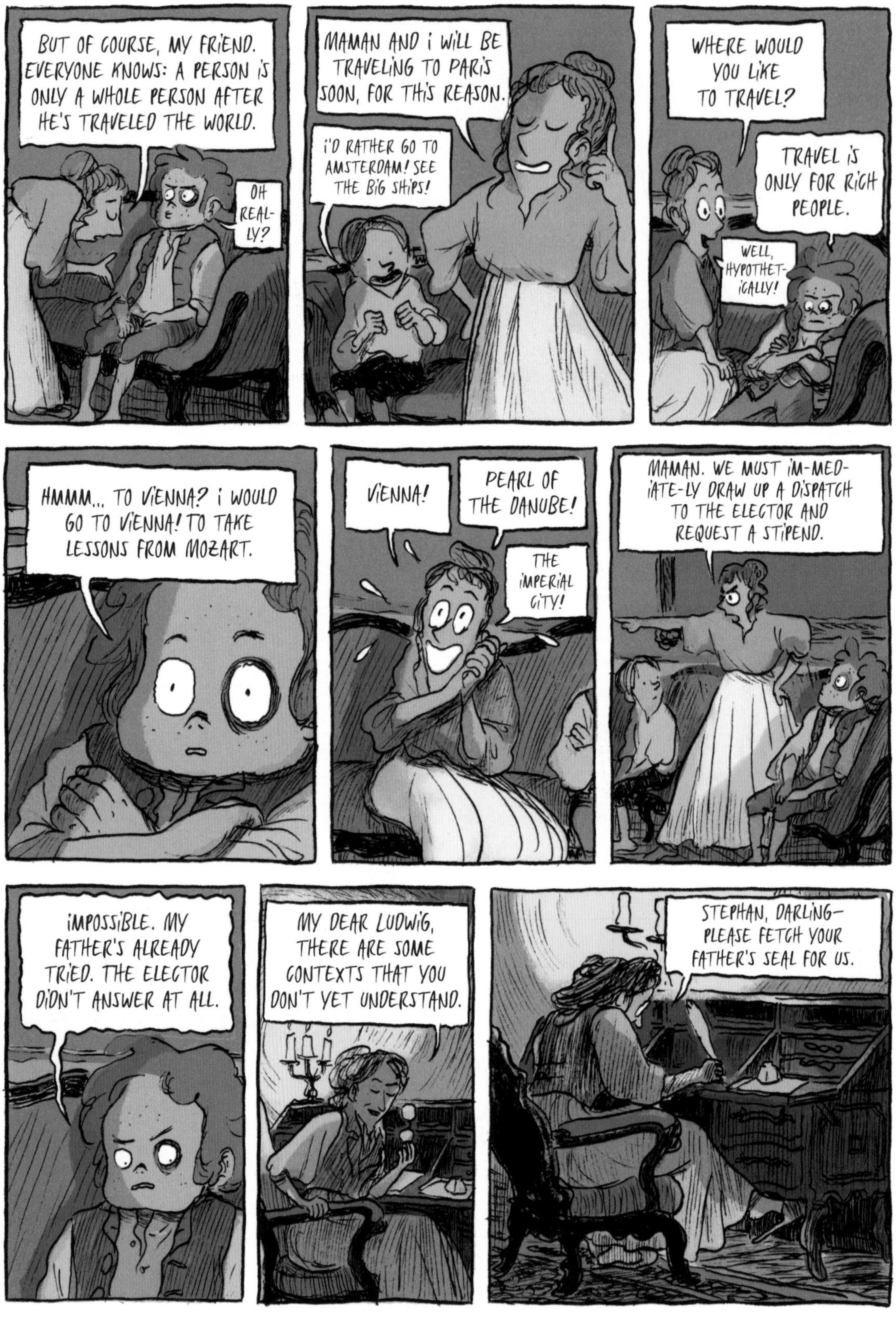
BUT OF COURSE, MY FRIEND. EVERYONE KNOWS: A PERSON IS ONLY A WHOLE PERSON AFTER HE'S TRAVELED THE WORLD.
OH REAL-LY?
MAMAN AND I WILL BE TRAVELING TO PARIS SOON, FOR THIS REASON.
I'D RATHER GO TO AMSTERDAM! SEE THE BIG SHIPS!
WHERE WOULD YOU LIKE TO TRAVEL?
TRAVEL IS ONLY FOR RICH PEOPLE.
WELL, HYPOTHET-ICALLY!
HMMM... TO VIENNA? I WOULD GO TO VIENNA! TO TAKE LESSONS FROM MOZART.
VIENNA!
PEARL OF THE DANUBE!
THE IMPERIAL CITY!
MAMAN. WE MUST IM-MED-IATE-LY DRAW UP A DISPATCH TO THE ELECTOR AND REQUEST A STIPEND.
IMPOSSIBLE. MY FATHER'S ALREADY TRIED. THE ELECTOR DIDN'T ANSWER AT ALL.
MY DEAR LUDWIG, THERE ARE SOME CONTEXTS THAT YOU DON'T YET UNDERSTAND.
STEPHAN, DARLING—PLEASE FETCH YOUR FATHER'S SEAL FOR US.

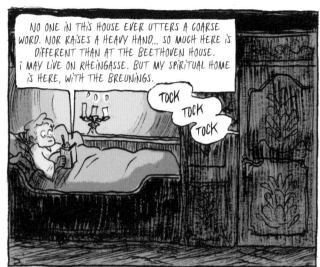

NO ONE IN THIS HOUSE EVER UTTERS A COARSE WORD. NOR RAISES A HEAVY HAND... SO MUCH HERE IS DIFFERENT THAN AT THE BEETHOVEN HOUSE. I MAY LIVE ON RHEINGASSE. BUT MY SPIRITUAL HOME IS HERE, WITH THE BREUNINGS.

TOCK
TOCK
TOCK

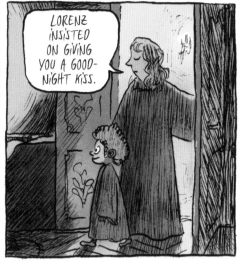

LORENZ INSISTED ON GIVING YOU A GOOD-NIGHT KISS.

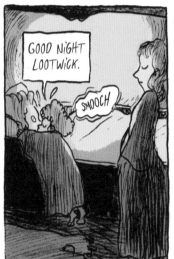

GOOD NIGHT LOOTWICK.

SMOOCH

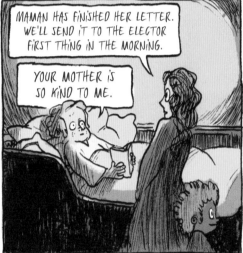

MAMAN HAS FINISHED HER LETTER. WE'LL SEND IT TO THE ELECTOR FIRST THING IN THE MORNING.

YOUR MOTHER IS SO KIND TO ME.

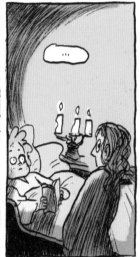

...

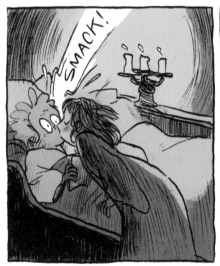

SMACK!

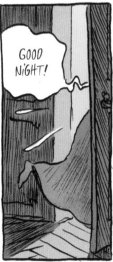

GOOD NIGHT!

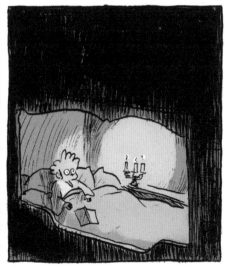

1786

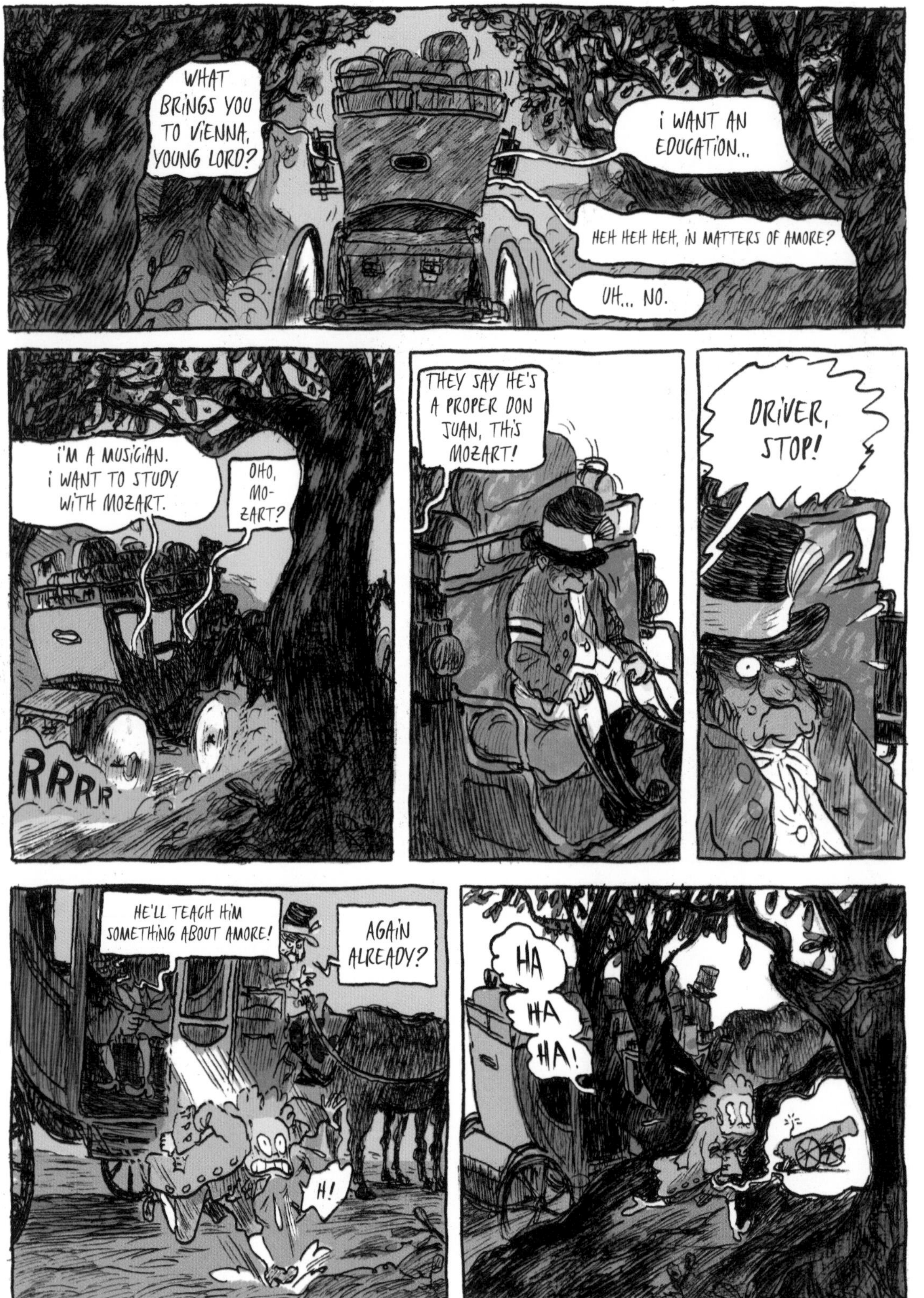
WHAT BRINGS YOU TO VIENNA, YOUNG LORD?
I WANT AN EDUCATION...
HEH HEH HEH, IN MATTERS OF AMORE?
UH... NO.
I'M A MUSICIAN. I WANT TO STUDY WITH MOZART.
OHO, MO-ZART?
RRRR
THEY SAY HE'S A PROPER DON JUAN, THIS MOZART!
DRIVER, STOP!
HE'LL TEACH HIM SOMETHING ABOUT AMORE!
AGAIN ALREADY?
H!
HA HA HA!

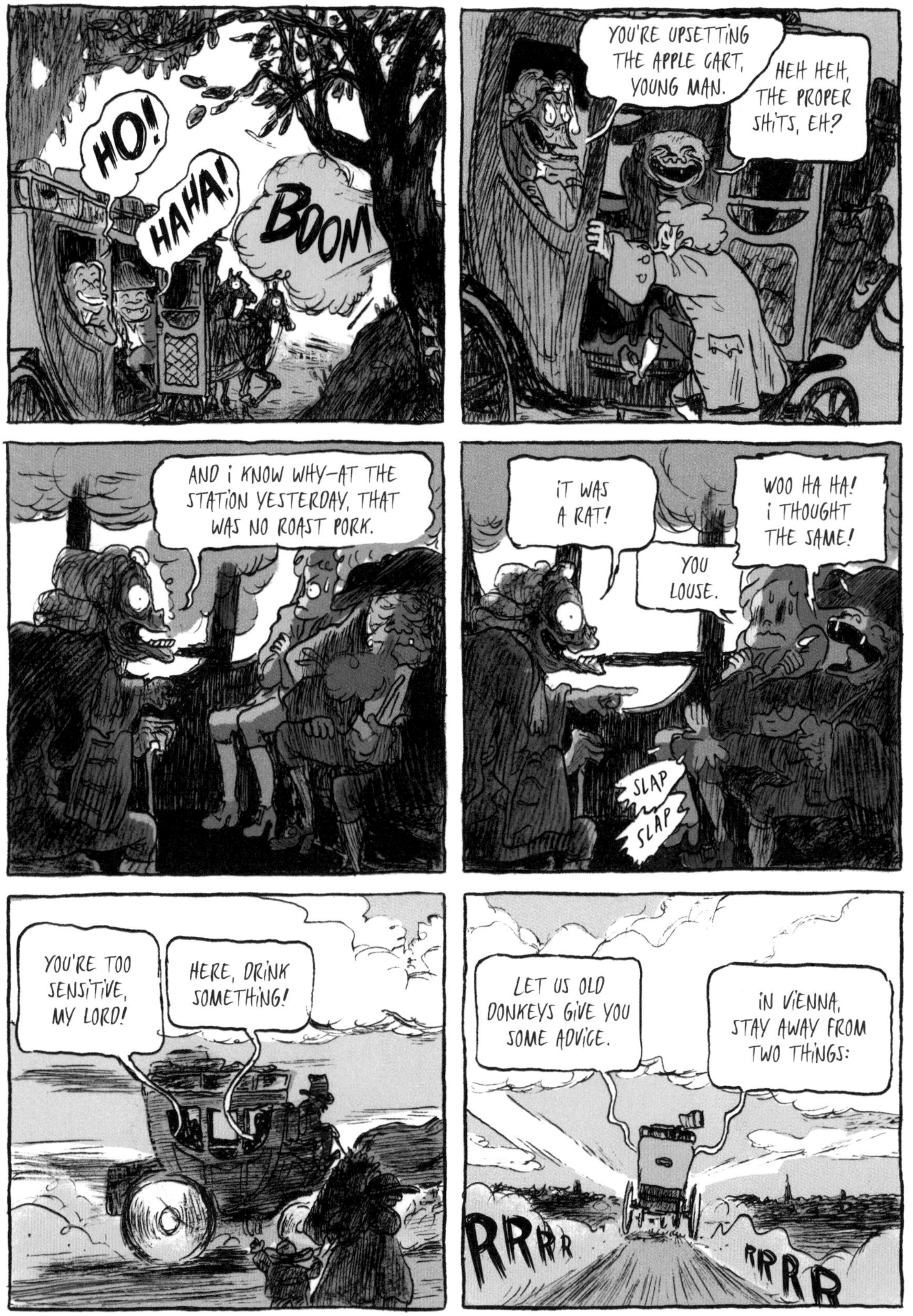
HO!
HAHA!
BOOM
YOU'RE UPSETTING THE APPLE CART, YOUNG MAN.
HEH HEH, THE PROPER SHITS, EH?
AND I KNOW WHY—AT THE STATION YESTERDAY, THAT WAS NO ROAST PORK.
IT WAS A RAT!
YOU LOUSE.
WOO HA HA! I THOUGHT THE SAME!
SLAP
SLAP
YOU'RE TOO SENSITIVE, MY LORD!
HERE, DRINK SOMETHING!
LET US OLD DONKEYS GIVE YOU SOME ADVICE.
IN VIENNA, STAY AWAY FROM TWO THINGS:
RRRR
RRRR

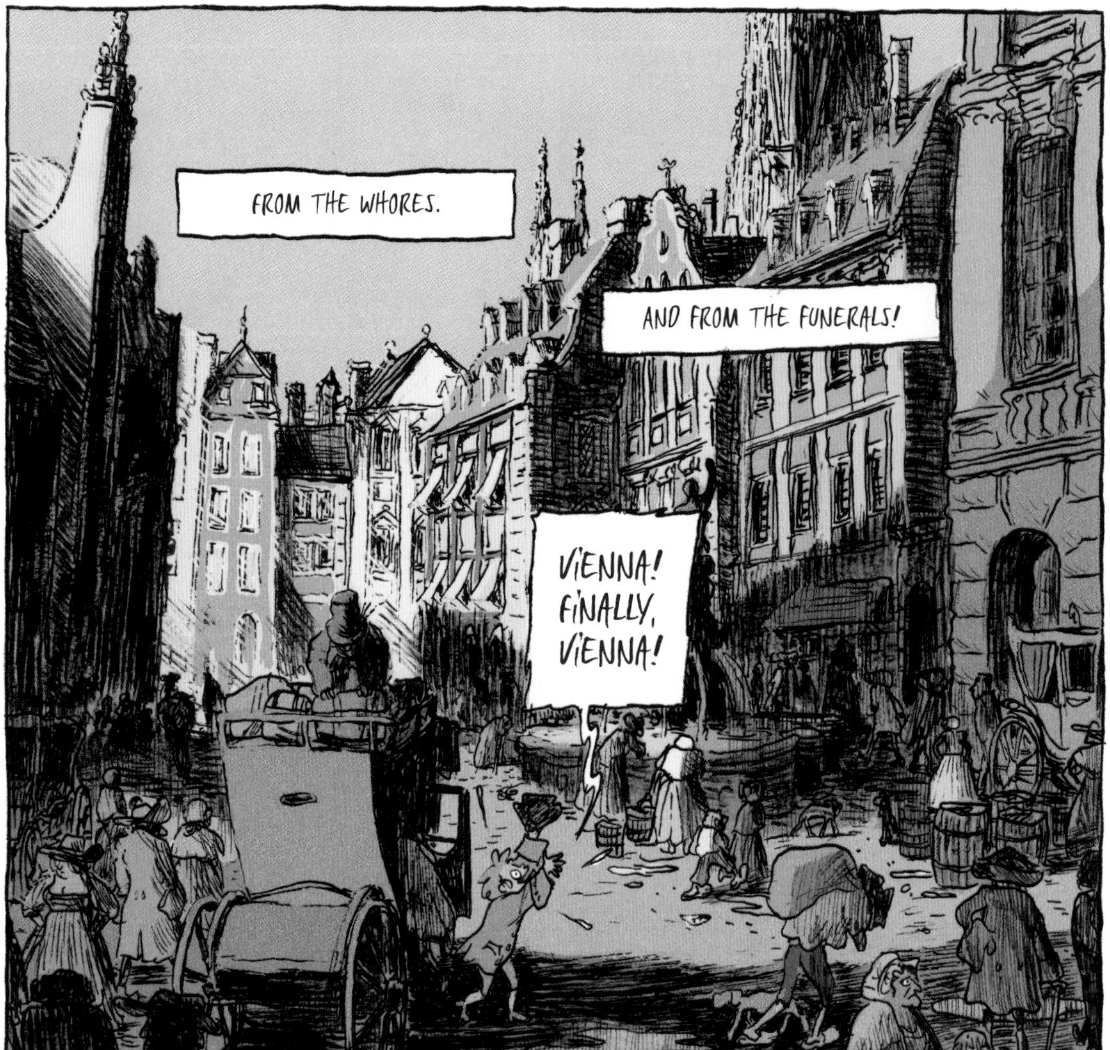
FROM THE WHORES.
AND FROM THE FUNERALS!
VIENNA! FINALLY, VIENNA!

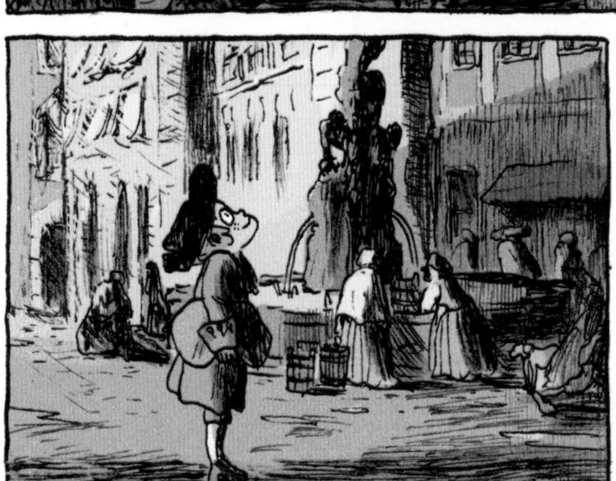

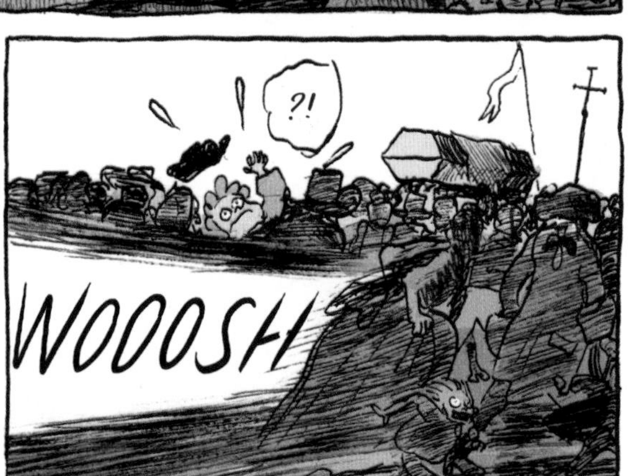
?!
WOOOSH

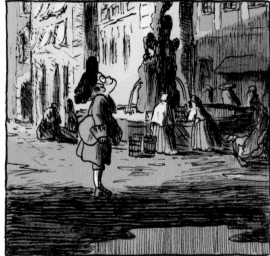

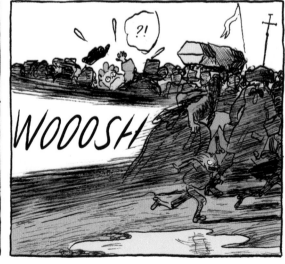

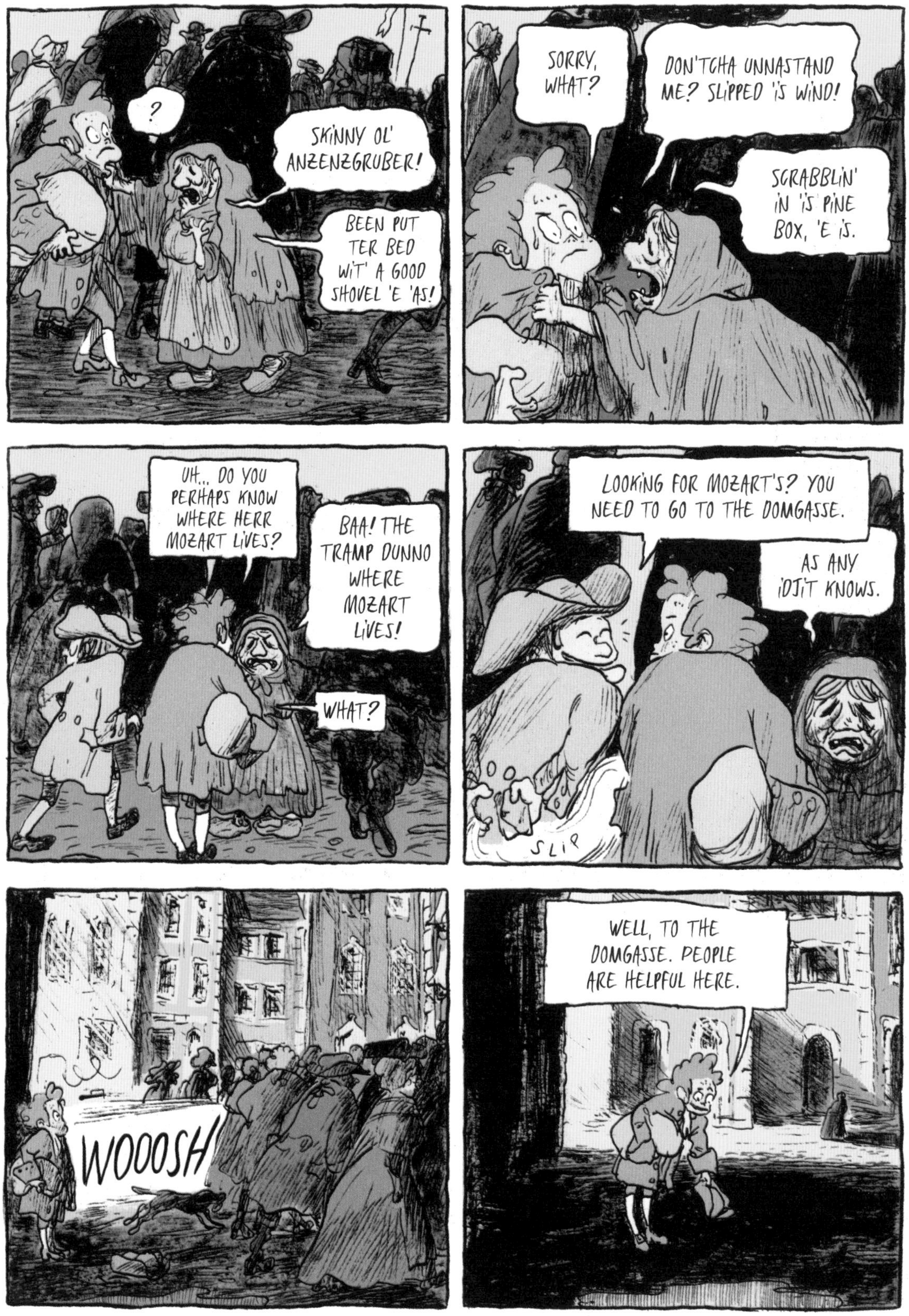
?
SKINNY OL' ANZENZGRUBER!
BEEN PUT TER BED WIT' A GOOD SHOVEL 'E 'AS!
SORRY, WHAT?
DON'TCHA UNNASTAND ME? SLIPPED 'IS WIND!
SCRABBLIN' IN 'IS PINE BOX, 'E IS.
UH... DO YOU PERHAPS KNOW WHERE HERR MOZART LIVES?
BAA! THE TRAMP DUNNO WHERE MOZART LIVES!
WHAT?
LOOKING FOR MOZART'S? YOU NEED TO GO TO THE DOMGASSE.
AS ANY IDJIT KNOWS.
SLIP
WOOOSH
WELL, TO THE DOMGASSE. PEOPLE ARE HELPFUL HERE.

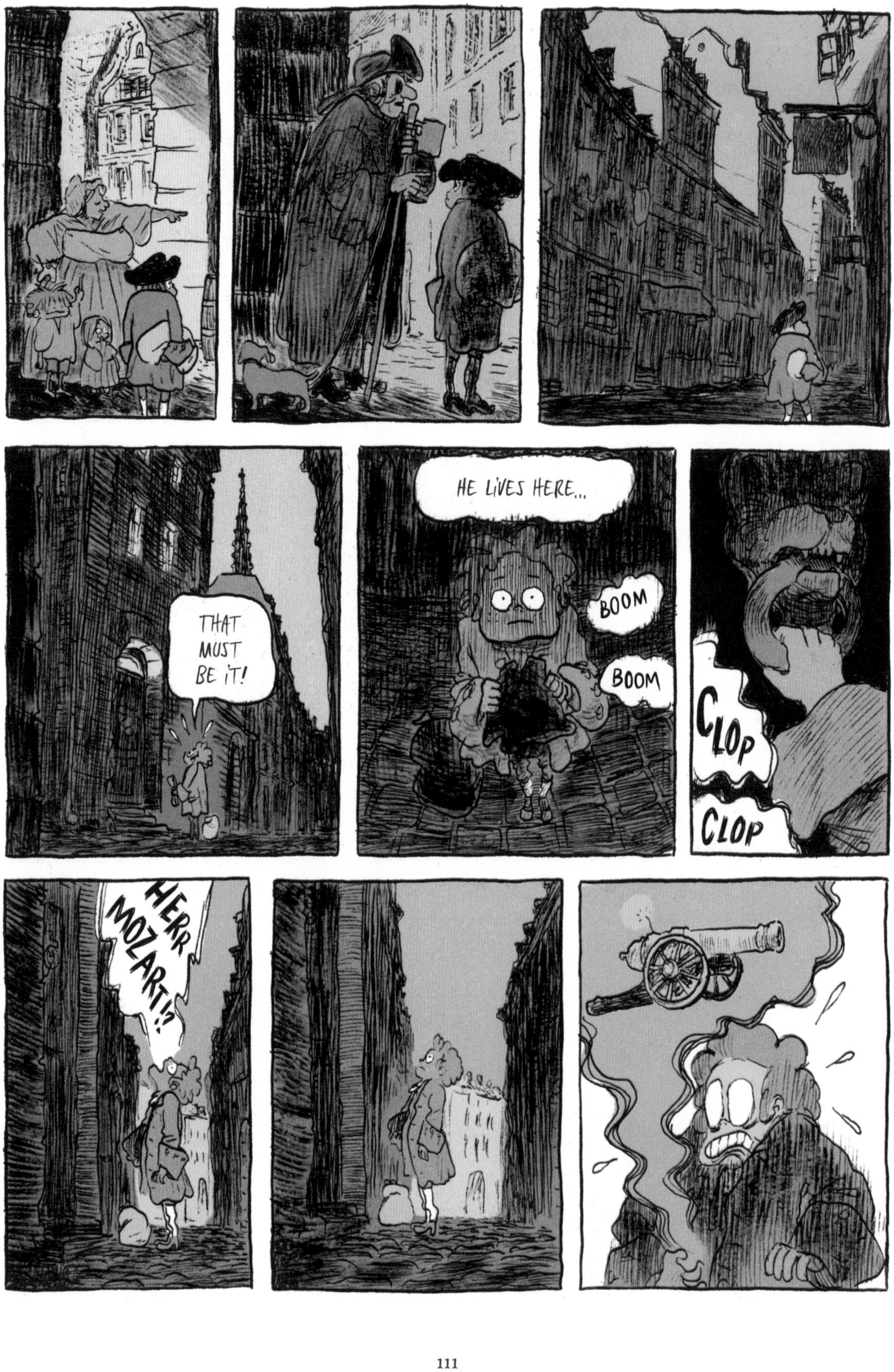
THAT MUST BE IT!
HE LIVES HERE...
BOOM
BOOM
CLOP
CLOP
HERR MOZART!?

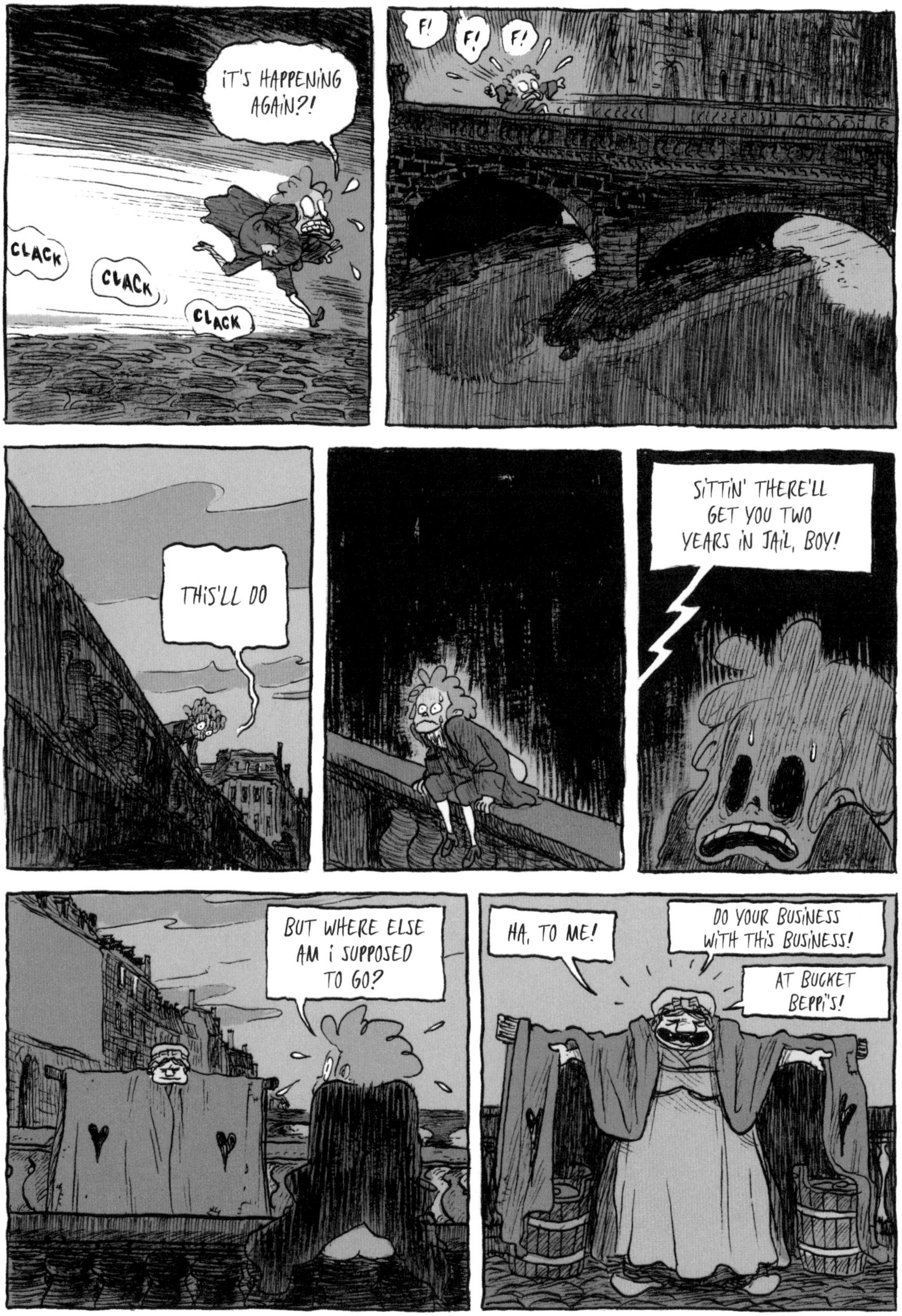
IT'S HAPPENING AGAIN?!
CLACK
CLACK
CLACK
F!
F!
F!
THIS'LL DO
SITTIN' THERE'LL GET YOU TWO YEARS IN JAIL, BOY!
BUT WHERE ELSE AM I SUPPOSED TO GO?
HA, TO ME!
DO YOUR BUSINESS WITH THIS BUSINESS!
AT BUCKET BEPPI'S!

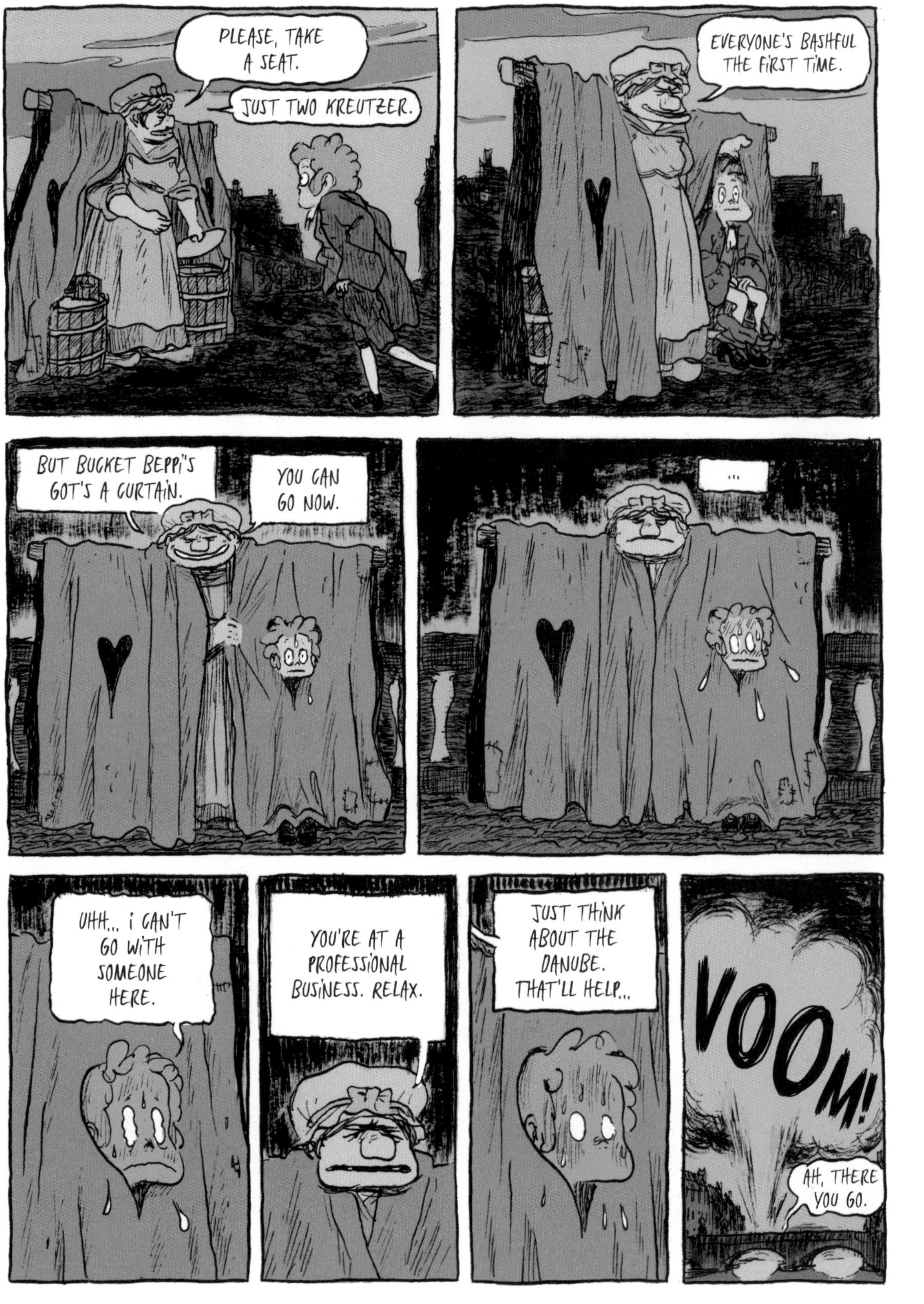
PLEASE, TAKE A SEAT.
JUST TWO KREUTZER.
EVERYONE'S BASHFUL THE FIRST TIME.
BUT BUCKET BEPPI'S GOT'S A CURTAIN.
YOU CAN GO NOW.
...
UHH... I CAN'T GO WITH SOMEONE HERE.
YOU'RE AT A PROFESSIONAL BUSINESS. RELAX.
JUST THINK ABOUT THE DANUBE. THAT'LL HELP...
VOOM!
AH, THERE YOU GO.

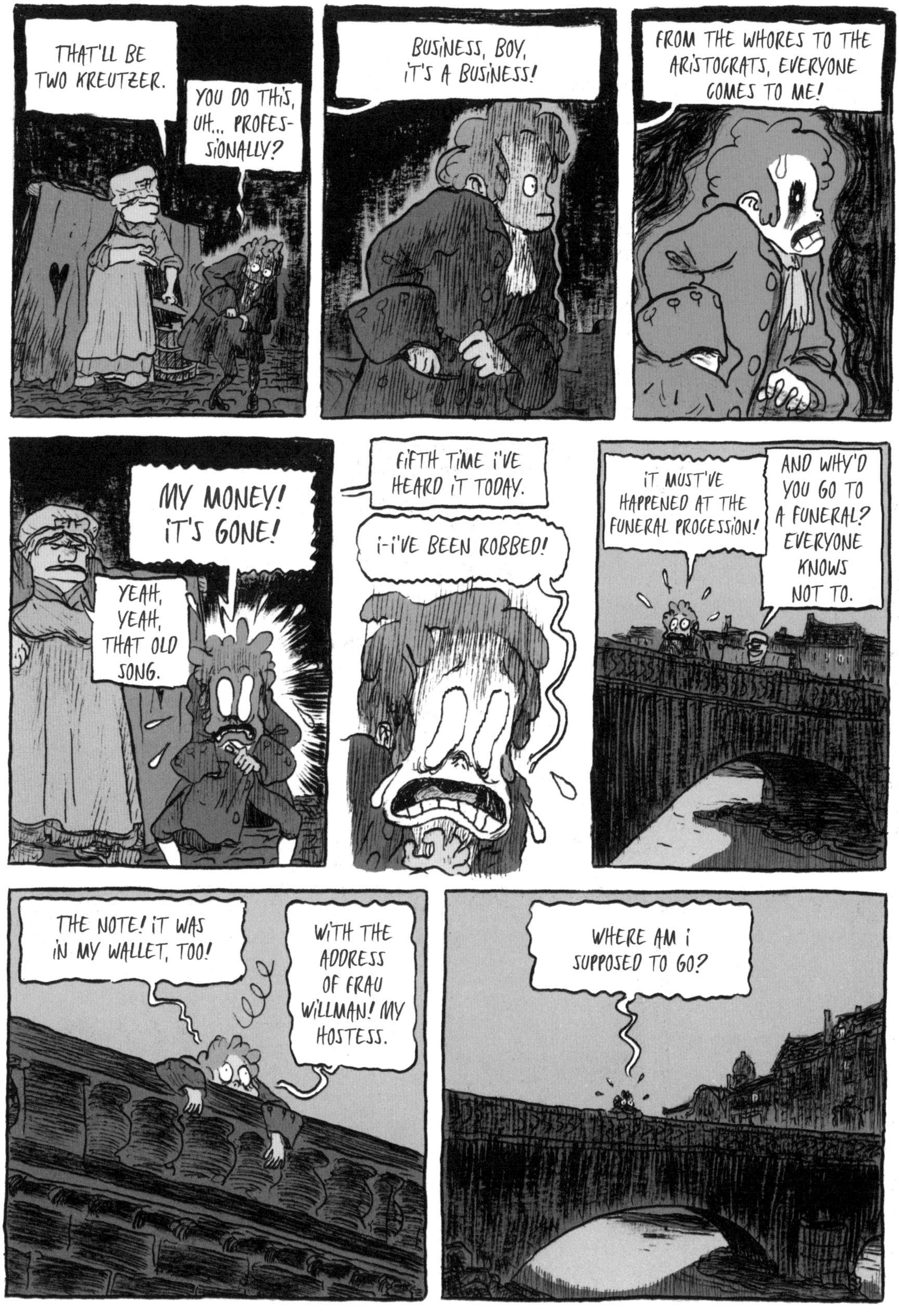
THAT'LL BE TWO KREUTZER.
YOU DO THIS, UH... PROFES-SIONALLY?
BUSINESS, BOY, IT'S A BUSINESS!
FROM THE WHORES TO THE ARISTOCRATS, EVERYONE COMES TO ME!
MY MONEY! IT'S GONE!
YEAH, YEAH, THAT OLD SONG.
FIFTH TIME I'VE HEARD IT TODAY.
I-I'VE BEEN ROBBED!
IT MUST'VE HAPPENED AT THE FUNERAL PROCESSION!
AND WHY'D YOU GO TO A FUNERAL? EVERYONE KNOWS NOT TO.
THE NOTE! IT WAS IN MY WALLET, TOO!
WITH THE ADDRESS OF FRAU WILLMAN! MY HOSTESS.
WHERE AM I SUPPOSED TO GO?

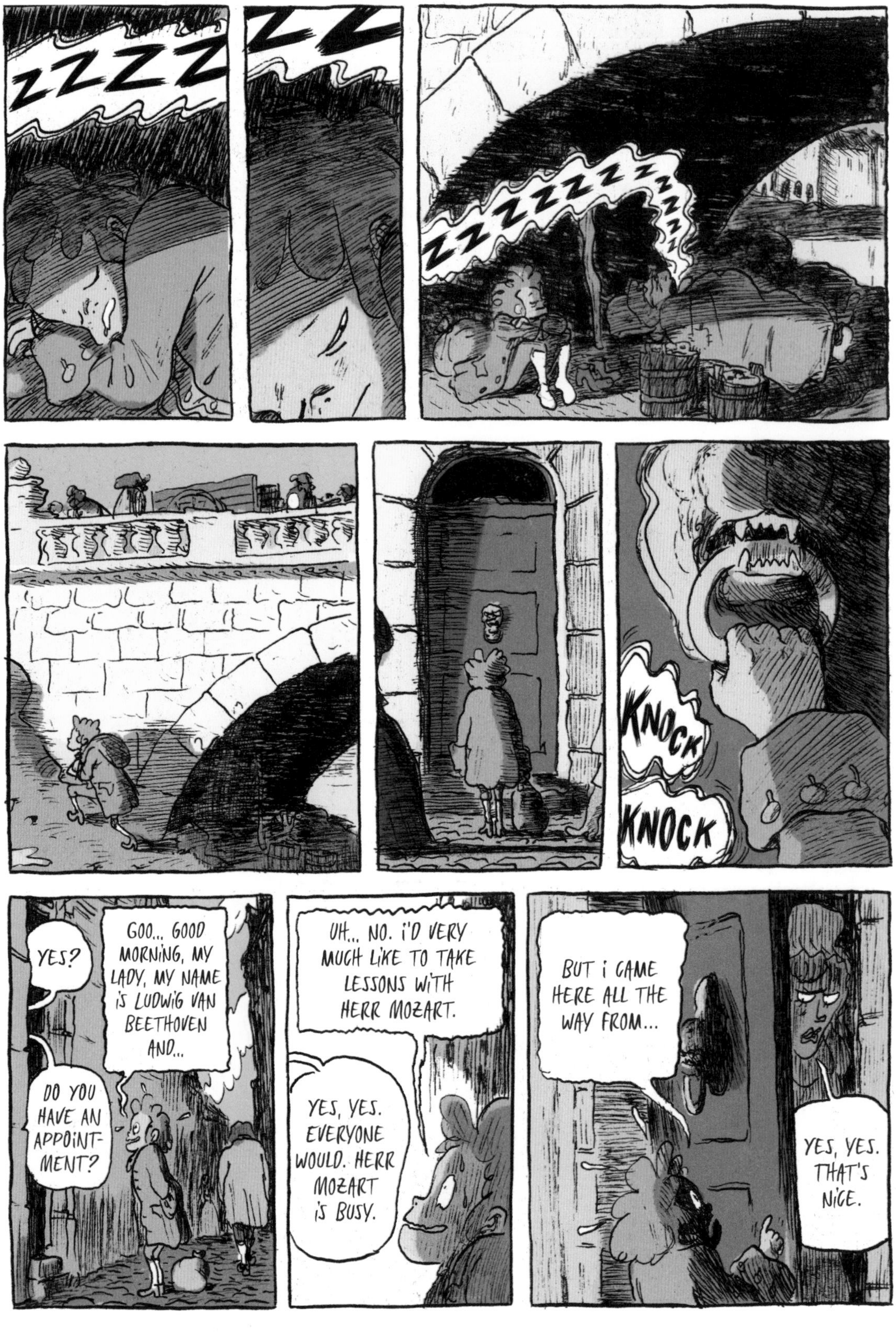
ZZZZZ
ZZ
ZZZZZZZZZZZ
KNOCK
KNOCK
YES?
GOO... GOOD MORNING, MY LADY, MY NAME iS LUDWiG VAN BEETHOVEN AND...
DO YOU HAVE AN APPOiNT-MENT?
UH... NO. i'D VERY MUCH LiKE TO TAKE LESSONS WiTH HERR MOZART.
YES, YES. EVERYONE WOULD. HERR MOZART iS BUSY.
BUT i CAME HERE ALL THE WAY FROM...
YES, YES. THAT'S NiCE.

THUD
...BONN.
SIGH.
DRAAAGG
WELL, BOY? FIND YOUR WALLET YET?
POOP PRINCESS!
AH, MY MOST FAMOUS CUSTOMER!
?

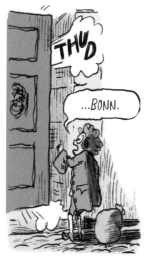

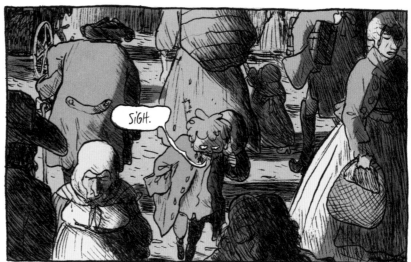

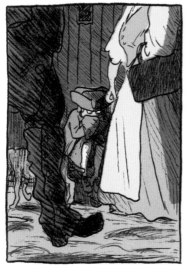

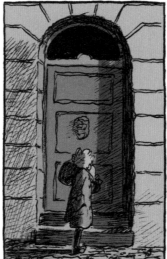

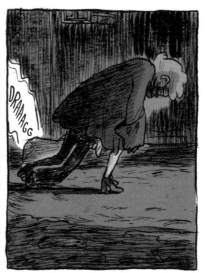

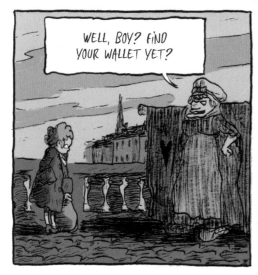

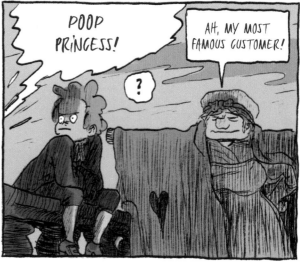

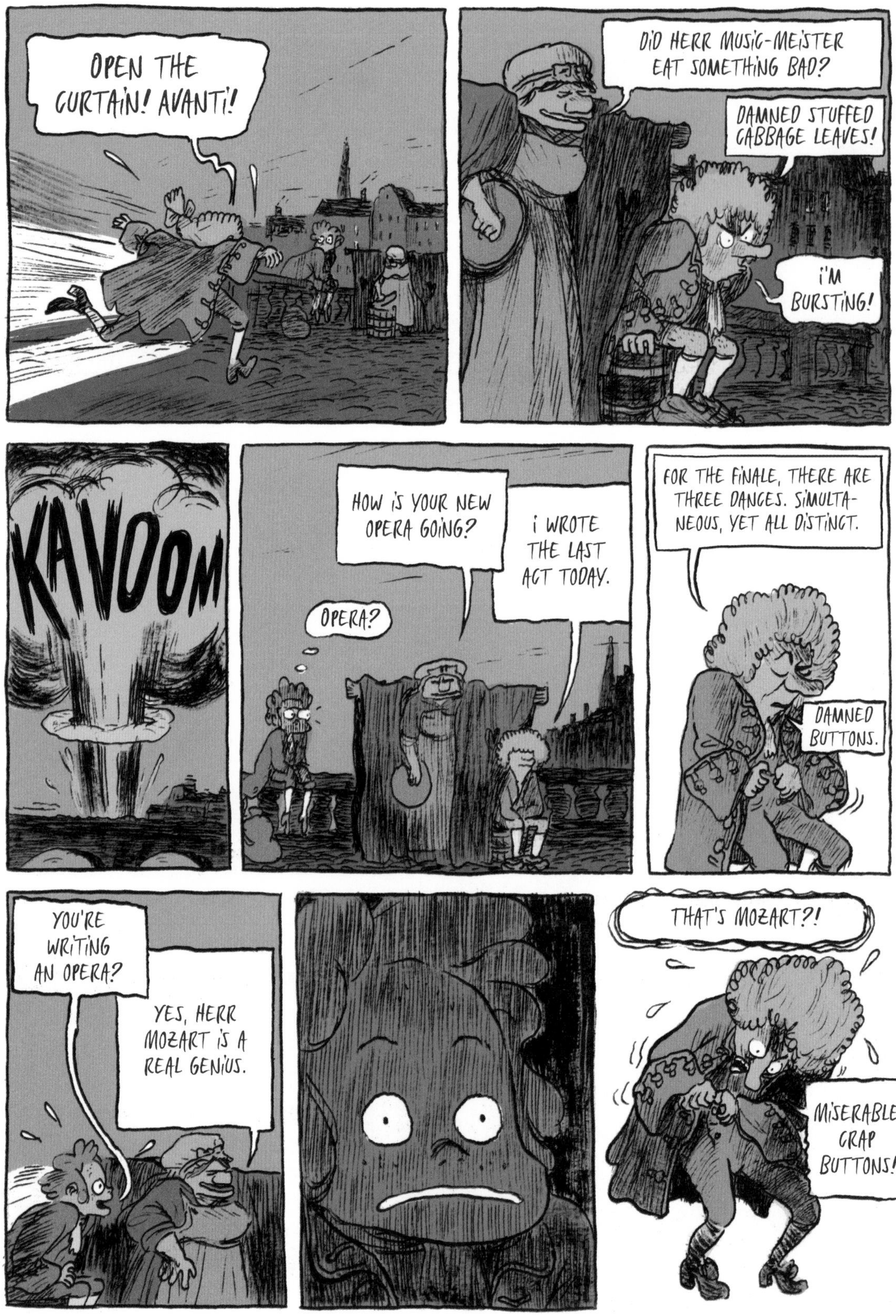
OPEN THE CURTAIN! AVANTI!
DID HERR MUSIC-MEISTER EAT SOMETHING BAD?
DAMNED STUFFED CABBAGE LEAVES!
I'M BURSTING!
KAVOOM
HOW IS YOUR NEW OPERA GOING?
I WROTE THE LAST ACT TODAY.
OPERA?
FOR THE FINALE, THERE ARE THREE DANCES. SIMULTANEOUS, YET ALL DISTINCT.
DAMNED BUTTONS.
YOU'RE WRITING AN OPERA?
YES, HERR MOZART IS A REAL GENIUS.
THAT'S MOZART?!
MISERABLE CRAP BUTTONS!

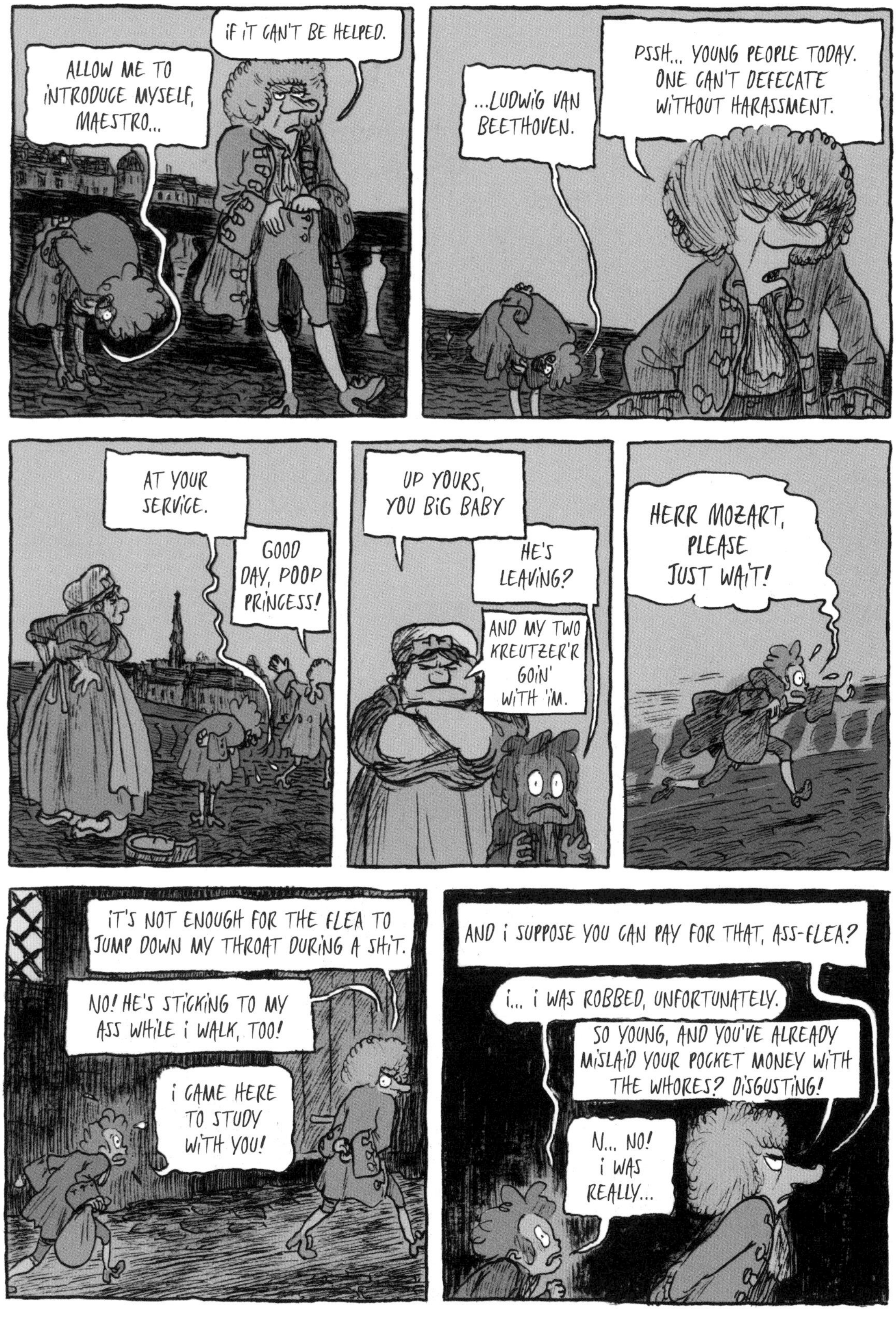
ALLOW ME TO INTRODUCE MYSELF, MAESTRO...
iF iT CAN'T BE HELPED.
...LUDWiG VAN BEETHOVEN.
PSSH... YOUNG PEOPLE TODAY. ONE CAN'T DEFECATE WiTHOUT HARASSMENT.
AT YOUR SERViCE.
GOOD DAY, POOP PRiNCESS!
UP YOURS, YOU BiG BABY
HE'S LEAViNG?
AND MY TWO KREUTZER'R GOiN' WiTH 'iM.
HERR MOZART, PLEASE JUST WAiT!
iT'S NOT ENOUGH FOR THE FLEA TO JUMP DOWN MY THROAT DURiNG A SHiT.
NO! HE'S STiCKiNG TO MY ASS WHiLE i WALK, TOO!
i CAME HERE TO STUDY WiTH YOU!
AND i SUPPOSE YOU CAN PAY FOR THAT, ASS-FLEA?
i... i WAS ROBBED, UNFORTUNATELY.
SO YOUNG, AND YOU'VE ALREADY MiSLAiD YOUR POCKET MONEY WiTH THE WHORES? DiSGUSTiNG!
N... NO! i WAS REALLY...

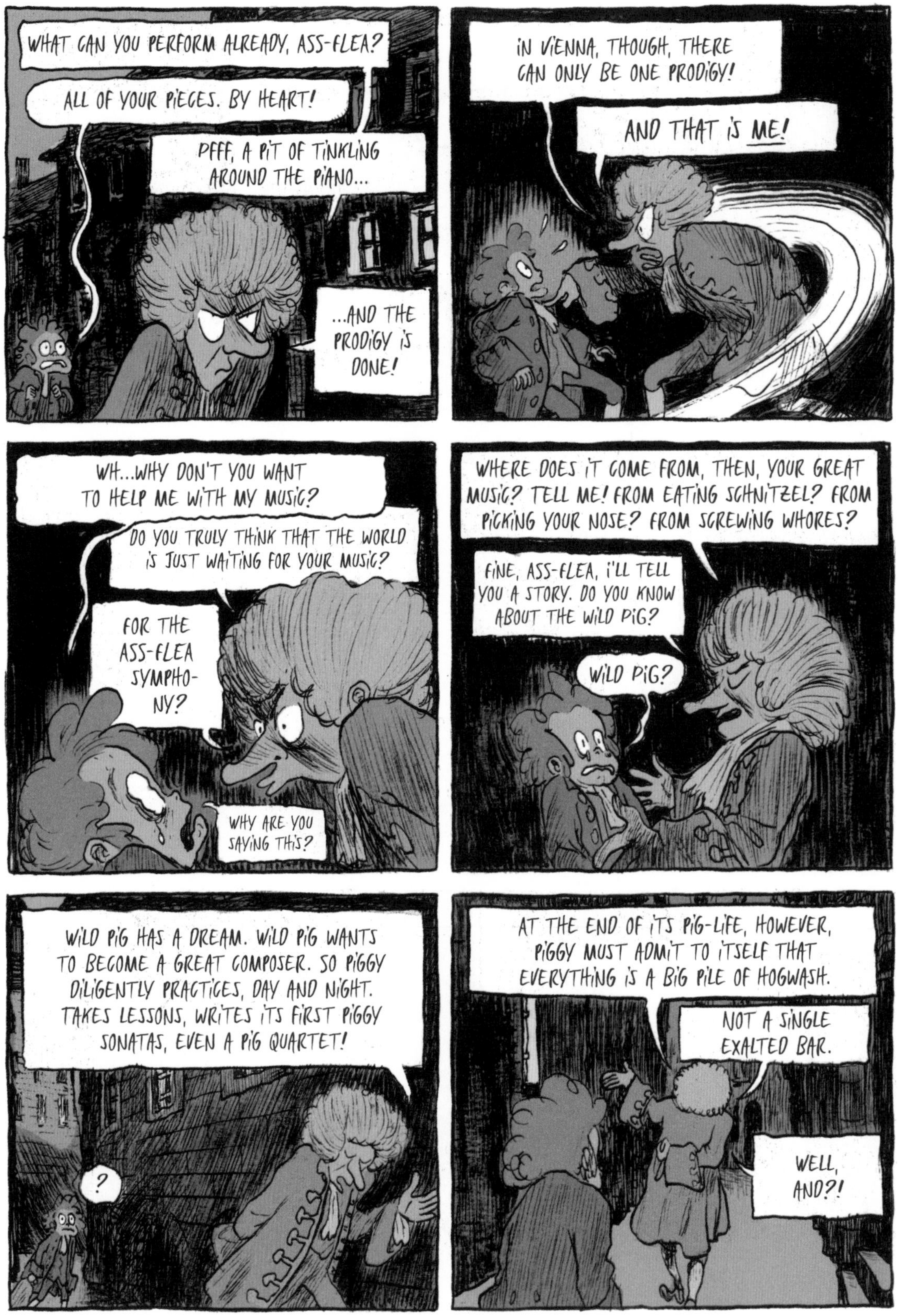
WHAT CAN YOU PERFORM ALREADY, ASS-FLEA?
ALL OF YOUR PIECES. BY HEART!
PFFF, A BIT OF TINKLING AROUND THE PIANO...
...AND THE PRODIGY IS DONE!
IN VIENNA, THOUGH, THERE CAN ONLY BE ONE PRODIGY!
AND THAT IS ME!
WH...WHY DON'T YOU WANT TO HELP ME WITH MY MUSIC?
DO YOU TRULY THINK THAT THE WORLD IS JUST WAITING FOR YOUR MUSIC?
FOR THE ASS-FLEA SYMPHO-NY?
WHY ARE YOU SAYING THIS?
WHERE DOES IT COME FROM, THEN, YOUR GREAT MUSIC? TELL ME! FROM EATING SCHNITZEL? FROM PICKING YOUR NOSE? FROM SCREWING WHORES?
FINE, ASS-FLEA, I'LL TELL YOU A STORY. DO YOU KNOW ABOUT THE WILD PIG?
WILD PIG?
WILD PIG HAS A DREAM. WILD PIG WANTS TO BECOME A GREAT COMPOSER. SO PIGGY DILIGENTLY PRACTICES, DAY AND NIGHT. TAKES LESSONS, WRITES ITS FIRST PIGGY SONATAS, EVEN A PIG QUARTET!
?
AT THE END OF ITS PIG-LIFE, HOWEVER, PIGGY MUST ADMIT TO ITSELF THAT EVERYTHING IS A BIG PILE OF HOGWASH.
NOT A SINGLE EXALTED BAR.
WELL, AND?!

A STUPID PIG SIMPLY REMAINS A STUPID PIG.
SAD, NO?
BUT WAIT, ASS-FLEA.
THE PLOT THICKENS!
THE BLACKBIRD!
WHAT?
THE BLACKBIRD HATCHES FROM THE EGG.
AND FROM THAT FIRST MOMENT, SHE HAS A SENSE FOR IT.
SHE OPENS HER BEAK AND...
...AND?
...AND SINGS!
THE BLACKBIRD SINGS!
DOESN'T NEED TO STUDY.
KNOWS NOTHING OF COUNTERPOINT AND BASSO CONTINUO.
AND SINGS ANYWAY.
JUST LIKE THAT.
YOU'RE MAKING FUN OF ME!
OF COURSE! WHAT ELSE?
COME ON, HELP ME OVER THE WALL, ASS-FLEA!

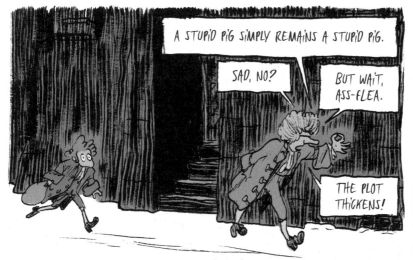

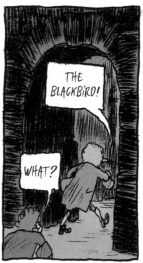

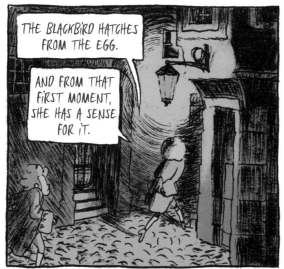

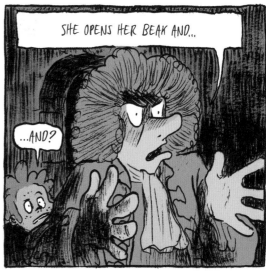

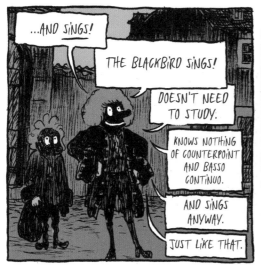

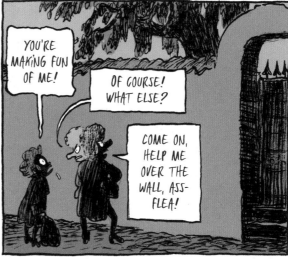

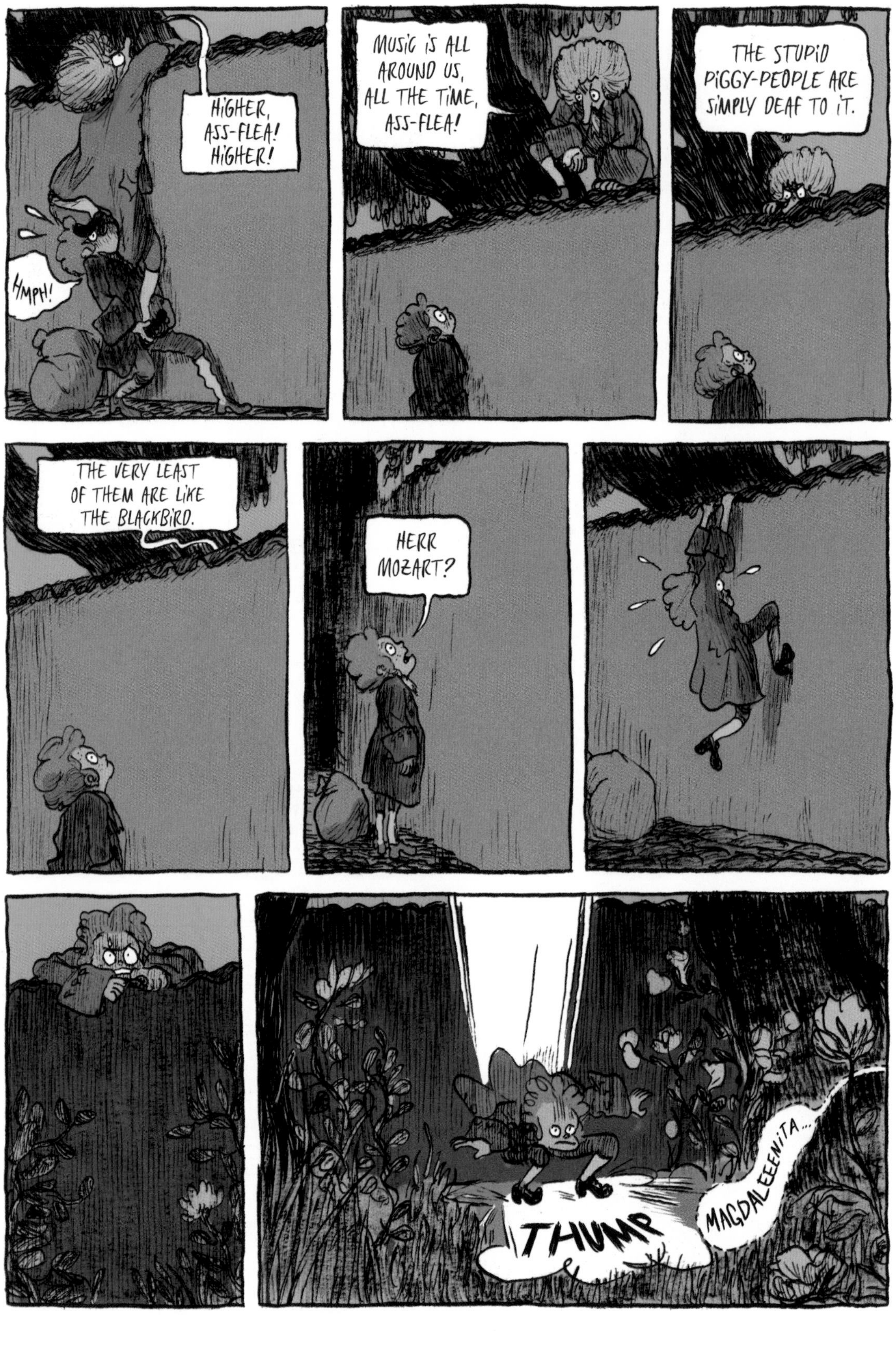
HIGHER, ASS-FLEA! HIGHER!
HMPH!
MUSIC IS ALL AROUND US, ALL THE TIME, ASS-FLEA!
THE STUPID PIGGY-PEOPLE ARE SIMPLY DEAF TO IT.
THE VERY LEAST OF THEM ARE LIKE THE BLACKBIRD.
HERR MOZART?
THUMP
MAGDALEEENITA...

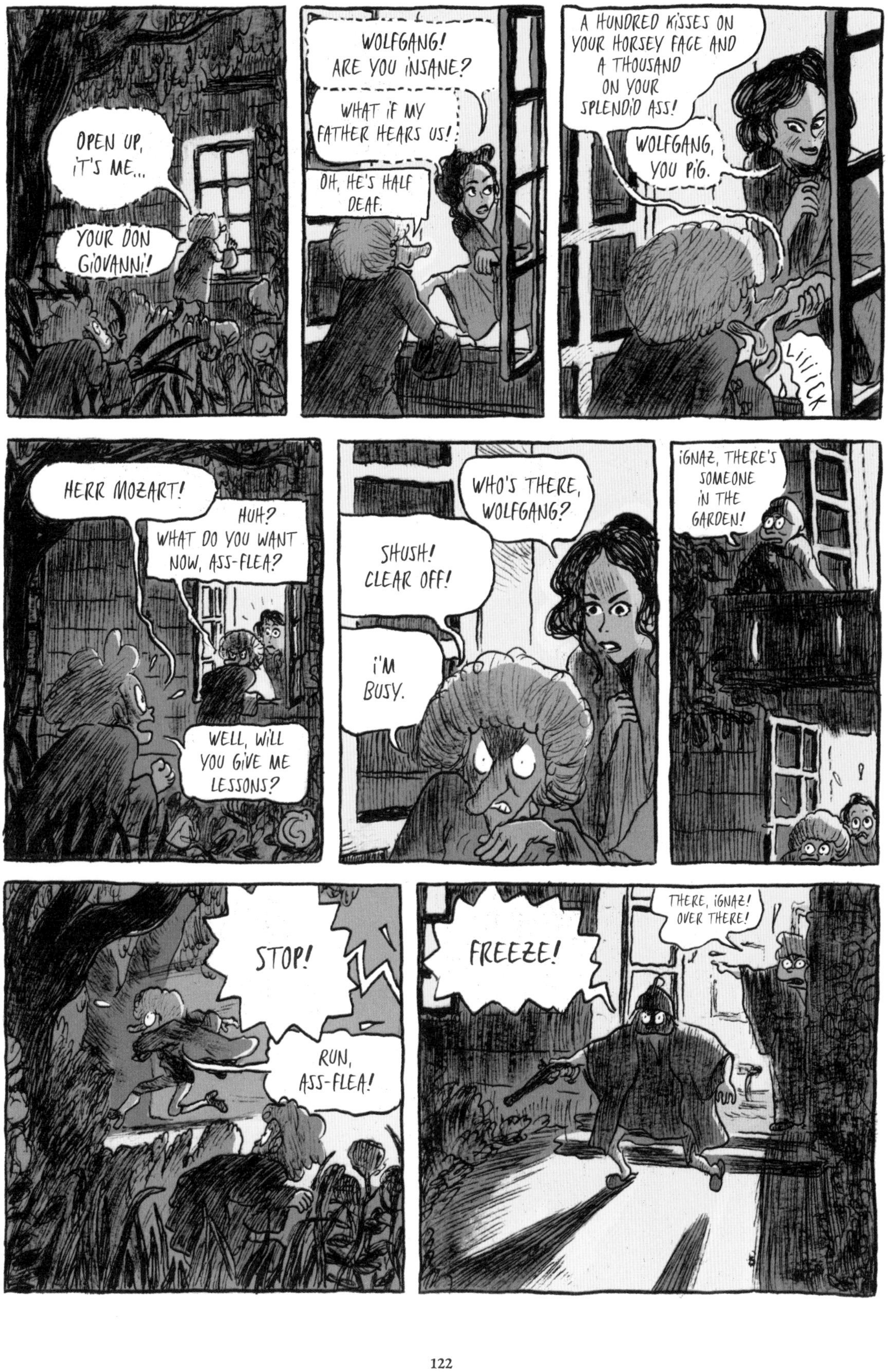
OPEN UP, IT'S ME...
YOUR DON GIOVANNI!
WOLFGANG! ARE YOU INSANE?
WHAT IF MY FATHER HEARS US!
OH, HE'S HALF DEAF.
A HUNDRED KISSES ON YOUR HORSEY FACE AND A THOUSAND ON YOUR SPLENDID ASS!
WOLFGANG, YOU PIG.
LIIIICK
HERR MOZART!
HUH? WHAT DO YOU WANT NOW, ASS-FLEA?
WELL, WILL YOU GIVE ME LESSONS?
WHO'S THERE, WOLFGANG?
SHUSH! CLEAR OFF!
I'M BUSY.
IGNAZ, THERE'S SOMEONE IN THE GARDEN!
STOP!
RUN, ASS-FLEA!
FREEZE!
THERE, IGNAZ! OVER THERE!

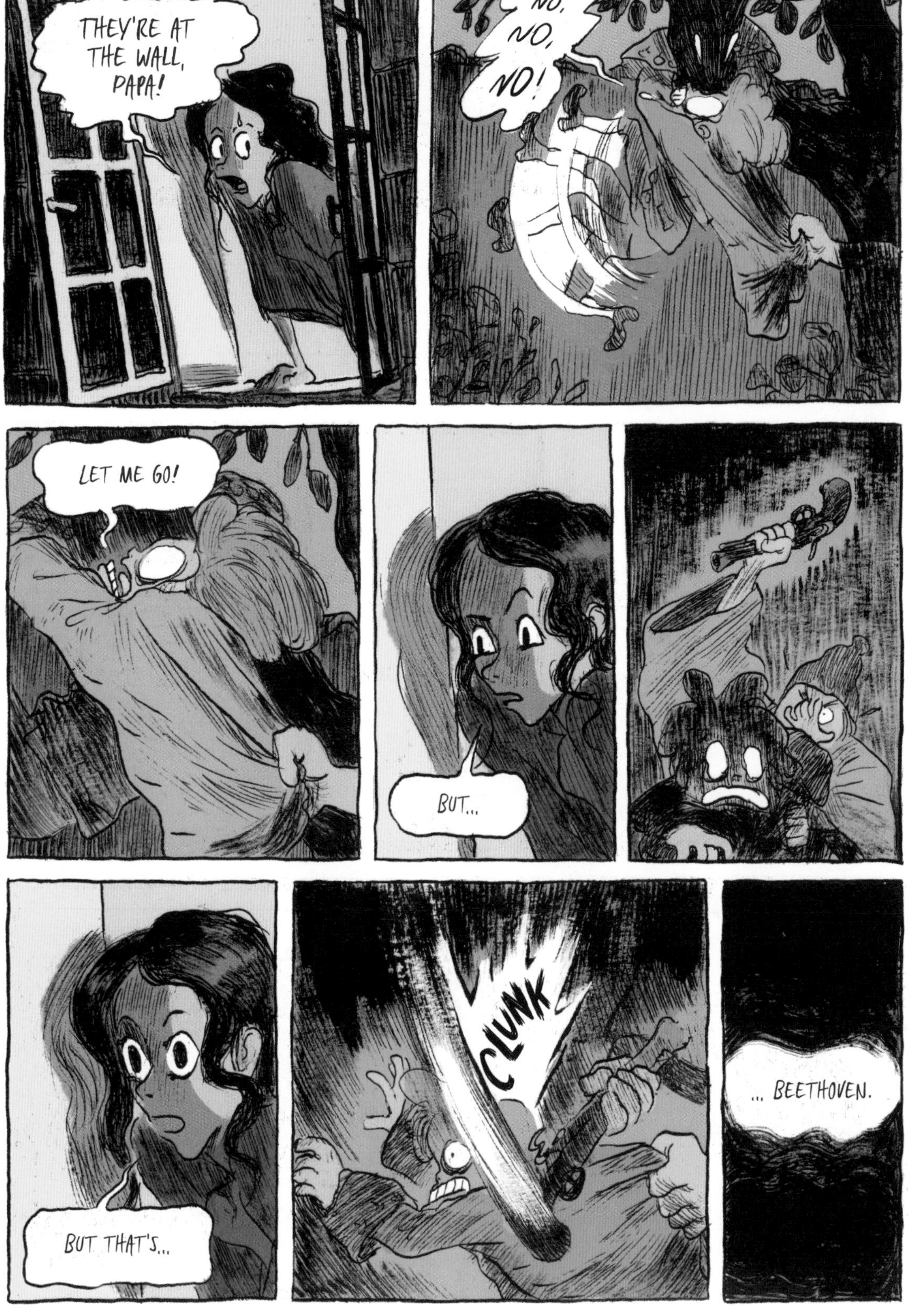
THEY'RE AT THE WALL, PAPA!
NO, NO, NO!
LET ME GO!
BUT...
BUT THAT'S...
CLUNK
... BEETHOVEN.

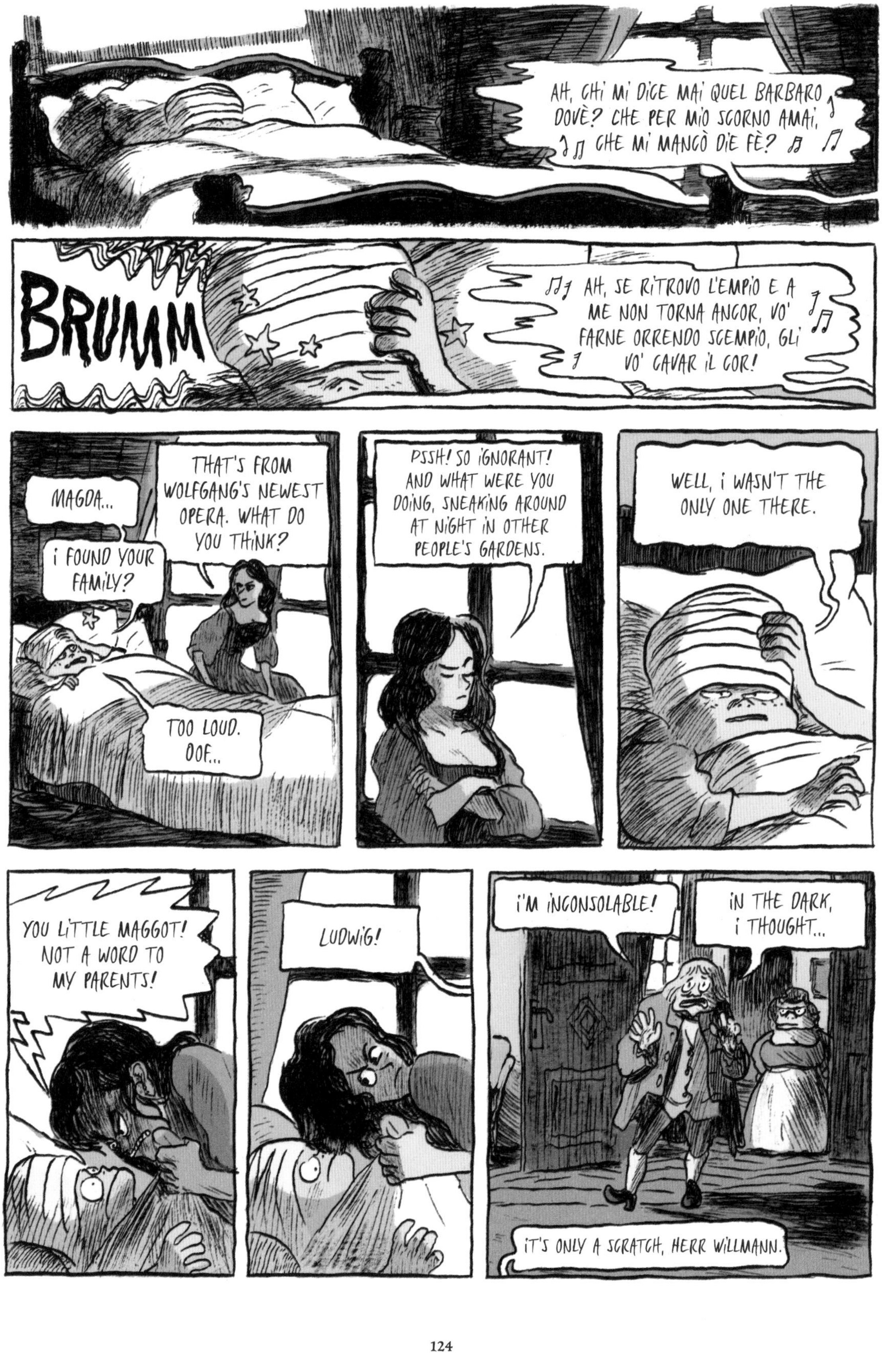
AH, CHi Mi DiCE MAi QUEL BARBARO DOVÈ? CHE PER MiO SCORNO AMAi, CHE Mi MANCÒ DiE FÈ?
BRUMM
AH, SE RiTROVO L'EMPiO E A ME NON TORNA ANCOR, VO' FARNE ORRENDO SCEMPiO, GLi VO' CAVAR iL COR!
MAGDA...
i FOUND YOUR FAMiLY?
THAT'S FROM WOLFGANG'S NEWEST OPERA. WHAT DO YOU THiNK?
TOO LOUD. OOF...
PSSH! SO iGNORANT! AND WHAT WERE YOU DOiNG, SNEAKiNG AROUND AT NiGHT iN OTHER PEOPLE'S GARDENS.
WELL, i WASN'T THE ONLY ONE THERE.
YOU LiTTLE MAGGOT! NOT A WORD TO MY PARENTS!
LUDWiG!
i'M iNCONSOLABLE!
iN THE DARK, i THOUGHT...
iT'S ONLY A SCRATCH, HERR WiLLMANN.

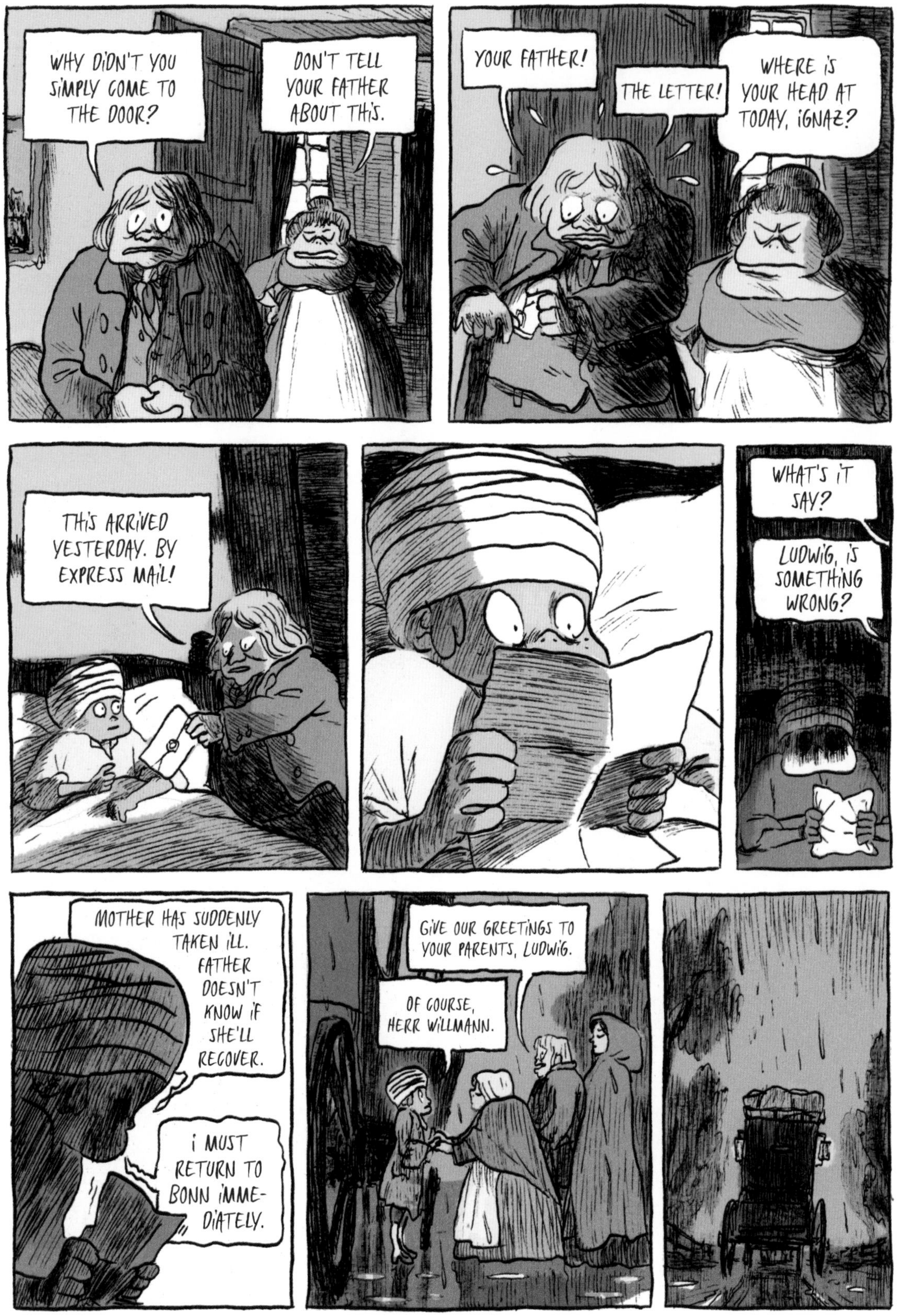
WHY DIDN'T YOU SIMPLY COME TO THE DOOR?
DON'T TELL YOUR FATHER ABOUT THIS.
YOUR FATHER!
THE LETTER!
WHERE IS YOUR HEAD AT TODAY, IGNAZ?
THIS ARRIVED YESTERDAY. BY EXPRESS MAIL!
WHAT'S IT SAY?
LUDWIG, IS SOMETHING WRONG?
MOTHER HAS SUDDENLY TAKEN ILL. FATHER DOESN'T KNOW IF SHE'LL RECOVER.
I MUST RETURN TO BONN IMME-DIATELY.
GIVE OUR GREETINGS TO YOUR PARENTS, LUDWIG.
OF COURSE, HERR WILLMANN.

1789

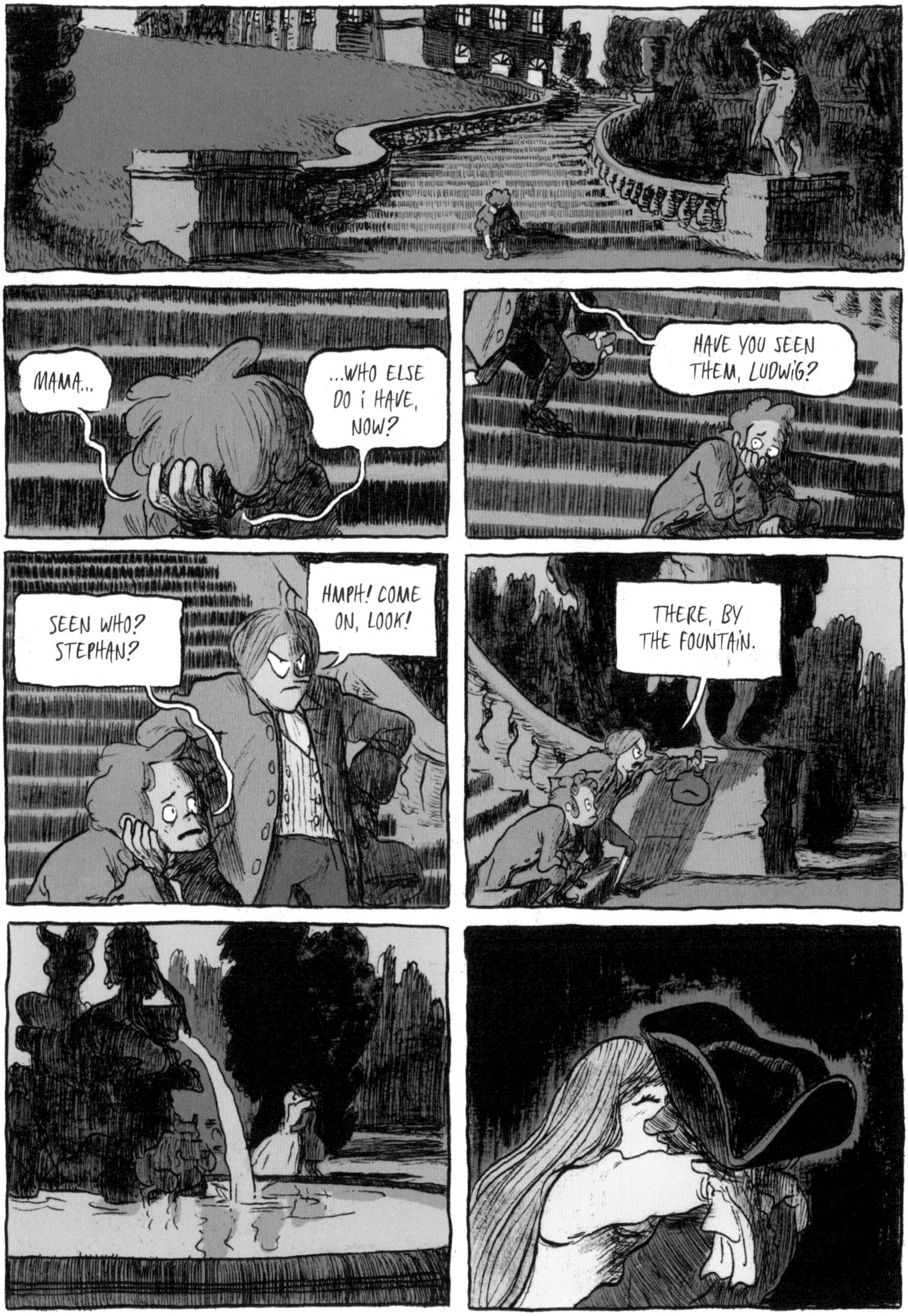
MAMA...
...WHO ELSE DO i HAVE, NOW?
HAVE YOU SEEN THEM, LUDWiG?
SEEN WHO? STEPHAN?
HMPH! COME ON, LOOK!
THERE, BY THE FOUNTAiN.

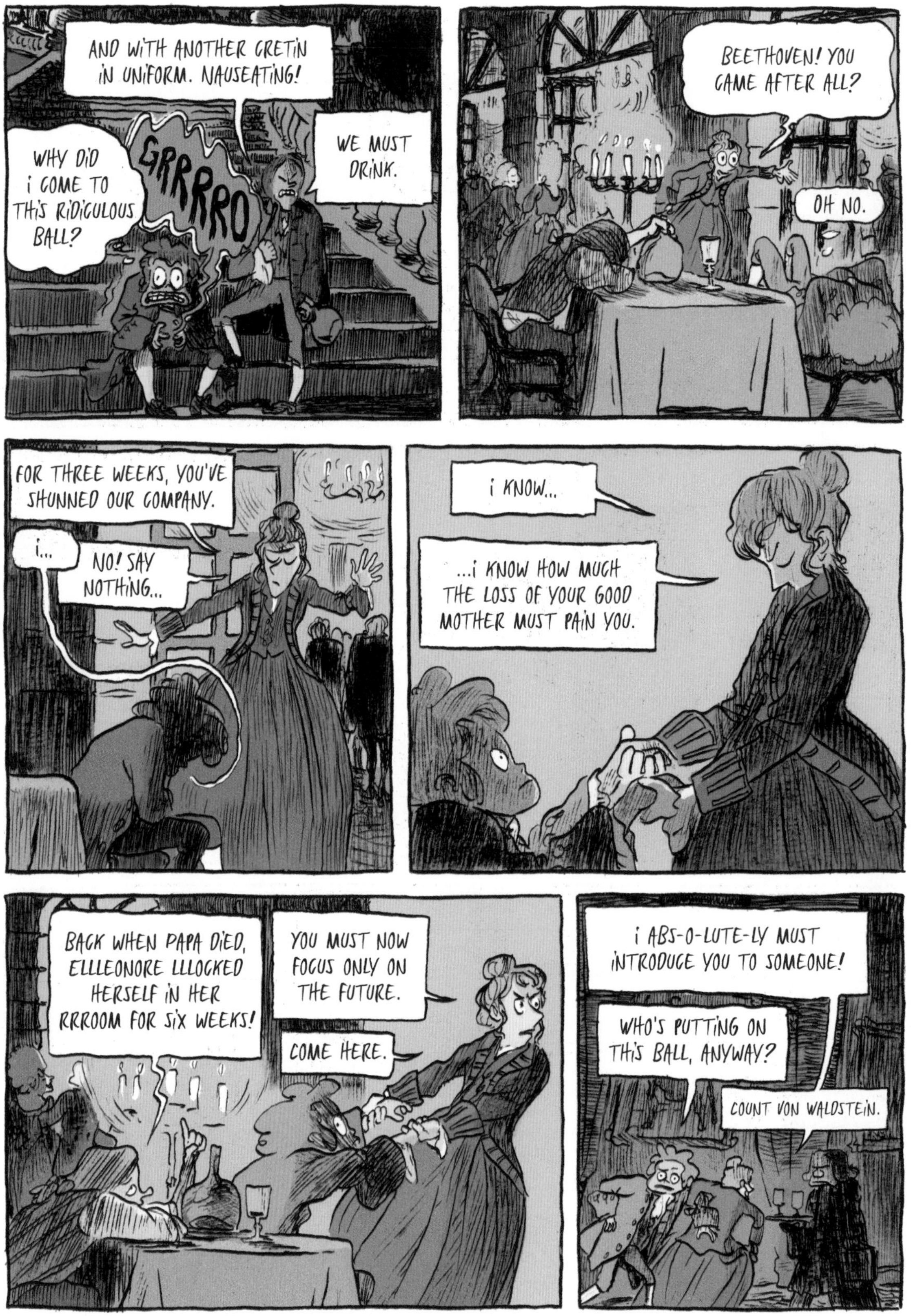
AND WITH ANOTHER CRETIN IN UNIFORM. NAUSEATING!
WHY DID I COME TO THIS RIDICULOUS BALL?
GRRRRRO
WE MUST DRINK.
BEETHOVEN! YOU CAME AFTER ALL?
OH NO.
FOR THREE WEEKS, YOU'VE SHUNNED OUR COMPANY.
I...
NO! SAY NOTHING...
I KNOW...
...I KNOW HOW MUCH THE LOSS OF YOUR GOOD MOTHER MUST PAIN YOU.
BACK WHEN PAPA DIED, ELLLEONORE LLLOCKED HERSELF IN HER RRROOM FOR SIX WEEKS!
YOU MUST NOW FOCUS ONLY ON THE FUTURE.
COME HERE.
I ABS-O-LUTE-LY MUST INTRODUCE YOU TO SOMEONE!
WHO'S PUTTING ON THIS BALL, ANYWAY?
COUNT VON WALDSTEIN.

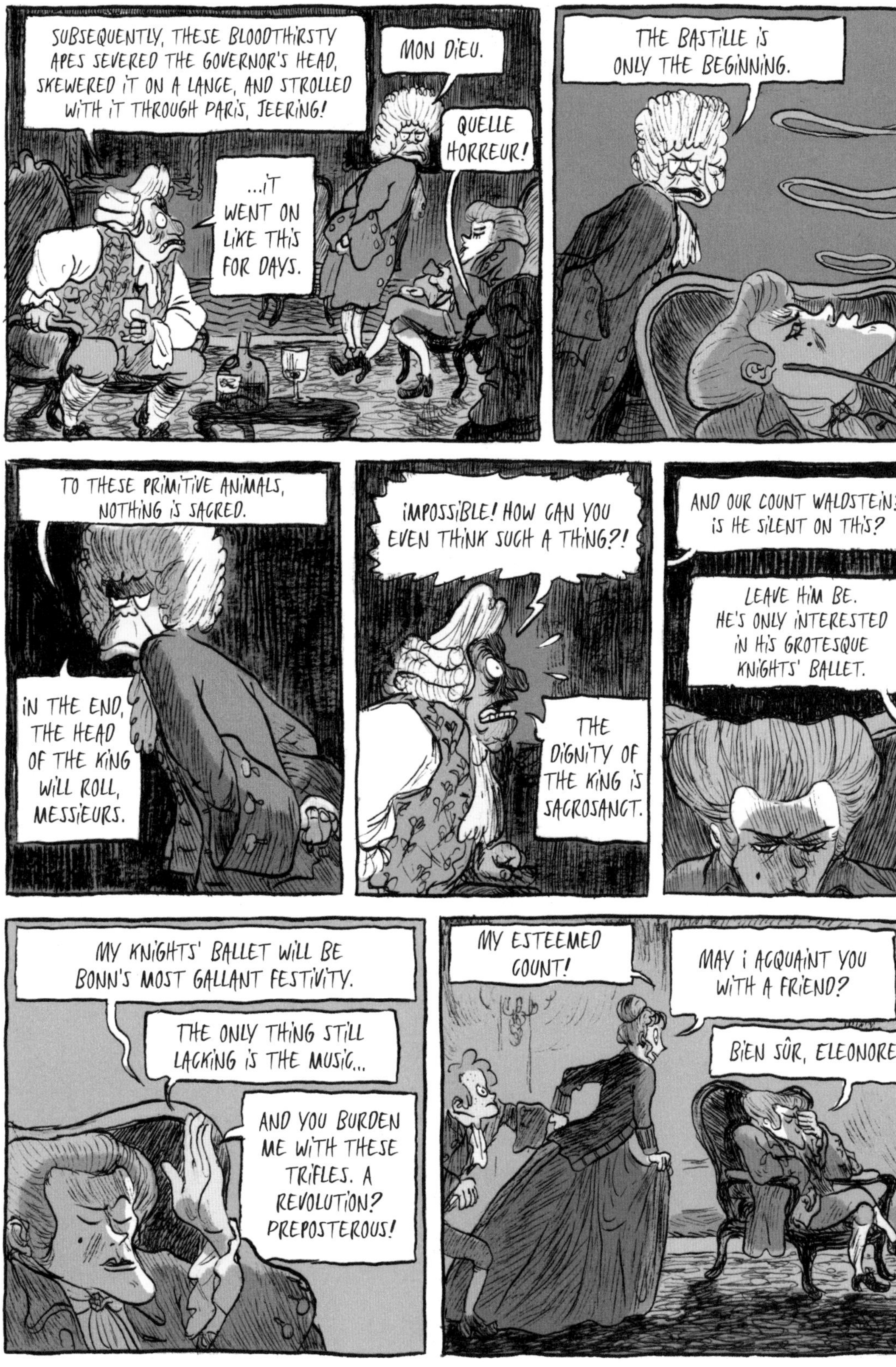
SUBSEQUENTLY, THESE BLOODTHIRSTY APES SEVERED THE GOVERNOR'S HEAD, SKEWERED IT ON A LANCE, AND STROLLED WITH IT THROUGH PARIS, JEERING!
...IT WENT ON LIKE THIS FOR DAYS.
MON DIEU.
QUELLE HORREUR!
THE BASTILLE IS ONLY THE BEGINNING.
TO THESE PRIMITIVE ANIMALS, NOTHING IS SACRED.
IN THE END, THE HEAD OF THE KING WILL ROLL, MESSIEURS.
IMPOSSIBLE! HOW CAN YOU EVEN THINK SUCH A THING?!
THE DIGNITY OF THE KING IS SACROSANCT.
AND OUR COUNT WALDSTEIN? IS HE SILENT ON THIS?
LEAVE HIM BE. HE'S ONLY INTERESTED IN HIS GROTESQUE KNIGHTS' BALLET.
MY KNIGHTS' BALLET WILL BE BONN'S MOST GALLANT FESTIVITY.
THE ONLY THING STILL LACKING IS THE MUSIC...
AND YOU BURDEN ME WITH THESE TRIFLES. A REVOLUTION? PREPOSTEROUS!
MY ESTEEMED COUNT!
MAY I ACQUAINT YOU WITH A FRIEND?
BIEN SÛR, ELEONORE.

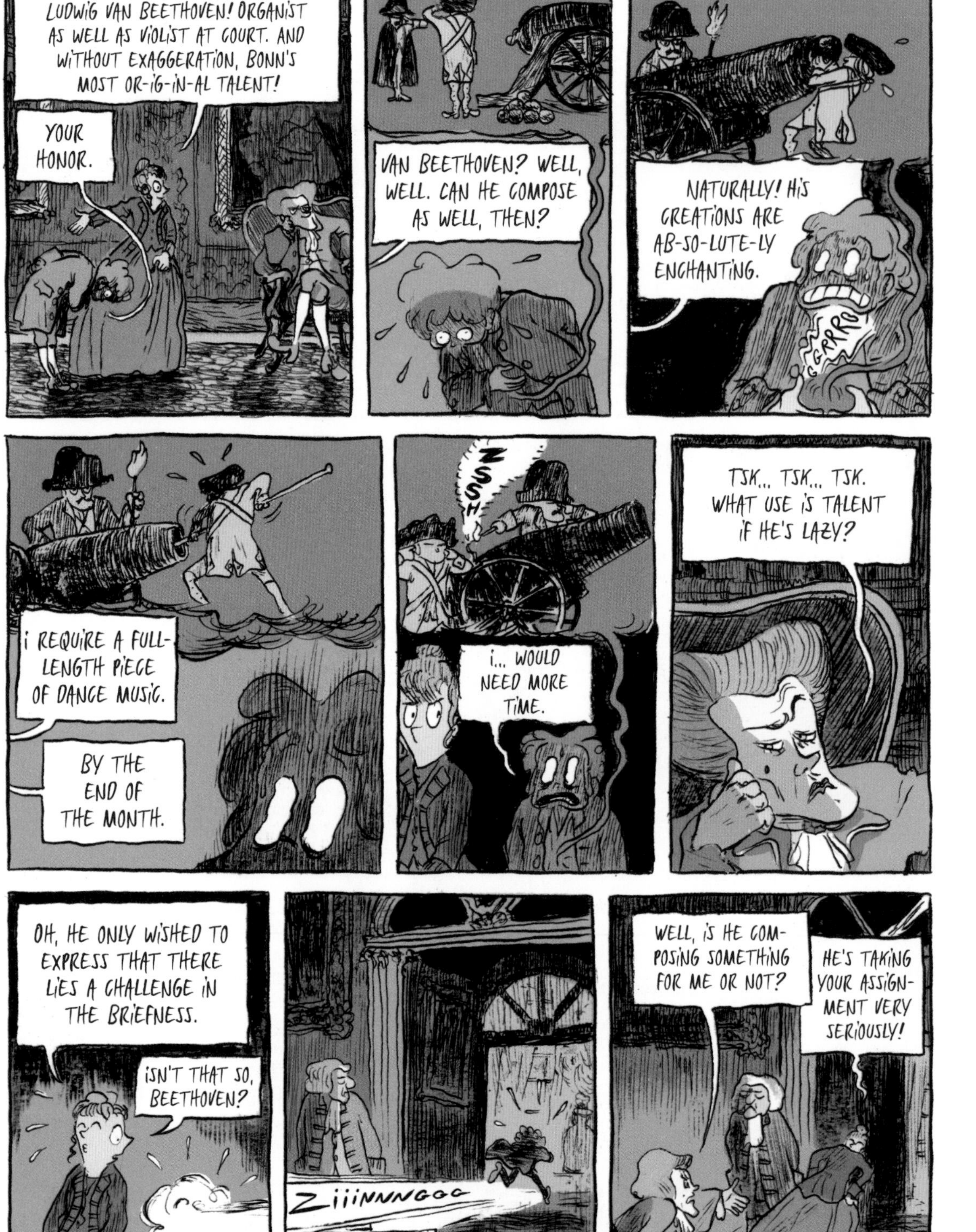
LUDWIG VAN BEETHOVEN! ORGANIST AS WELL AS VIOLIST AT COURT. AND WITHOUT EXAGGERATION, BONN'S MOST OR-IG-IN-AL TALENT!
YOUR HONOR.
VAN BEETHOVEN? WELL, WELL. CAN HE COMPOSE AS WELL, THEN?
NATURALLY! HIS CREATIONS ARE AB-SO-LUTE-LY ENCHANTING.
GGRRRR
I REQUIRE A FULL-LENGTH PIECE OF DANCE MUSIC.
BY THE END OF THE MONTH.
ZSSH
I... WOULD NEED MORE TIME.
TSK... TSK... TSK. WHAT USE IS TALENT IF HE'S LAZY?
OH, HE ONLY WISHED TO EXPRESS THAT THERE LIES A CHALLENGE IN THE BRIEFNESS.
ISN'T THAT SO, BEETHOVEN?
ZIIINNNGGG
BEETHOVEN!
WELL, IS HE COMPOSING SOMETHING FOR ME OR NOT?
HE'S TAKING YOUR ASSIGNMENT VERY SERIOUSLY!

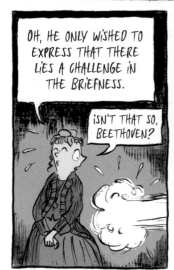

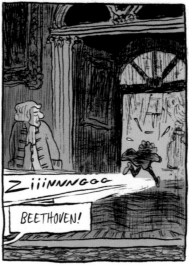

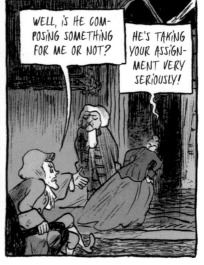

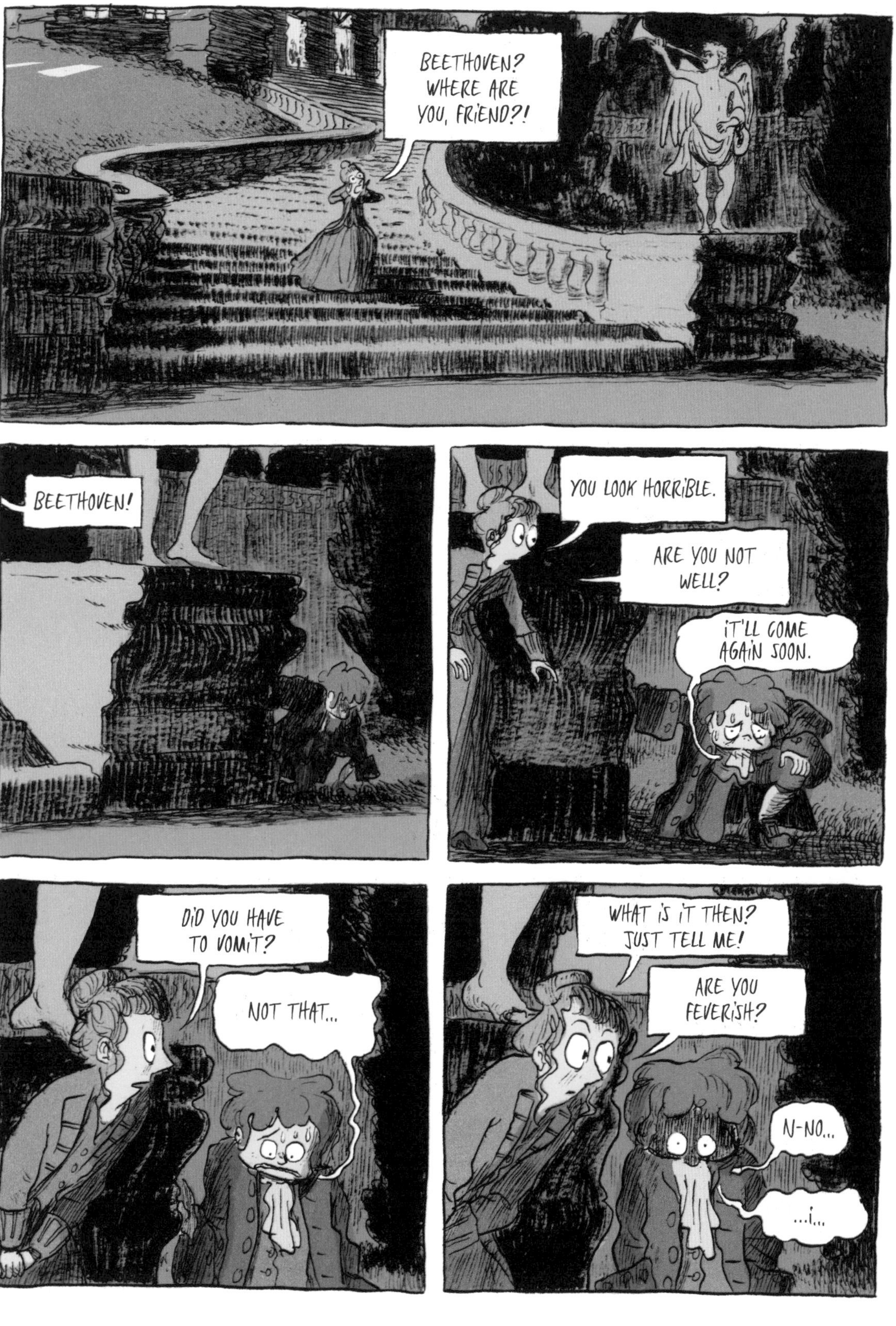
BEETHOVEN? WHERE ARE YOU, FRIEND?!
BEETHOVEN!
YOU LOOK HORRIBLE.
ARE YOU NOT WELL?
IT'LL COME AGAIN SOON.
DID YOU HAVE TO VOMIT?
NOT THAT...
WHAT IS IT THEN? JUST TELL ME!
ARE YOU FEVERISH?
N-NO...
...I...

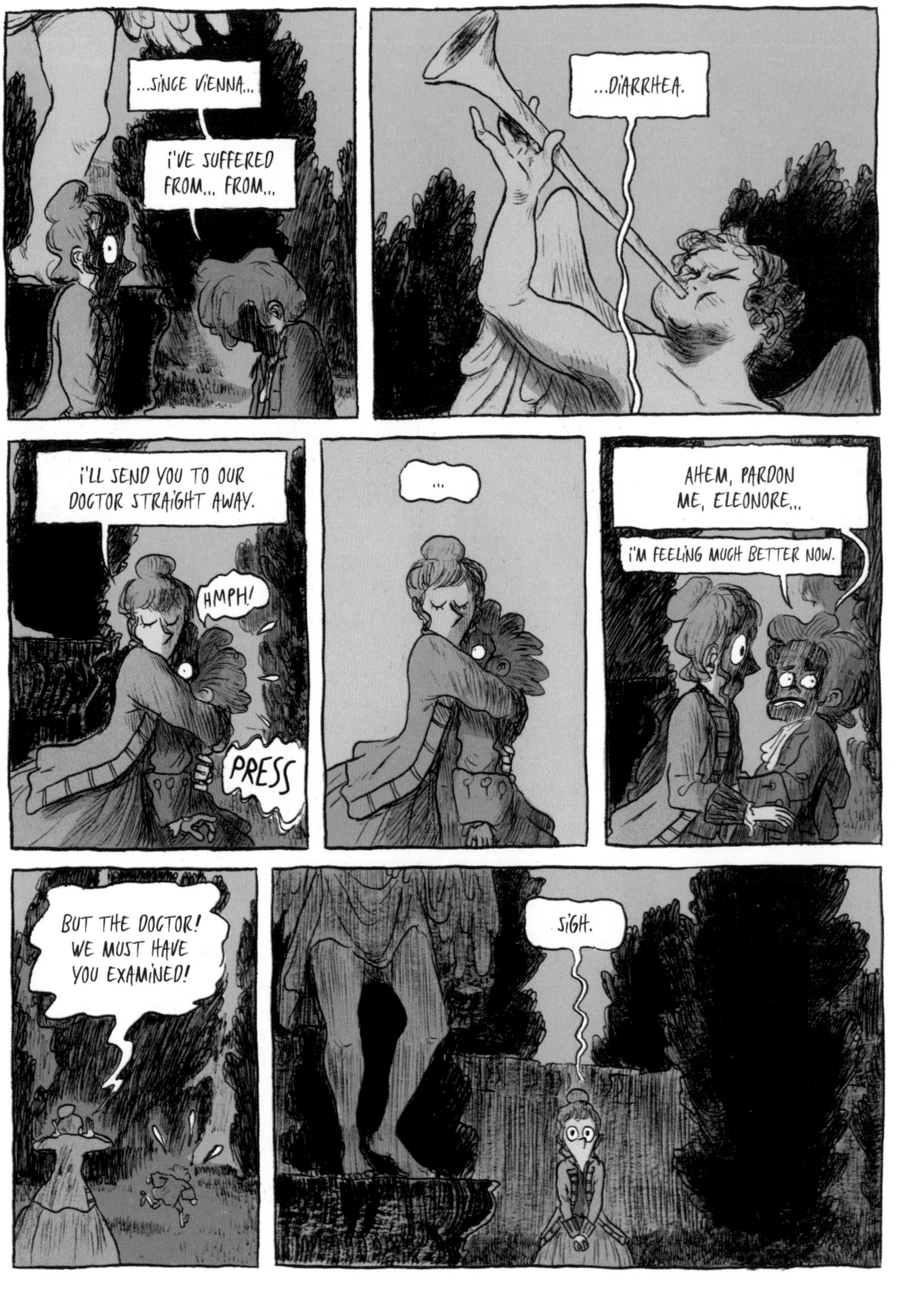
...SINCE VIENNA...
I'VE SUFFERED FROM... FROM...
...DIARRHEA.
I'LL SEND YOU TO OUR DOCTOR STRAIGHT AWAY.
HMPH!
PRESS
...
AHEM, PARDON ME, ELEONORE...
I'M FEELING MUCH BETTER NOW.
BUT THE DOCTOR! WE MUST HAVE YOU EXAMINED!
SIGH.

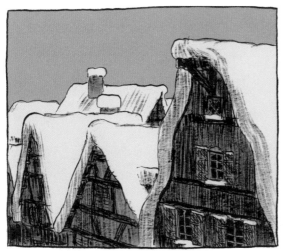

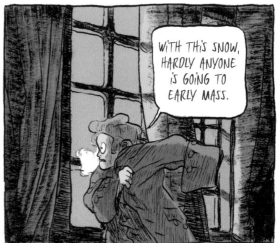

WITH THIS SNOW, HARDLY ANYONE IS GOING TO EARLY MASS.

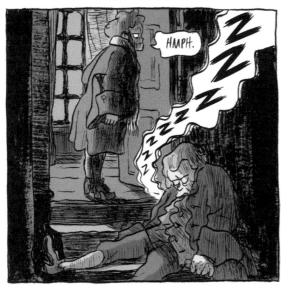

HMPH.

ZZZZZZ

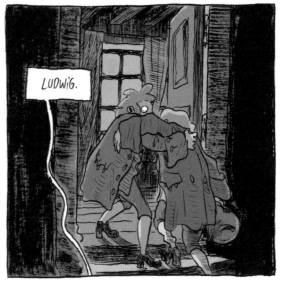

LUDWIG.

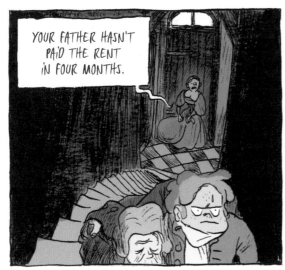

YOUR FATHER HASN'T PAID THE RENT IN FOUR MONTHS.

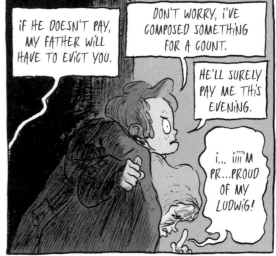

IF HE DOESN'T PAY, MY FATHER WILL HAVE TO EVICT YOU.

DON'T WORRY, I'VE COMPOSED SOMETHING FOR A COUNT.

HE'LL SURELY PAY ME THIS EVENING.

I... IiiiI'M PR...PROUD OF MY LUDWIG!

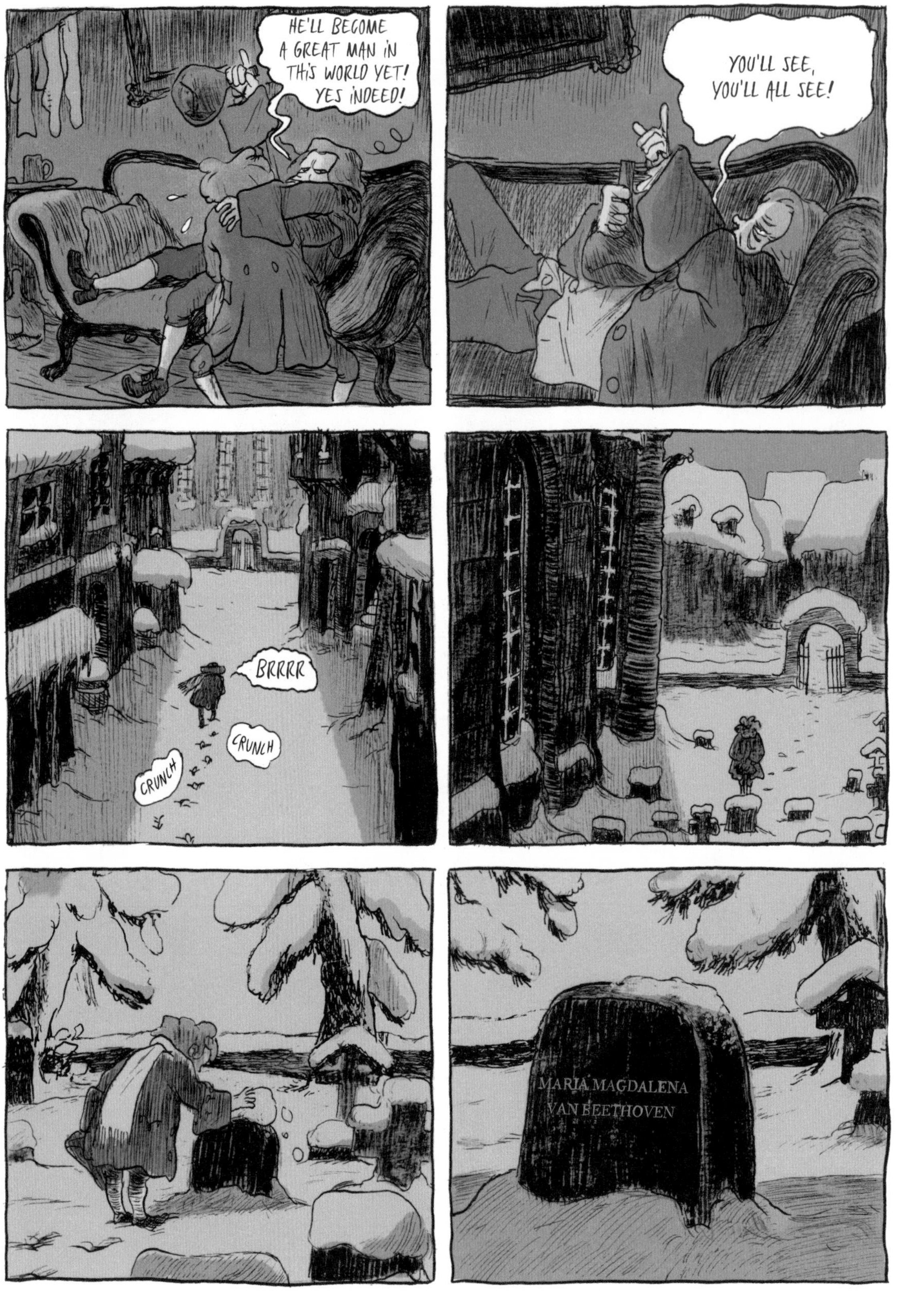
HE'LL BECOME A GREAT MAN IN THIS WORLD YET! YES INDEED!
YOU'LL SEE, YOU'LL ALL SEE!
BRRRR
CRUNCH
CRUNCH
MARIA MAGDALENA VAN BEETHOVEN

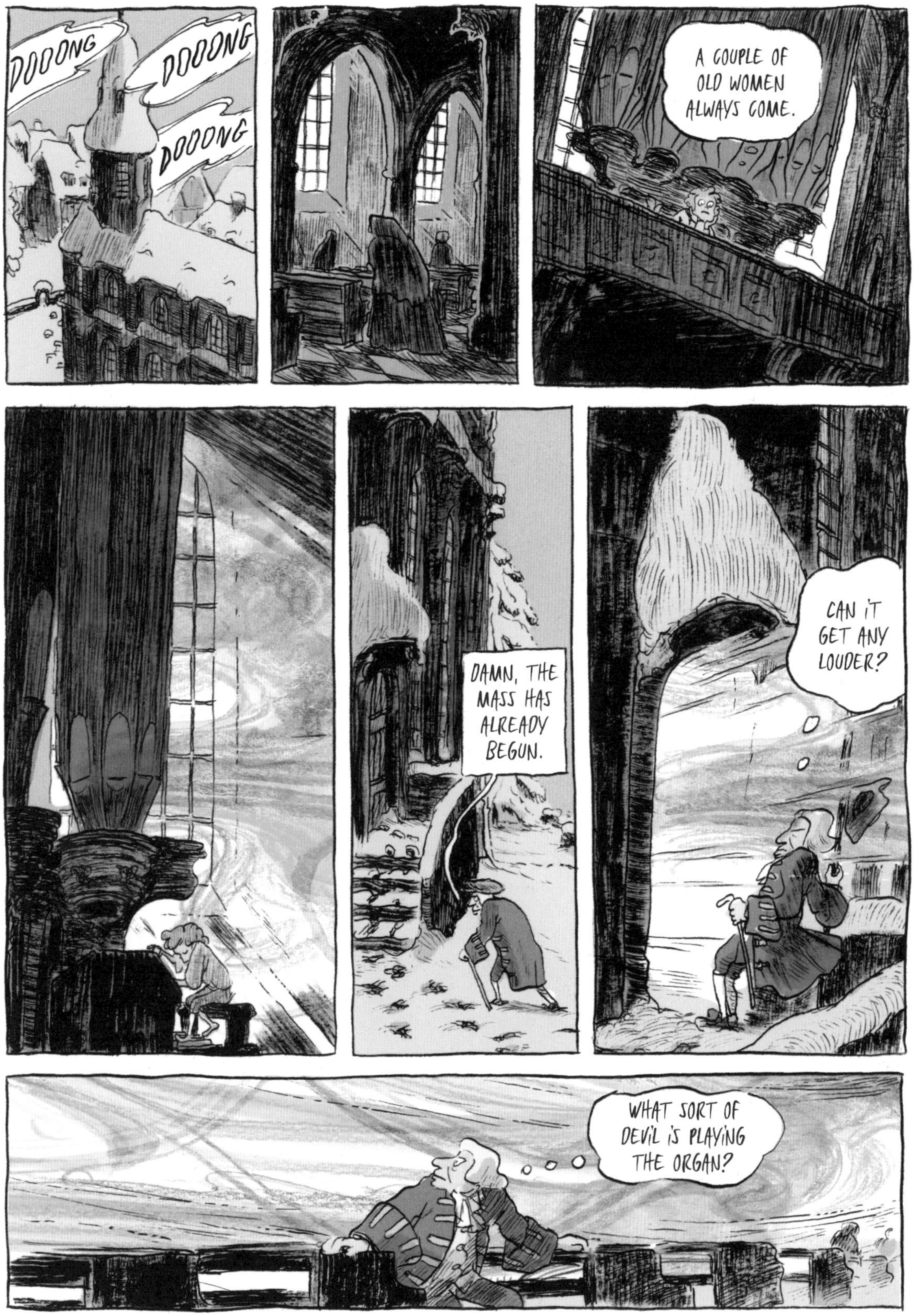
DOOONG
DOOONG
DOOONG
A COUPLE OF OLD WOMEN ALWAYS COME.
DAMN, THE MASS HAS ALREADY BEGUN.
CAN IT GET ANY LOUDER?
WHAT SORT OF DEVIL IS PLAYING THE ORGAN?

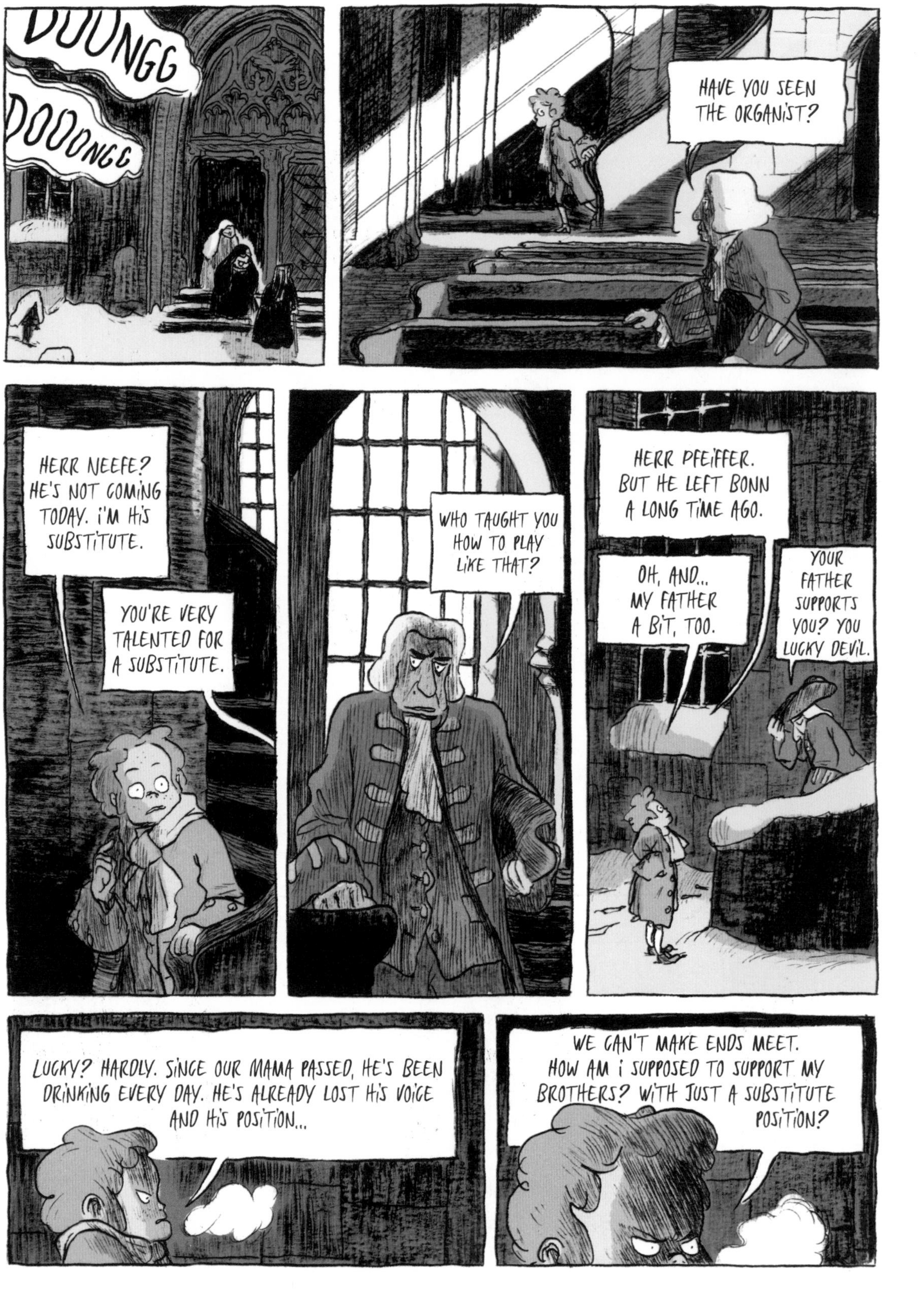
DOONGG
DOOOONGG
HAVE YOU SEEN THE ORGANIST?
HERR NEEFE? HE'S NOT COMING TODAY. I'M HIS SUBSTITUTE.
YOU'RE VERY TALENTED FOR A SUBSTITUTE.
WHO TAUGHT YOU HOW TO PLAY LIKE THAT?
HERR PFEIFFER. BUT HE LEFT BONN A LONG TIME AGO.
OH, AND... MY FATHER A BIT, TOO.
YOUR FATHER SUPPORTS YOU? YOU LUCKY DEVIL.
LUCKY? HARDLY. SINCE OUR MAMA PASSED, HE'S BEEN DRINKING EVERY DAY. HE'S ALREADY LOST HIS VOICE AND HIS POSITION...
WE CAN'T MAKE ENDS MEET. HOW AM I SUPPOSED TO SUPPORT MY BROTHERS? WITH JUST A SUBSTITUTE POSITION?

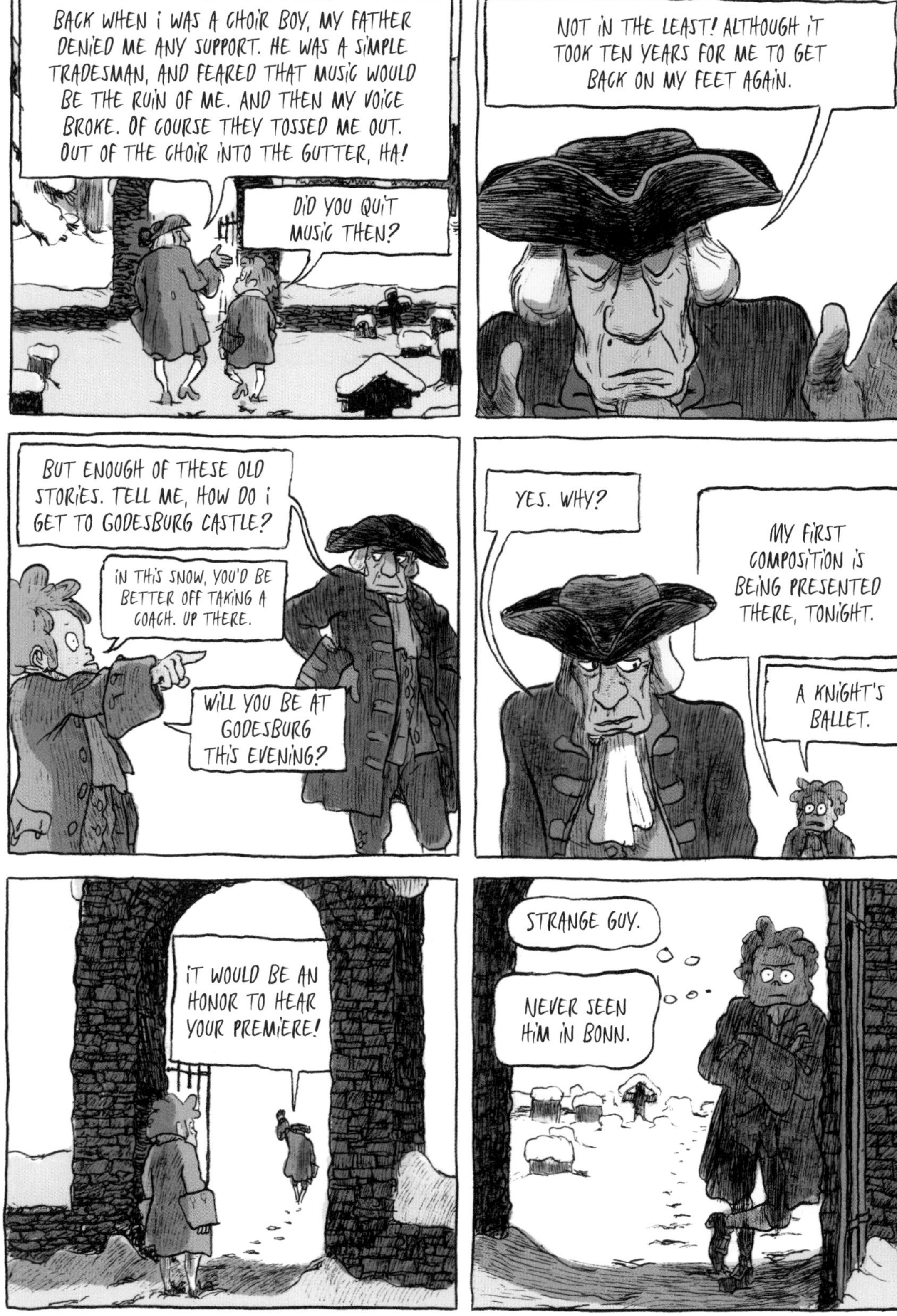
BACK WHEN I WAS A CHOIR BOY, MY FATHER DENIED ME ANY SUPPORT. HE WAS A SIMPLE TRADESMAN, AND FEARED THAT MUSIC WOULD BE THE RUIN OF ME. AND THEN MY VOICE BROKE. OF COURSE THEY TOSSED ME OUT. OUT OF THE CHOIR INTO THE GUTTER, HA!
DID YOU QUIT MUSIC THEN?
NOT IN THE LEAST! ALTHOUGH IT TOOK TEN YEARS FOR ME TO GET BACK ON MY FEET AGAIN.
BUT ENOUGH OF THESE OLD STORIES. TELL ME, HOW DO I GET TO GODESBURG CASTLE?
IN THIS SNOW, YOU'D BE BETTER OFF TAKING A COACH. UP THERE.
WILL YOU BE AT GODESBURG THIS EVENING?
YES. WHY?
MY FIRST COMPOSITION IS BEING PRESENTED THERE, TONIGHT.
A KNIGHT'S BALLET.
IT WOULD BE AN HONOR TO HEAR YOUR PREMIERE!
STRANGE GUY.
NEVER SEEN HIM IN BONN.

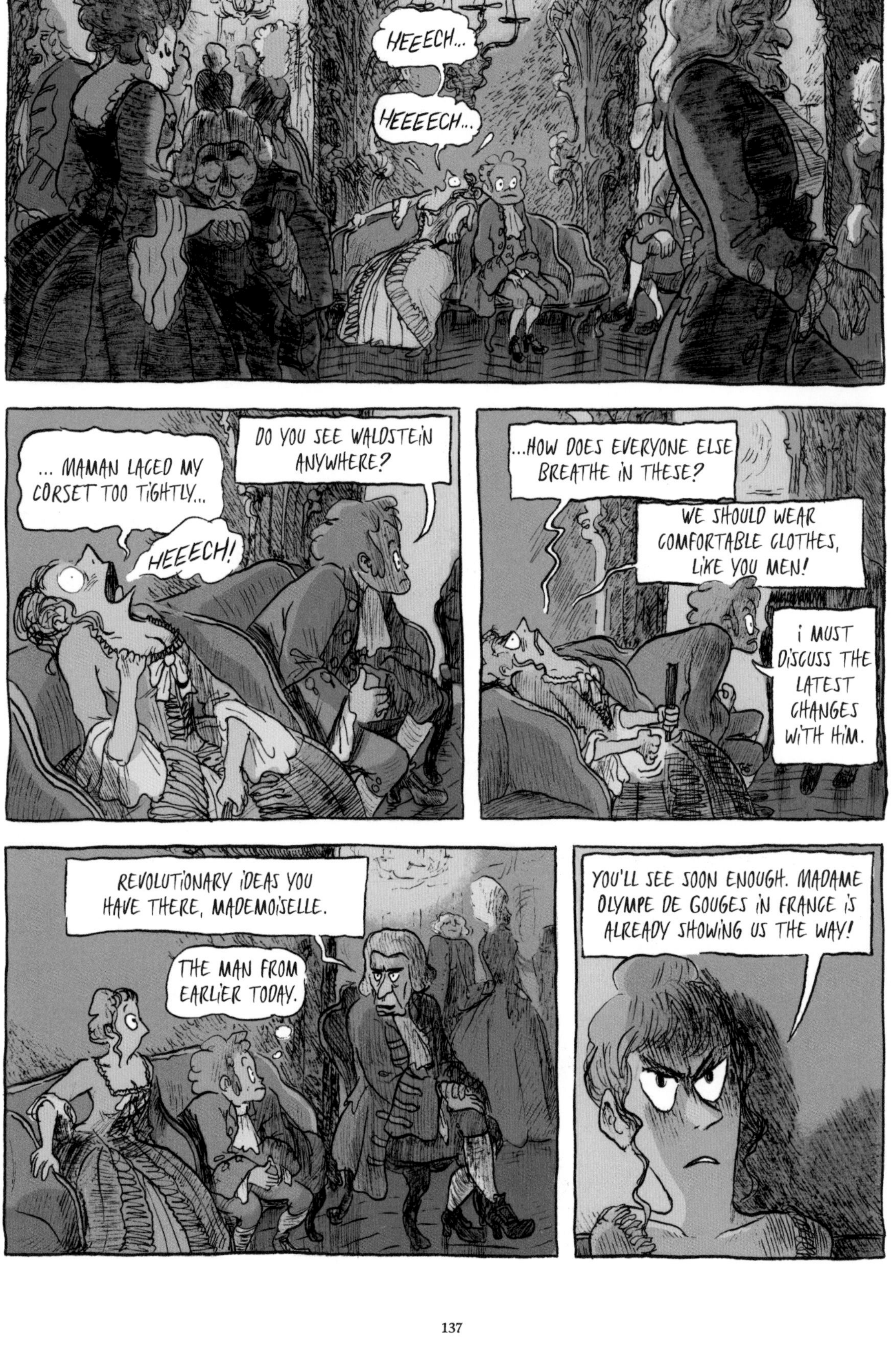
HEEECH...
HEEEECH...
... MAMAN LACED MY CORSET TOO TIGHTLY...
DO YOU SEE WALDSTEIN ANYWHERE?
HEEECH!
...HOW DOES EVERYONE ELSE BREATHE IN THESE?
WE SHOULD WEAR COMFORTABLE CLOTHES, LIKE YOU MEN!
I MUST DISCUSS THE LATEST CHANGES WITH HIM.
REVOLUTIONARY IDEAS YOU HAVE THERE, MADEMOISELLE.
THE MAN FROM EARLIER TODAY.
YOU'LL SEE SOON ENOUGH. MADAME OLYMPE DE GOUGES IN FRANCE IS ALREADY SHOWING US THE WAY!

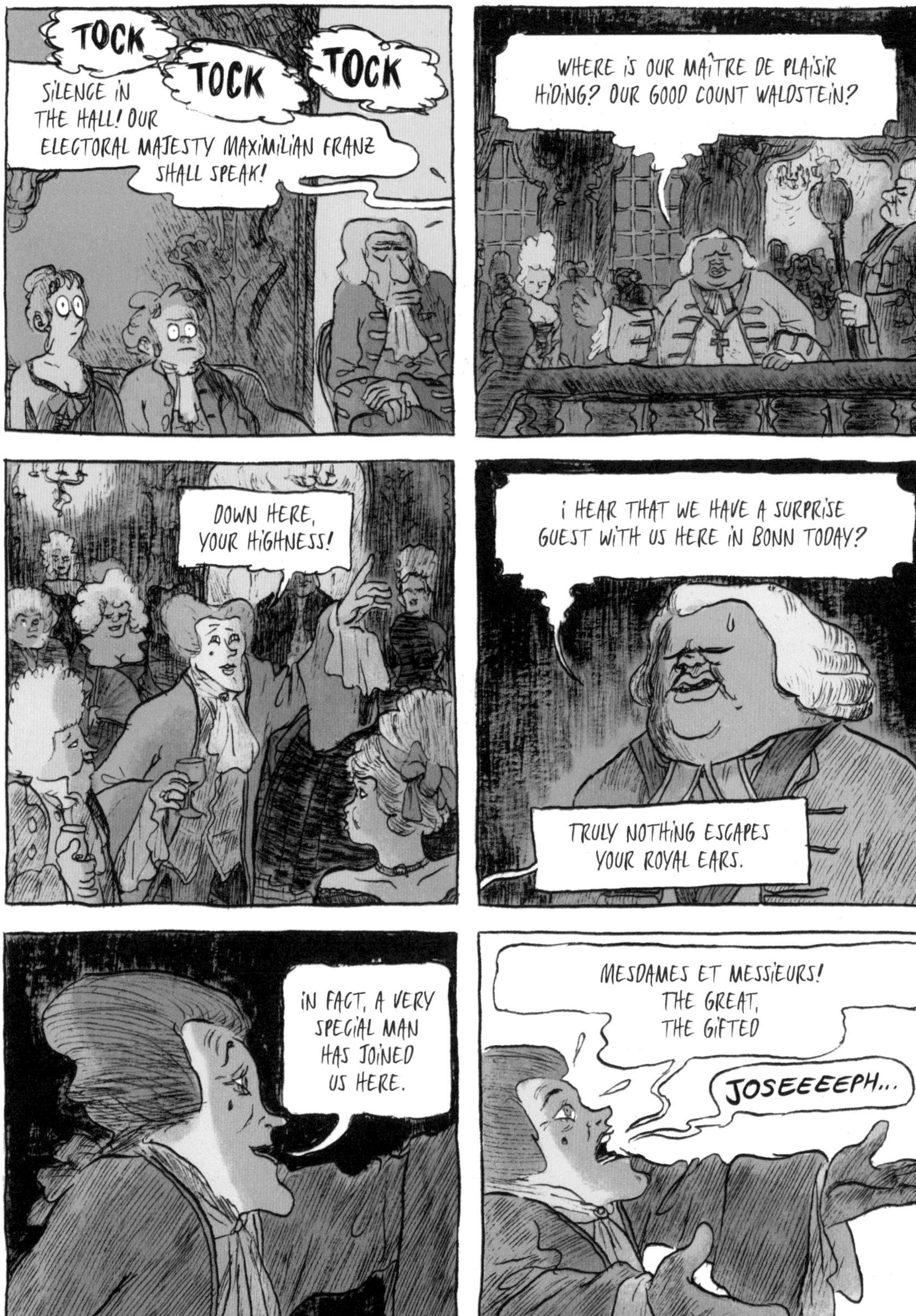
TOCK
TOCK
TOCK
SILENCE IN THE HALL! OUR ELECTORAL MAJESTY MAXIMILIAN FRANZ SHALL SPEAK!
WHERE IS OUR MAÎTRE DE PLAISIR HIDING? OUR GOOD COUNT WALDSTEIN?
DOWN HERE, YOUR HIGHNESS!
I HEAR THAT WE HAVE A SURPRISE GUEST WITH US HERE IN BONN TODAY?
TRULY NOTHING ESCAPES YOUR ROYAL EARS.
IN FACT, A VERY SPECIAL MAN HAS JOINED US HERE.
MESDAMES ET MESSIEURS! THE GREAT, THE GIFTED
JOSEEEEPH...

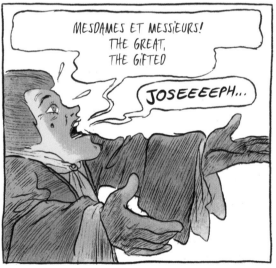

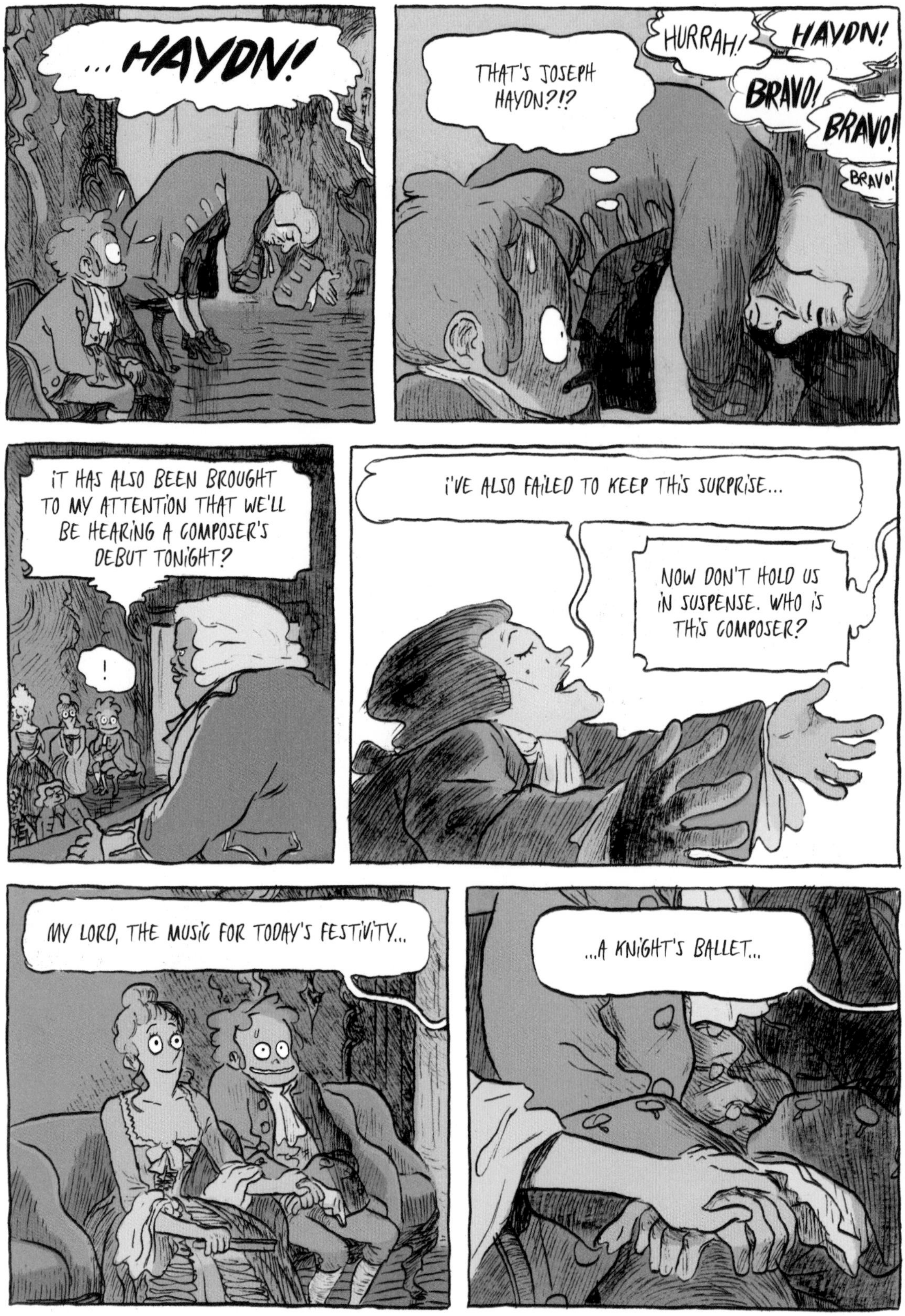
...HAYDN!
THAT'S JOSEPH HAYDN?!?
HURRAH!
HAYDN!
BRAVO!
BRAVO!
BRAVO!
IT HAS ALSO BEEN BROUGHT TO MY ATTENTION THAT WE'LL BE HEARING A COMPOSER'S DEBUT TONIGHT?
!
I'VE ALSO FAILED TO KEEP THIS SURPRISE...
NOW DON'T HOLD US IN SUSPENSE. WHO IS THIS COMPOSER?
MY LORD, THE MUSIC FOR TODAY'S FESTIVITY...
...A KNIGHT'S BALLET...

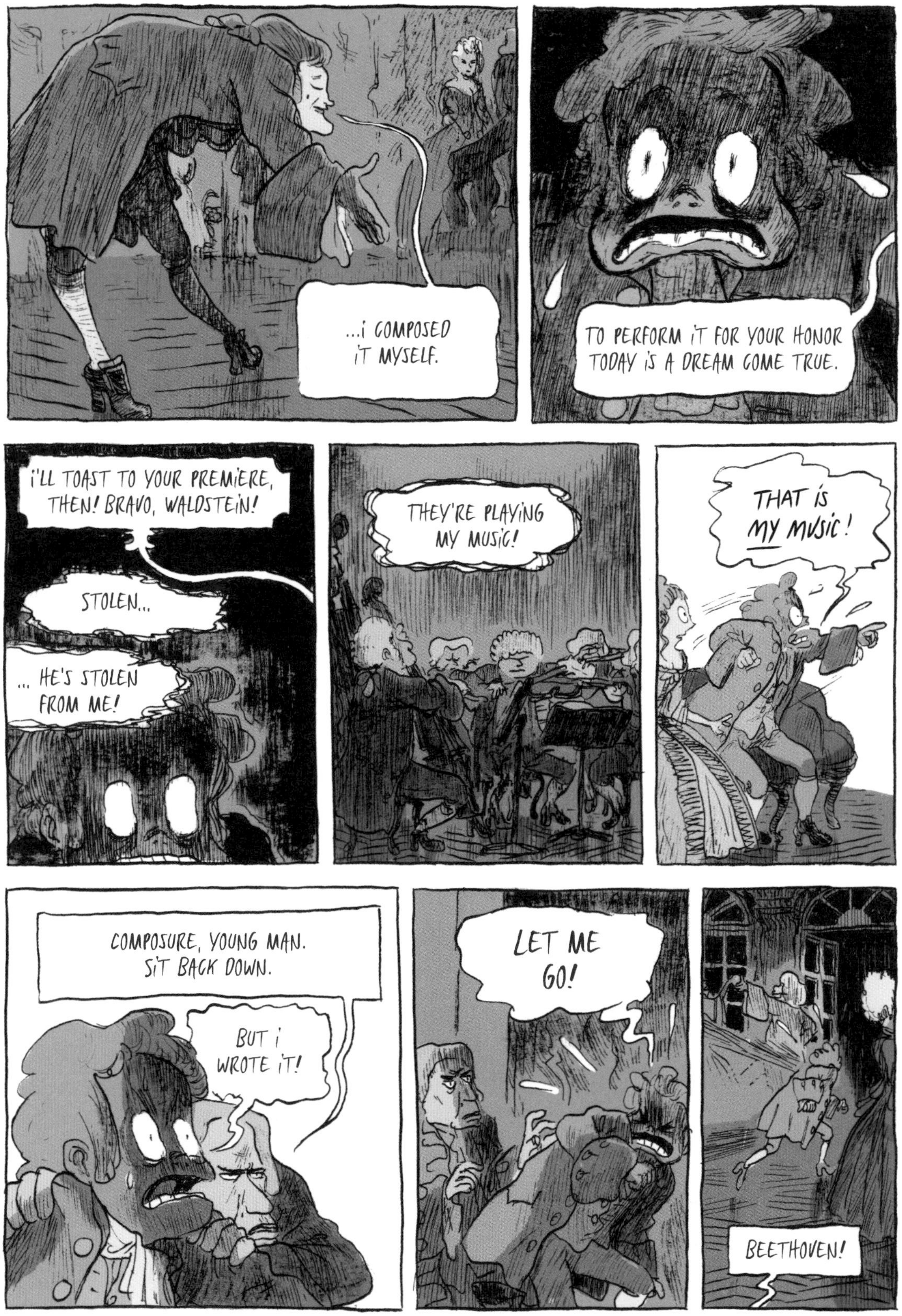
...i COMPOSED iT MYSELF.
TO PERFORM iT FOR YOUR HONOR TODAY iS A DREAM COME TRUE.
i'LL TOAST TO YOUR PREMiERE, THEN! BRAVO, WALDSTEiN!
STOLEN...
... HE'S STOLEN FROM ME!
THEY'RE PLAYiNG MY MUSiC!
THAT iS MY MUSiC!
COMPOSURE, YOUNG MAN. SiT BACK DOWN.
BUT i WROTE iT!
LET ME GO!
BEETHOVEN!

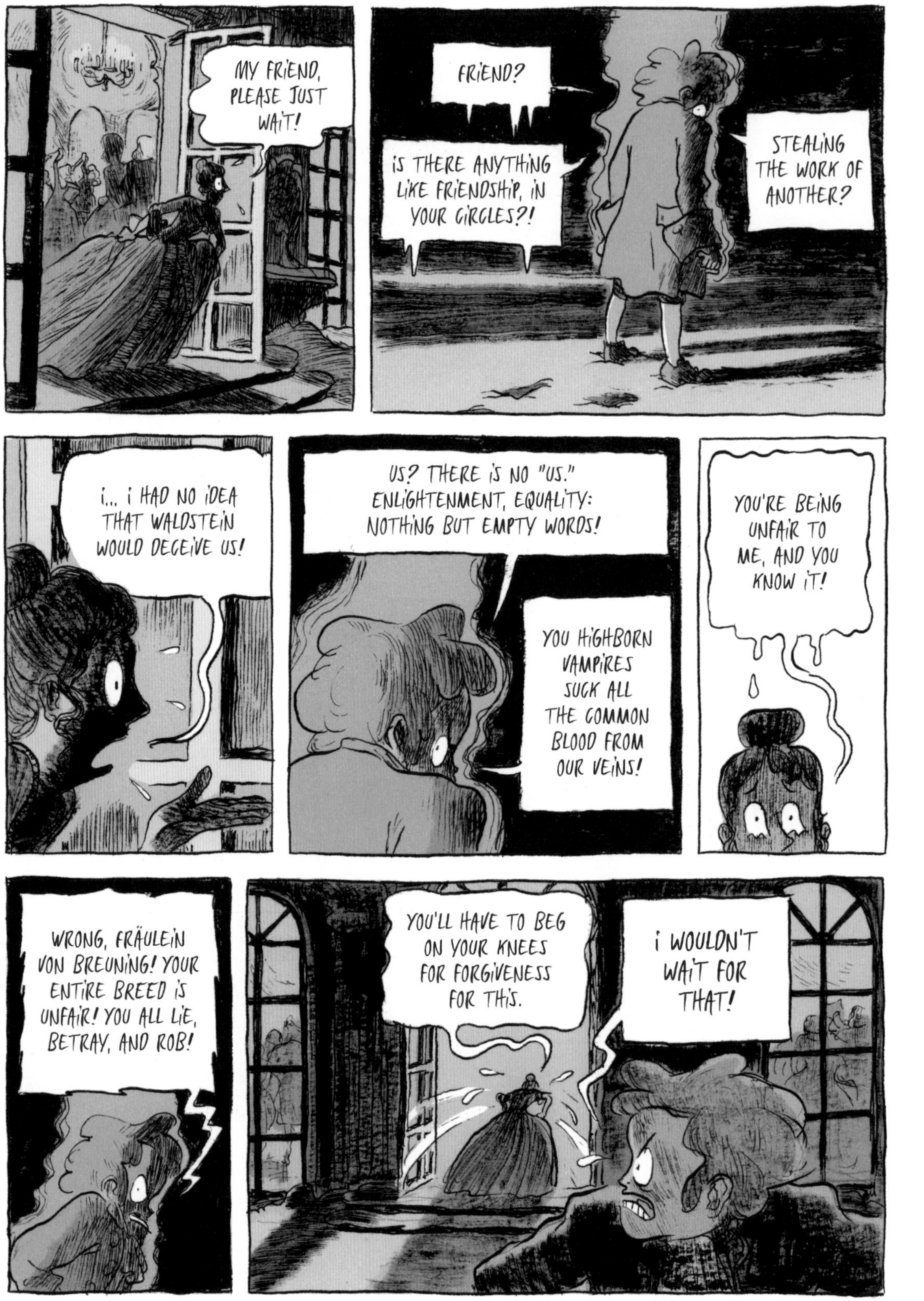
MY FRIEND, PLEASE JUST WAIT!
FRIEND?
IS THERE ANYTHING LIKE FRIENDSHIP, IN YOUR CIRCLES?!
STEALING THE WORK OF ANOTHER?
I... I HAD NO IDEA THAT WALDSTEIN WOULD DECEIVE US!
US? THERE IS NO "US." ENLIGHTENMENT, EQUALITY: NOTHING BUT EMPTY WORDS!
YOU HIGHBORN VAMPIRES SUCK ALL THE COMMON BLOOD FROM OUR VEINS!
YOU'RE BEING UNFAIR TO ME, AND YOU KNOW IT!
WRONG, FRÄULEIN VON BREUNING! YOUR ENTIRE BREED IS UNFAIR! YOU ALL LIE, BETRAY, AND ROB!
YOU'LL HAVE TO BEG ON YOUR KNEES FOR FORGIVENESS FOR THIS.
I WOULDN'T WAIT FOR THAT!

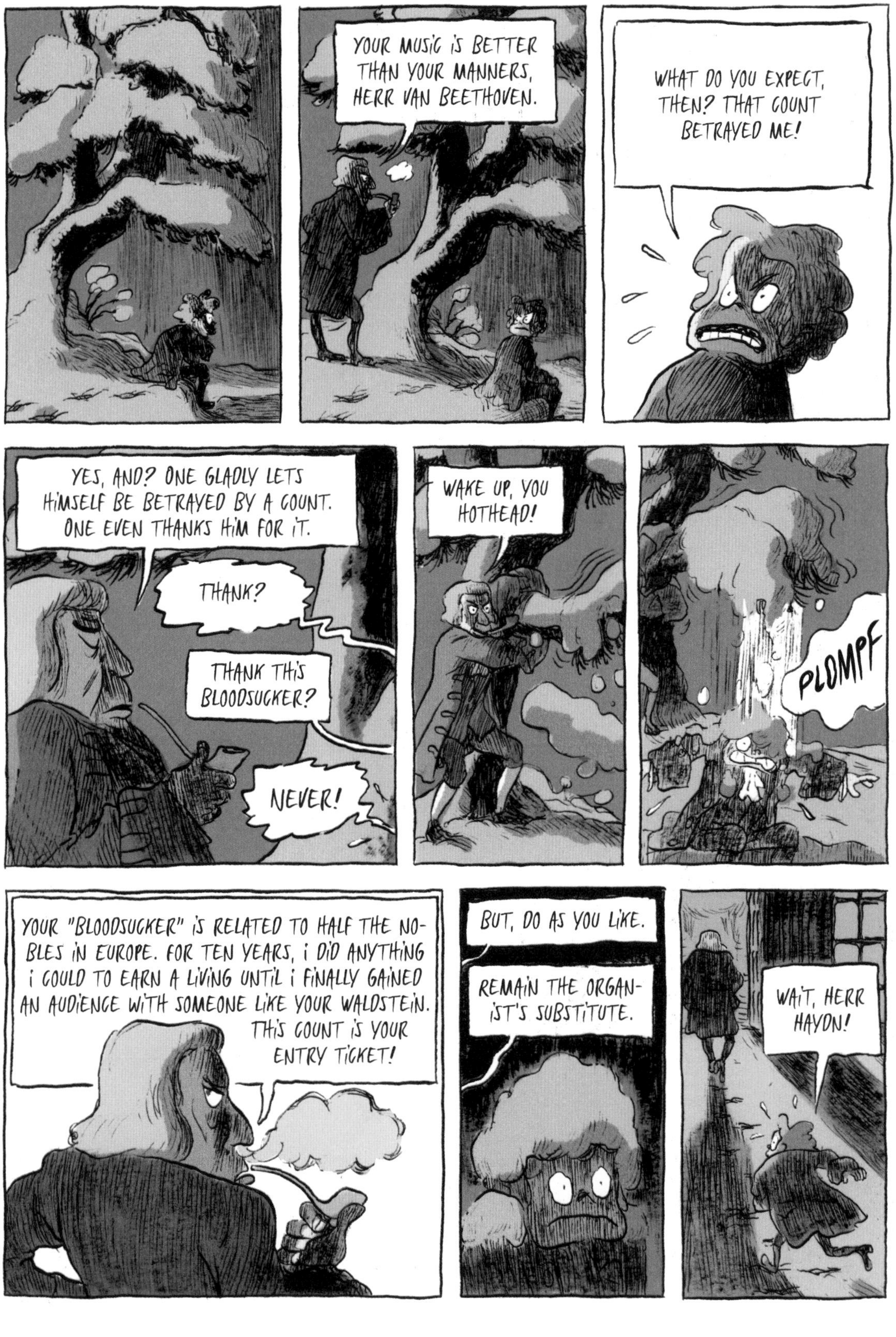
YOUR MUSIC IS BETTER THAN YOUR MANNERS, HERR VAN BEETHOVEN.
WHAT DO YOU EXPECT, THEN? THAT COUNT BETRAYED ME!
YES, AND? ONE GLADLY LETS HIMSELF BE BETRAYED BY A COUNT. ONE EVEN THANKS HIM FOR IT.
THANK?
THANK THIS BLOODSUCKER?
NEVER!
WAKE UP, YOU HOTHEAD!
PLOMPF
YOUR "BLOODSUCKER" IS RELATED TO HALF THE NOBLES IN EUROPE. FOR TEN YEARS, I DID ANYTHING I COULD TO EARN A LIVING UNTIL I FINALLY GAINED AN AUDIENCE WITH SOMEONE LIKE YOUR WALDSTEIN. THIS COUNT IS YOUR ENTRY TICKET!
BUT, DO AS YOU LIKE.
REMAIN THE ORGANIST'S SUBSTITUTE.
WAIT, HERR HAYDN!

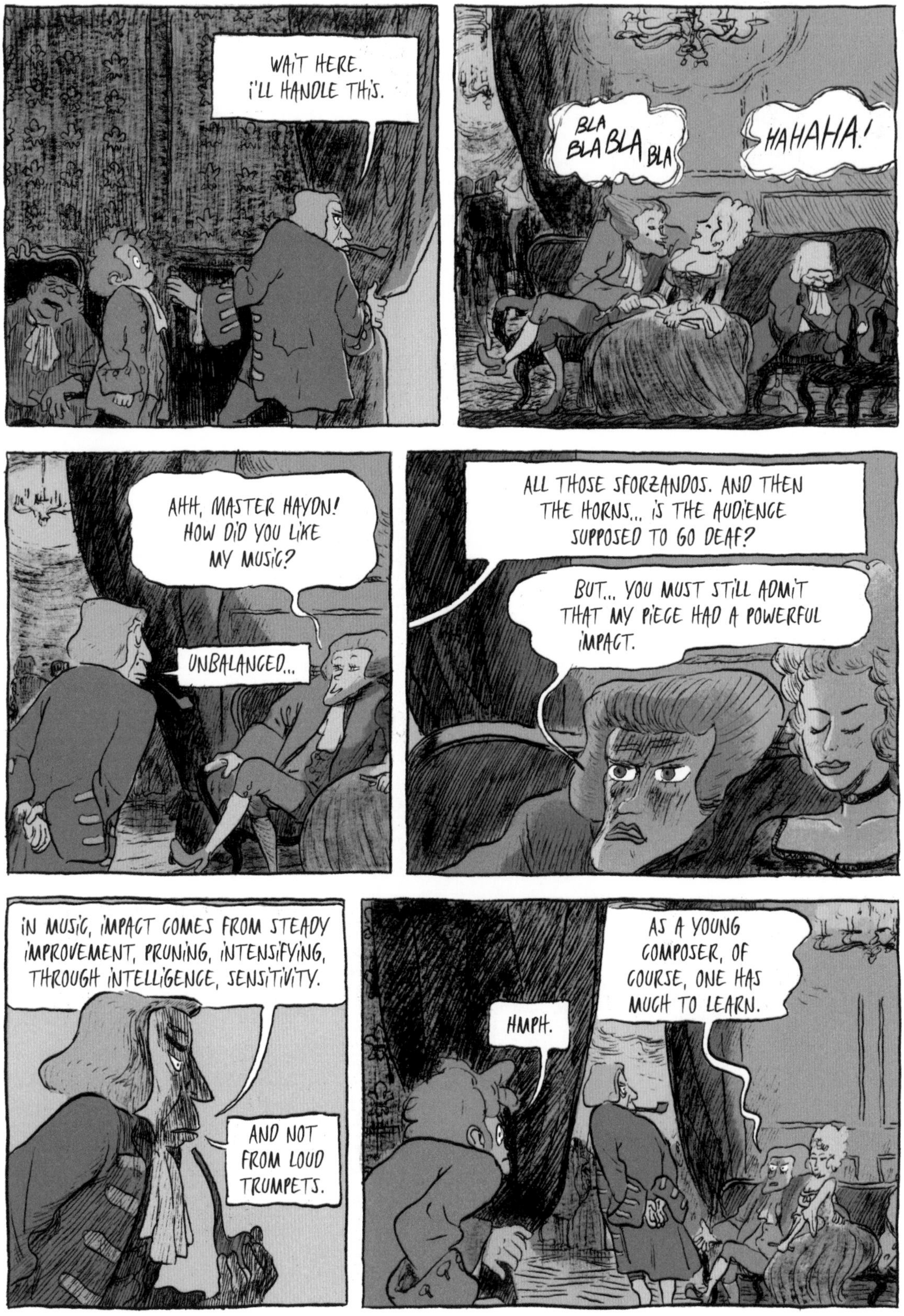
WAIT HERE. I'LL HANDLE THIS.
BLA BLA BLA BLA BLA
HAHAHA!
AHH, MASTER HAYDN! HOW DID YOU LIKE MY MUSIC?
UNBALANCED...
ALL THOSE SFORZANDOS. AND THEN THE HORNS... IS THE AUDIENCE SUPPOSED TO GO DEAF?
BUT... YOU MUST STILL ADMIT THAT MY PIECE HAD A POWERFUL IMPACT.
IN MUSIC, IMPACT COMES FROM STEADY IMPROVEMENT, PRUNING, INTENSIFYING, THROUGH INTELLIGENCE, SENSITIVITY.
AND NOT FROM LOUD TRUMPETS.
HMPH.
AS A YOUNG COMPOSER, OF COURSE, ONE HAS MUCH TO LEARN.

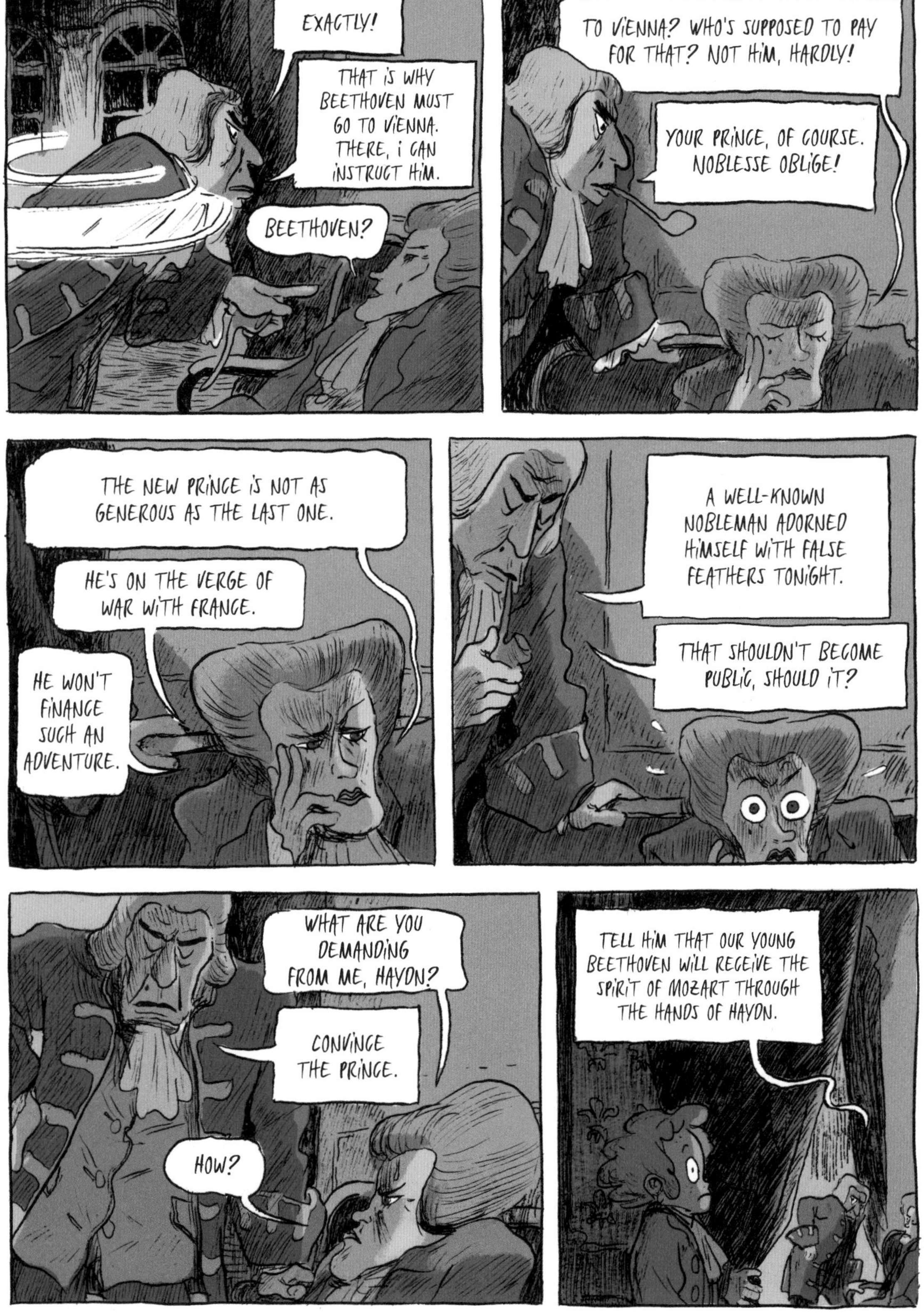
EXACTLY!
THAT IS WHY BEETHOVEN MUST GO TO VIENNA. THERE, I CAN INSTRUCT HIM.
BEETHOVEN?
TO VIENNA? WHO'S SUPPOSED TO PAY FOR THAT? NOT HIM, HARDLY!
YOUR PRINCE, OF COURSE. NOBLESSE OBLIGE!
THE NEW PRINCE IS NOT AS GENEROUS AS THE LAST ONE.
HE'S ON THE VERGE OF WAR WITH FRANCE.
HE WON'T FINANCE SUCH AN ADVENTURE.
A WELL-KNOWN NOBLEMAN ADORNED HIMSELF WITH FALSE FEATHERS TONIGHT.
THAT SHOULDN'T BECOME PUBLIC, SHOULD IT?
WHAT ARE YOU DEMANDING FROM ME, HAYDN?
CONVINCE THE PRINCE.
HOW?
TELL HIM THAT OUR YOUNG BEETHOVEN WILL RECEIVE THE SPIRIT OF MOZART THROUGH THE HANDS OF HAYDN.

1792

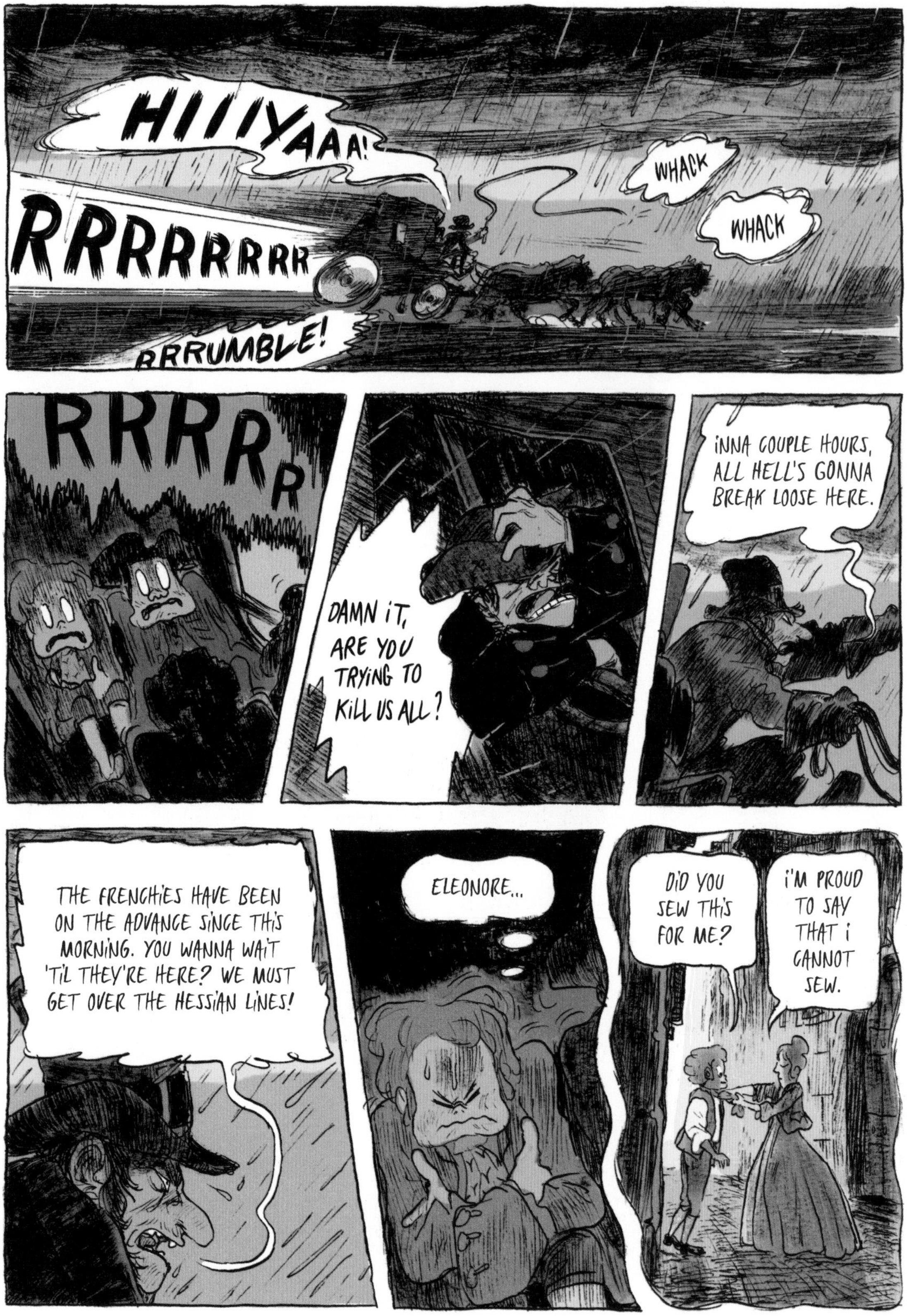

HIIIYAAA!
RRRRRRRRR
WHACK
WHACK
RRRUMBLE!
RRRRRR
DAMN IT, ARE YOU TRYING TO KILL US ALL?
INNA COUPLE HOURS, ALL HELL'S GONNA BREAK LOOSE HERE.
THE FRENCHIES HAVE BEEN ON THE ADVANCE SINCE THIS MORNING. YOU WANNA WAIT 'TIL THEY'RE HERE? WE MUST GET OVER THE HESSIAN LINES!
ELEONORE...
DID YOU SEW THIS FOR ME?
I'M PROUD TO SAY THAT I CANNOT SEW.

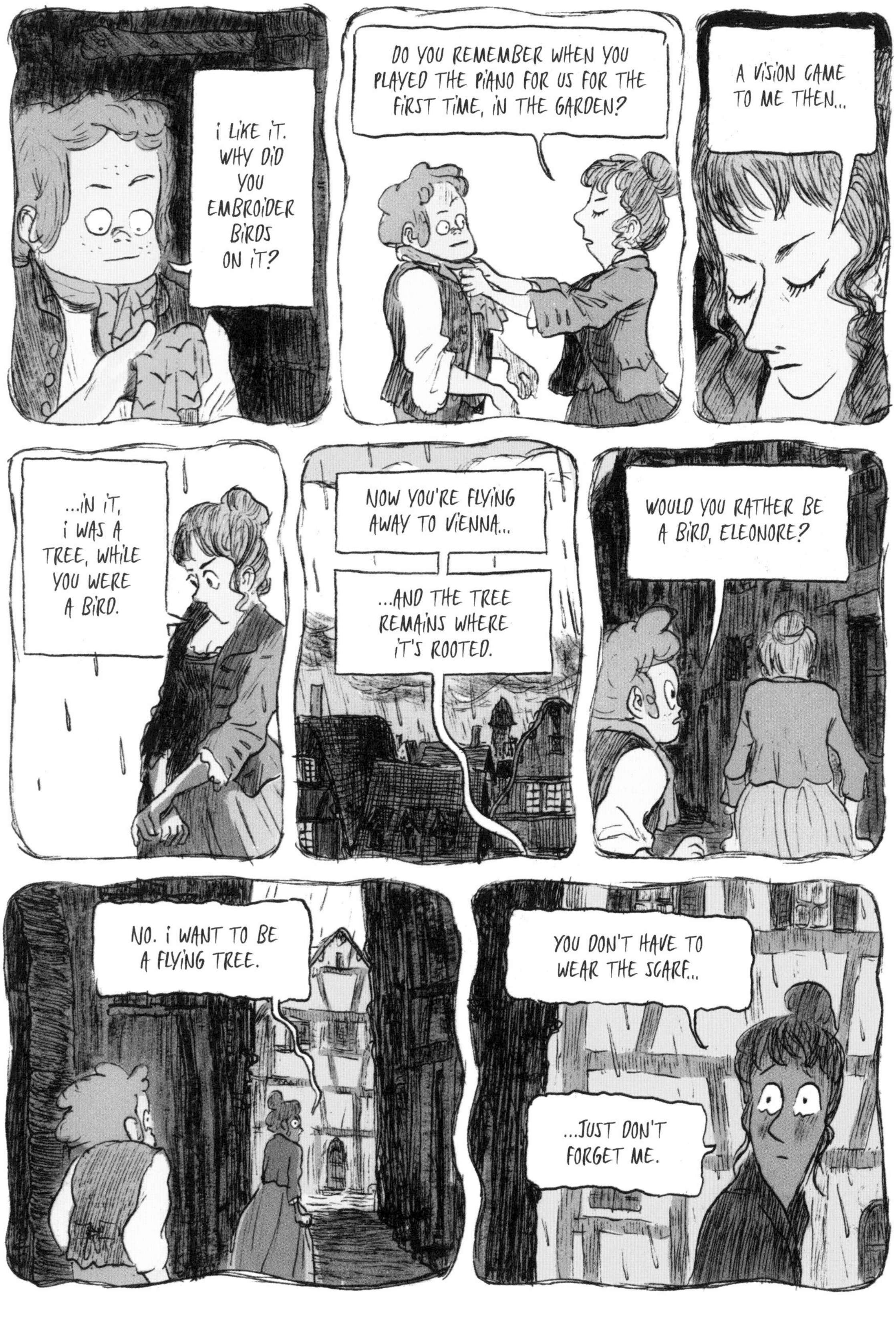
I LIKE IT. WHY DID YOU EMBROIDER BIRDS ON IT?
DO YOU REMEMBER WHEN YOU PLAYED THE PIANO FOR US FOR THE FIRST TIME, IN THE GARDEN?
A VISION CAME TO ME THEN...
...IN IT, I WAS A TREE, WHILE YOU WERE A BIRD.
NOW YOU'RE FLYING AWAY TO VIENNA...
...AND THE TREE REMAINS WHERE IT'S ROOTED.
WOULD YOU RATHER BE A BIRD, ELEONORE?
NO. I WANT TO BE A FLYING TREE.
YOU DON'T HAVE TO WEAR THE SCARF...
...JUST DON'T FORGET ME.

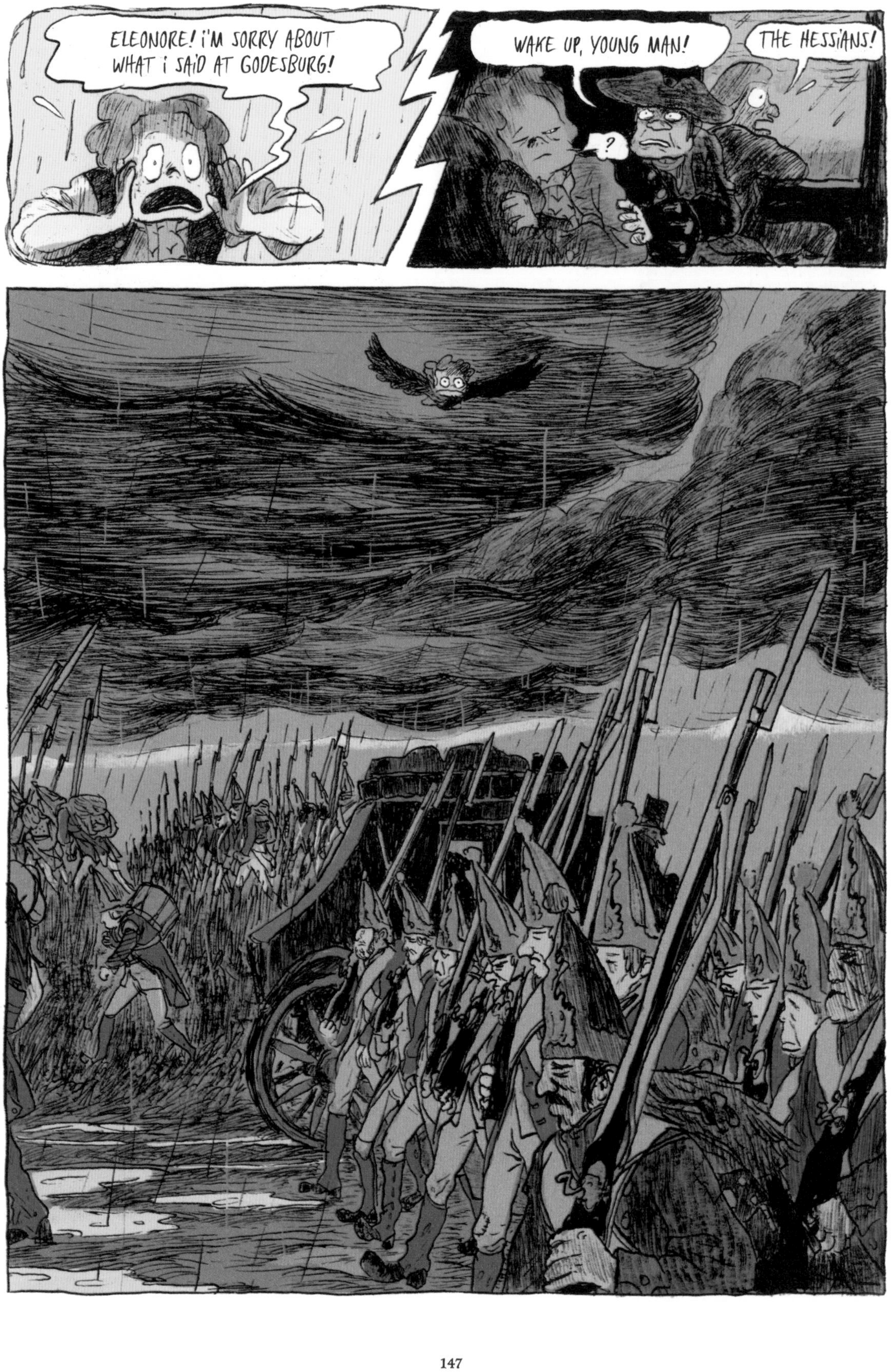
ELEONORE! I'M SORRY ABOUT WHAT I SAID AT GODESBURG!
WAKE UP, YOUNG MAN!
?
THE HESSIANS!

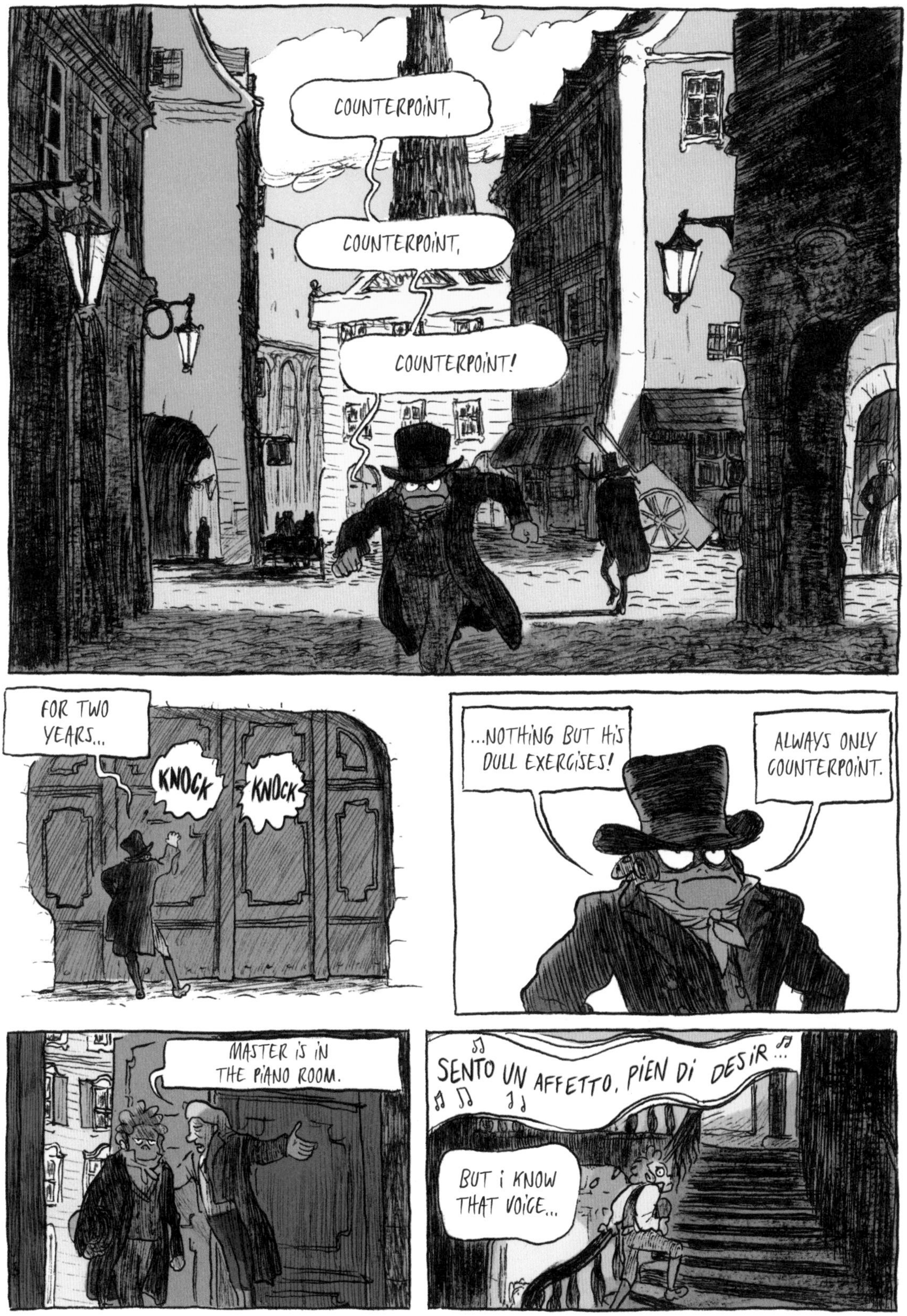
COUNTERPOINT,
COUNTERPOINT,
COUNTERPOINT!
FOR TWO YEARS...
KNOCK
KNOCK
...NOTHING BUT HIS DULL EXERCISES!
ALWAYS ONLY COUNTERPOINT.
MASTER IS IN THE PIANO ROOM.
SENTO UN AFFETTO, PIEN DI DESIR...
BUT I KNOW THAT VOICE...

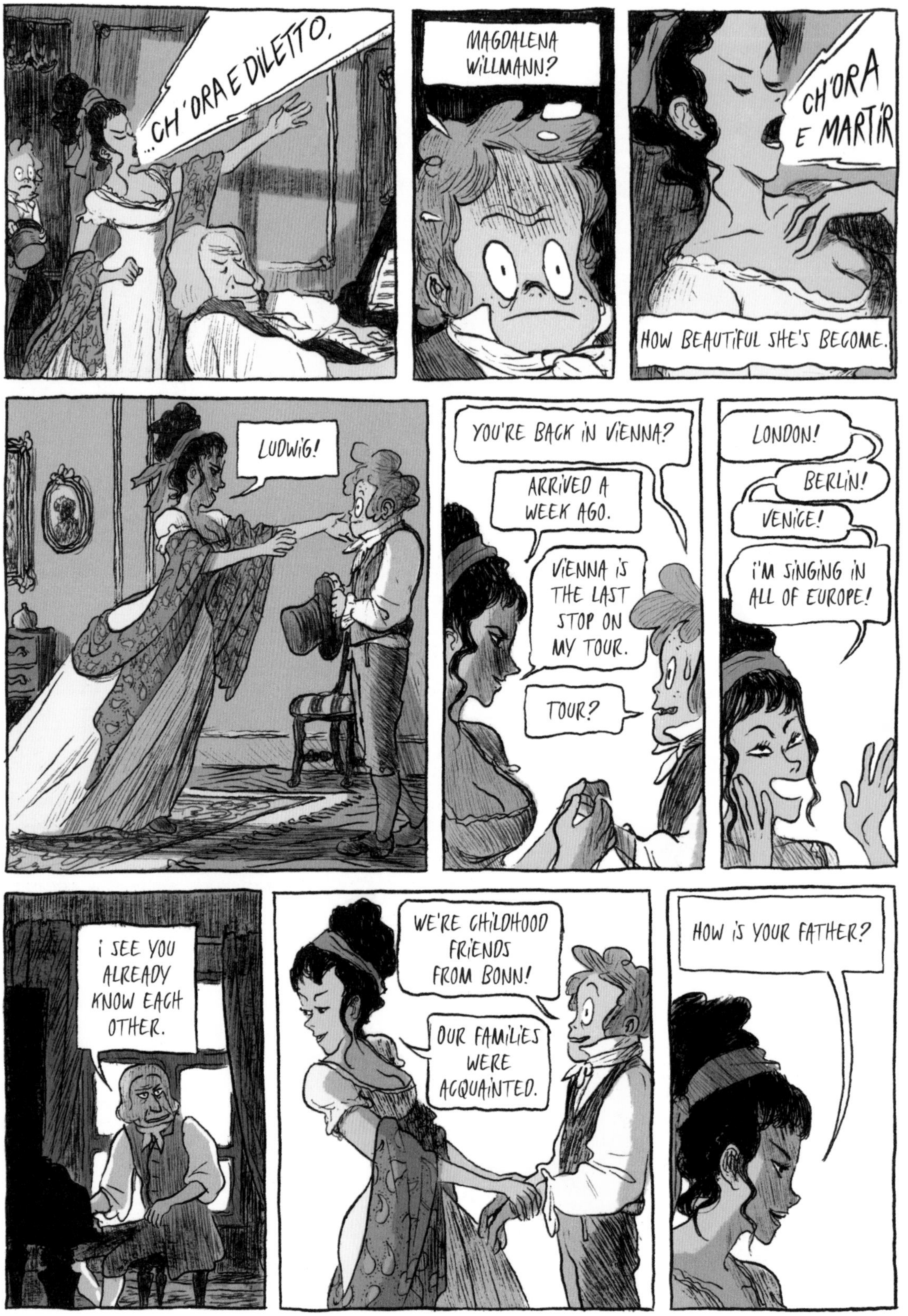
...CH'ORA E DILETTO,
MAGDALENA WILLMANN?
CH'ORA E MARTIR
HOW BEAUTIFUL SHE'S BECOME.
LUDWIG!
YOU'RE BACK IN VIENNA?
ARRIVED A WEEK AGO.
VIENNA IS THE LAST STOP ON MY TOUR.
TOUR?
LONDON!
BERLIN!
VENICE!
I'M SINGING IN ALL OF EUROPE!
I SEE YOU ALREADY KNOW EACH OTHER.
WE'RE CHILDHOOD FRIENDS FROM BONN!
OUR FAMILIES WERE ACQUAINTED.
HOW IS YOUR FATHER?

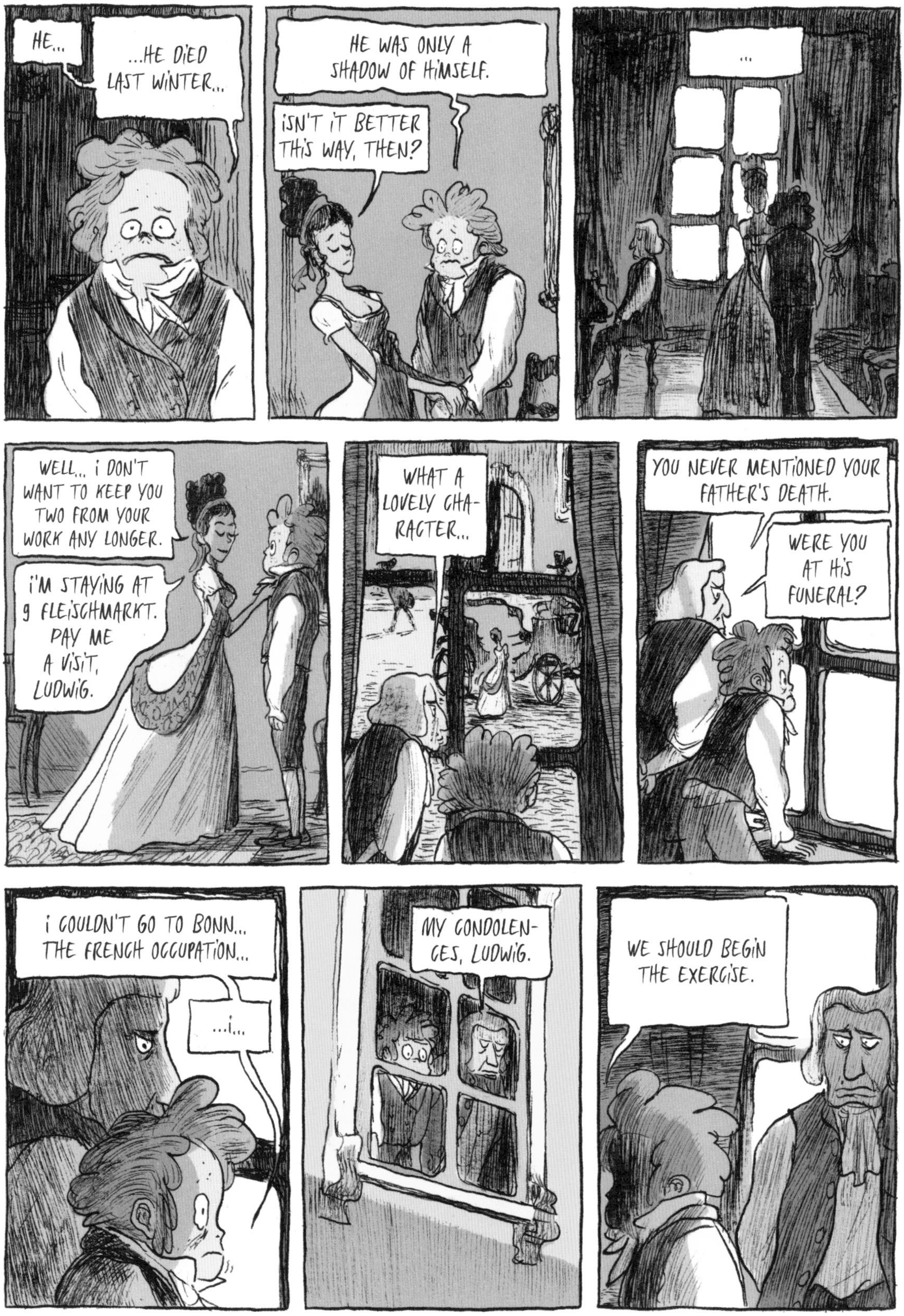
HE...
...HE DIED LAST WINTER...
HE WAS ONLY A SHADOW OF HIMSELF.
ISN'T IT BETTER THIS WAY, THEN?
...
WELL... I DON'T WANT TO KEEP YOU TWO FROM YOUR WORK ANY LONGER.
I'M STAYING AT 9 FLEISCHMARKT. PAY ME A VISIT, LUDWIG.
WHAT A LOVELY CHA-RACTER...
YOU NEVER MENTIONED YOUR FATHER'S DEATH.
WERE YOU AT HIS FUNERAL?
I COULDN'T GO TO BONN... THE FRENCH OCCUPATION...
...I...
MY CONDOLEN-CES, LUDWIG.
WE SHOULD BEGIN THE EXERCISE.

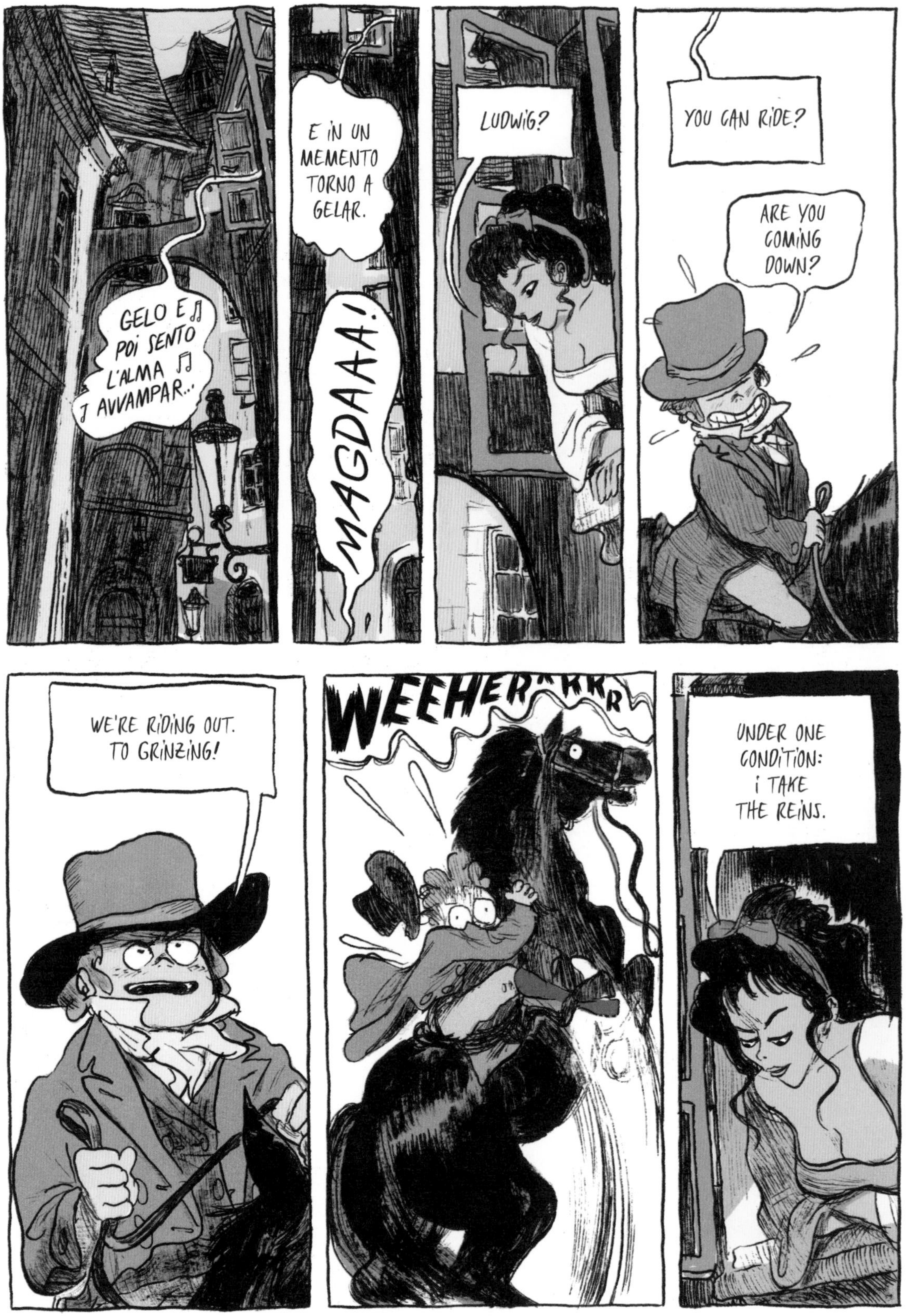
GELO E ♫ POI SENTO L'ALMA ♫ J AVVAMPAR...
E IN UN MEMENTO TORNO A GELAR.
MAGDAAA!
LUDWIG?
YOU CAN RIDE?
ARE YOU COMING DOWN?
WE'RE RIDING OUT. TO GRINZING!
WEEHERRRRR
UNDER ONE CONDITION: I TAKE THE REINS.

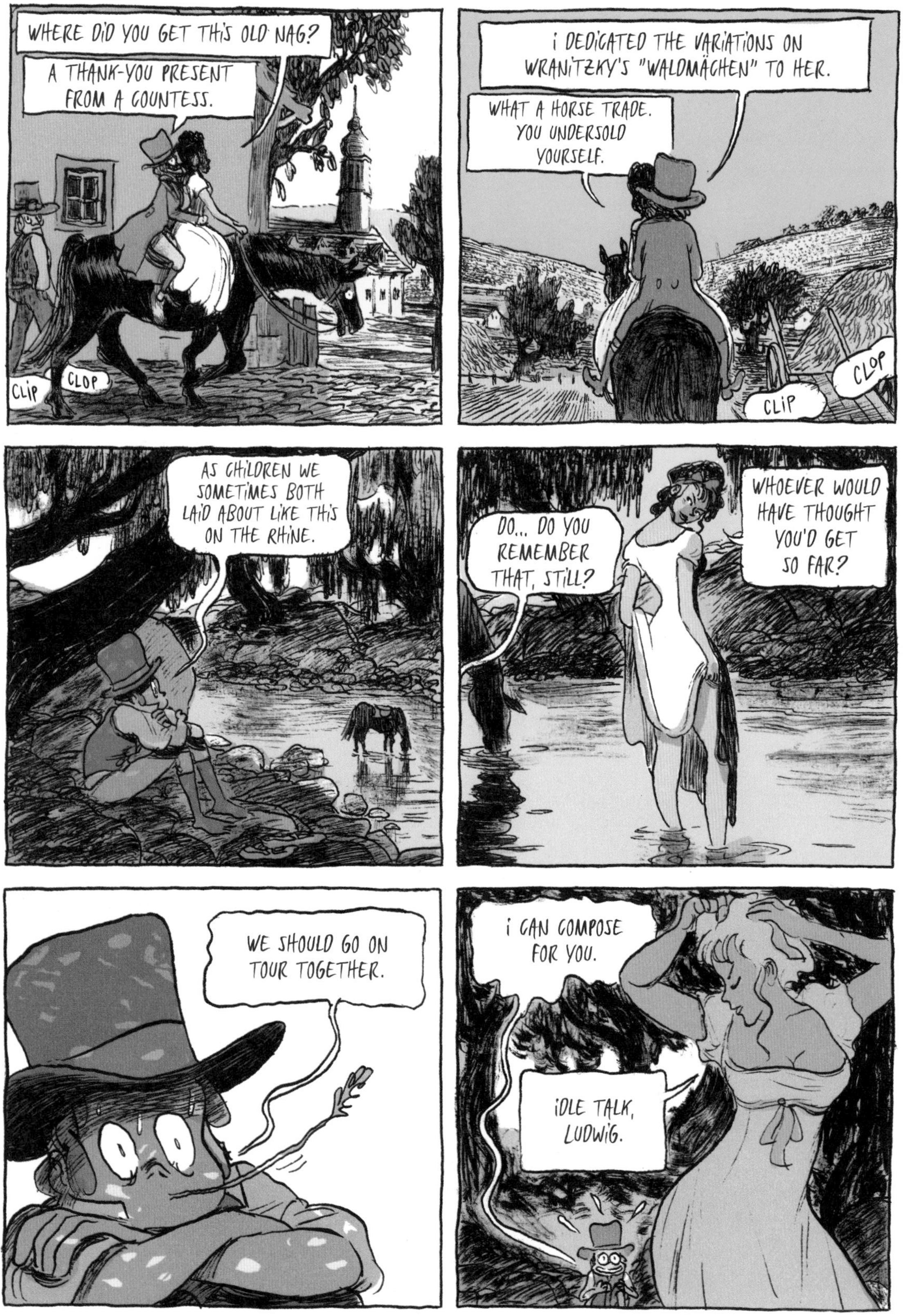
WHERE DID YOU GET THIS OLD NAG?
A THANK-YOU PRESENT FROM A COUNTESS.
CLIP
CLOP
I DEDICATED THE VARIATIONS ON WRANITZKY'S "WALDMÄCHEN" TO HER.
WHAT A HORSE TRADE. YOU UNDERSOLD YOURSELF.
CLIP
CLOP
AS CHILDREN WE SOMETIMES BOTH LAID ABOUT LIKE THIS ON THE RHINE.
DO... DO YOU REMEMBER THAT, STILL?
WHOEVER WOULD HAVE THOUGHT YOU'D GET SO FAR?
WE SHOULD GO ON TOUR TOGETHER.
I CAN COMPOSE FOR YOU.
IDLE TALK, LUDWIG.

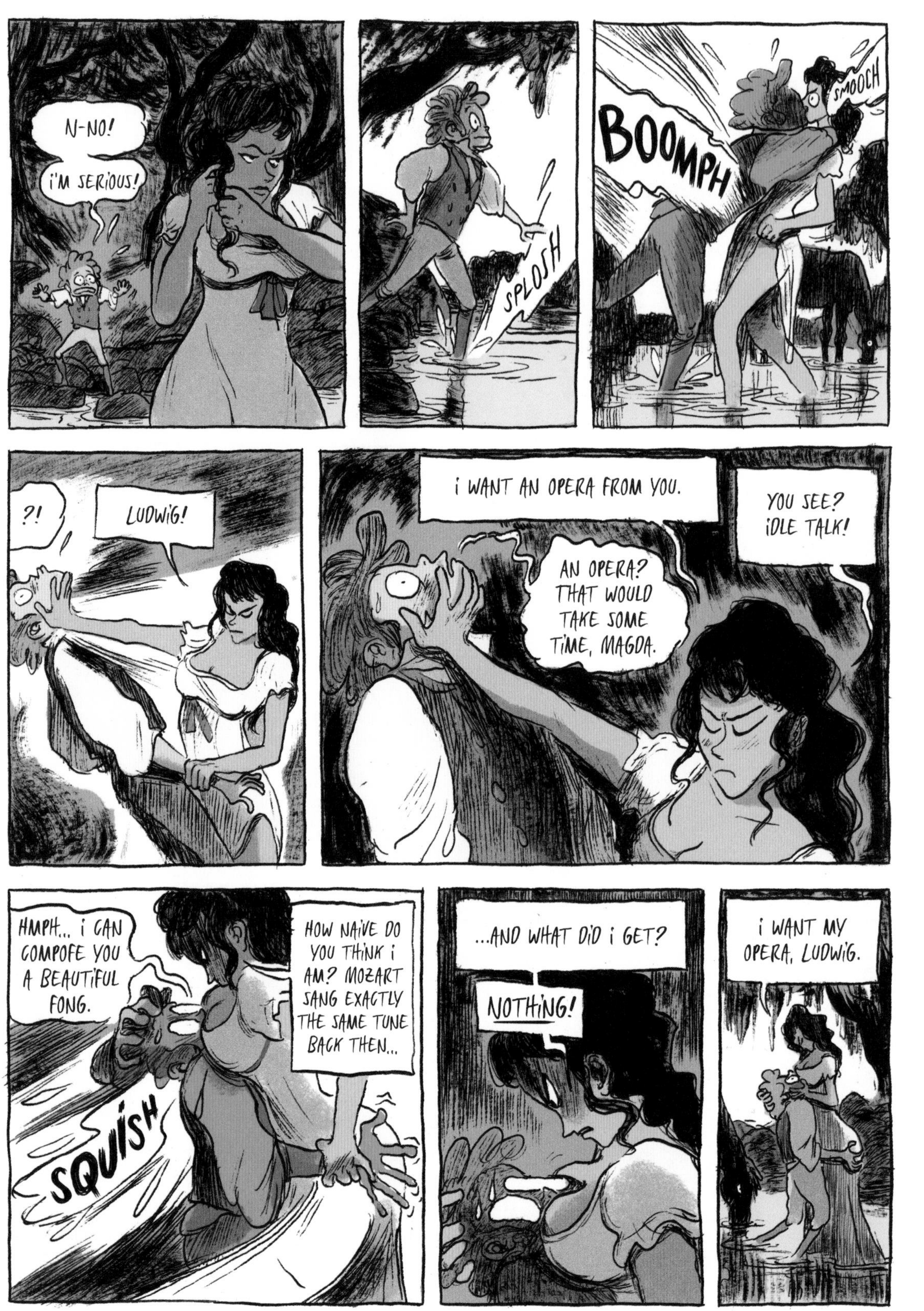
N-NO!
i'M SERiOUS!
SPLOSH
BOOMPH
SMOOCH
?!
LUDWiG!
i WANT AN OPERA FROM YOU.
AN OPERA? THAT WOULD TAKE SOME TiME, MAGDA.
YOU SEE? iDLE TALK!
HMPH... i CAN COMPOFE YOU A BEAUTiFUL FONG.
HOW NAiVE DO YOU THiNK i AM? MOZART SANG EXACTLY THE SAME TUNE BACK THEN...
SQUiSH
...AND WHAT DiD i GET?
NOTHiNG!
i WANT MY OPERA, LUDWiG.

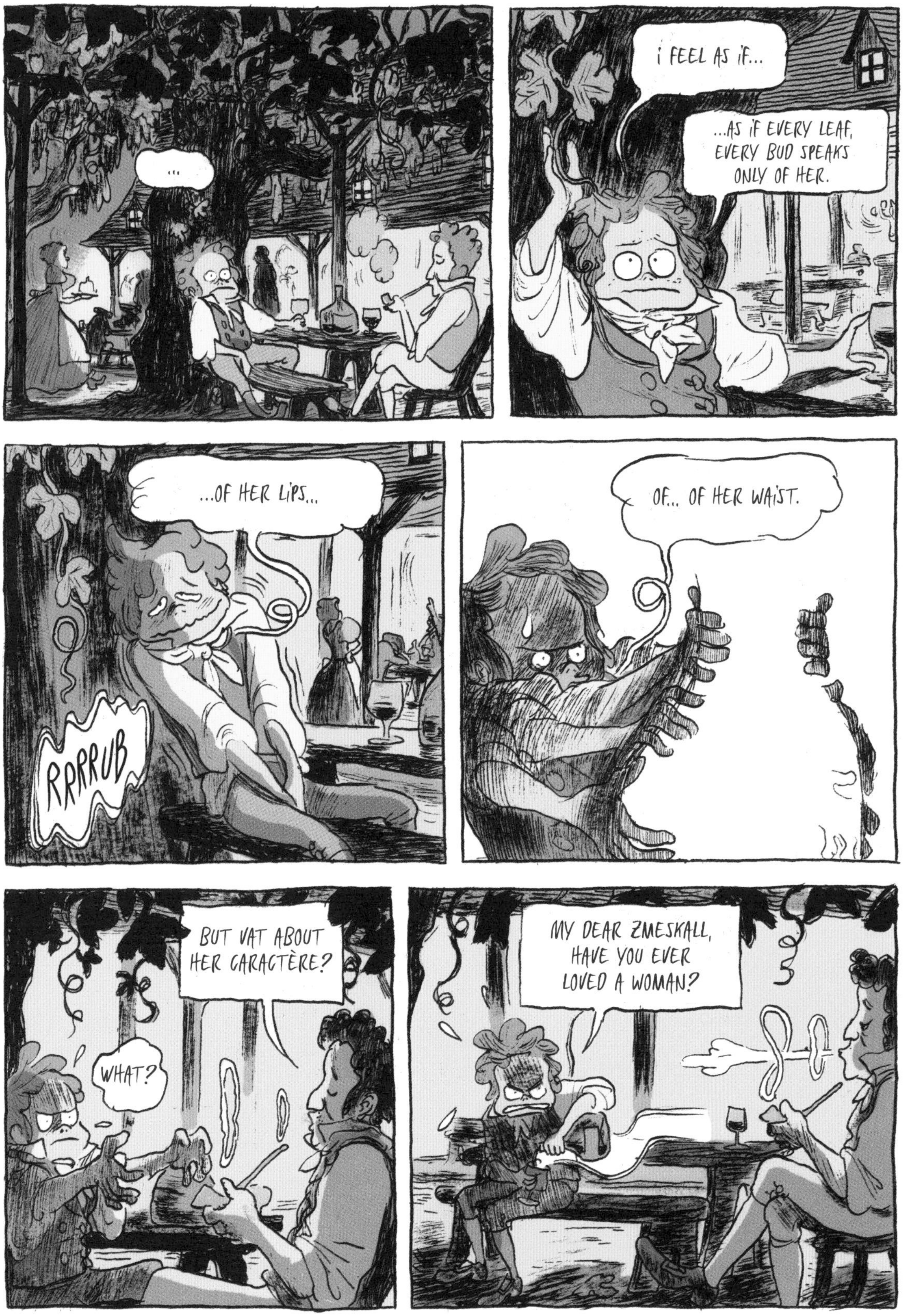
...
I FEEL AS IF...
...AS IF EVERY LEAF, EVERY BUD SPEAKS ONLY OF HER.
...OF HER LIPS...
RRRRUB
OF... OF HER WAIST.
BUT VAT ABOUT HER CARACTÈRE?
WHAT?
MY DEAR ZMESKALL, HAVE YOU EVER LOVED A WOMAN?

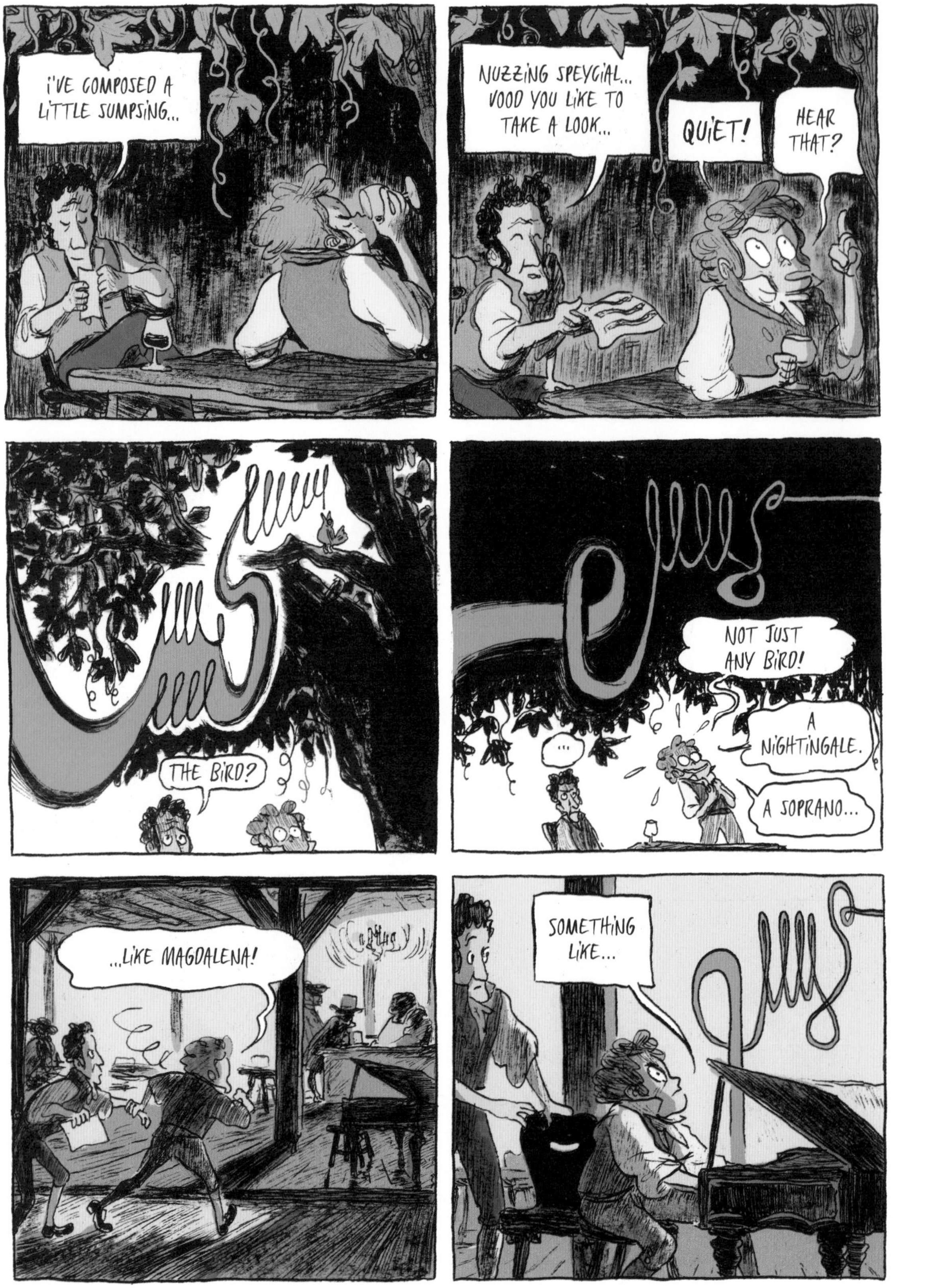
I'VE COMPOSED A LITTLE SUMPSING...
NUZZING SPEYCIAL... VOOD YOU LIKE TO TAKE A LOOK...
QUIET!
HEAR THAT?
THE BIRD?
NOT JUST ANY BIRD!
...
A NIGHTINGALE.
A SOPRANO...
...LIKE MAGDALENA!
SOMETHING LIKE...

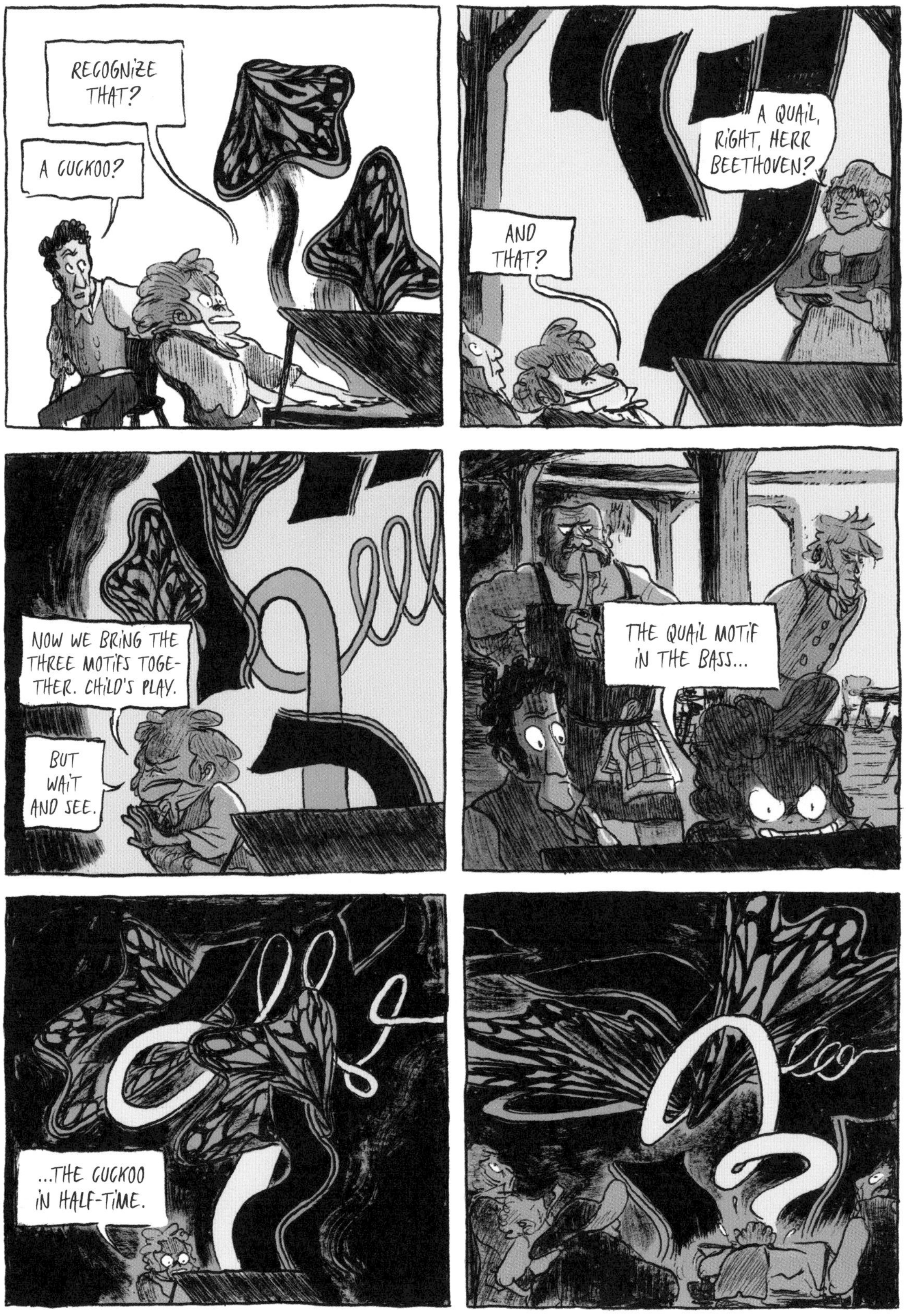
RECOGNIZE THAT?
A CUCKOO?
A QUAIL, RIGHT, HERR BEETHOVEN?
AND THAT?
NOW WE BRING THE THREE MOTIFS TOGETHER. CHILD'S PLAY.
BUT WAIT AND SEE.
THE QUAIL MOTIF IN THE BASS...
...THE CUCKOO IN HALF-TIME.

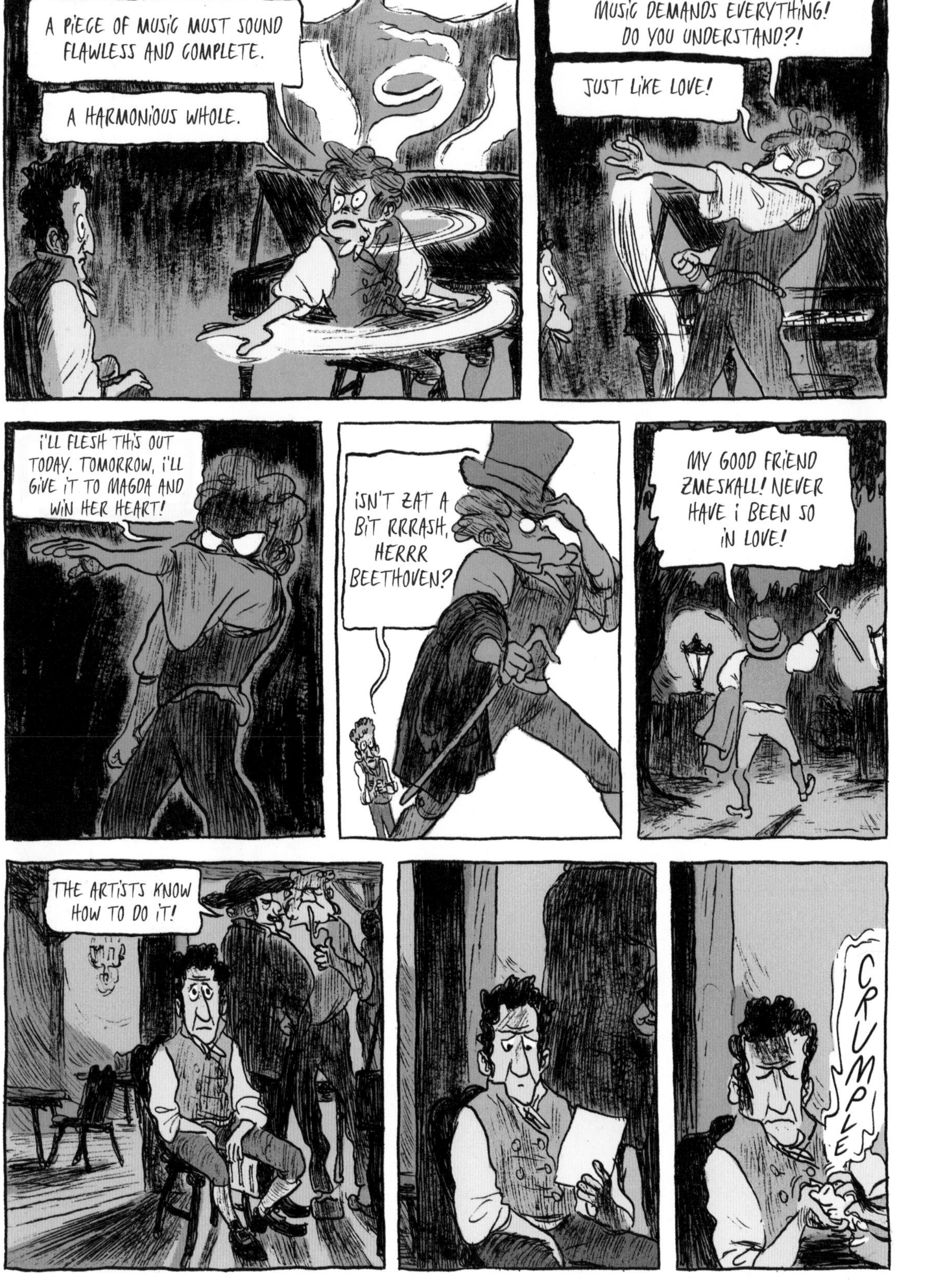
A PIECE OF MUSIC MUST SOUND FLAWLESS AND COMPLETE.
A HARMONIOUS WHOLE.
MUSIC DEMANDS EVERYTHING! DO YOU UNDERSTAND?!
JUST LIKE LOVE!
I'LL FLESH THIS OUT TODAY. TOMORROW, I'LL GIVE IT TO MAGDA AND WIN HER HEART!
ISN'T ZAT A BIT RRRASH, HERRR BEETHOVEN?
MY GOOD FRIEND ZMESKALL! NEVER HAVE I BEEN SO IN LOVE!
THE ARTISTS KNOW HOW TO DO IT!
CRUMPLE

MAGDAAA
WHAT DO YOU WANT?
i'VE WRiTTEN SOMETHiNG FOR YOU. SHALL WE TRY iT OUT?
i DON'T HAVE TiME.
WHAT'S HAP-PENiNG WiTH MY OPERA?
HAVE YOU PUBLiSHED ANYTHiNG AT ALL?
i WANTED TO RELEASE MY PiANO TRiOS.
BUT HAYDN THiNKS THEY'RE TOO COMPLEX FOR THE ViENNESE.
AND WHY ARE YOU PERFORMiNG NOWHERE iN ViENNA?
HAYDN SAYS iT'S STiLL TOO EARLY FOR THAT...
...BECAUSE OF THE FiNANCiAL RiSKS...
HAYDN THiS, HAYDN THAT...
iS HE YOUR NANNY, OR WHAT?
YOU DiSAPPOiNT ME.

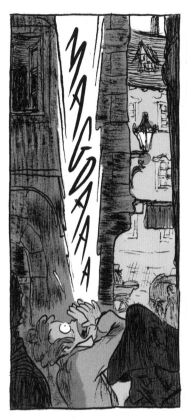

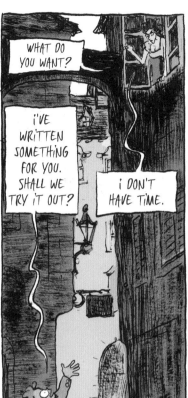

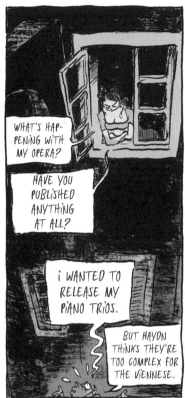

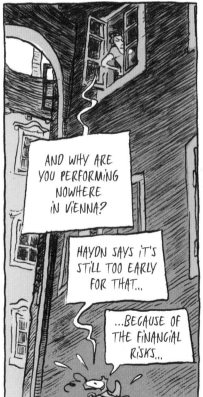

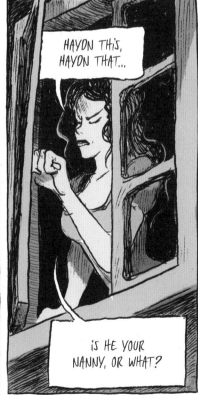

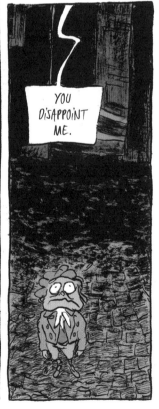

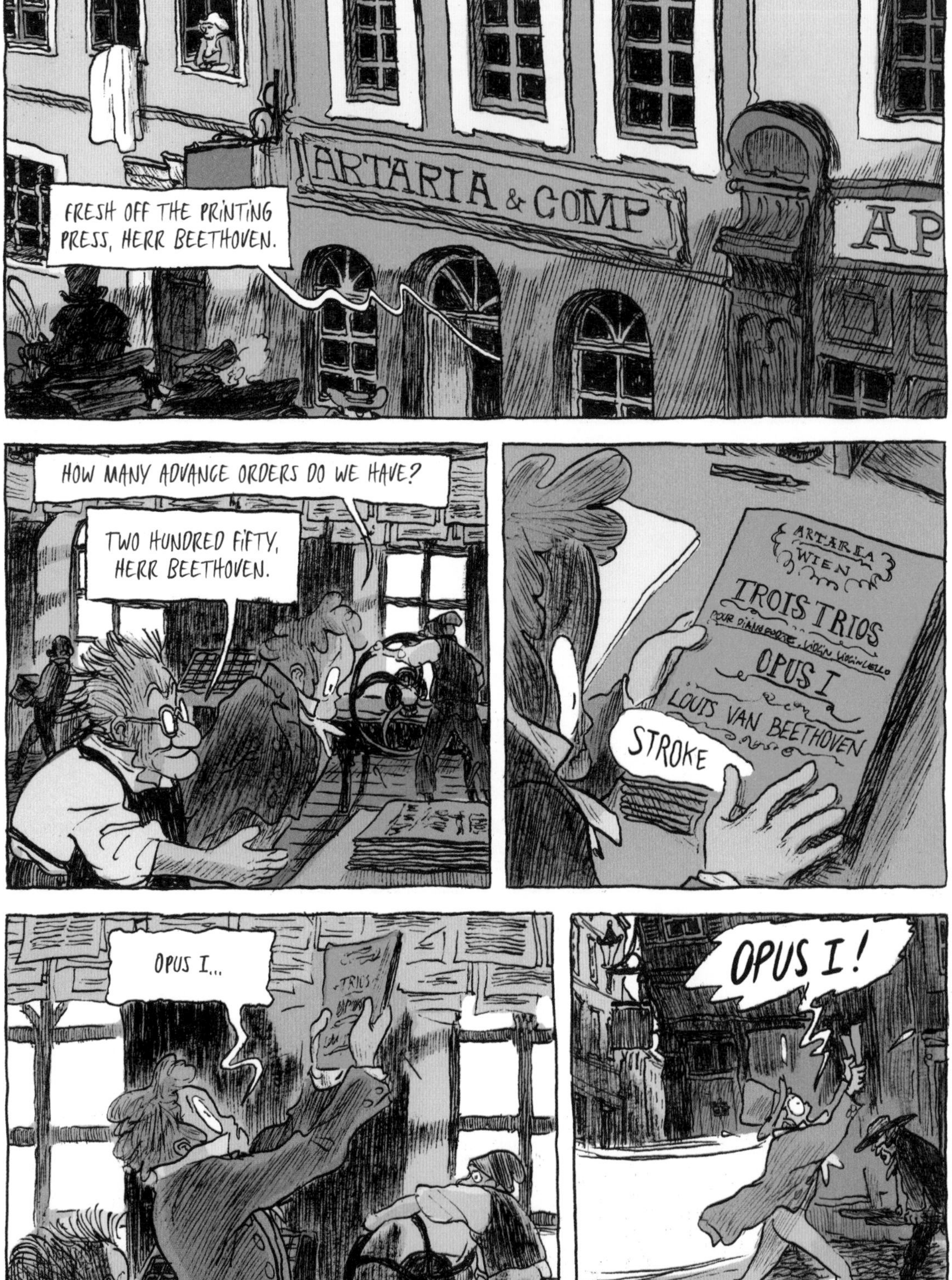
ARTARIA & COMP
AP
FRESH OFF THE PRINTING PRESS, HERR BEETHOVEN.
HOW MANY ADVANCE ORDERS DO WE HAVE?
TWO HUNDRED FIFTY, HERR BEETHOVEN.
ARTARIA WIEN
TROIS TRIOS
OPUS I
LOUIS VAN BEETHOVEN
STROKE
OPUS I...
OPUS I!

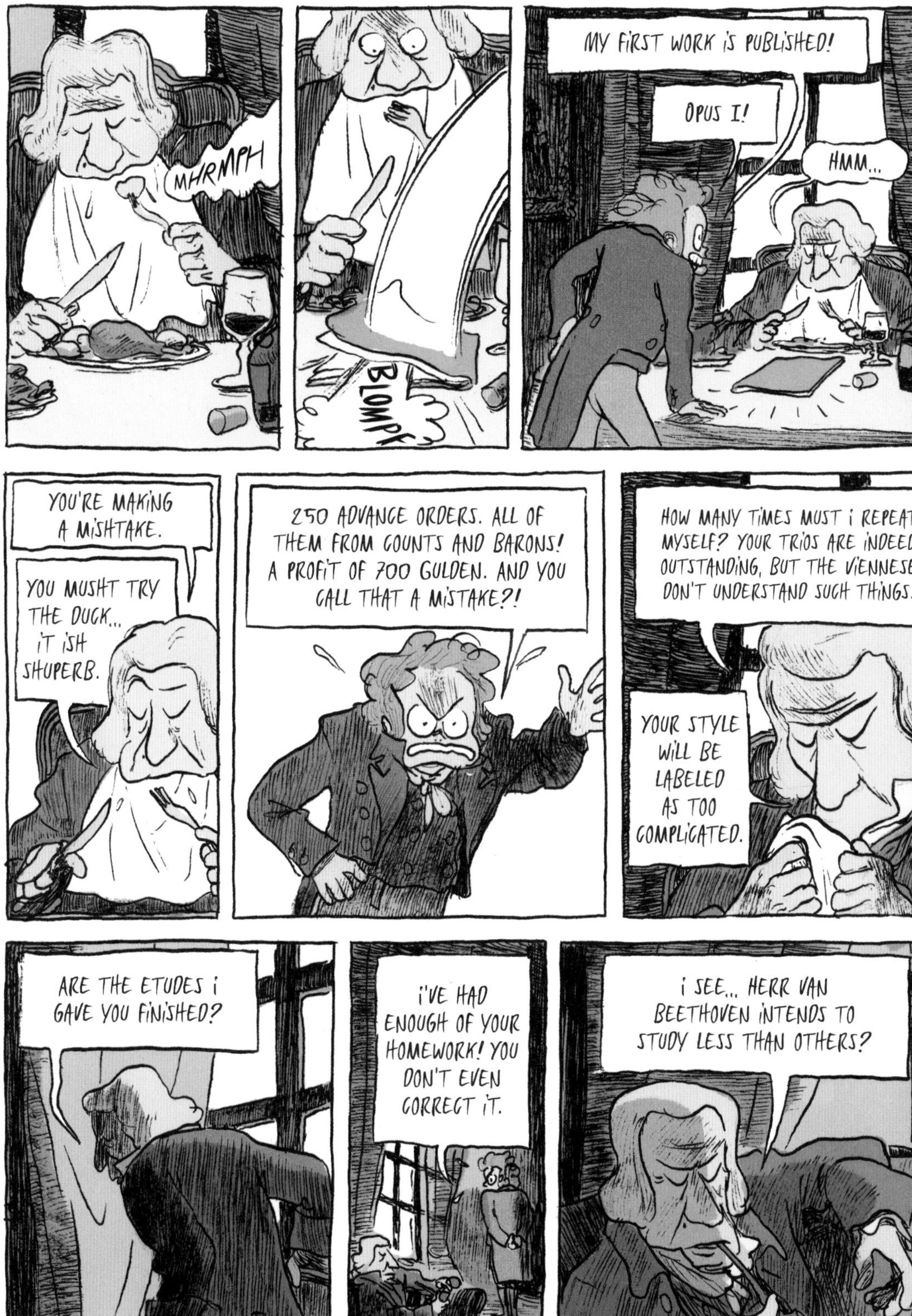
MHRMPH
BLOMPF
MY FIRST WORK IS PUBLISHED!
OPUS I!
HMM...
YOU'RE MAKING A MISHTAKE.
YOU MUSHT TRY THE DUCK... IT ISH SHUPERB.
250 ADVANCE ORDERS. ALL OF THEM FROM COUNTS AND BARONS! A PROFIT OF 700 GULDEN. AND YOU CALL THAT A MISTAKE?!
HOW MANY TIMES MUST I REPEAT MYSELF? YOUR TRIOS ARE INDEED OUTSTANDING, BUT THE VIENNESE DON'T UNDERSTAND SUCH THINGS.
YOUR STYLE WILL BE LABELED AS TOO COMPLICATED.
ARE THE ETUDES I GAVE YOU FINISHED?
I'VE HAD ENOUGH OF YOUR HOMEWORK! YOU DON'T EVEN CORRECT IT.
I SEE... HERR VAN BEETHOVEN INTENDS TO STUDY LESS THAN OTHERS?

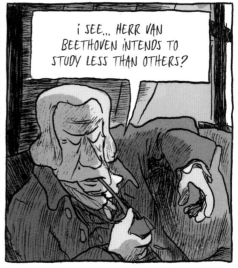

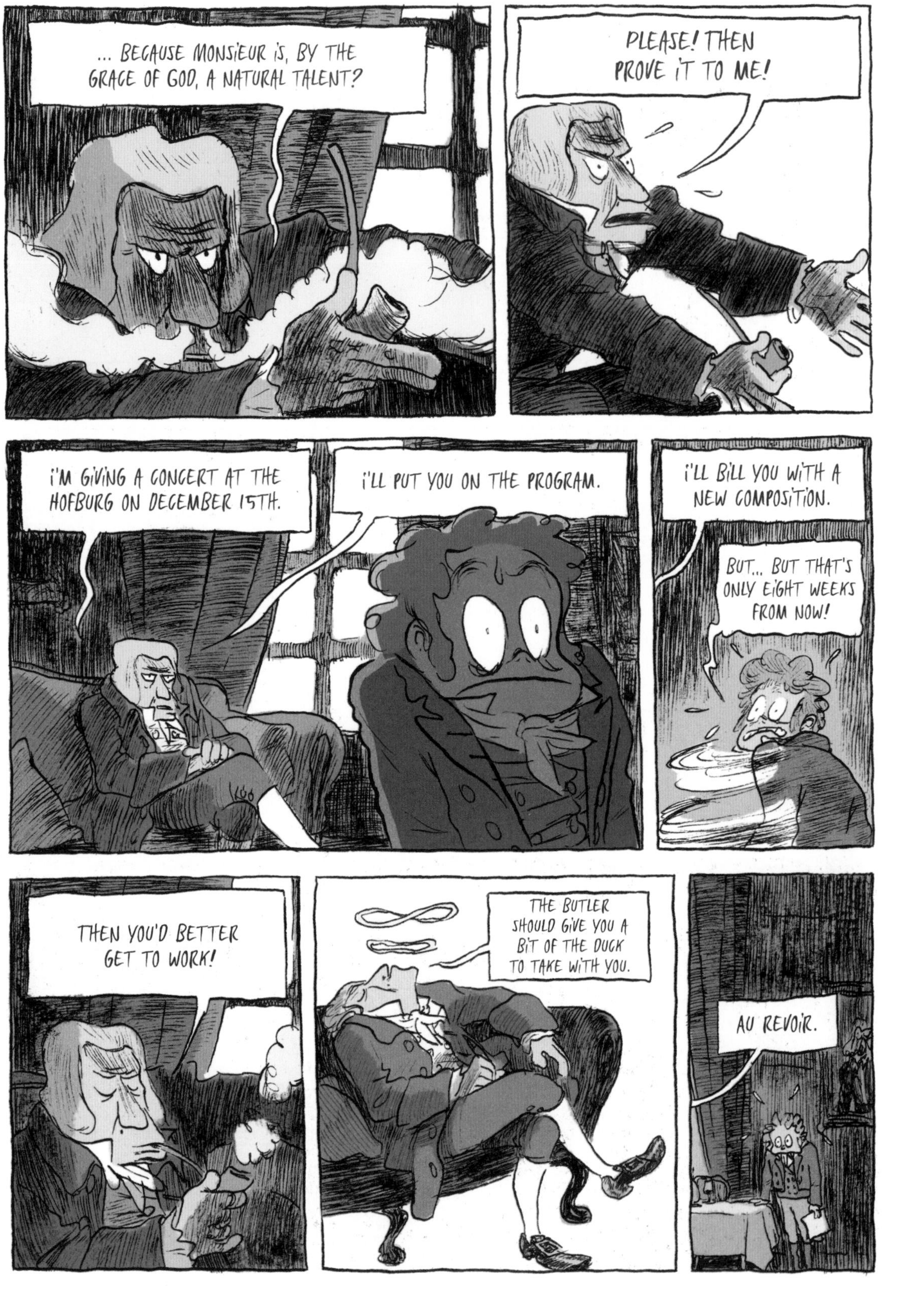

... BECAUSE MONSIEUR IS, BY THE GRACE OF GOD, A NATURAL TALENT?
PLEASE! THEN PROVE IT TO ME!
I'M GIVING A CONCERT AT THE HOFBURG ON DECEMBER 15TH.
I'LL PUT YOU ON THE PROGRAM.
I'LL BILL YOU WITH A NEW COMPOSITION.
BUT... BUT THAT'S ONLY EIGHT WEEKS FROM NOW!
THEN YOU'D BETTER GET TO WORK!
THE BUTLER SHOULD GIVE YOU A BIT OF THE DUCK TO TAKE WITH YOU.
AU REVOIR.

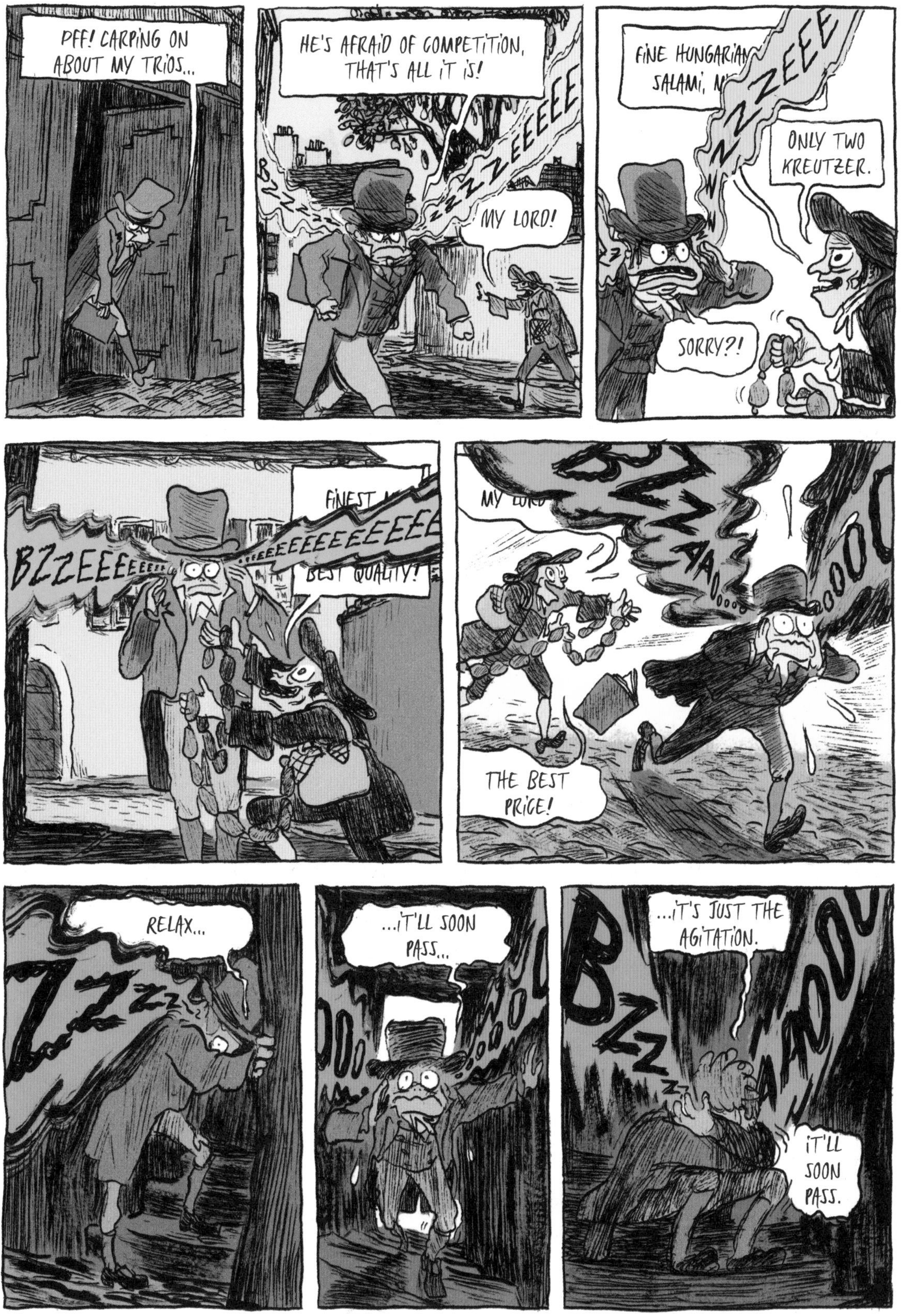

PFF! CARPING ON ABOUT MY TRIOS...
HE'S AFRAID OF COMPETITION, THAT'S ALL IT IS!
BZZZZEEEEEEE
MY LORD!
FINE HUNGARIAN SALAMI,
ZZZEEE
ONLY TWO KREUTZER.
SORRY?!
BZZEEEEEEE...EEEEEEEEEEE
FINEST
BEST QUALITY!
BZZAAOOOO
THE BEST PRICE!
RELAX...
...IT'LL SOON PASS...
...IT'S JUST THE AGITATION.
IT'LL SOON PASS.

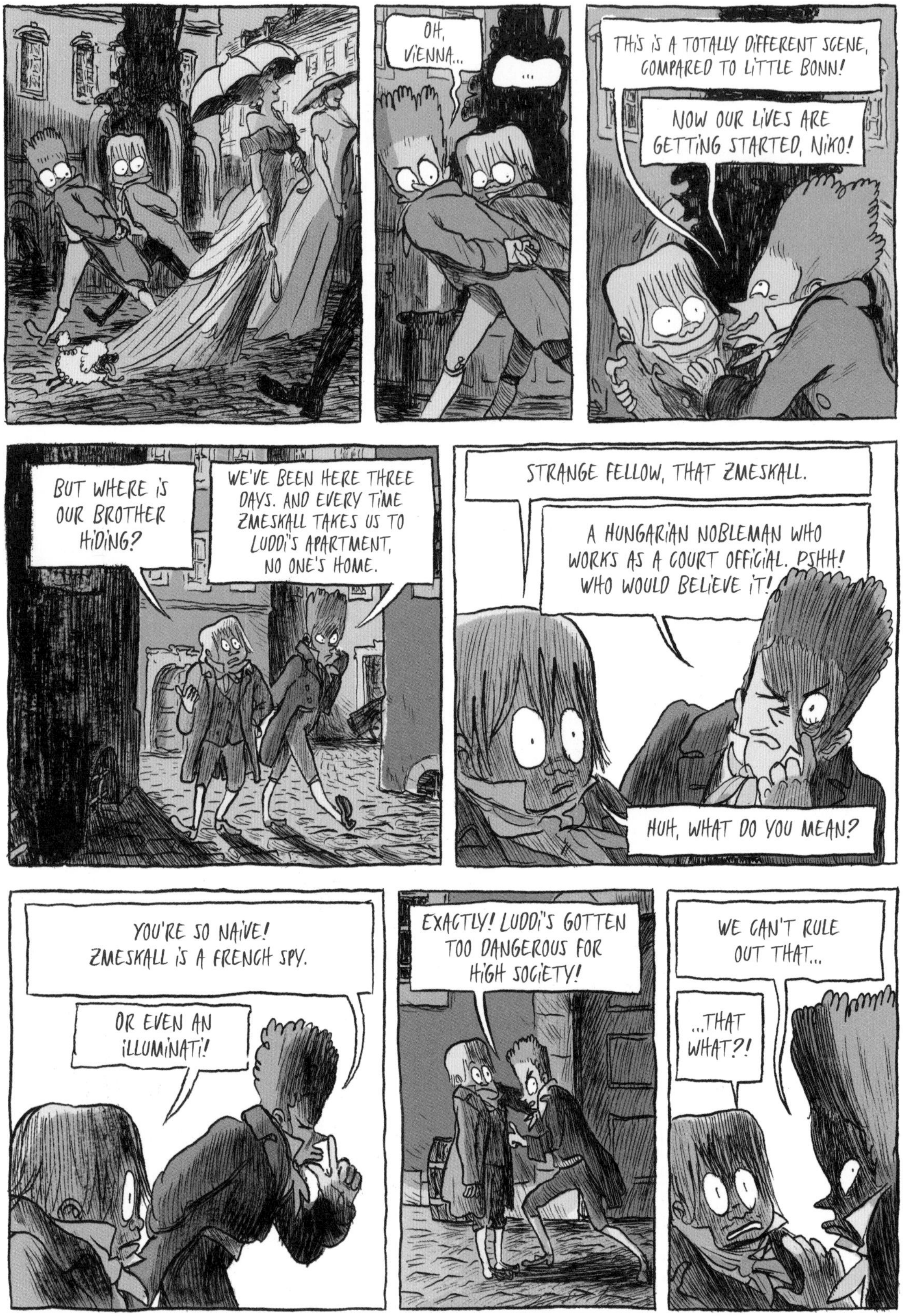
OH, VIENNA...
...
THIS IS A TOTALLY DIFFERENT SCENE, COMPARED TO LITTLE BONN!
NOW OUR LIVES ARE GETTING STARTED, NIKO!
BUT WHERE IS OUR BROTHER HIDING?
WE'VE BEEN HERE THREE DAYS. AND EVERY TIME ZMESKALL TAKES US TO LUDDI'S APARTMENT, NO ONE'S HOME.
STRANGE FELLOW, THAT ZMESKALL.
A HUNGARIAN NOBLEMAN WHO WORKS AS A COURT OFFICIAL. PSHH! WHO WOULD BELIEVE IT!
HUH, WHAT DO YOU MEAN?
YOU'RE SO NAIVE! ZMESKALL IS A FRENCH SPY.
OR EVEN AN ILLUMINATI!
EXACTLY! LUDDI'S GOTTEN TOO DANGEROUS FOR HIGH SOCIETY!
WE CAN'T RULE OUT THAT...
...THAT WHAT?!

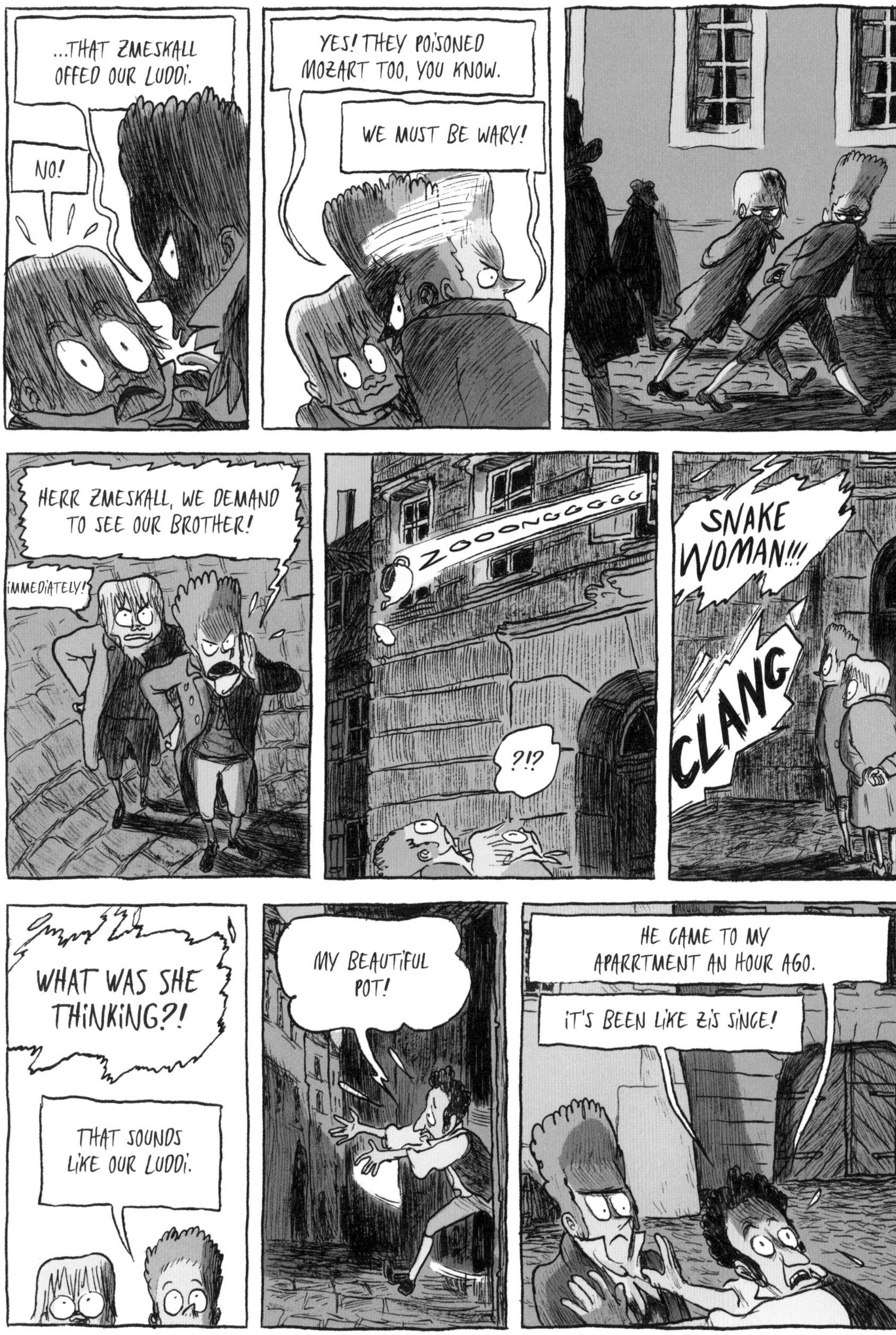
...THAT ZMESKALL OFFED OUR LUDDi.
NO!
YES! THEY POiSONED MOZART TOO, YOU KNOW.
WE MUST BE WARY!
HERR ZMESKALL, WE DEMAND TO SEE OUR BROTHER!
iMMEDiATELY!
ZOOONGGGGG
?!?
SNAKE WOMAN!!!
CLANG
WHAT WAS SHE THiNKiNG?!
THAT SOUNDS LiKE OUR LUDDi.
MY BEAUTiFUL POT!
HE CAME TO MY APARRTMENT AN HOUR AGO.
iT'S BEEN LiKE ZiS SiNCE!

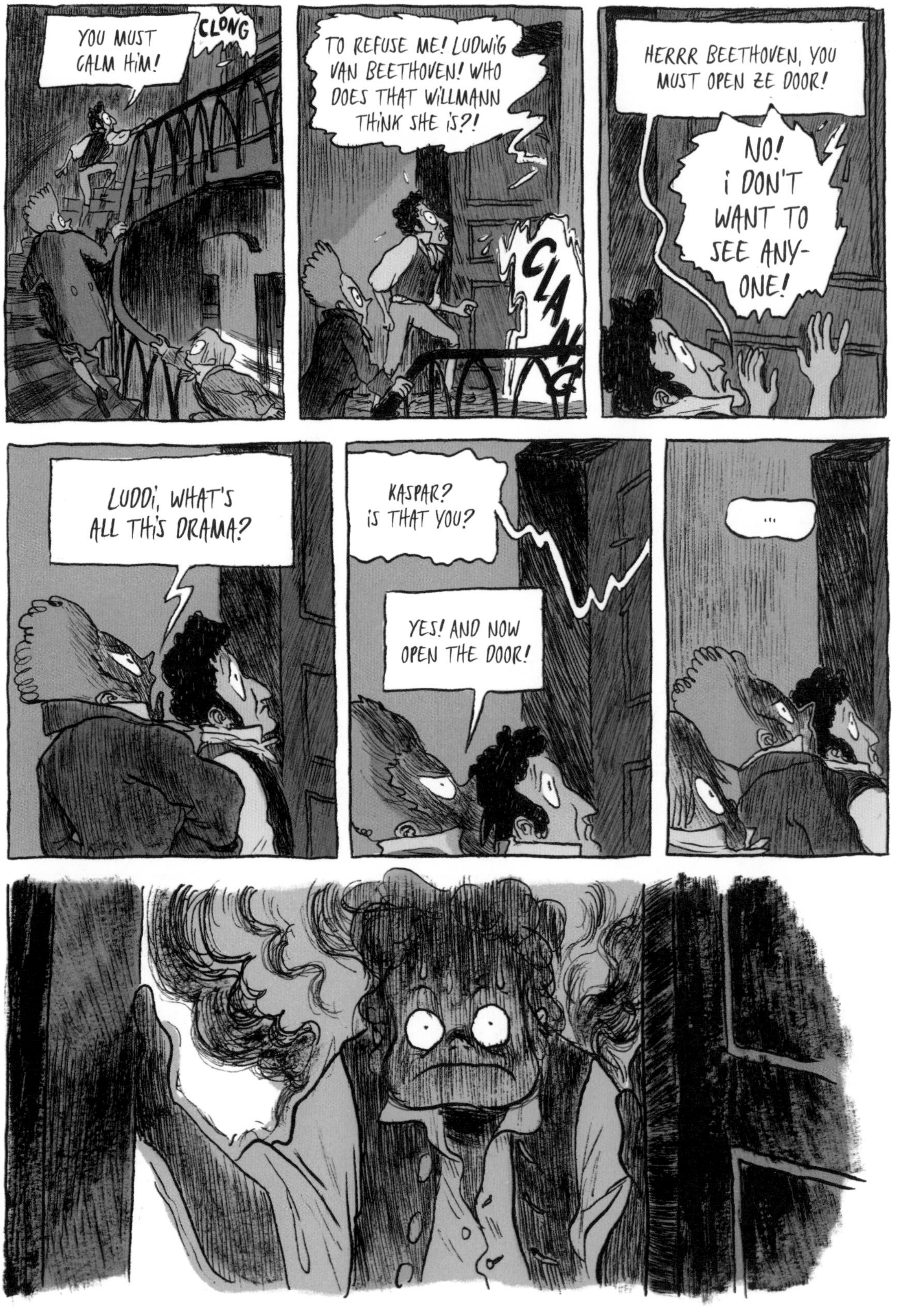
YOU MUST CALM HIM!
CLONG
TO REFUSE ME! LUDWIG VAN BEETHOVEN! WHO DOES THAT WILLMANN THINK SHE IS?!
CLANG
HERRR BEETHOVEN, YOU MUST OPEN ZE DOOR!
NO! I DON'T WANT TO SEE ANY-ONE!
LUDDI, WHAT'S ALL THIS DRAMA?
KASPAR? IS THAT YOU?
YES! AND NOW OPEN THE DOOR!
...

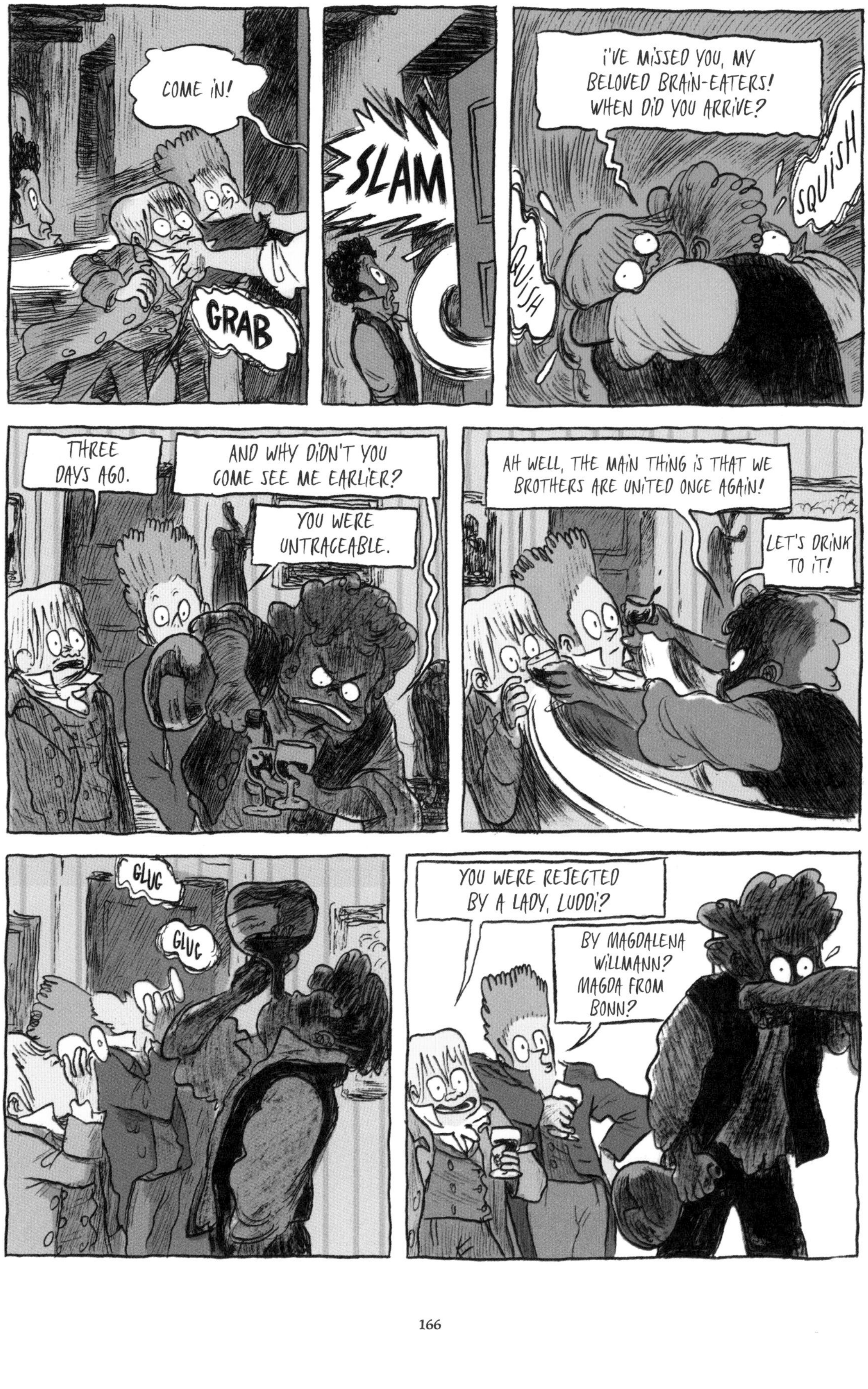
COME IN!
GRAB
SLAM
I'VE MISSED YOU, MY BELOVED BRAIN-EATERS! WHEN DID YOU ARRIVE?
SQUISH
SQUISH
THREE DAYS AGO.
AND WHY DIDN'T YOU COME SEE ME EARLIER?
YOU WERE UNTRACEABLE.
AH WELL, THE MAIN THING IS THAT WE BROTHERS ARE UNITED ONCE AGAIN!
LET'S DRINK TO IT!
GLUG
GLUG
YOU WERE REJECTED BY A LADY, LUDDI?
BY MAGDALENA WILLMANN? MAGDA FROM BONN?

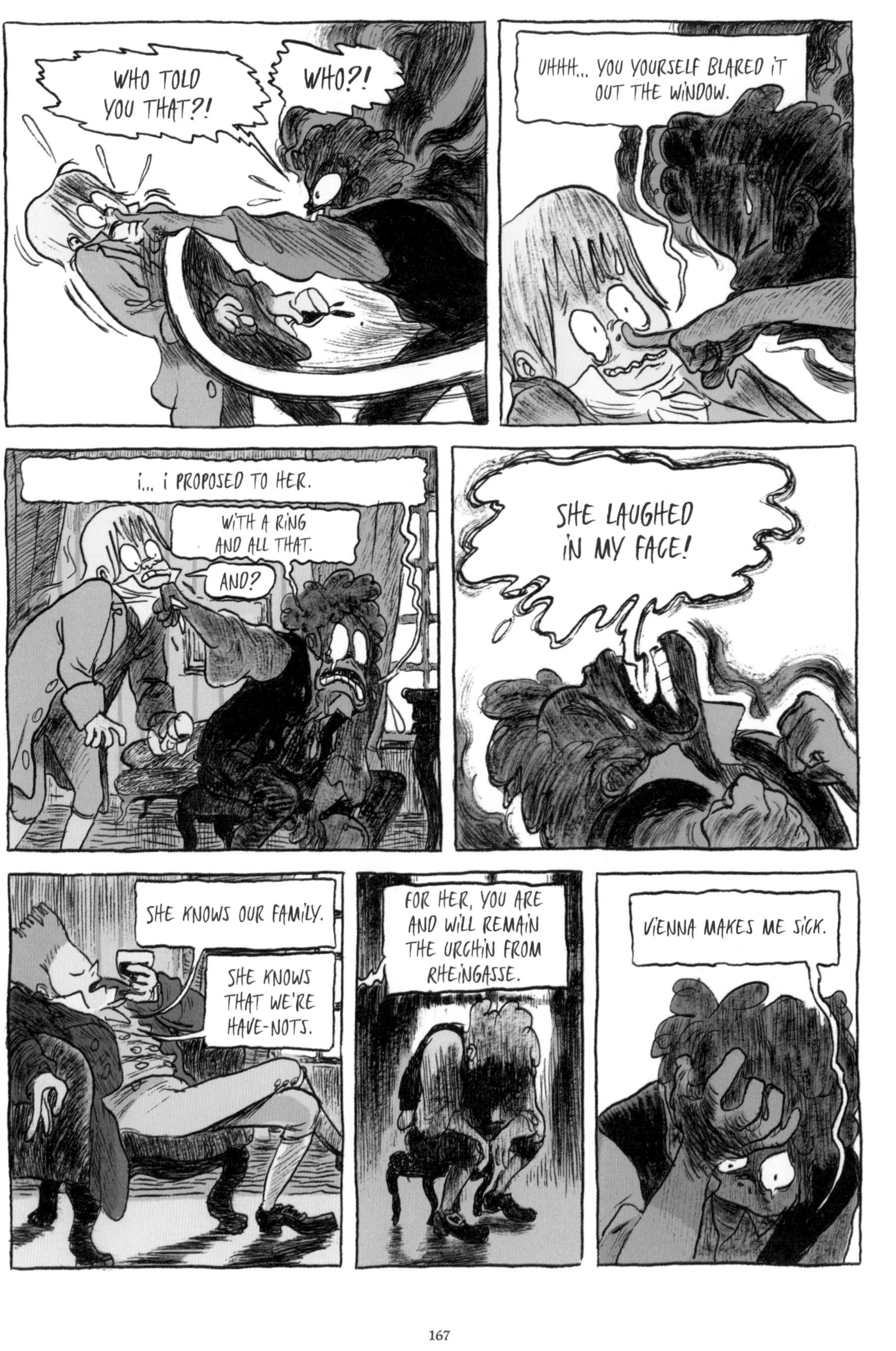
WHO TOLD YOU THAT?!
WHO?!
UHHH... YOU YOURSELF BLARED IT OUT THE WINDOW.
I... I PROPOSED TO HER.
WITH A RING AND ALL THAT.
AND?
SHE LAUGHED IN MY FACE!
SHE KNOWS OUR FAMILY.
SHE KNOWS THAT WE'RE HAVE-NOTS.
FOR HER, YOU ARE AND WILL REMAIN THE URCHIN FROM RHEINGASSE.
VIENNA MAKES ME SICK.

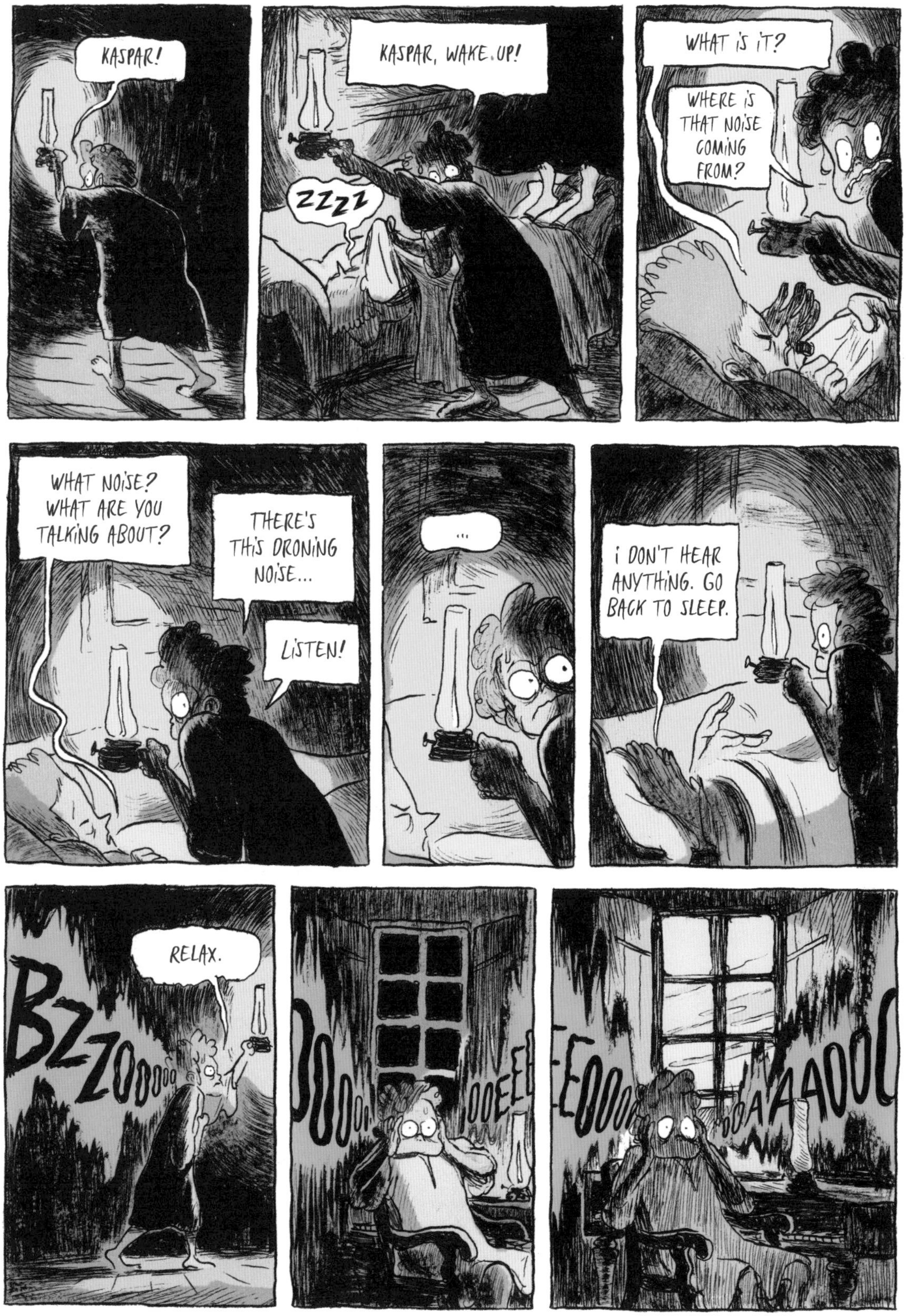
KASPAR!
KASPAR, WAKE UP!
ZZZZ
WHAT IS IT?
WHERE IS THAT NOISE COMING FROM?
WHAT NOISE? WHAT ARE YOU TALKING ABOUT?
THERE'S THIS DRONING NOISE...
LISTEN!
...
I DON'T HEAR ANYTHING. GO BACK TO SLEEP.
RELAX.
BZZOOOooo
OOOOooo
OOEEE
EEOOOO
OOAAAOOO

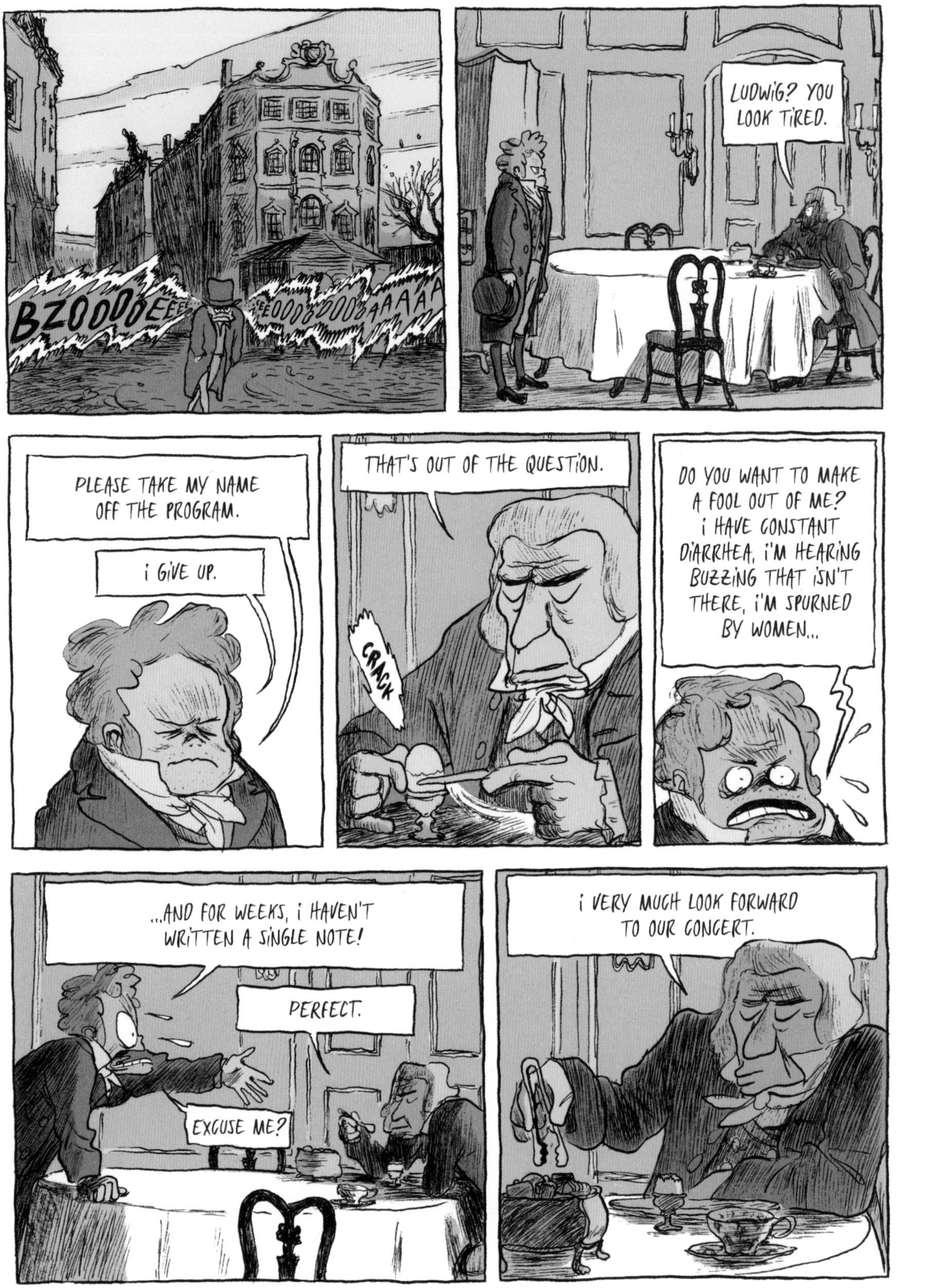
BZOODOEEEEEEOOOBOOOBAAAAA
LUDWIG? YOU LOOK TIRED.
PLEASE TAKE MY NAME OFF THE PROGRAM.
I GIVE UP.
THAT'S OUT OF THE QUESTION.
CRACK
DO YOU WANT TO MAKE A FOOL OUT OF ME? I HAVE CONSTANT DIARRHEA, I'M HEARING BUZZING THAT ISN'T THERE, I'M SPURNED BY WOMEN...
...AND FOR WEEKS, I HAVEN'T WRITTEN A SINGLE NOTE!
PERFECT.
EXCUSE ME?
I VERY MUCH LOOK FORWARD TO OUR CONCERT.

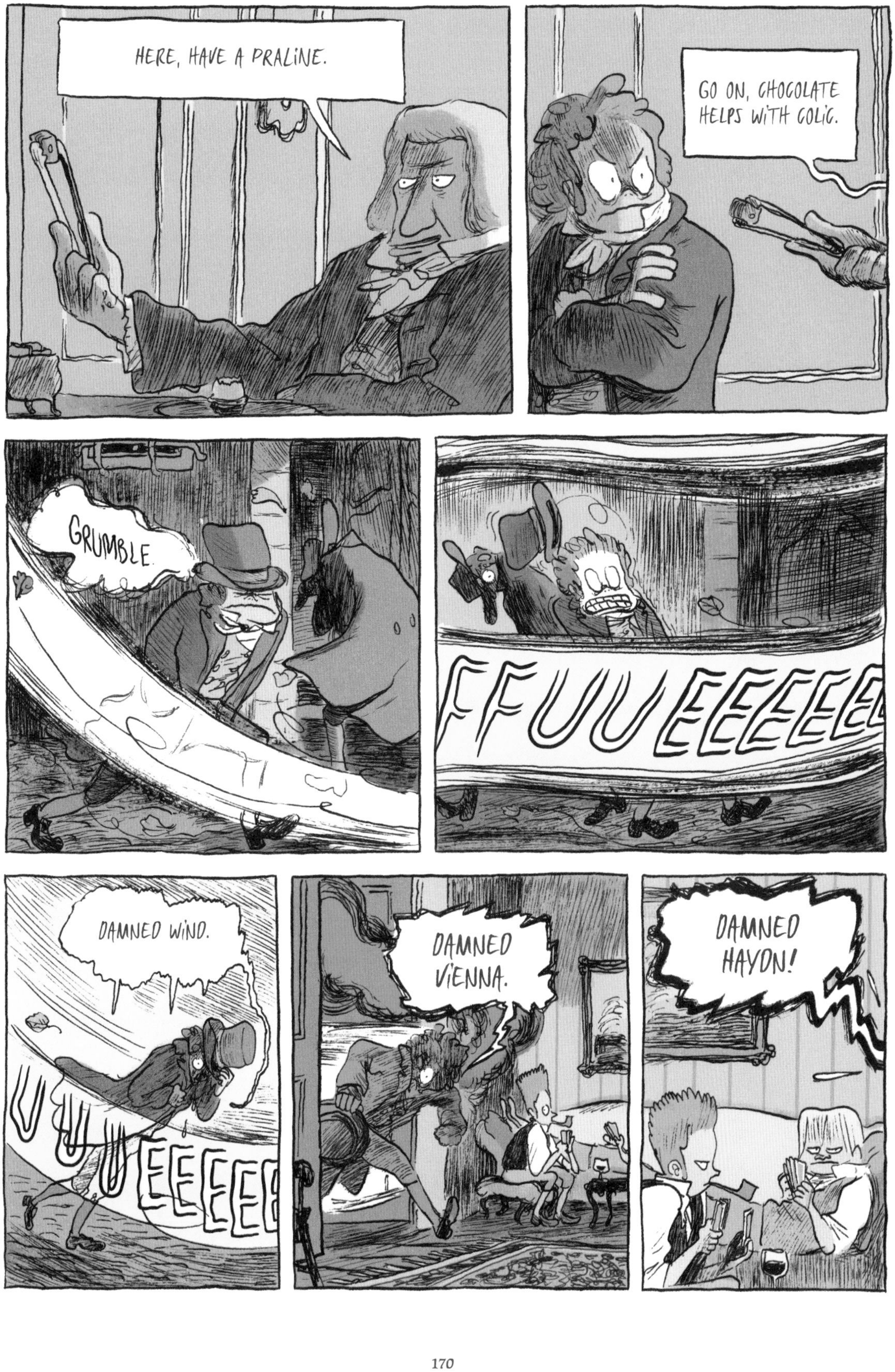
HERE, HAVE A PRALINE.
GO ON, CHOCOLATE HELPS WITH COLIC.
GRUMBLE.
FFUUEEEEEE
DAMNED WIND.
UUUEEEEEE
DAMNED VIENNA.
DAMNED HAYDN!

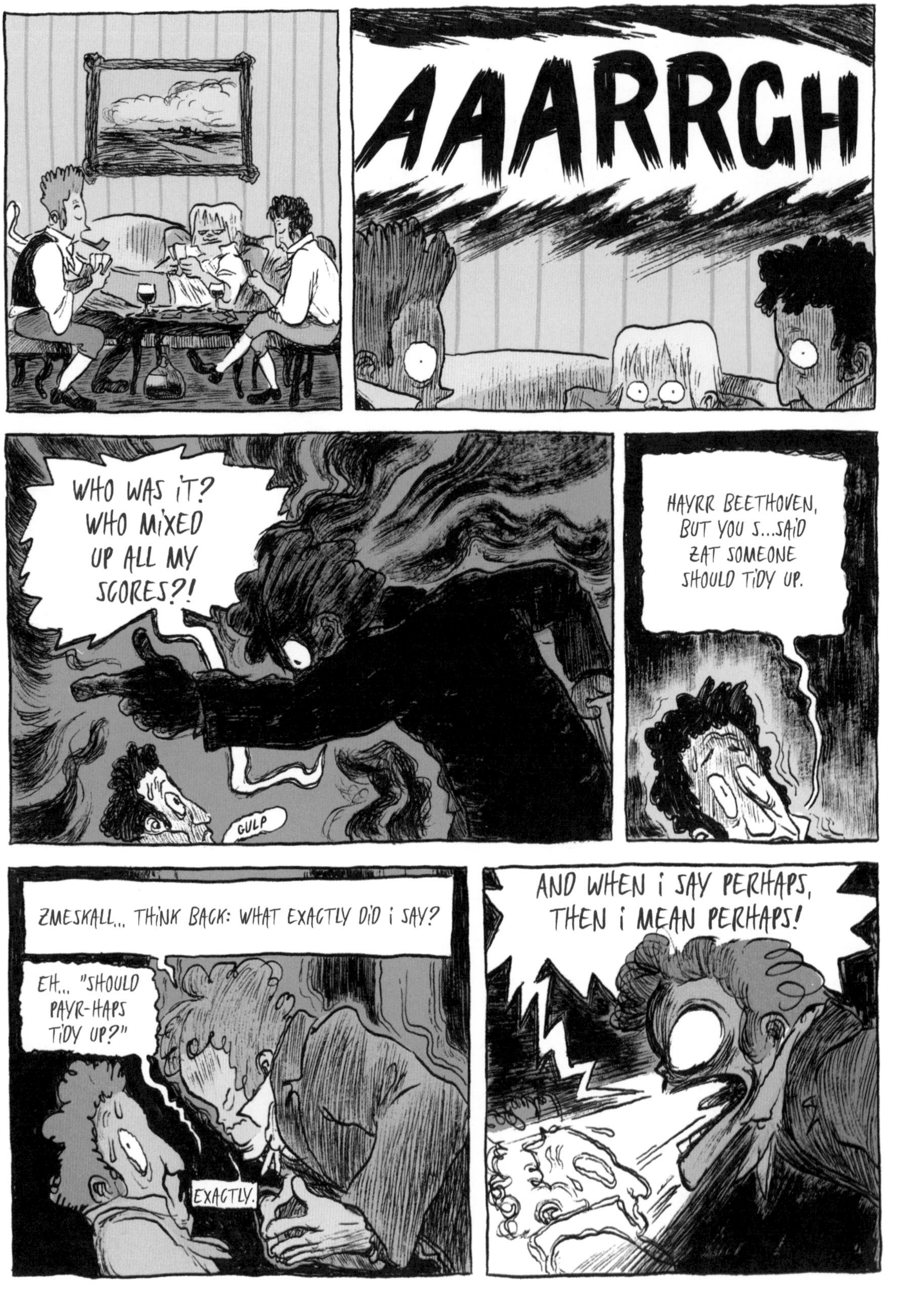
AAARRGH
WHO WAS iT? WHO MiXED UP ALL MY SCORES?!
GULP
HAYRR BEETHOVEN, BUT YOU S...SAiD ZAT SOMEONE SHOULD TiDY UP.
ZMESKALL... THiNK BACK: WHAT EXACTLY DiD i SAY?
EH... "SHOULD PAYR-HAPS TiDY UP?"
EXACTLY.
AND WHEN i SAY PERHAPS, THEN i MEAN PERHAPS!

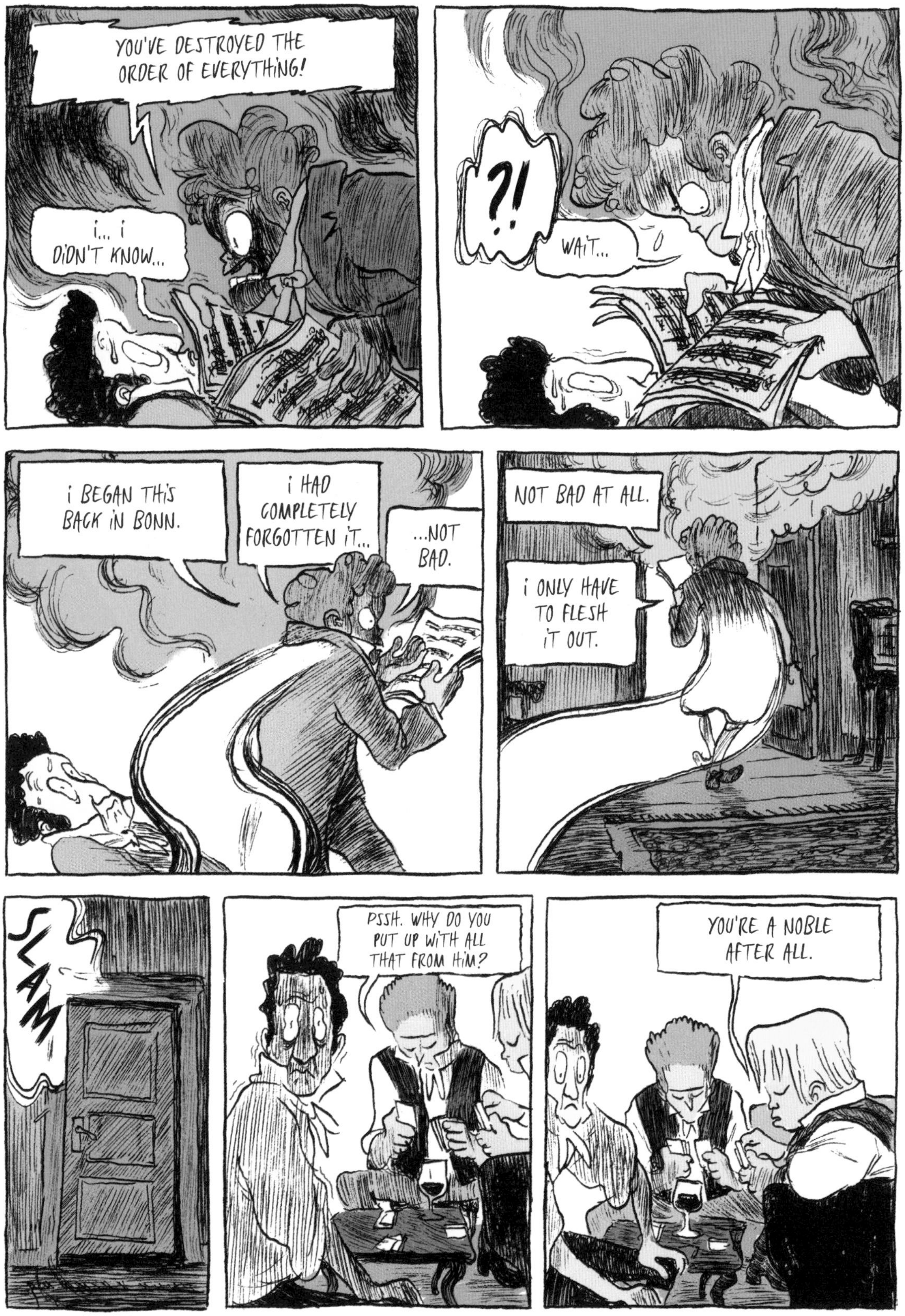
YOU'VE DESTROYED THE ORDER OF EVERYTHING!
I... I DIDN'T KNOW...
?!
WAIT...
I BEGAN THIS BACK IN BONN.
I HAD COMPLETELY FORGOTTEN IT...
...NOT BAD.
NOT BAD AT ALL.
I ONLY HAVE TO FLESH IT OUT.
SLAM
PSSH. WHY DO YOU PUT UP WITH ALL THAT FROM HIM?
YOU'RE A NOBLE AFTER ALL.

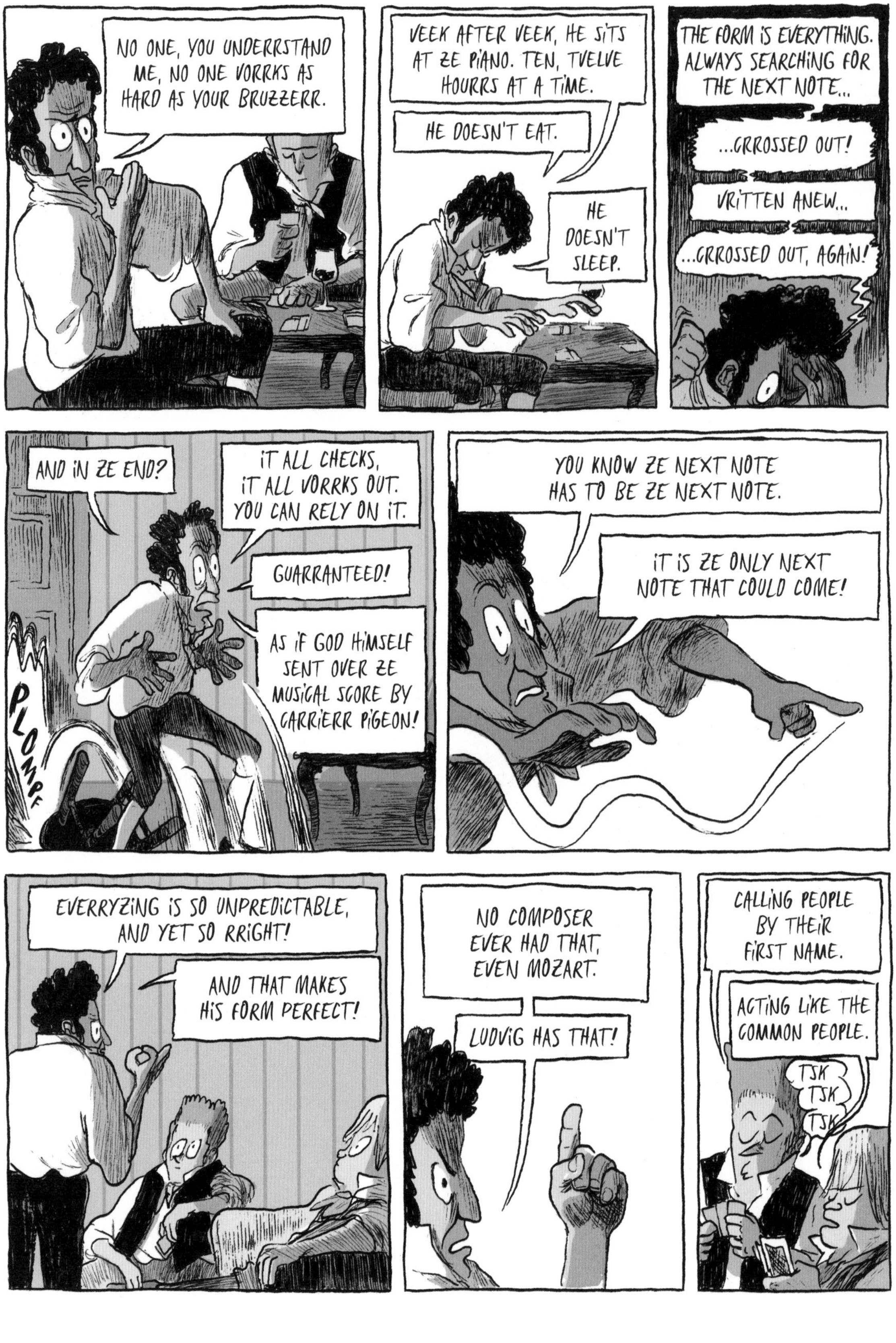
NO ONE, YOU UNDERRSTAND ME, NO ONE VORRKS AS HARD AS YOUR BRUZZERR.
VEEK AFTER VEEK, HE SITS AT ZE PIANO. TEN, TVELVE HOURRS AT A TIME.
HE DOESN'T EAT.
HE DOESN'T SLEEP.
THE FORM IS EVERYTHING. ALWAYS SEARCHING FOR THE NEXT NOTE...
...CRROSSED OUT!
VRITTEN ANEW...
...CRROSSED OUT, AGAIN!
AND IN ZE END?
IT ALL CHECKS, IT ALL VORRKS OUT. YOU CAN RELY ON IT.
GUARRANTEED!
AS IF GOD HIMSELF SENT OVER ZE MUSICAL SCORE BY CARRIERR PIGEON!
PLOMRF
YOU KNOW ZE NEXT NOTE HAS TO BE ZE NEXT NOTE.
IT IS ZE ONLY NEXT NOTE THAT COULD COME!
EVERRYZING IS SO UNPREDICTABLE, AND YET SO RRIGHT!
AND THAT MAKES HIS FORM PERFECT!
NO COMPOSER EVER HAD THAT, EVEN MOZART.
LUDVIG HAS THAT!
CALLING PEOPLE BY THEIR FIRST NAME.
ACTING LIKE THE COMMON PEOPLE.
TSK
TSK
TSK

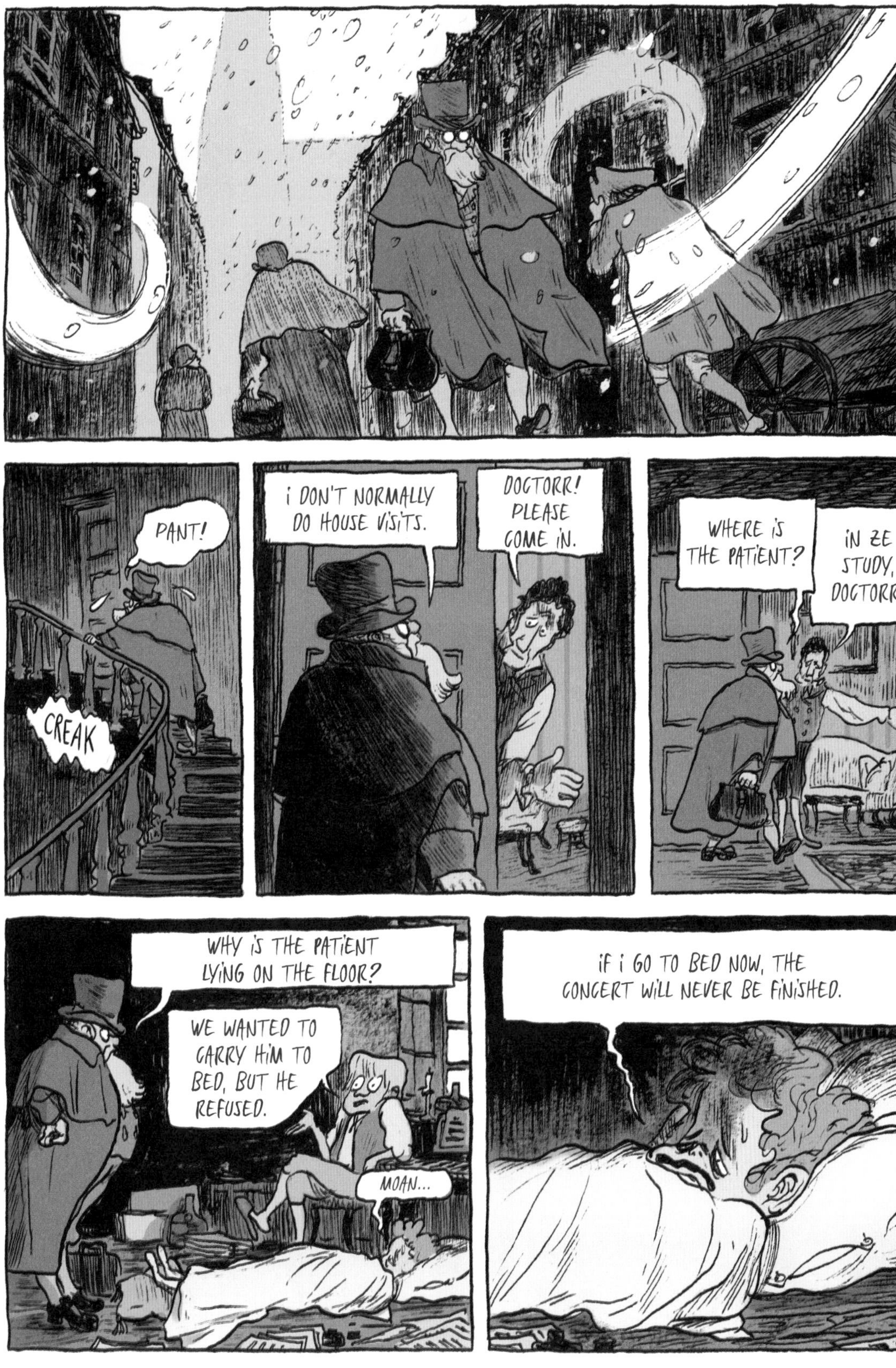
PANT!
CREAK
I DON'T NORMALLY DO HOUSE VISITS.
DOCTORR! PLEASE COME IN.
WHERE IS THE PATIENT?
IN ZE STUDY, DOCTORR.
WHY IS THE PATIENT LYING ON THE FLOOR?
WE WANTED TO CARRY HIM TO BED, BUT HE REFUSED.
MOAN...
IF I GO TO BED NOW, THE CONCERT WILL NEVER BE FINISHED.

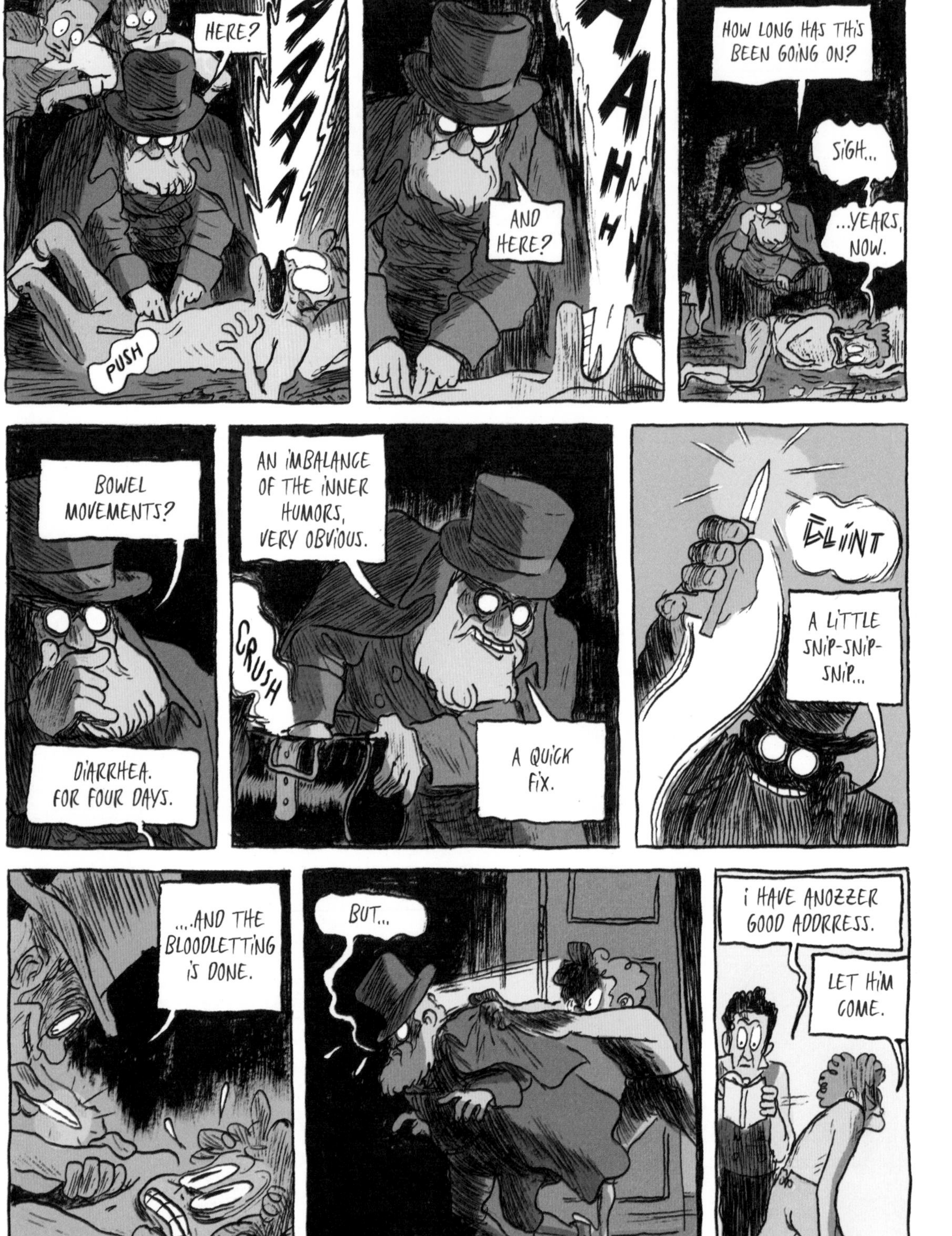
HERE?
AAAAAA
PUSH
AND HERE?
AAHHHH
HOW LONG HAS THIS BEEN GOING ON?
SIGH...
...YEARS, NOW.
BOWEL MOVEMENTS?
DIARRHEA. FOR FOUR DAYS.
AN IMBALANCE OF THE INNER HUMORS, VERY OBVIOUS.
CRUSH
A QUICK FIX.
GLINT
A LITTLE SNIP-SNIP-SNIP...
...AND THE BLOODLETTING IS DONE.
BUT...
I HAVE ANOZZER GOOD ADDRRESS.
LET HIM COME.

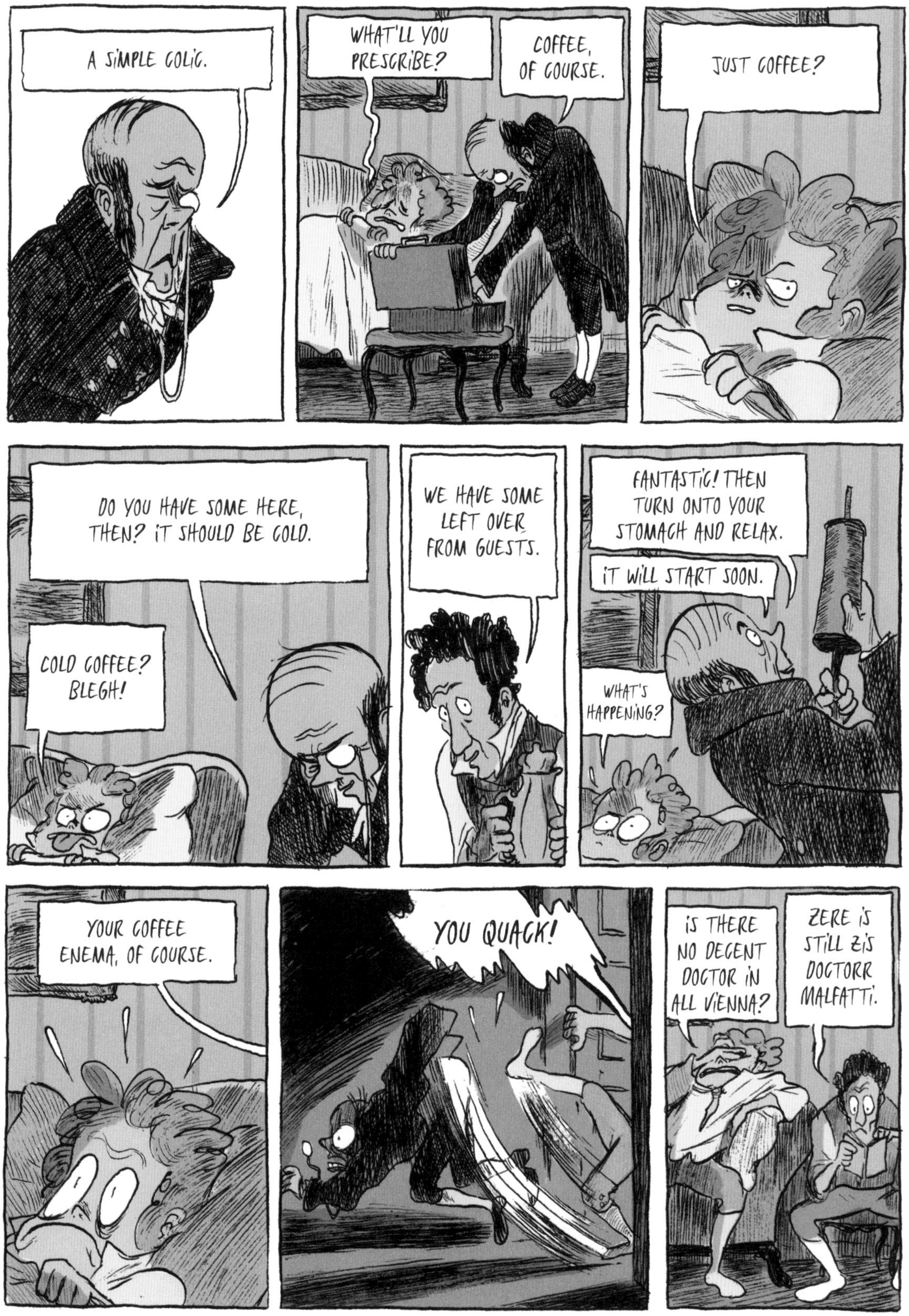
A SIMPLE COLIC.
WHAT'LL YOU PRESCRIBE?
COFFEE, OF COURSE.
JUST COFFEE?
DO YOU HAVE SOME HERE, THEN? IT SHOULD BE COLD.
COLD COFFEE? BLEGH!
WE HAVE SOME LEFT OVER FROM GUESTS.
FANTASTIC! THEN TURN ONTO YOUR STOMACH AND RELAX.
IT WILL START SOON.
WHAT'S HAPPENING?
YOUR COFFEE ENEMA, OF COURSE.
YOU QUACK!
IS THERE NO DECENT DOCTOR IN ALL VIENNA?
ZERE IS STILL ZIS DOCTORR MALFATTI.

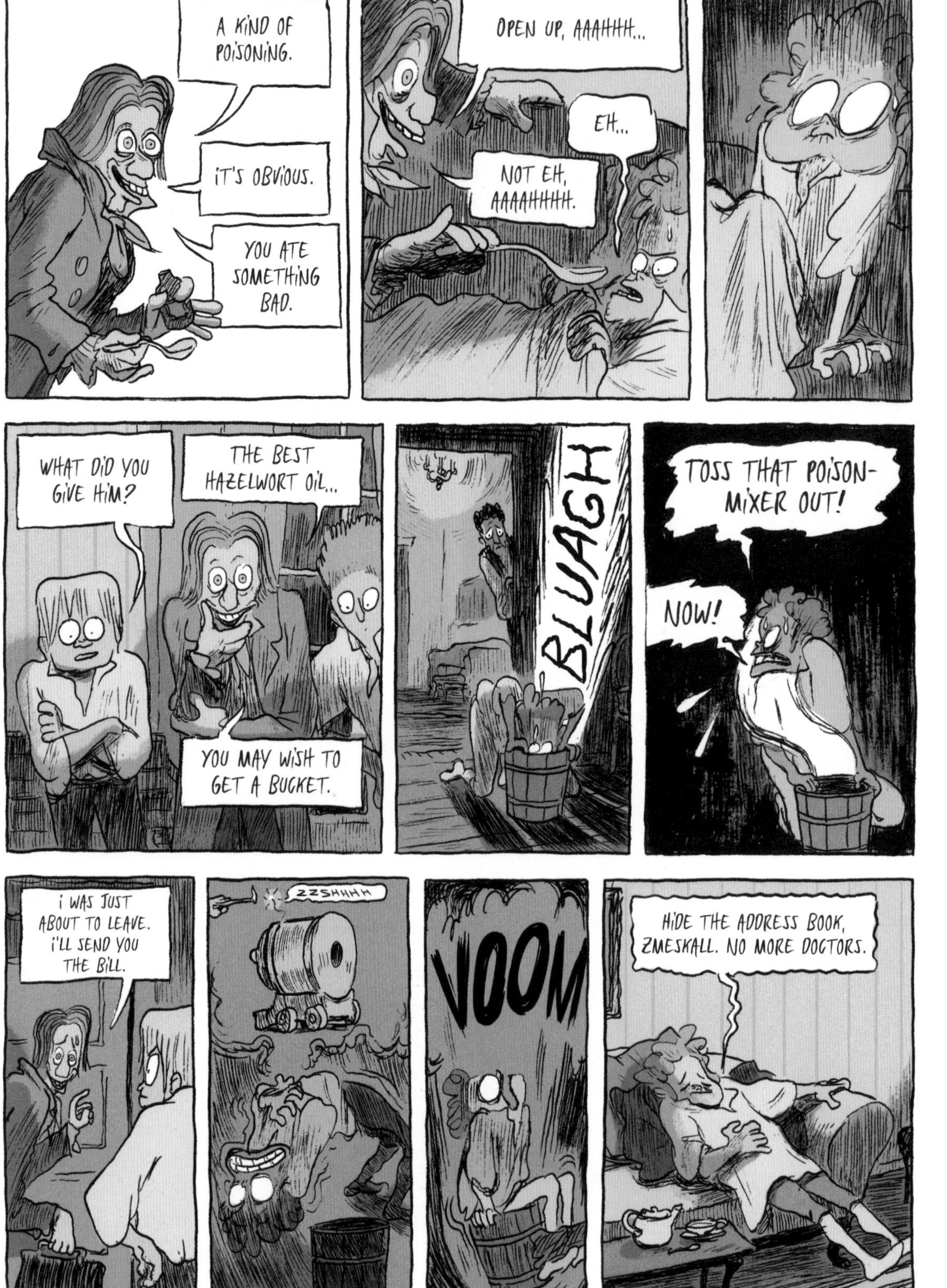
A KIND OF POISONING.
IT'S OBVIOUS.
YOU ATE SOMETHING BAD.
OPEN UP, AAAHHH...
EH...
NOT EH, AAAAHHHH.
WHAT DID YOU GIVE HIM?
THE BEST HAZELWORT OIL...
YOU MAY WISH TO GET A BUCKET.
BLUAGH
TOSS THAT POISON-MIXER OUT!
NOW!
I WAS JUST ABOUT TO LEAVE. I'LL SEND YOU THE BILL.
ZZSHHHH
VOOM
HIDE THE ADDRESS BOOK, ZMESKALL. NO MORE DOCTORS.

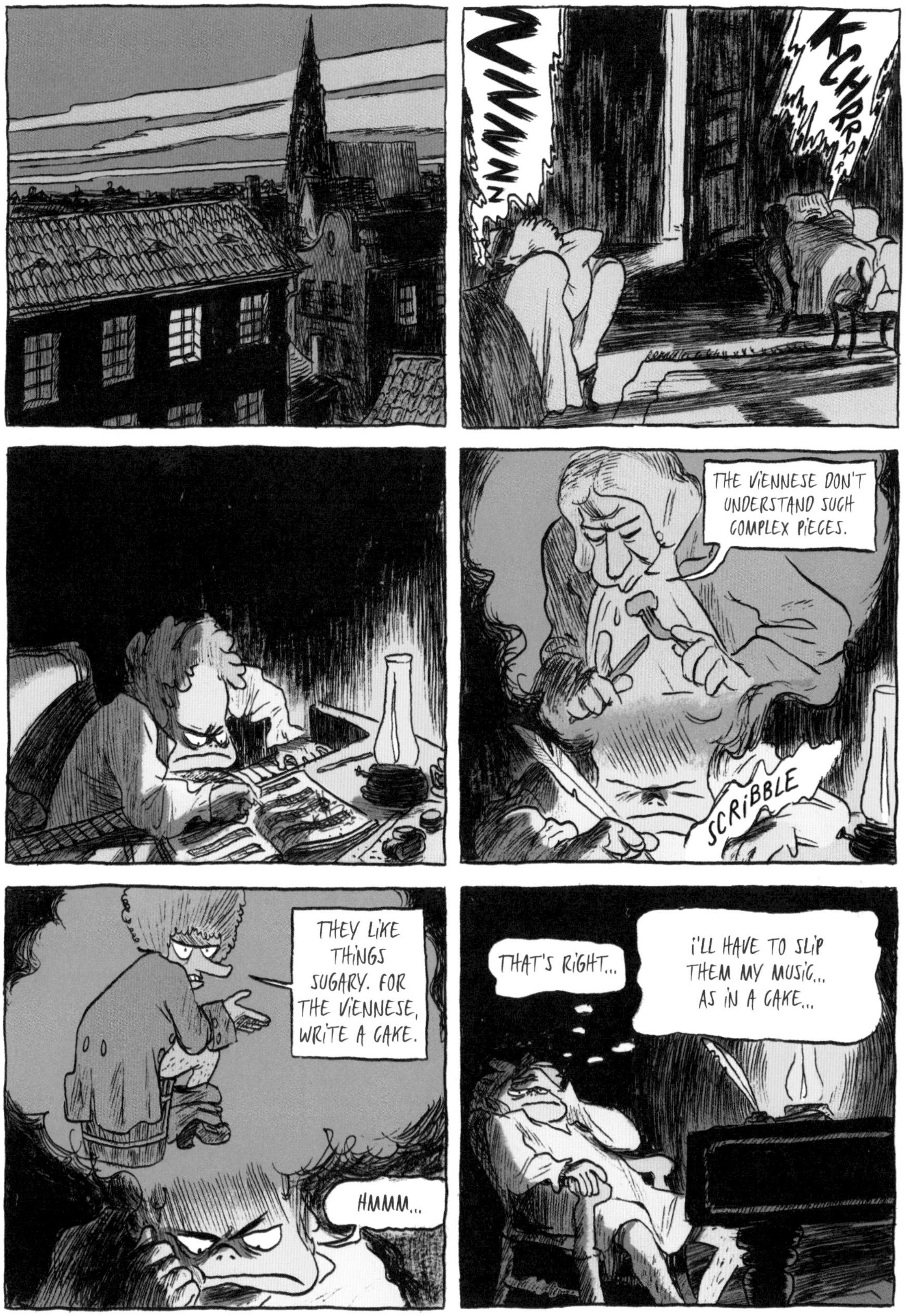
ZZZZZZZ
KCHRRRRR
THE VIENNESE DON'T UNDERSTAND SUCH COMPLEX PIECES.
SCRIBBLE
THEY LIKE THINGS SUGARY. FOR THE VIENNESE, WRITE A CAKE.
HMMM...
THAT'S RIGHT...
I'LL HAVE TO SLIP THEM MY MUSIC... AS IN A CAKE...

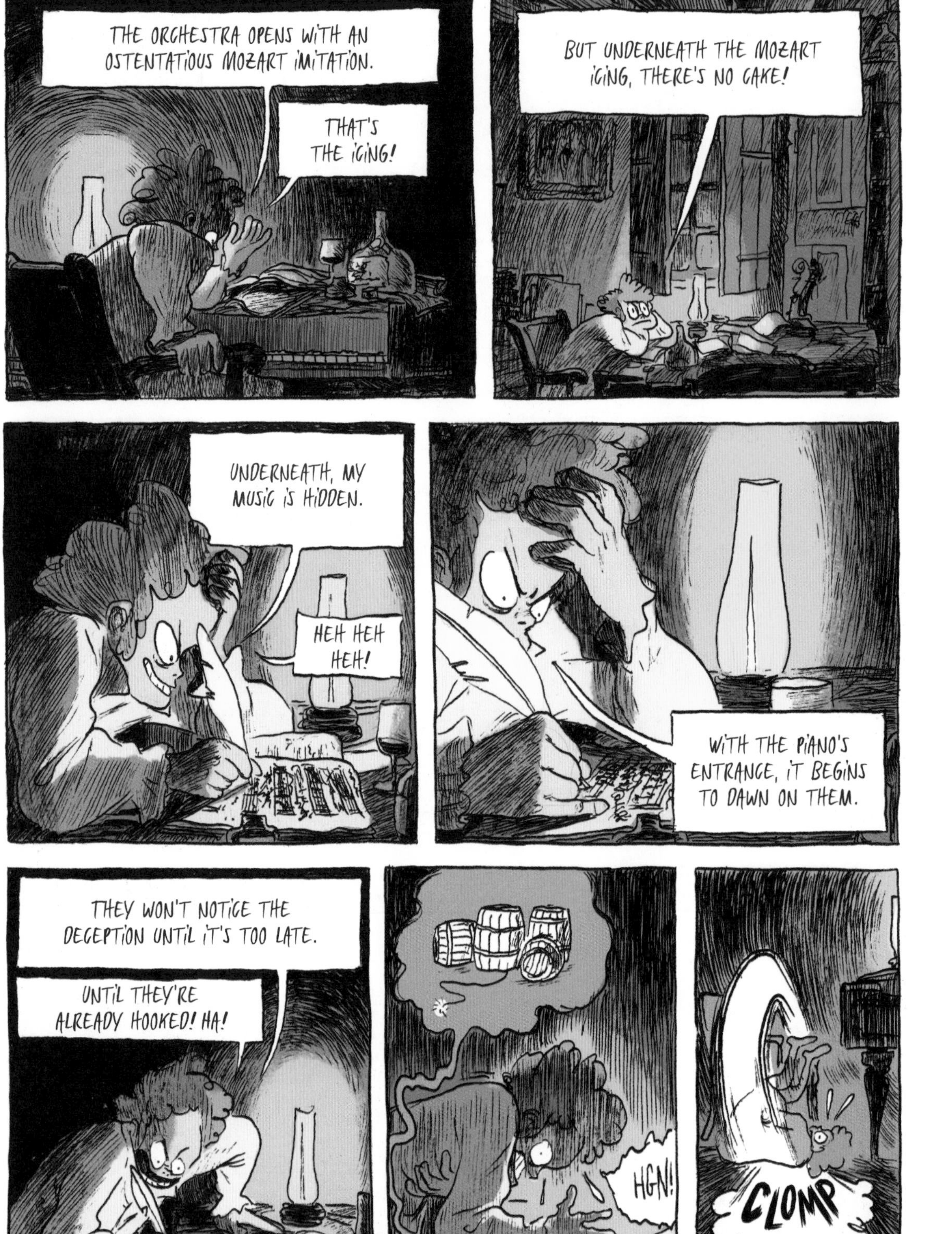
THE ORCHESTRA OPENS WITH AN OSTENTATIOUS MOZART IMITATION.
THAT'S THE ICING!
BUT UNDERNEATH THE MOZART ICING, THERE'S NO CAKE!
UNDERNEATH, MY MUSIC IS HIDDEN.
HEH HEH HEH!
WITH THE PIANO'S ENTRANCE, IT BEGINS TO DAWN ON THEM.
THEY WON'T NOTICE THE DECEPTION UNTIL IT'S TOO LATE.
UNTIL THEY'RE ALREADY HOOKED! HA!
HGN!
CLOMP

TRAITOR.
TRAITOROUS BODY.
A SLIMY WORM THAT CRAWLS ACROSS THE EARTH...
... AND DREAMS OF HEAVENLY MUSIC.
CRAWL ON, WORM!

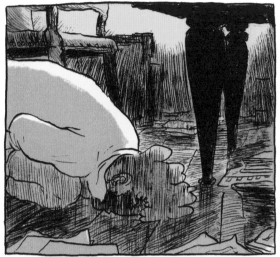

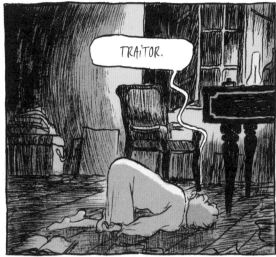

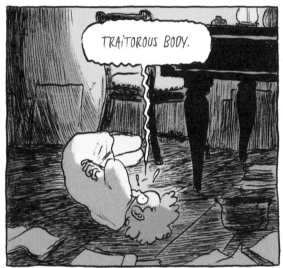

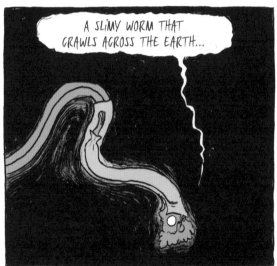

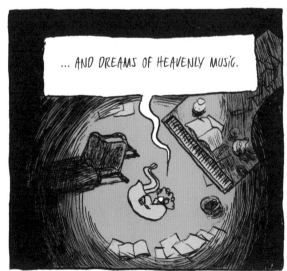

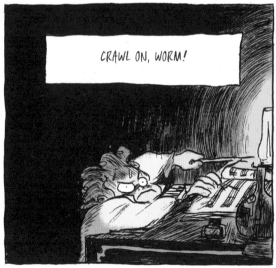

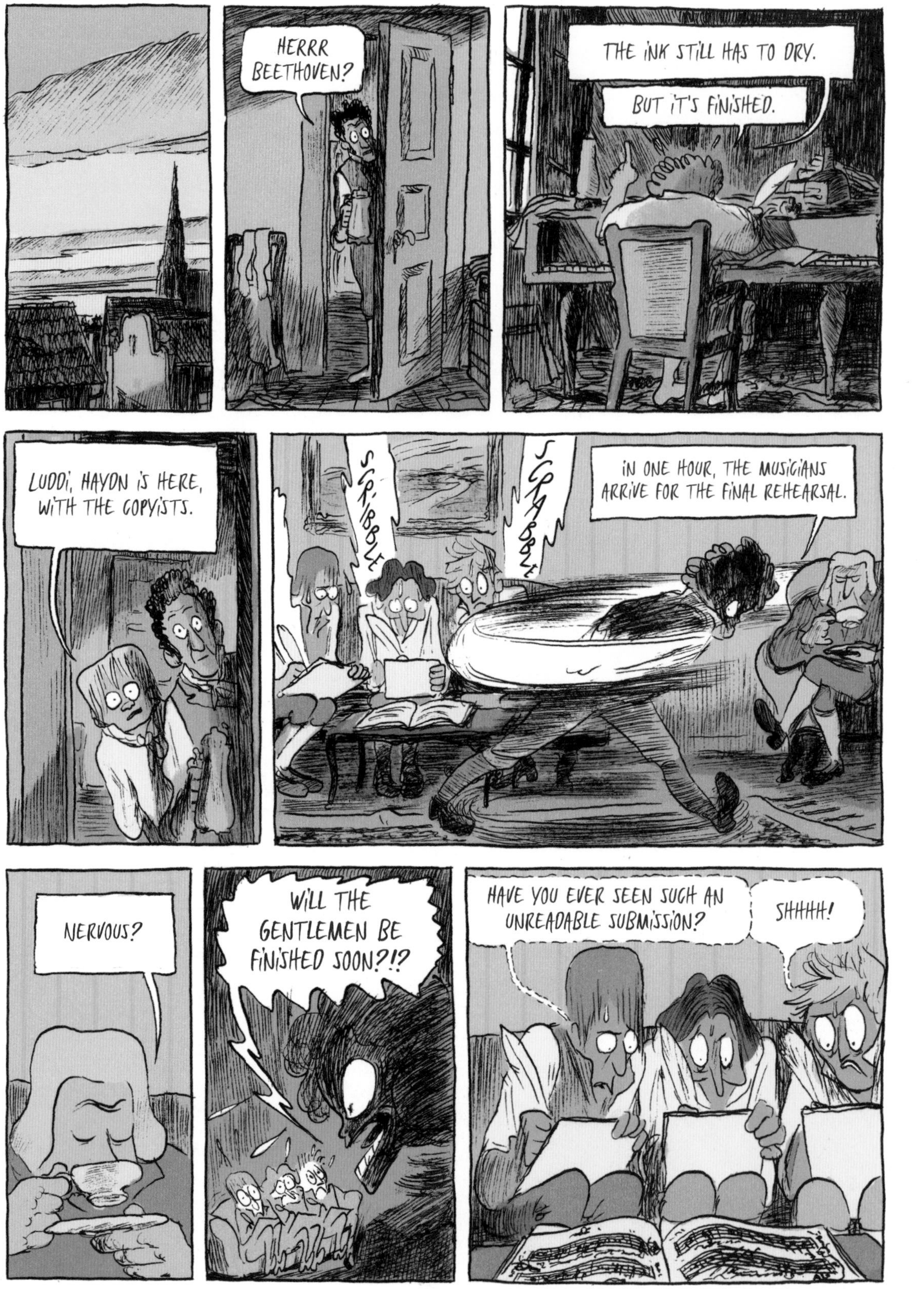
HERRR BEETHOVEN?
THE INK STILL HAS TO DRY.
BUT IT'S FINISHED.
LUDDI, HAYDN IS HERE, WITH THE COPYISTS.
SCRIBBLE
SCRABBLE
IN ONE HOUR, THE MUSICIANS ARRIVE FOR THE FINAL REHEARSAL.
NERVOUS?
WILL THE GENTLEMEN BE FINISHED SOON?!?
HAVE YOU EVER SEEN SUCH AN UNREADABLE SUBMISSION?
SHHHH!

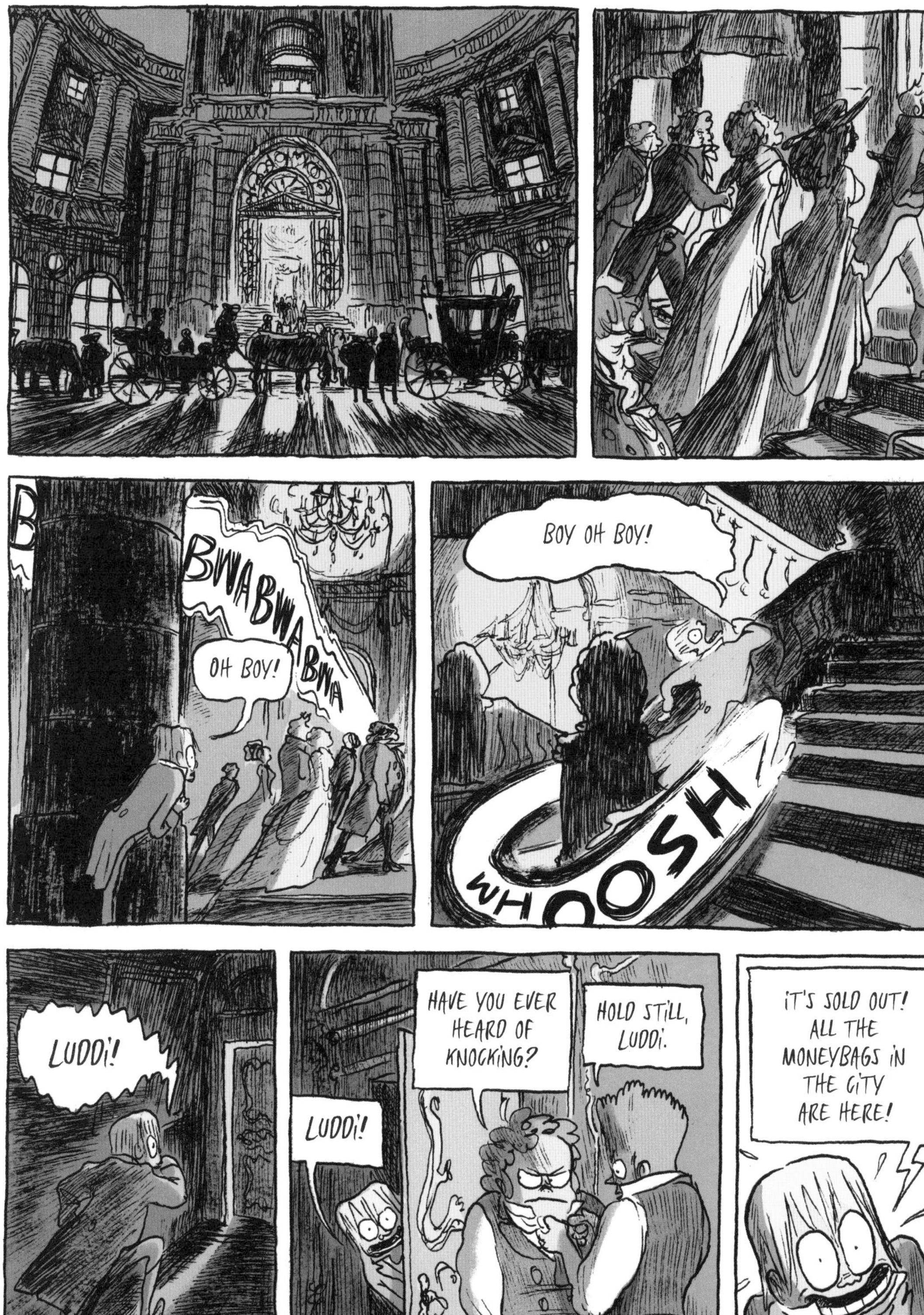
B
BWABWABWA
OH BOY!
BOY OH BOY!
WHOOSH
LUDDi!
LUDDi!
HAVE YOU EVER HEARD OF KNOCKiNG?
HOLD STiLL, LUDDi.
iT'S SOLD OUT! ALL THE MONEYBAGS iN THE CiTY ARE HERE!

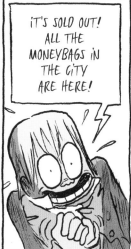

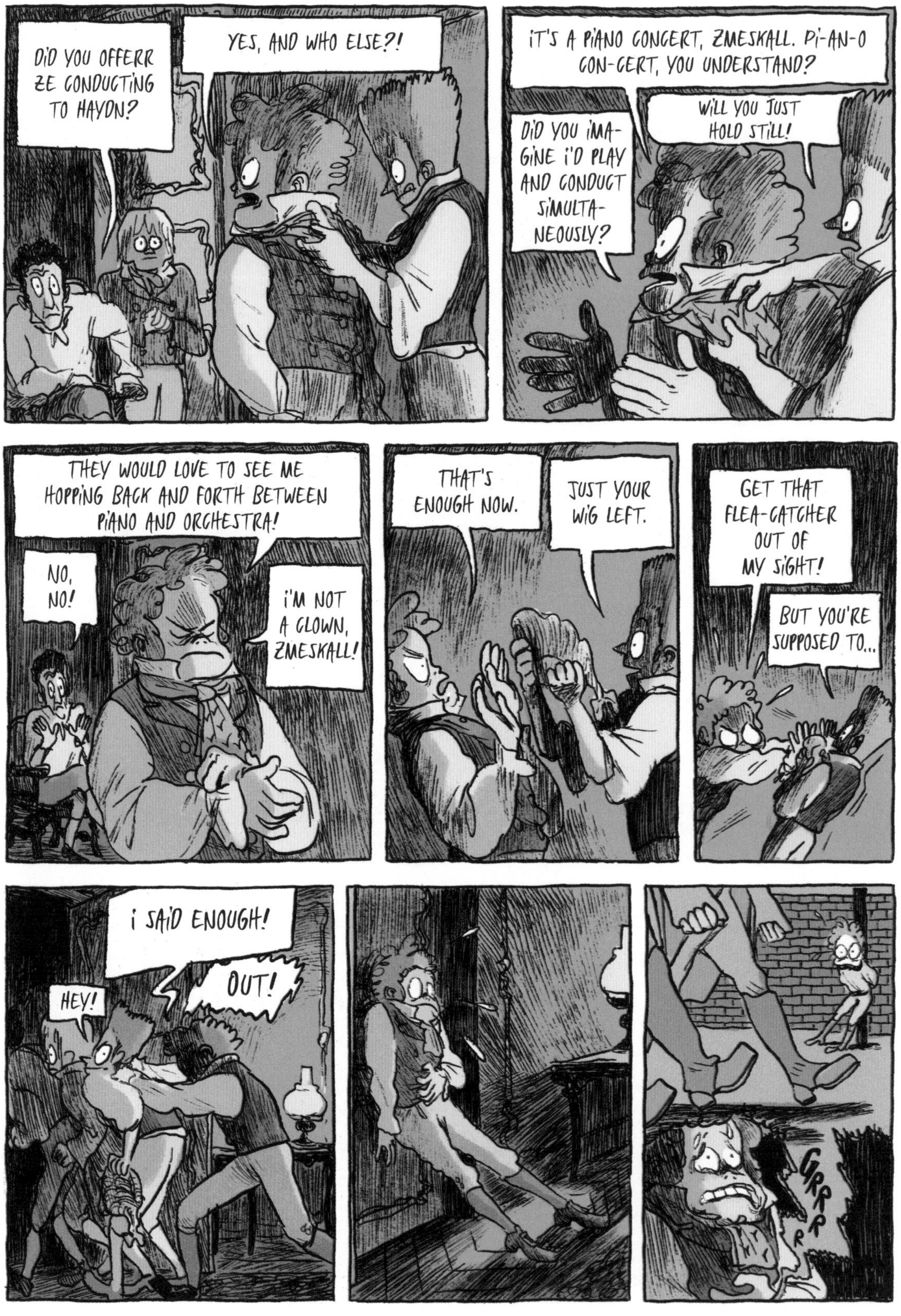
DID YOU OFFERR ZE CONDUCTING TO HAYDN?
YES, AND WHO ELSE?!
IT'S A PIANO CONCERT, ZMESKALL. PI-AN-O CON-CERT, YOU UNDERSTAND?
DID YOU IMAGINE I'D PLAY AND CONDUCT SIMULTANEOUSLY?
WILL YOU JUST HOLD STILL!
THEY WOULD LOVE TO SEE ME HOPPING BACK AND FORTH BETWEEN PIANO AND ORCHESTRA!
NO, NO!
I'M NOT A CLOWN, ZMESKALL!
THAT'S ENOUGH NOW.
JUST YOUR WIG LEFT.
GET THAT FLEA-CATCHER OUT OF MY SIGHT!
BUT YOU'RE SUPPOSED TO...
I SAID ENOUGH!
HEY!
OUT!
GRRRR

BLAM
WHAT HELL iS THiS.

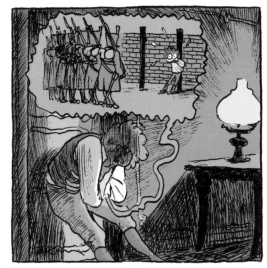

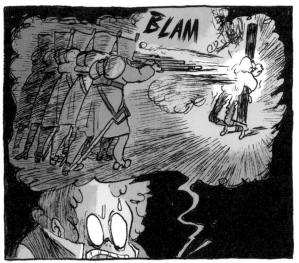

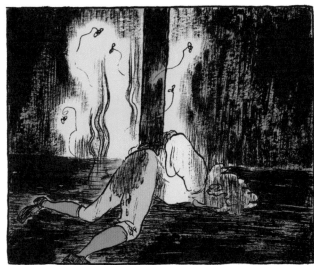

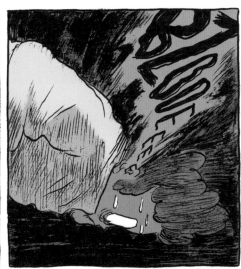

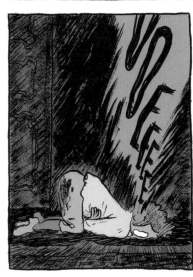

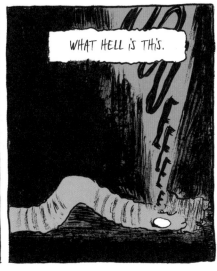

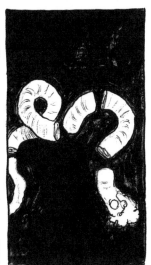

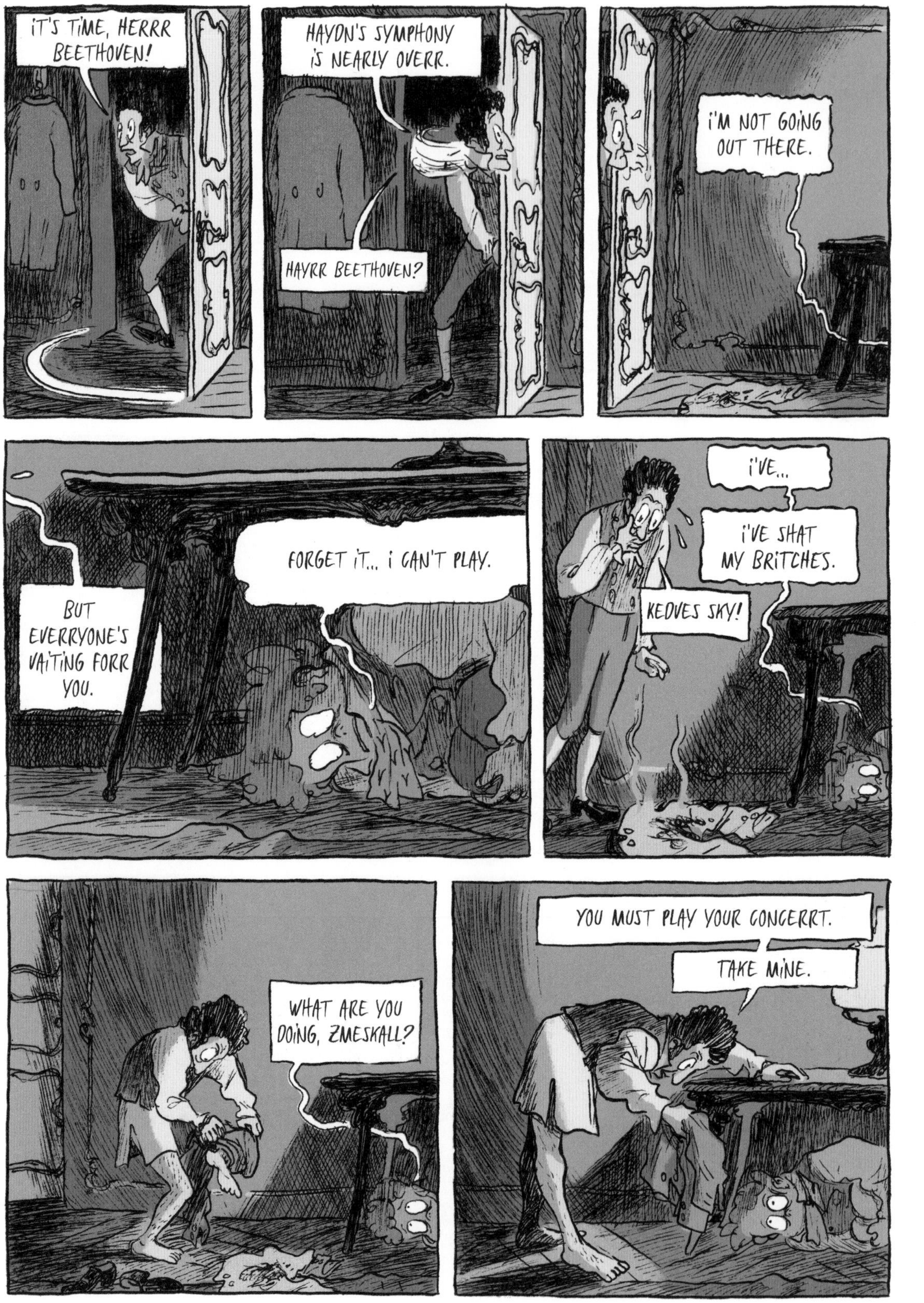

IT'S TIME, HERRR BEETHOVEN!
HAYDN'S SYMPHONY IS NEARLY OVERR.
HAYRR BEETHOVEN?
I'M NOT GOING OUT THERE.
BUT EVERRYONE'S VAITING FORR YOU.
FORGET IT... I CAN'T PLAY.
I'VE...
I'VE SHAT MY BRITCHES.
KEDVES SKY!
WHAT ARE YOU DOING, ZMESKALL?
YOU MUST PLAY YOUR CONCERRT.
TAKE MINE.

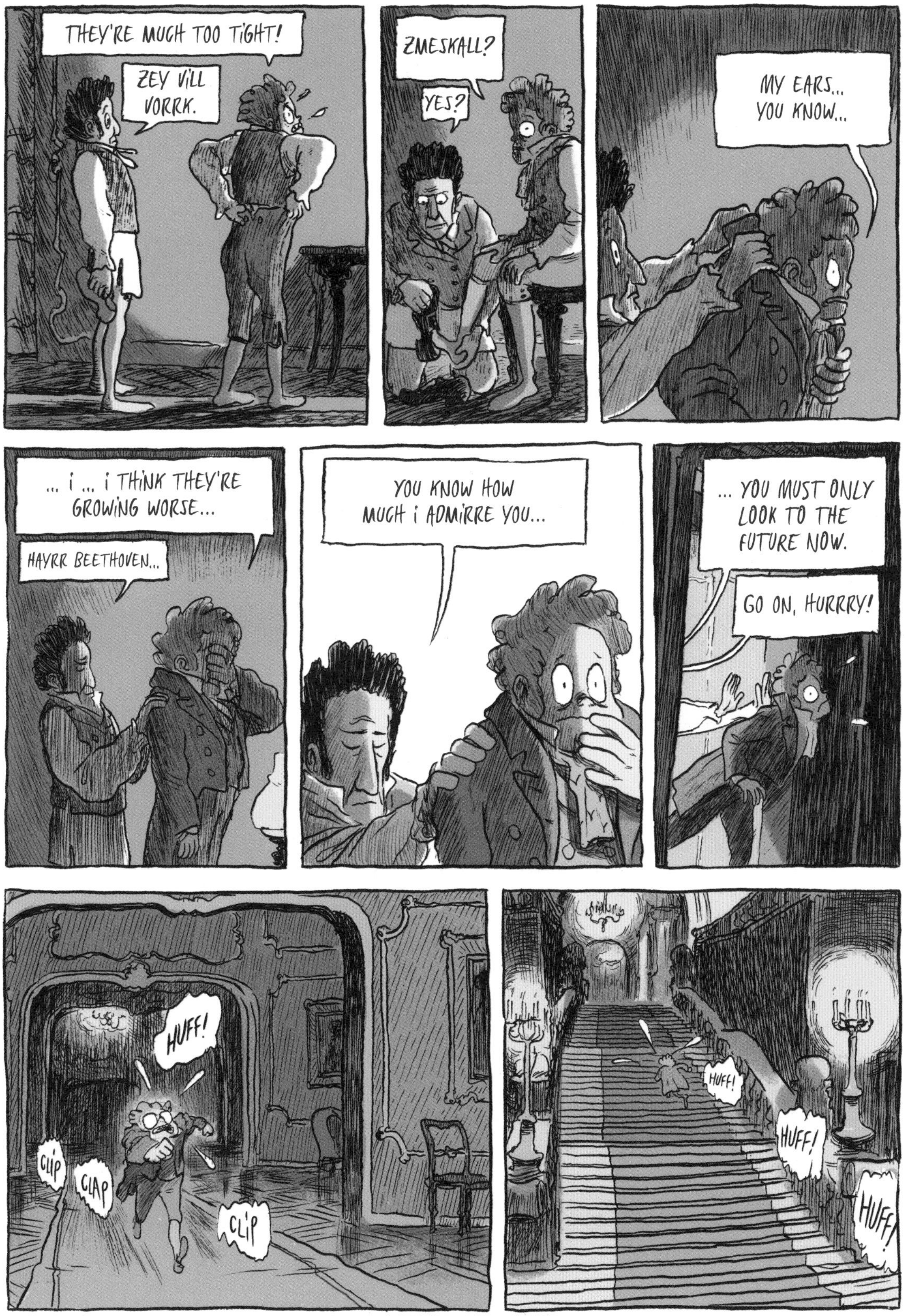
THEY'RE MUCH TOO TIGHT!
ZEY VILL VORRK.
ZMESKALL?
YES?
MY EARS... YOU KNOW...
... I ... I THINK THEY'RE GROWING WORSE...
HAYRR BEETHOVEN...
YOU KNOW HOW MUCH I ADMIRRE YOU...
... YOU MUST ONLY LOOK TO THE FUTURE NOW.
GO ON, HURRRY!
HUFF!
CLIP
CLAP
CLIP
HUFF!
HUFF!
HUFF!

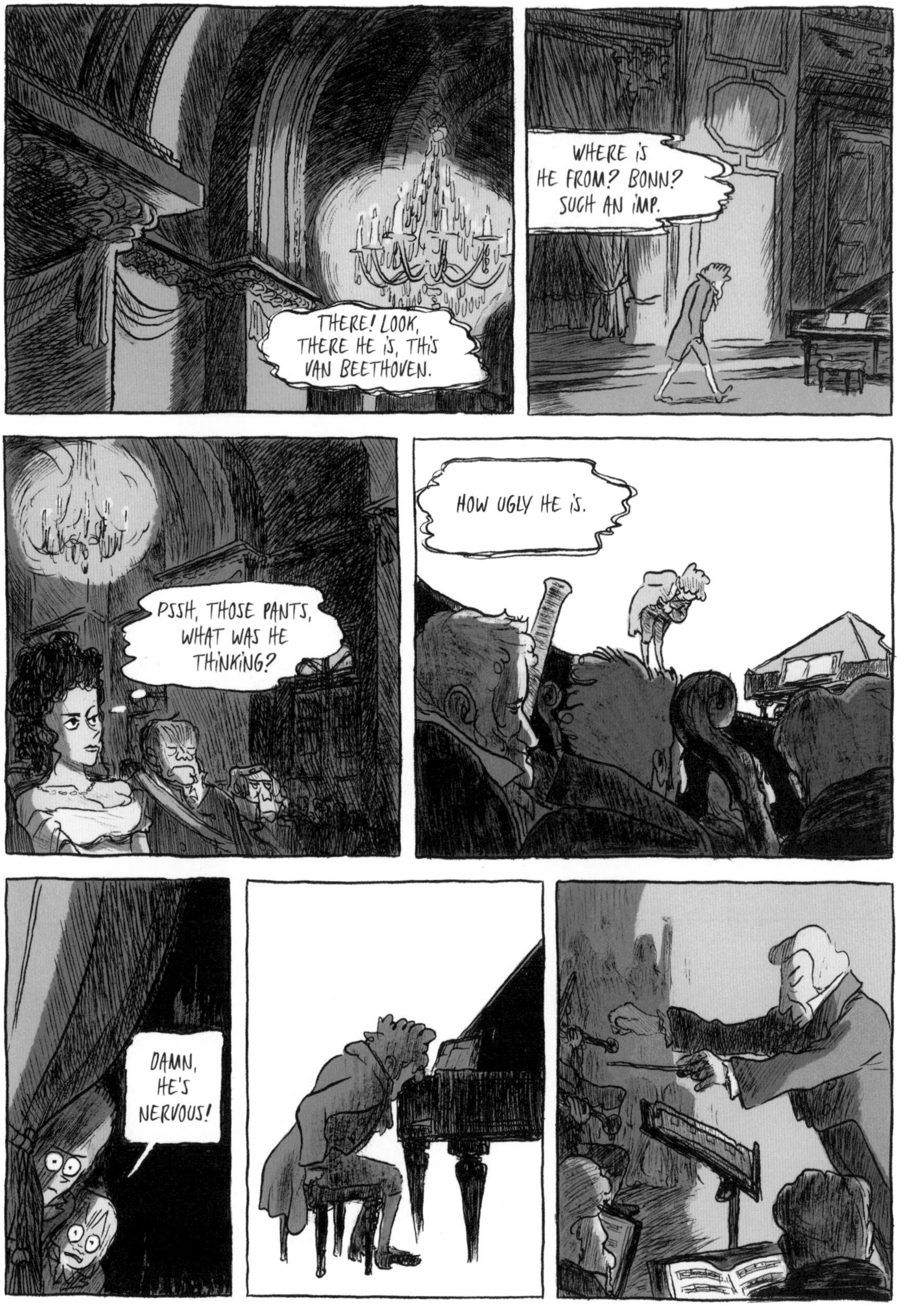
THERE! LOOK, THERE HE IS, THIS VAN BEETHOVEN.
WHERE IS HE FROM? BONN? SUCH AN IMP.
PSSH, THOSE PANTS, WHAT WAS HE THINKING?
HOW UGLY HE IS.
DAMN, HE'S NERVOUS!

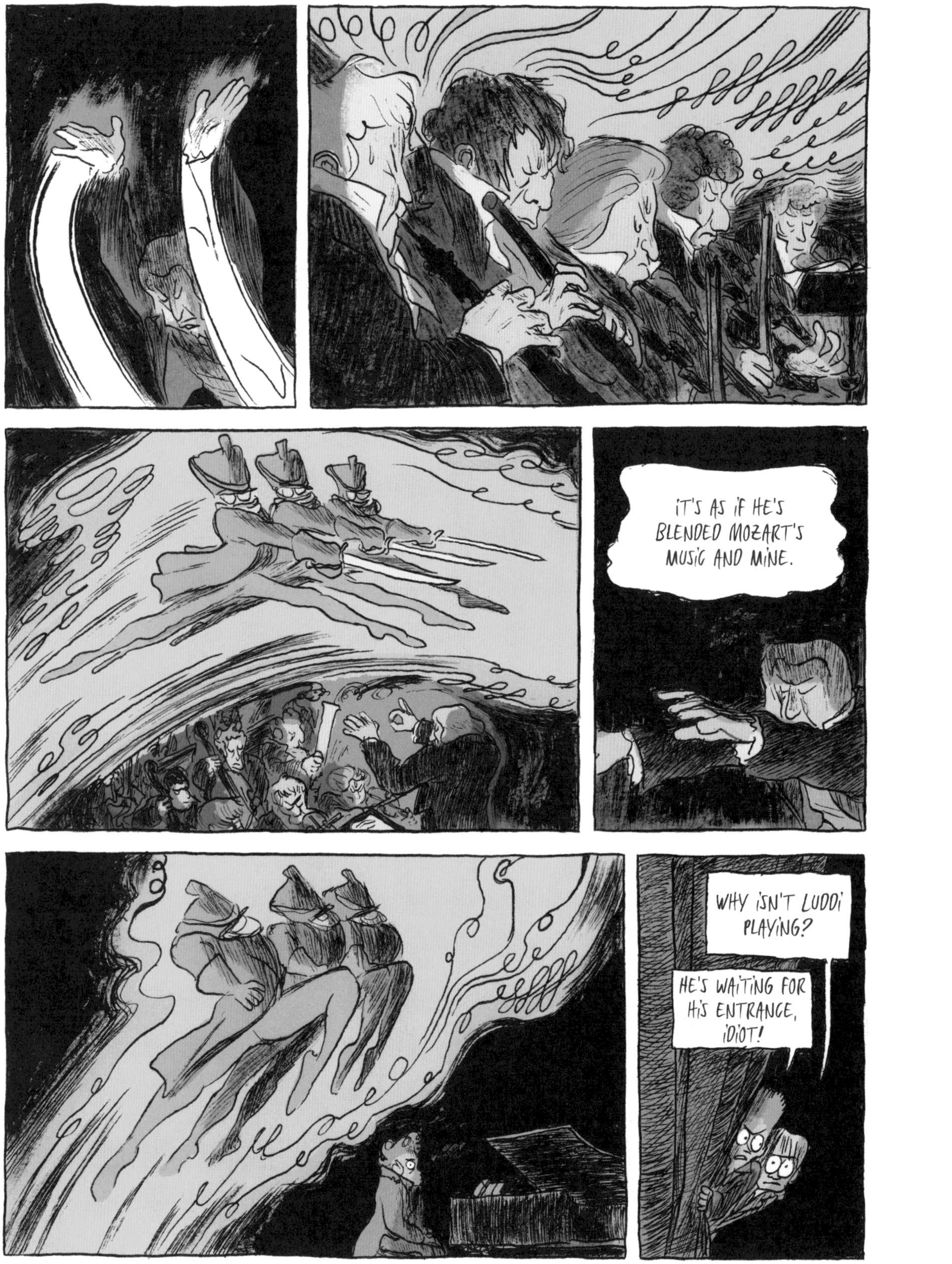

IT'S AS IF HE'S BLENDED MOZART'S MUSIC AND MINE.
WHY ISN'T LUDDI PLAYING?
HE'S WAITING FOR HIS ENTRANCE, IDIOT!

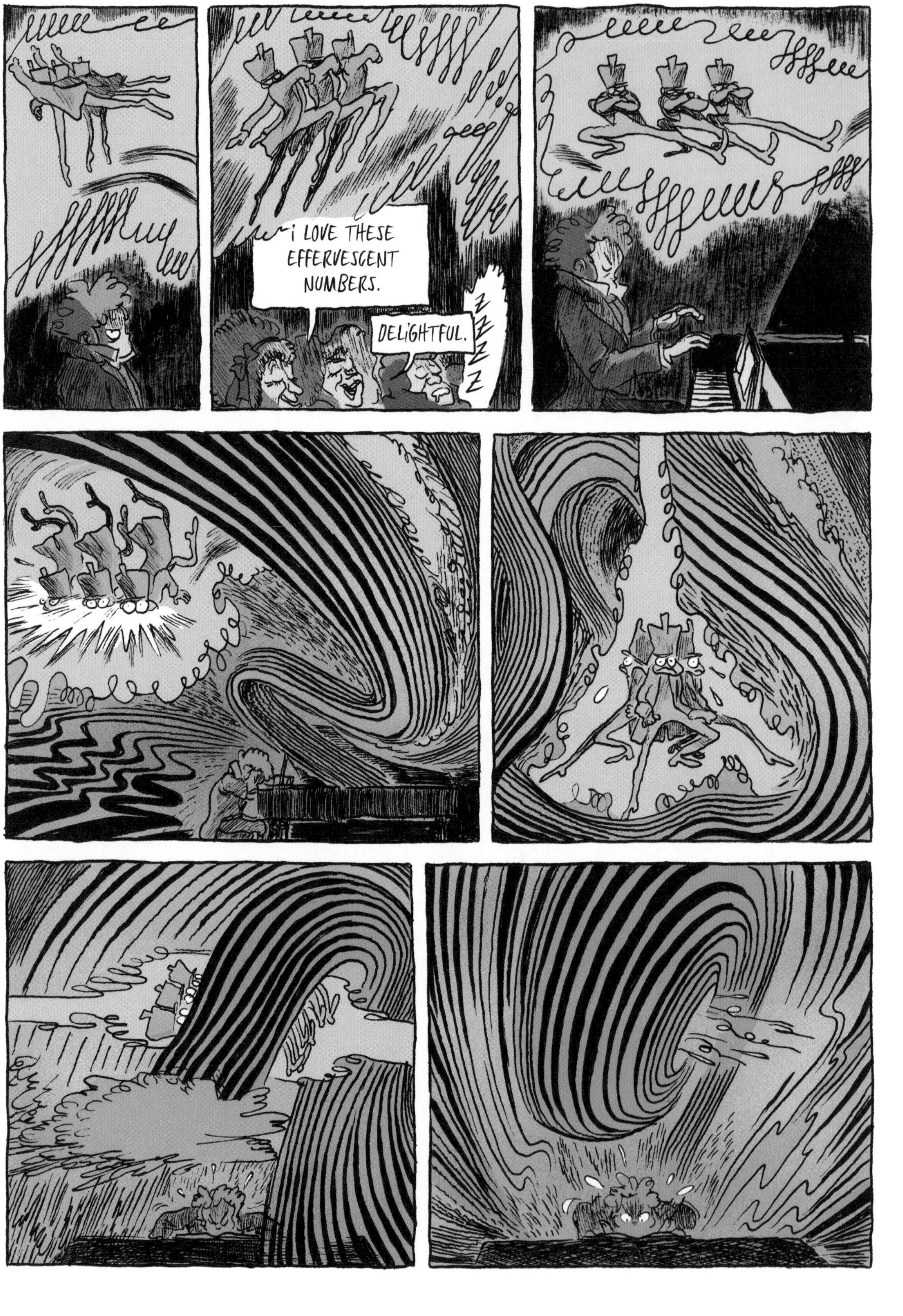
I LOVE THESE EFFERVESCENT NUMBERS.
DELIGHTFUL.
ZZZZZZ

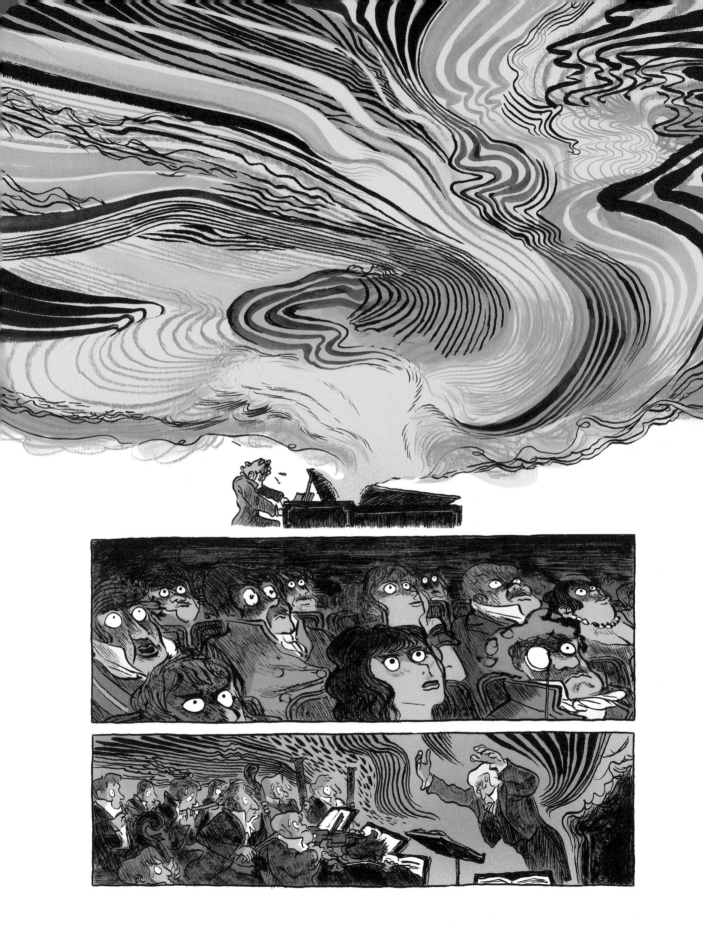

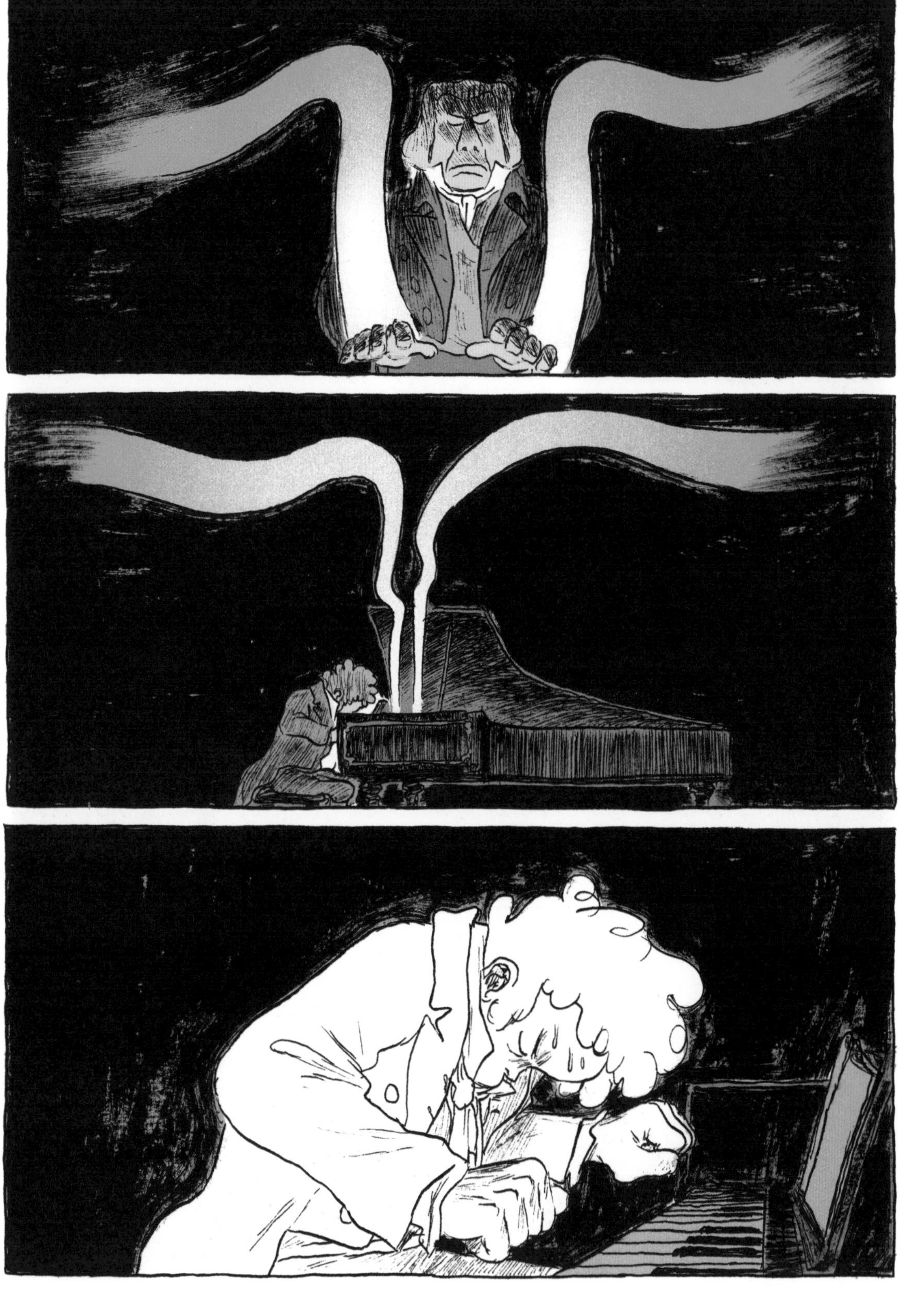

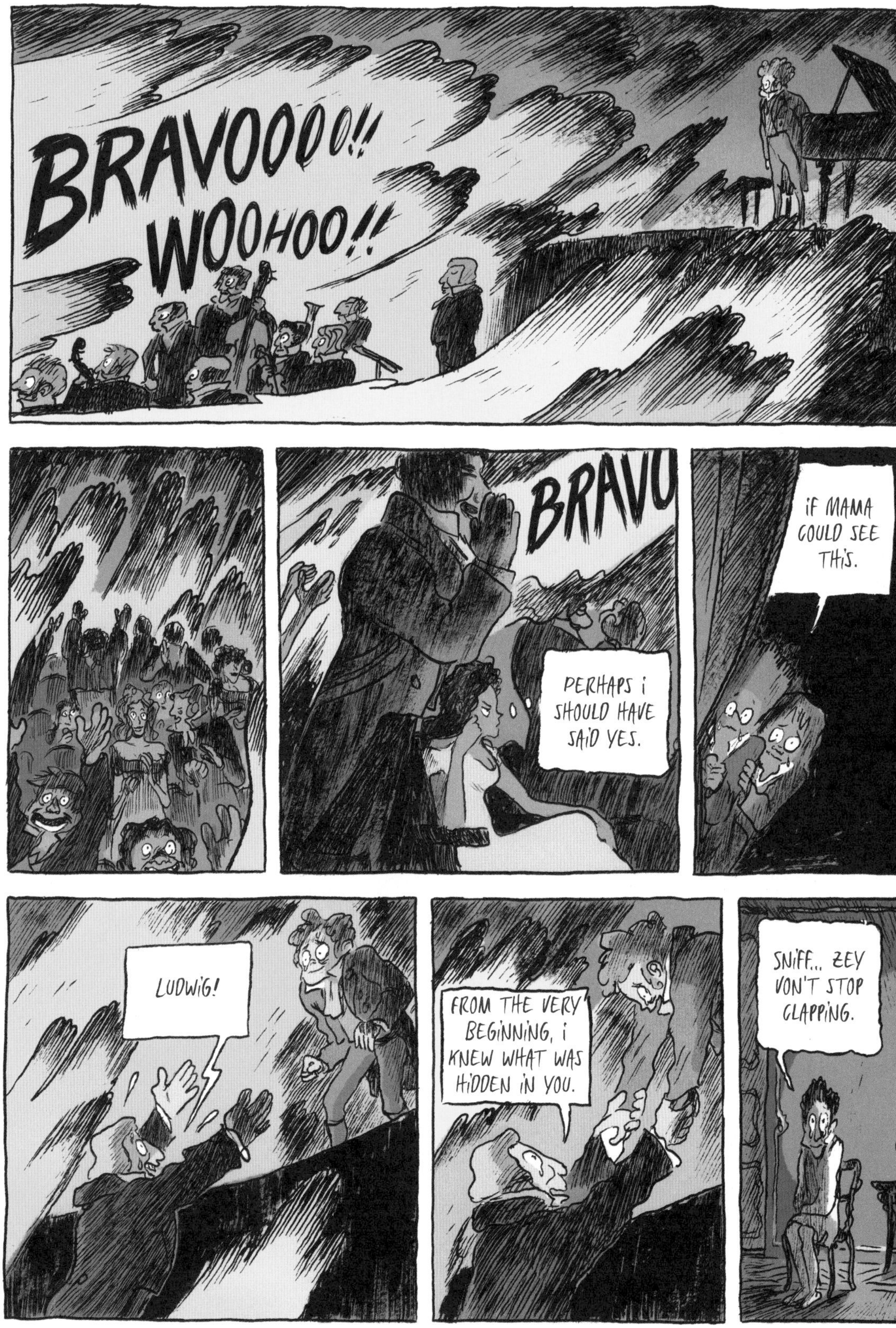
BRAVOOOO!!
WOOHOO!!
BRAVO
PERHAPS I SHOULD HAVE SAID YES.
IF MAMA COULD SEE THIS.
LUDWIG!
FROM THE VERY BEGINNING, I KNEW WHAT WAS HIDDEN IN YOU.
SNIFF... ZEY VON'T STOP CLAPPING.

ENCORE!!
ENCORE
ENCORE
ENCORE!!!
BRAVO!

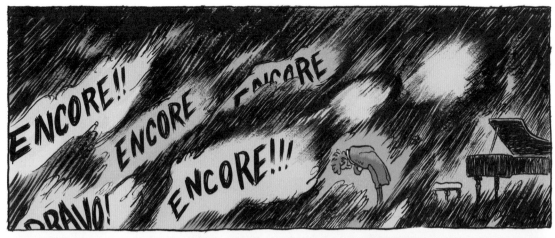

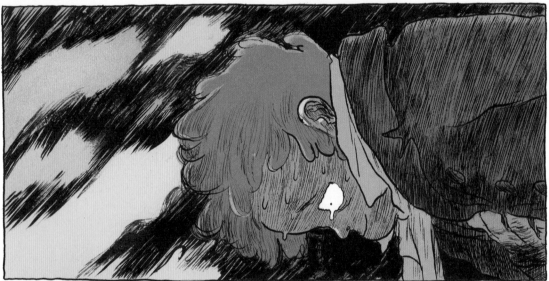

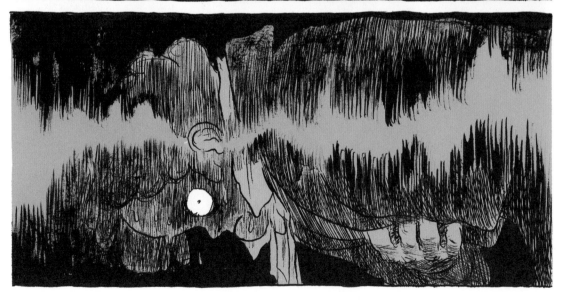

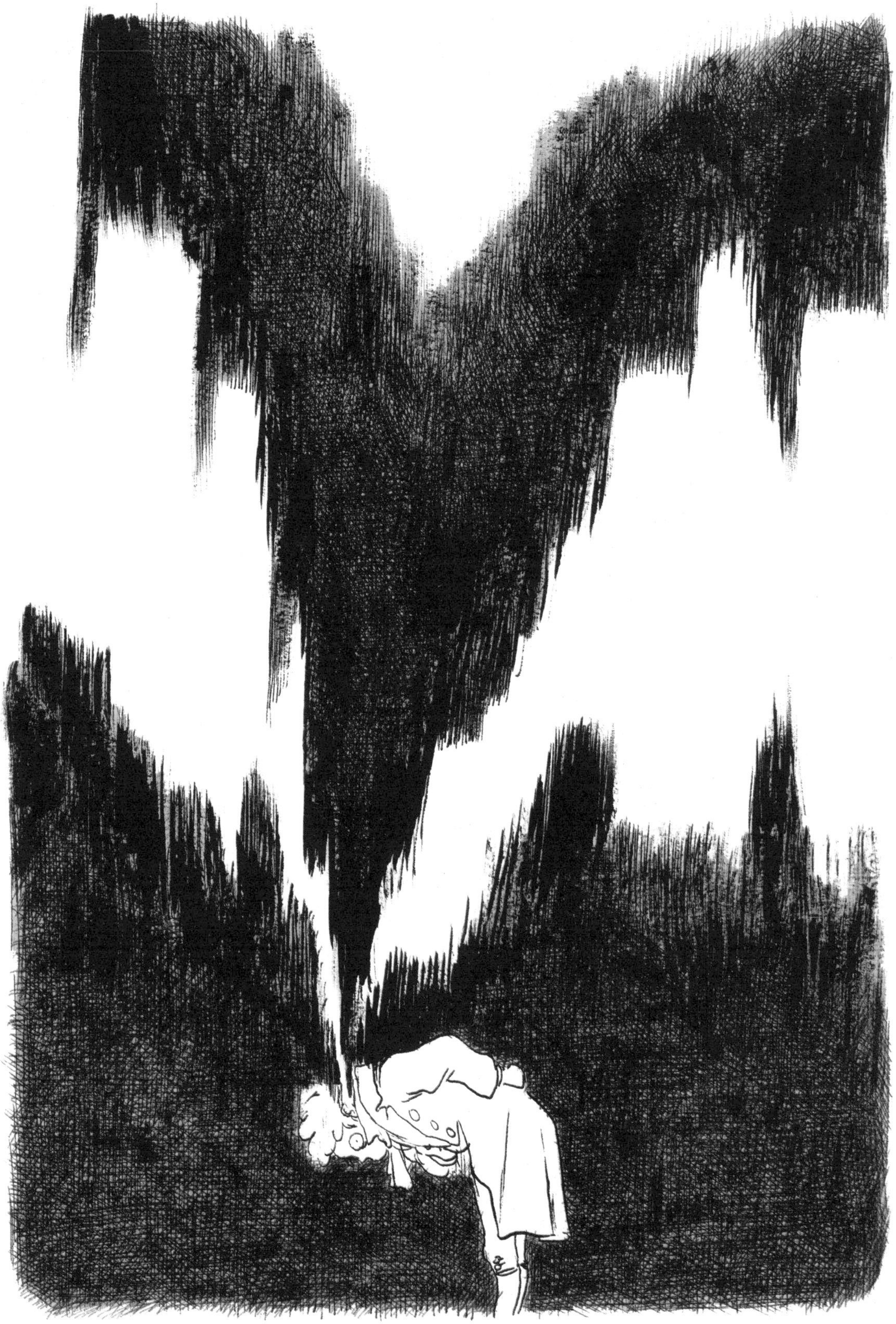

MIKAËL ROSS '2020

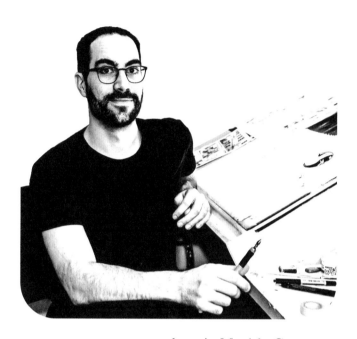

MIKAEL ROSS was born in Munich, Germany, in 1984. After apprenticing as a theater tailor with the Bavarian State Opera, he attended the Weissensee Academy of Art in Berlin for four years before spending a year abroad in Brussels, studying comics at the Saint-Luc School of the Arts. He has done an artist's residency in the grand comics town of Angoulême, exhibited his work in Lucerne (Switzerland), Hamburg, and Frankfurt, and taught comic workshops in Berlin. In between comics he works as an educator and illustrator. His previous graphic novel, *The Thud*, was published by Fantagraphics Books in 2021.

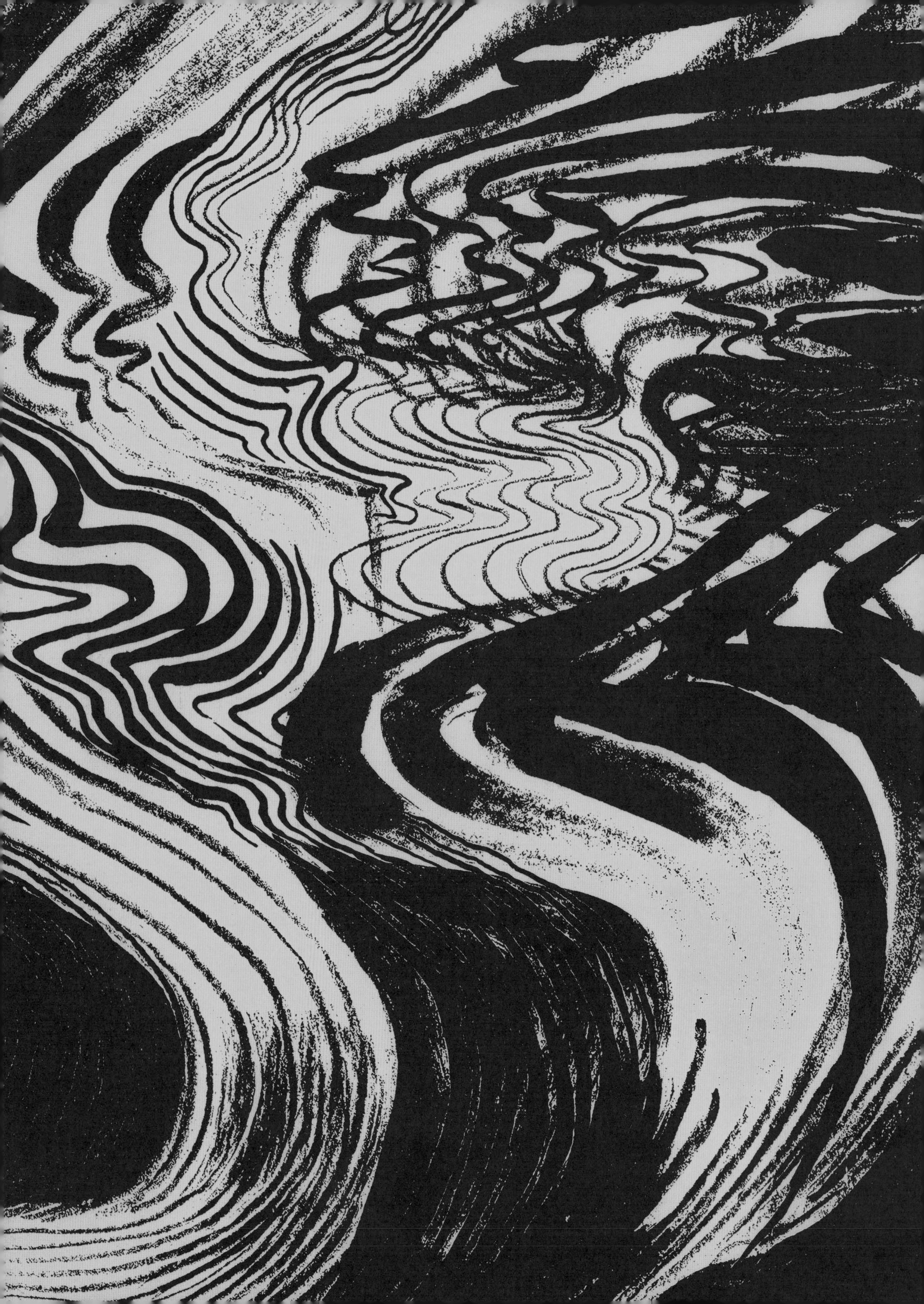

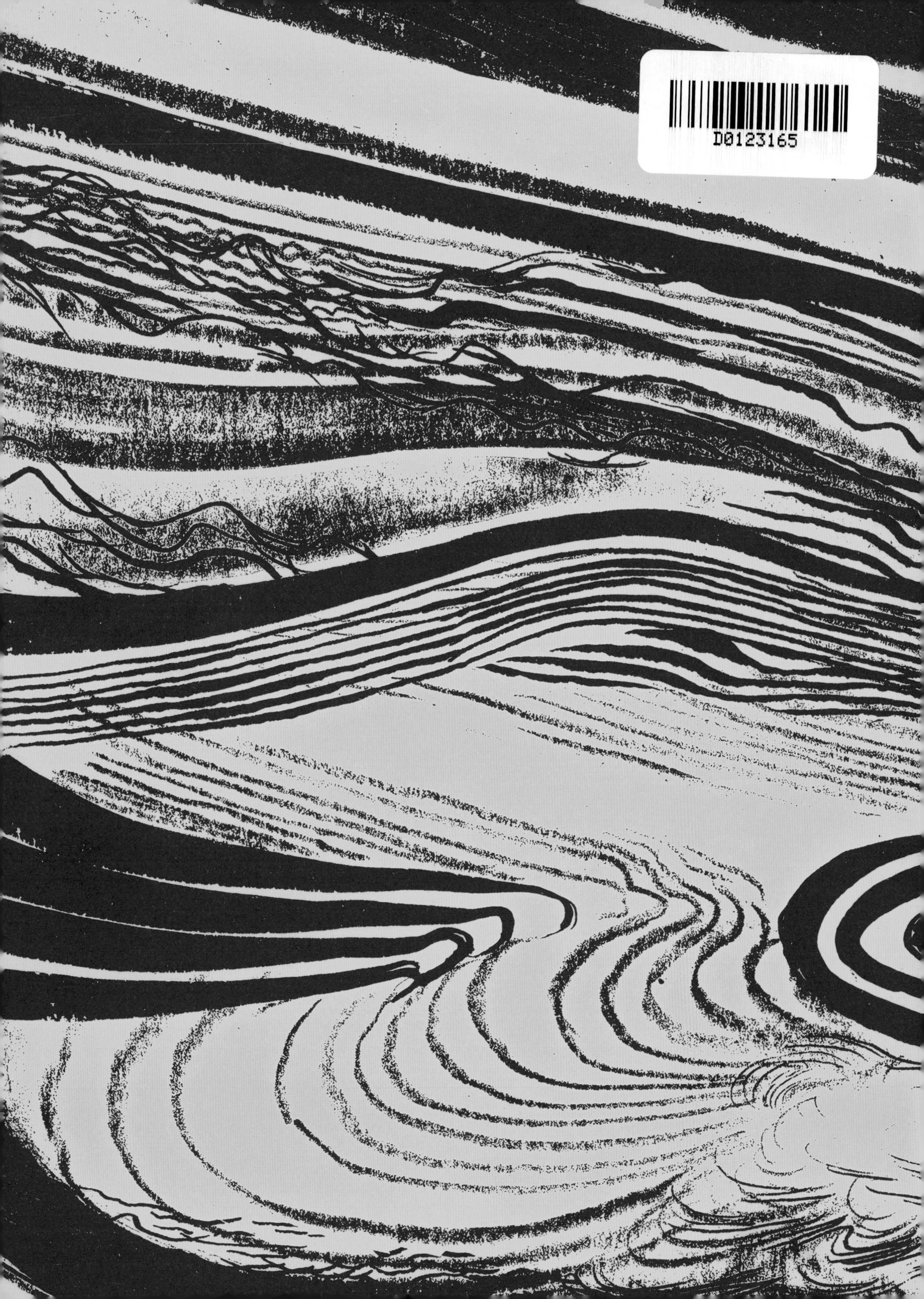